CAMBRIDGE

Official Cambridge Exam Preparation

CB081859

PREPARE

TEACHER'S BOOK

A2

LEVEL 2

Emma Heyderman

Second Edition

Cambridge University Press
www.cambridge.org/elt

Cambridge Assessment English
www.cambridgeenglish.org

Information on this title: www.cambridge.org/9781108385947

First published 2015
Second Edition 2019

20 19 18 17 16 15 14 13 12 11 10 9 8 7 6 5 4 3

Printed in Italy by Rotolito S.p.A.

A catalogue record for this publication is available from the British Library

ISBN 978-1-108-38594-7 Teacher's Book with Downloadable Resource Pack
ISBN 978-1-108-43328-0 Student's Book
ISBN 978-1-108-38059-1 Student's Book and Online Workbook
ISBN 978-1-108-38093-5 Workbook with Audio Download
(Class Audio, Video, Photocopiable Worksheets)

CONTENTS

CAMBRIDGE

Official Cambridge Exam Preparation

DEAR TEACHERS

I'm delighted that you've chosen our official preparation materials to prepare for a Cambridge English Qualification.

We take great pride in the fact that our materials draw on the expertise of a whole team of writers, teachers, assessors and exam experts. These are materials that you can really trust.

Our preparation materials are unique in many ways:

- They combine the skills and knowledge of the teams at Cambridge Assessment English, who create the tests, and the teams at Cambridge University Press, who create the English Language Teaching materials.
- They draw upon the experience of millions of previous exam candidates – where they succeed and where they have difficulties. We target exercises and activities precisely at these areas so that you can actively 'learn' from previous test takers' mistakes.
- Every single task in our materials has been carefully checked to be an accurate reflection of what test takers find in the test.

In addition, we listen to what you tell us at every stage of the development process. This allows us to design the most user-friendly courses, practice tests and supplementary training. We create materials using in-depth knowledge, research and practical understanding. Prepare for Cambridge English Qualifications with confidence in the knowledge that you have the best materials available to support you on your way to success.

We wish you the very best on your journey with us.

With kind regards,

Pamela Baxter
Director
Cambridge Exams Publishing

PS. If you have any feedback at all on our support materials for exams, please write to us at cambridgeexams@cambridge.org

WELCOME TO PREPARE

STUDENT'S BOOK OVERVIEW

Each unit begins with **About you**, where students can talk about themselves and their lives.

Clear **grammar presentation** and practice is extended in the Grammar reference and practice section at the back of the book.

There is comprehensive coverage of **pronunciation** in the Student's Book.

Vocabulary sets are informed by English Vocabulary Profile to ensure they are appropriate for the level.

Motivating, topic-based **texts** specifically chosen to engage and inform students.

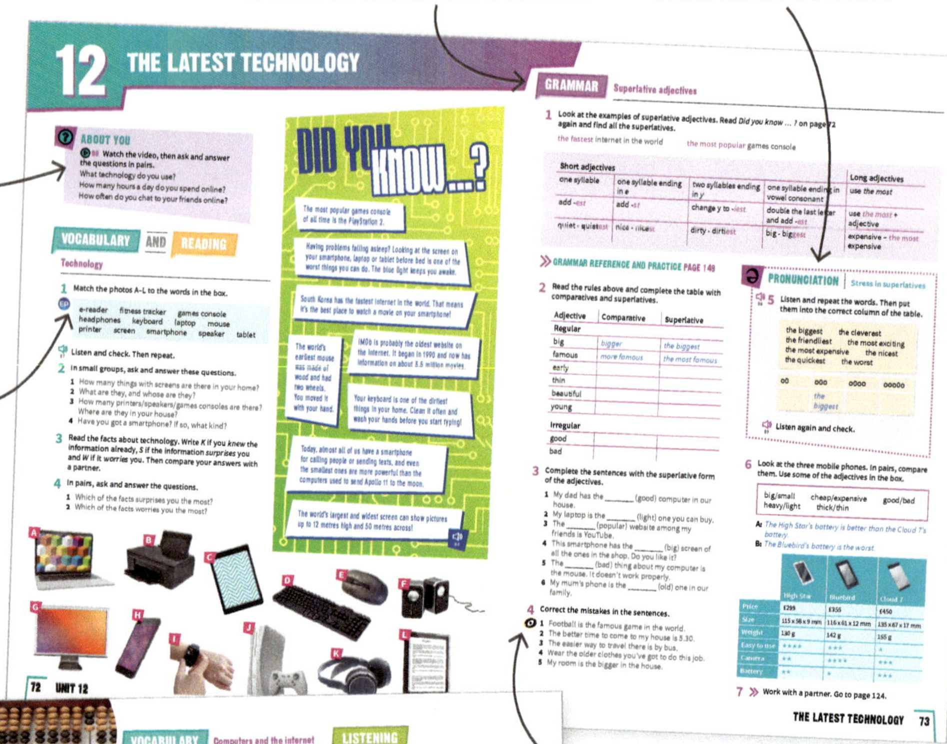

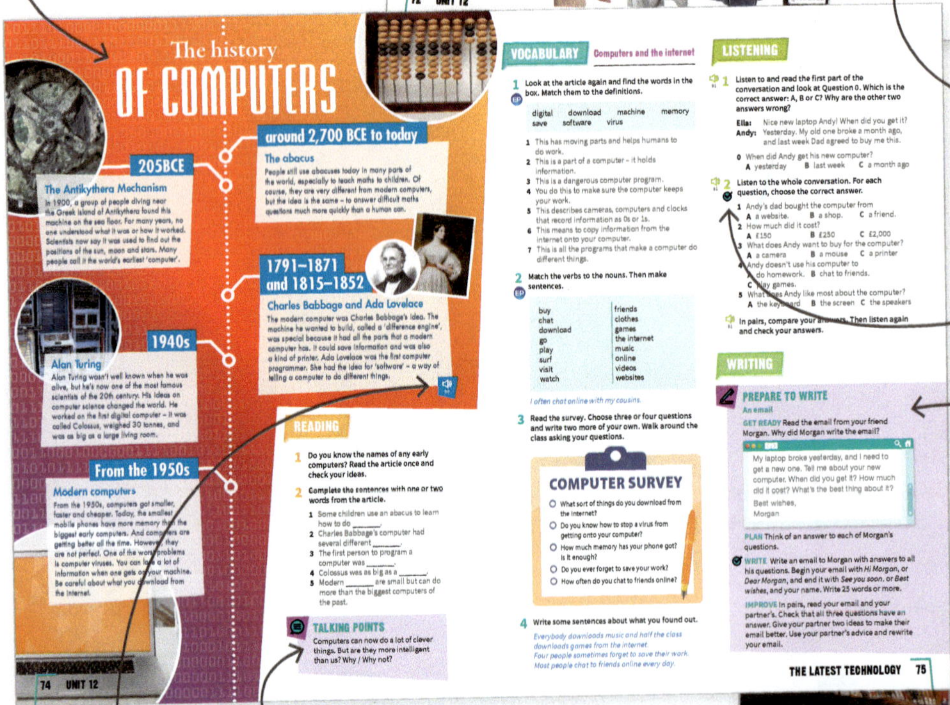

Common mistakes relevant to your students' level are identified in the grammar activities marked with the **Cambridge Learner Corpus icon.**

A2 Key for Schools **exam tasks** are clearly marked by the exam icon.

The stages in **Prepare to Write** help students prepare, plan, produce and improve their own written texts.

All reading texts are recorded, giving the option to listen and read or listen and check answers where appropriate.

Talking points provides opportunities to personalise language and encourage students to say what they think about the topic in the unit.

Video interviews show real teens giving their opinion on the topic of the unit. Each video comes with a worksheet containing comprehension and discussion questions.

There is a **Culture** or **Life Skills** lesson after every two units.
The **Culture** lessons highlight interesting aspects of culture in English-speaking countries.

In the **videos** that are found at the end of each Culture lesson, students can watch interesting documentaries about the culture topics. Each video comes with a worksheet for students to complete as they watch.

Life Skills lessons help students develop important skills for their everyday lives.

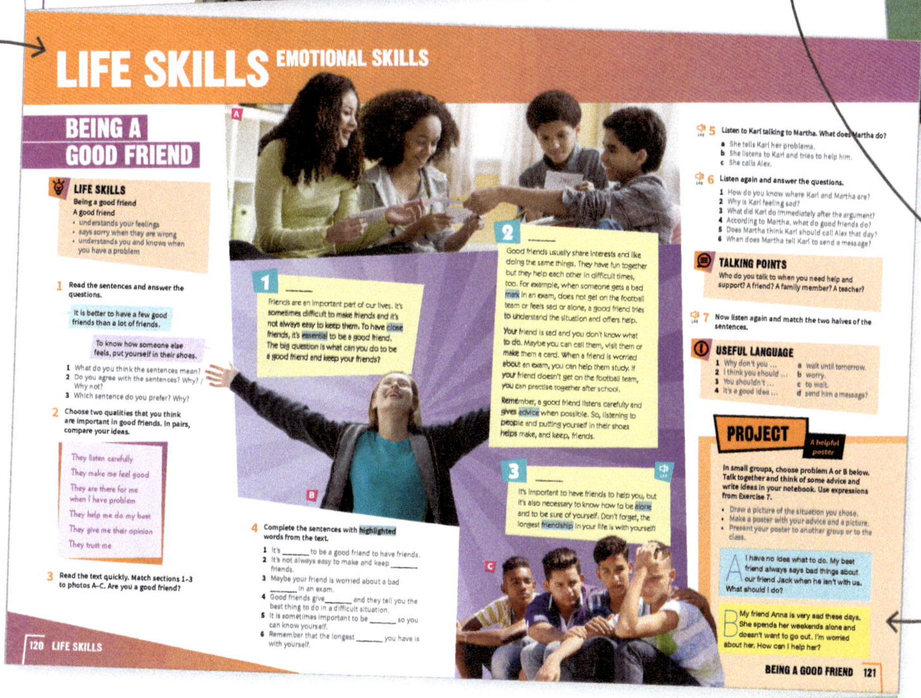

Projects in the Culture and Life Skills lessons encourage students to work together to create something fun and expand their learning.

Review pages after every four units give further practice of language and skills.

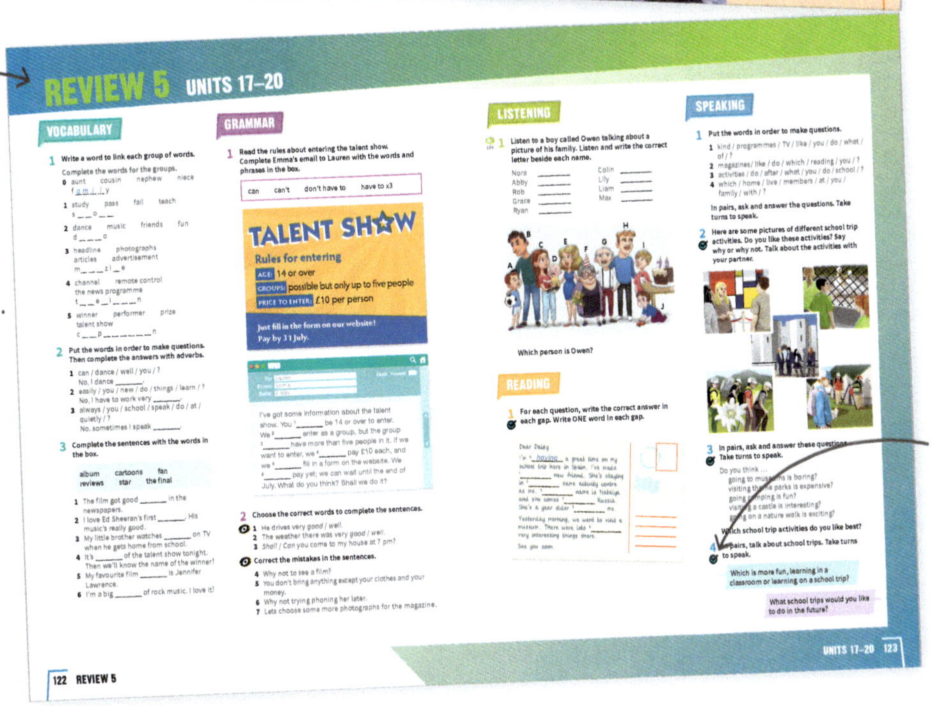

Exam tasks in the review sections provide additional practice of the *A2 Key for schools* exam tasks found in the units.

COMPONENT LINE UP

Student's Book

The Student's Book combines teen-appeal topics with preparation for the revised 2020 *A2 Key for Schools* exam. With a starter unit, twenty lively core units, Reviews, Culture and Life Skills sections, a Vocabulary list, and a Grammar reference and practice section, the Student's Book has all the material you need to create interactive, personalised lessons. Full audio and extensive video to accompany the Student's Book is available for teachers online or to download.

Workbook with Audio Download

The Workbook gives additional practice of all the language from the Student's Book. It also provides students with comprehensive skills development work and further exposure to exam tasks. The Workbook is suitable for use both in the classroom and for homework. Learners can access and download the audio files from e-Source using the code provided.

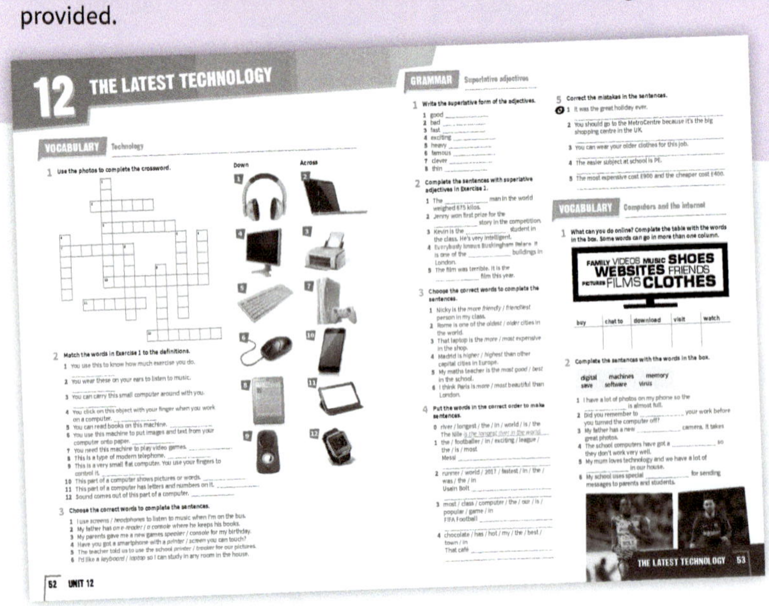

Online Workbook

The Online Workbook, delivered via the Cambridge Learning Management System, is a digital version of the Workbook with interactive exercises and tasks which provide further practice of the language and skills in the Student's Book. The Online Workbook also allows you to track your students' progress, highlighting areas of strength and weakness for ongoing performance improvement.

Teacher's Book with Downloadable Resource Pack

The interleaved Teacher's Book contains complete teaching notes for all of the Student's Book tasks, in addition to answer keys and audioscripts. With a wealth of lesson ideas, warmers, coolers and extension tasks, the Teacher's Book helps you manage mixed-ability classes and work with fast finishers. Information panels include background information about themes, topics and cultural events, and guidance for all exam tasks. Clear indications direct you to additional resources which support and extend learning.

The Downloadable Resource Pack, accessed via e-Source, includes Class Audio, Video and Photocopiable Worksheets. These provide an extensive suite of downloadable teacher's resources to use in class and include:

- Grammar worksheets (available at two levels of challenge: standard and plus)
- Vocabulary worksheets (available at two levels of challenge: standard and plus)
- Review games
- Literature worksheets
- Speaking worksheets
- Writing worksheets
- Video worksheets
- Culture video worksheets

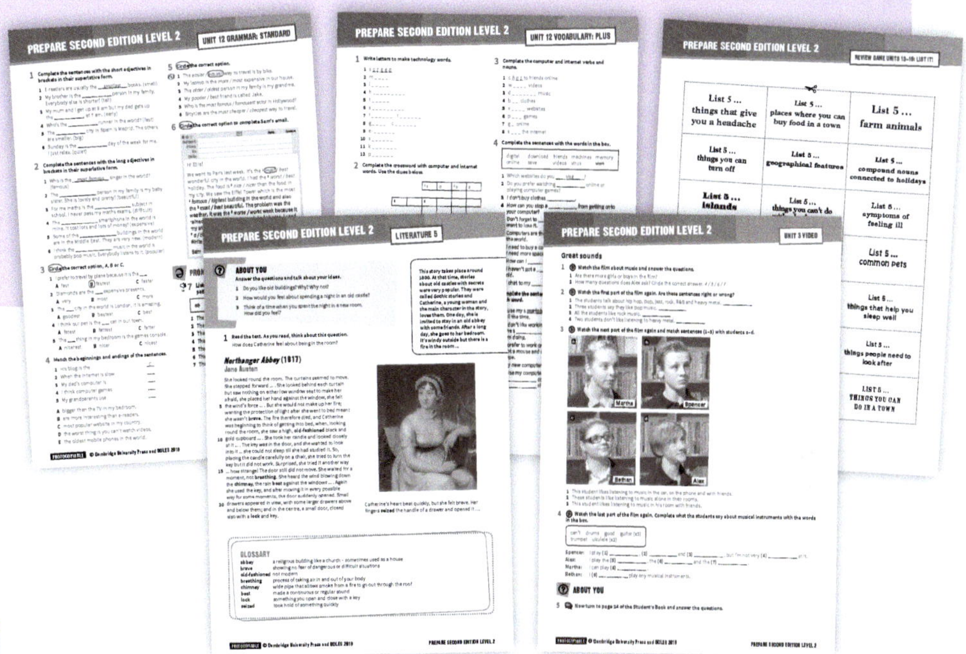

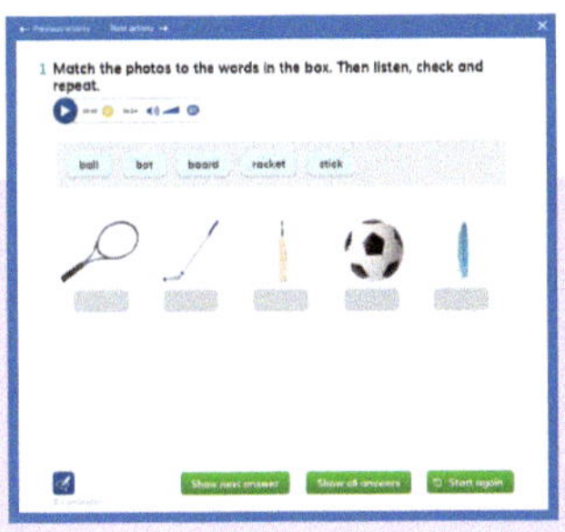

Presentation Plus

Presentation Plus is easy-to-use, interactive classroom presentation software that helps you deliver effective and engaging lessons. It includes all the Student's Book and Workbook content and allows you to present and annotate content, and link to the Photocopiable Worksheets.

Test Generator

The Test Generator allows you to download ready-made tests for each unit, term and end-of-year assessment or to build your own tests easily and quickly. All the tests are available at two levels of challenge: standard and plus, to help assess learners of mixed abilities.

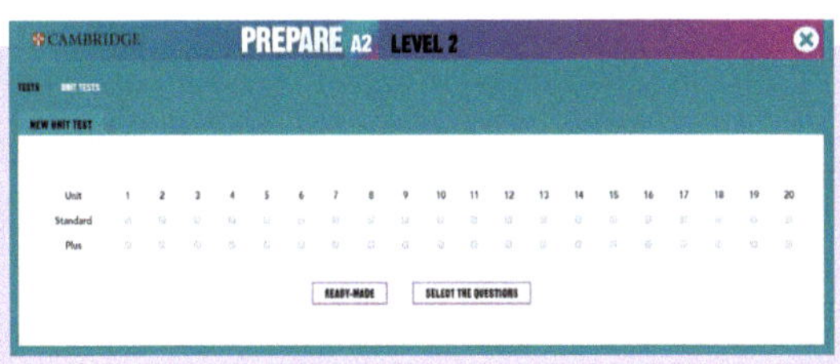

THE PREPARE EXAM JOURNEY

The *Prepare* Exam Journey combines teen-appeal topics with extensive preparation for Cambridge English Qualifications. Levels 2 and 3 of *Prepare Second Edition* take students on a two-year journey towards the revised 2020 *A2 Key for Schools* exam. This approach builds confidence every step of the way from the first experiences of exam tasks to skills development, from language discovery to understanding how English works in the real world.

LEVEL 2

Prepare Level 2 gradually introduces authentic *A2 Key for Schools* exam tasks, ensuring students become familiar with every part of the exam.

- Exam tasks are discreetly labelled with the exam icon in **Level 2 Student's Book.**

35 **2** **Listen to five short conversations. For each question, choose the correct picture (A, B or C).**

1 What was Bella happy with at the party?

- **Level 2 Workbook** offers further exposure to each part of the exam.

2 **For each question, choose the correct answer.**

1

A The blankets are all big.
B There's a special offer on these blankets.
C The blankets are only £35 each today.

- Information for each part of the exam is included in **Level 2 Teacher's Book.**

35 2 A2 Key for Schools Listening Part 1.

In this part, students listen to five short conversations and answer a question by choosing the correct picture, A, B or C. They listen to each conversation twice. Before they listen, ask the students to read each question again and say how each of the three pictures answers it. Do the first as an example: *What was Bella happy with at the party? In A Bella was happy about the people, in B she was happy about the food and in C she was happy about the music.* The students then listen to the three conversations and choose the right picture for each one. After they listen for the first time, encourage them to compare their answers with a partner and to say why they think their answer is correct. Play the recording for a second time for the students to check their ideas. With a weaker class, play the recording for a third time and stop it after the correct answer is given. With a stronger class, ask the students to say why the other pictures are not correct, e.g. *In 1 Bella says the music wasn't great and there weren't many people there.* They can do this by listening again.

LEVEL 3

Prepare Level 3 provides complete coverage of the *A2 Key for Schools* exam, driving students to exam success.

- Each exam task is highlighted clearly in the *Prepare for the Exam* features in **Level 3 Student's Book.**

PREPARE FOR THE EXAM

Speaking Part 2

6 **Look at the photos A–K on page 20. Discuss the questions with your partner.**

1 Do you like these different ways of travelling? Why? / Why not?
2 Do you think riding a bike is difficult? Why? / Why not?
3 Do you think going in a boat or a ship is enjoyable? Why? / Why not?
4 Now tell your partner which of these ways of travelling you like best.
5 How do you like to travel when it's very hot?
6 Do you prefer going on holiday to the sea or in the mountains?

» PREPARE FOR THE EXAM PAGE 134

- The *Prepare for the Exam* section in **Level 3 Student's Book** includes further guidance and support with practice tasks.

Writing Part 7 Picture story
(Unit 4, Unit 18, Review 1)

EXAM INFORMATION
What is Part 7?
There is a story writing task.
What do I have to do?
You have to write a story based on three pictures.

1 **Read the exam task and the sample answer. Is there something about every picture? What tense is the story in? Why?**

Look at the three pictures.
Write the story shown in the pictures.
Write **35 words** or more.

- **Level 3 Workbook** consolidates each exam task and includes Exam Tips.

PREPARE FOR THE EXAM

Listening Part 5

1 **For each question, choose the correct answer.**

You will hear Martha talking to a friend about a trip to the zoo. Which animal was each person most interested in?

People		What they liked best	
0 brother	E	A bears	E monkeys
1 sister		B dolphins	F penguins
2 dad		C elephants	G snakes
3 mum		D giraffes	H wild dogs
4 grandad			
5 grandma			

EXAM TIPS

- Always read the instructions, the questions (1–5) and all the answer options (A–H) before you listen.
- You can only use an answer A–H once. Remember you can't use the example!

- **Level 3 Teacher's Book** details each part of the exam and suggests teaching tips for the classroom.

PREPARE FOR THE EXAM

A2 KEY FOR SCHOOLS
Listening Part 5

In this part, students listen to a dialogue. They need to match five items to eight options. They are listening for specific information such as objects, places and feelings. They hear the recording twice.

Tip Tell the students that there are five questions plus an example, and eight answers, so there are two answers they don't need to use. They may hear two or more words from the list of answers for each question, but only one will be correct. They must listen for the meaning to choose the right one.

A2 KEY FOR SCHOOLS EXAM OVERVIEW

PAPER / TIMING	PART	WHAT DO CANDIDATES HAVE TO DO?	PRACTICE IN LEVEL 2
Reading and Writing 1 hour Reading	**Part 1** Six 3-option multiple-choice questions	Read six short real-world texts for the main message.	Student's Book page 51, 57 Workbook page 38
	Part 2 Seven 3-option multiple matching questions	Read seven questions and three short texts on the same topic, then match the questions to the texts.	Student's Book page 20 Workbook page 14
	Part 3 Five 3-option multiple-choice questions	Read one long text for detailed understanding and main ideas.	Student's Book page 42 Workbook page 30
	Part 4 Six 3-option multiple-choice cloze questions	Read a factual text and choose the correct vocabulary items to complete the gaps.	Student's Book page 96 Workbook page 70
	Part 5 Six open cloze questions	Complete gaps in an email (and sometimes the reply too) using one word.	Student's Book page 119, 123 Workbook page 86
Writing	**Part 6** One guided writing task	Write a short email or note of 25 words or more.	Student's Book page 75 Workbook page 55
	Part 7 One Picture Story task	Write a short story of 35 words or more based on three picture prompts.	Student's Book page 97, 101 Workbook page 71
Listening About 30 minutes	**Part 1** Five 3-option multiple-choice questions	Identify key information in five short dialogues and choose the correct picture.	Student's Book page 31, 35 Workbook page 23
	Part 2 Five gap fill questions	Listen to a monologue and complete gaps in a page of notes.	Student's Book page 112 Workbook page 83
	Part 3 Five 3-option multiple-choice questions	Listen to a dialogue for key information and answer five 3-option questions.	Student's Book page 75 Workbook page 54
	Part 4 Five 3-option multiple-choice questions	Identify the main idea, message, gist or topic in five short monologues or dialogues and answer five 3-option questions.	Student's Book page 65, 79 Workbook page 47
	Part 5 Five matching questions	Listen to a dialogue for key information and match five items.	Student's Book page 87, 101 Workbook page 63
Speaking 8–10 minutes: Part 1, 3–4 minutes; Part 2, 5–6 minutes	**Part 1** Interlocutor asks questions to each candidate in turn	Respond to questions, giving factual or personal information.	Student's Book page 25, 27, 35, 57, 79, 101
	Part 2 Discussion task with visual stimulus	Candidates discuss likes, dislikes and give reasons.	Student's Book page 27, 123

LISTENING	SPEAKING	WRITING	VIDEO
	Classroom language Ask and answer questions about personal details ə The alphabet		
An interview about an unusual sport	Talking about sports		
A description of a morning routine Interviews about getting up in the morning		A paragraph about your routine	
			Paralympic athletes
A conversation about music and musical instruments A conversation about a music school ə Email addresses, phone numbers and names	Giving opinions about music and musical instruments Speaking Parts 1 and 2		Great Sounds
Conversations about experiences Five short conversations Listening Part 1		A description of a party	
Listening Part 1	Speaking Part 1		
An interview about a moment in history	Giving a presentation about a moment in history		
A conversation about work experience		A paragraph about work	Jobs
			Summer camp
A conversation about holidays A description of a journey	Telling a travel story		Holidays
Descriptions of favourite places		A description of a favourite place	
	Speaking Part 1		
Descriptions of unusual things to use to make clothes	Describing what someone is wearing		
Five short conversations Listening Part 4		A story about a problem buying something online	
			Street fairs everywhere

Key to symbols:
ə Pronunciation ✓ *A2 Key for Schools* exam task ▶ Video

LISTENING	SPEAKING	WRITING	VIDEO
A conversation about a street food festival	Ordering food		Street foods
A conversation about a new computer Listening Part 3		An email to a friend Writing Part 6	Technology
Listening Part 4	Speaking Part 1 Phase 2		
Conversations about health problems A conversation about a race	Giving advice		Health problems
A conversation about a visit to Edinburgh Listening Part 5		An article about a city	
			A view of Scotland
A story about looking for the Loch Ness monster	A story about a strange animal		
An interview about looking after pets		A story Writing Part 7	Animals
Listening Part 5	Speaking Part 1	Writing Part 7	
A conversation about watching a football match A conversation about a talent show	Talking about TV programmes		
A conversation about a school magazine A review of a film		A review of a film, play or book	Books we like
			The world of British TV
A talk about a school trip Listening Part 2 A description of a boarding school	Giving a presentation about your perfect school		School life
A talk about a family tree Descriptions of families		A description of your family Reading Part 5	
	Speaking Part 2		

GET STARTED!

VOCABULARY Things in the classroom

1 Match the words in the box to the letters A–P in the photo.

EP

bag	board	chair	coat
computer	door	exercise book	
map	pencil case	pen	
poster	rubber	ruler	
teacher	textbook	window	

01 Then listen, check and repeat.

GRAMMAR Verb *be*

I am
he/she/it is
you/we/they are

1 What colour is each thing? Write five sentences. In pairs, ask and answer the questions.

A: *It's blue and white.*
B: *Is it the coat?*
A: *Yes, it is.*

there is / there are

2 Look at the photo and read the sentences. Write *yes* or *no*.

0 There's a rubber on the table. *yes*
1 There are five students in the classroom.
2 There's a red pencil case on the table.
3 There's a blue bag on a chair.
4 There's a computer near the window.
5 There's a poster on the wall.
6 There's a bag on the floor.

02 **3** Look at the photo and listen to the questions. Complete the table with a tick (✓) for the right answers.

	Yes, there is.	Yes, there are.	No, there isn't.	No, there aren't.
1		✓		
2				
3				
4				
5				

4 Work with a partner. Student A, look around your classroom for 60 seconds, and then close your eyes. Student B, ask questions about the classroom.

B: *Is there a green bag under my desk?*
A: *Yes, there is. / No, there isn't.*
A: *Are there any coats near the door?*
B: *No, there aren't.*

GET STARTED!

Unit Overview

TOPIC	My classroom and classmates
VOCABULARY	Things in the classroom
GRAMMAR	Verb *be*; *there is / there are*; *have got*
SPEAKING	Classroom language; ask and answer questions about personal details
PRONUNCIATION	The alphabet
VOCABULARY	Numbers; Dates
GRAMMAR	*can*; Present simple
SPEAKING	Find out about your partner

Resources

GRAMMAR REFERENCE AND PRACTICE: SB pages 137 and 138; TB page 247
WORKBOOK: pages 4–7
TEST GENERATOR: Diagnostic test

WARMER
Divide the class into small groups. Appoint a secretary for each group and give them a few minutes to write down as many things in the classroom as they can, e.g. *desk, board*. Don't go through the lists with them yet. Collect in the lists and check them while the students are doing Exercise 1. Award points for correctly spelled words.

VOCABULARY Things in the classroom

1 Ask the students to look at the photo first and to say what they can see. Then, ask them to look at the words. Check that they can pronounce them correctly; in particular remind them that *board* /bɔːd/ and *coat* /kəʊt/ are one syllable. Then, ask the students to match the words to the lettered objects in the photo. If you did the Warmer activity, give the lists back and ask them to compare their lists with the words in the book. If they enjoy competition, award extra points for every word they have written which is *not* in the book.

01

Answers
The answers are recorded for the students to check and then repeat.
A board B map C poster D door E teacher F window G computer H bag I coat J chair K textbook L pen M pencil case N ruler O rubber P exercise book

GRAMMAR Verb *be*

1 First, revise the names of the colours by pointing to things in the classroom and inviting volunteers to name the colours. Write them on the board. Remind students that with the verb *be*, we use *is* for singular objects and *are* for plural objects. If necessary, remind the students of the question and short answer form. Ask the students to write at least five sentences about the objects in the photo using *It's / They're* + colour, e.g. *It's green and white* (the rubber), *it's blue* (the chair). Then, demonstrate the pairwork activity by inviting a student to read out one of their sentences, e.g.:

Student: *It's red and black.*
Teacher: *Is it a coat?*
Student: *No, it isn't.*
Teacher: *Is it a pencil case?*
Student: *Yes, it is.*

Answers
Students' own answers

there is / there are

2 Read the first sentence as a class and encourage the students to look at the photo and to say if the sentence is correct (*yes*) or incorrect (*no*). They then do the exercise on their own.

Answers
1 no 2 yes 3 no 4 no 5 yes 6 yes

02
3 Draw the table onto the board. Play the recording and stop it after the first question. Ask the students to repeat the question, then look at the photo and say the answer. Invite a volunteer to put a tick in the correct space on the table on the board. Play the rest of the recording for the students to complete the table in their books or notebooks. With a stronger class, play the recording again and ask the students to *say* the complete correct answer, e.g. *Yes, there is.*

MIXED ABILITY
Stop the recording after each question, ask the class to repeat the question, and if necessary write it on the board. Give them time to look at the photo, compare their ideas with a partner and then put up their hand when they think they know the correct answer.

Answers
Ticks should be under:
1 Yes, there are.
2 Yes, there is.
3 Yes, there are.
4 No, there isn't.
5 No, there aren't.

» AUDIOSCRIPT TB PAGE 265

4 Play questions 1 and 2 from the recording in Exercise 3 again and invite volunteers to write the two questions on the board. Remind the students that we use *Are there any … ?* with plural things and *Is there a … ?* with singular things. If necessary, revise *my* and *your*. They should take turns to close their eyes while their partner asks at least three questions.

Answers
Students' own answers

BACKGROUND INFORMATION

Research suggest that backpacks should not weigh more than 10% of a students' body weight. Students should try to keep as many books and material as possible at school and they should regularly clean out their bag to check they are not carrying unnecessary items, like heavy toys. Students should also make sure they spread the weight of their bag evenly over both shoulders using both straps and not carry it on just one.

have got

5 In pairs, ask the students to look at things (A–H) and say what they are. Then, ask them to read about Simon's bag and tick the things in his bag.

Answers

B textbooks G exercise books F pencil case
C bottle of water E sandwich H money

6 On the board, write: *What have you got in your bag today? Have you got a/an/any … in your bag today?* Remind students that we use *a/an* with singular things (*an* before a vowel sound) and *any* with plural things. Encourage them to ask you questions about your bag first. Then, in pairs, they ask and answer about their bags. They will need to remember their partner's answer because they will have to write some sentences about their partner's bag.

Allow them some time to ask and answer their questions, then challenge volunteers to come to the board to write some sentences, both positive and negative, about your bag, e.g. *Mrs Fulton has got a bottle of water in her bag. She hasn't got a football.*

They must write at least five sentences about their partner's bag.

Answers

Students' own answers

» GRAMMAR REFERENCE AND PRACTICE ANSWER KEY TB PAGE 247

SPEAKING

PRONUNCIATION | The alphabet

03 1 Play the recording and ask the students to listen and repeat the letters of the alphabet. If necessary, write some groups of letters on the board that students often confuse, e.g. the vowels A E I O U, and consonants G/J, B/V/W.

Audioscript

The alphabet is recorded for the students to listen and repeat.

2 Ask the students to look at the table in their books and ask 'Why is H under A, and why is C under B?' (*because they have the same vowel sound*) Ask the students to write the letters of the alphabet in the right column, according to the vowel sound. Play the recording again (or say the letters yourself) if the students need help.

04 **Answers**

The answers are recorded for students to listen and check.
A: H J K
B: C D E G P T V
F: L M N S X Z
I: Y
O:
U: Q W
R:

3 Tell the students to complete the questions (1–6) before they match them to their answers (a–f). If time allows, ask them in pairs to take turns to ask and answer the questions.

FAST FINISHERS

In pairs, fast finishers ask each other variations on these questions, e.g. *How do you say 'pizarra' in English? How do you spell 'pencil case'?*

Answers

1 repeat – d 2 say – f 3 page – e 4 spell – a 5 borrow – b
6 mean – c

COOLER

Have a spelling race. Divide the class into teams of four or five. Choose a word from this unit and spell it out quickly. The first team to put up their hand, say the word and spell it correctly gets a point. With a stronger class, the students can continue playing in groups.

have got

5 Read what Simon says. Tick (✓) the things he's got in his bag.

My bag's really heavy today! I've got three textbooks, four exercise books and my pencil case. I've also got a bottle of water because I've got football club after school. I've got a sandwich and some money too. I haven't got my phone – that's at home in my bedroom.

6 In pairs, ask and answer the questions.

A: *What have you got in your bag today?*
B: *I've got* ________ *...*
A: *Have you got a/an/any* ________ *in your bag today?*
B: *Yes, I have. / No, I haven't.*

Write five sentences about your partner.

» GRAMMAR REFERENCE AND PRACTICE PAGE 137

SPEAKING

ə PRONUNCIATION | The alphabet

03 **1** Listen and repeat.

Aa	Bb	Cc	Dd
Ee	Ff	Gg	Hh
Ii	Jj	Kk	Ll
Mm	Nn	Oo	Pp
Qq	Rr	Ss	Tt
Uu	Vv	Ww	
Xx	Yy	Zz	

2 In pairs, read out the names of the letters and complete the table with the letters that sound the same. Two columns have no additional letters!

A	B	F	I	O	U	R
H	*C*					

04 Listen and check.

3 Complete questions 1–6 with the words in the box. Then match the questions to answers a–f.

borrow mean page
repeat say spell

1 I'm sorry, can you ________ that, please?
2 How do you ________ *bonjour* in English?
3 What ________ are we on?
4 How do you ________ 'because'?
5 Can I ________ your ruler?
6 What does 'in pairs' ________?

a B-E-C-A-U-S-E.
b Sure, here you are.
c With your partner.
d I said, 'please do Exercise 3'.
e 19, I think.
f Hello.

VOCABULARY Numbers

10 ten | 20 twenty | 30 thirty | 40 forty
50 fifty | 60 sixty | 70 seventy | 80 eighty
90 ninety | 100 a hundred

1 Listen and repeat. (05)

2 Listen and choose the numbers you hear. (06)

a	25	75	39
b	13	30	70
c	41	61	91
d	14	16	40
e	17	19	90
f	15	50	80

Dates

3 Say the months in the correct order.

November, September, March, January
May, December, August, July
February, October, April, June

4 Listen and write the dates. (07)

> When we **say** dates, we **say** *the* and *of*:
> *My birthday is on* **the** *ninth* **of** *June.*
> When we **write** dates, we don't write *the* or *of*:
> *My birthday is on 9th June.*

1 *1st March*

In pairs, compare your answers. Say the dates.

5 In small groups, ask and answer the questions.

- When / your birthday?
- What / today's date?
- When / your mum's/dad's birthday?

Write the dates of all the students in your group.

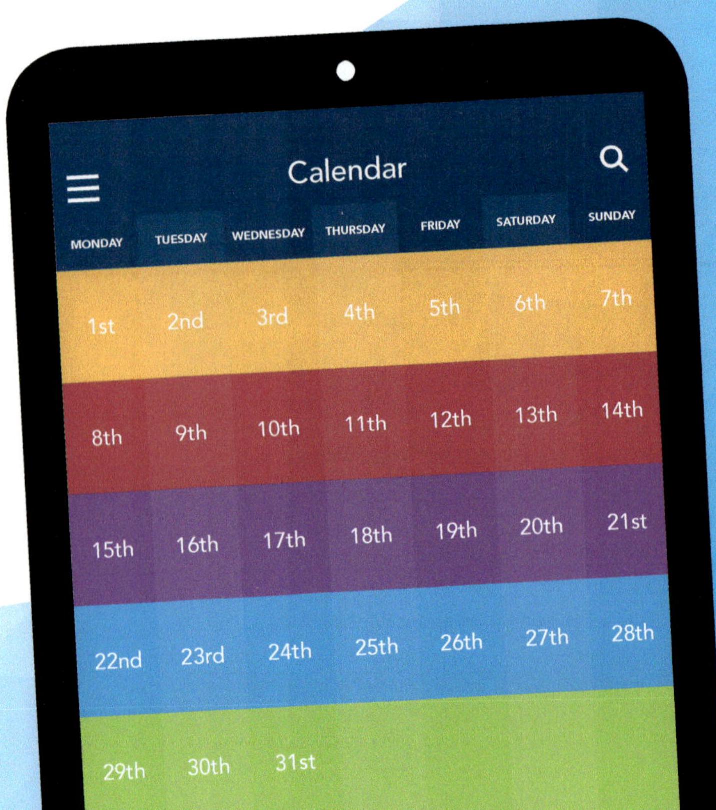

VOCABULARY Numbers

WARMER

Play *I Spy* with the class using the things in the classroom in Exercise 1 on Student's Book page 10. Begin by saying 'I spy with my little eye, something beginning with B'. Encourage the students to ask you questions before they guess what the word is. For example:

Teacher: *I spy with my little eye something beginning with B.*
Student A: *Is it big?*
Teacher: *Yes, it is.*
Student B: *Is it near the door?*
Teacher: *Yes, it is.*
Student C: *Is it the board?*
Teacher: *Yes, it is.*

With a stronger class, the students play the game in small groups.

05 **1** Ask the students to notice how these numbers are always said with the stress on the first part of the word, e.g. *twenty*.

Audioscript

The numbers are recorded for the students to listen and repeat.

06 **2** Encourage the students to work in pairs and say the numbers in this exercise first, before they listen to the recording. If time allows, after the students have completed the activity, ask them in pairs to take turns to say another number for their partner to choose the right number; e.g. a 25, b 13.

Answers / Audioscript

a 75 b 30 c 91 d 14 e 19 f 50

Dates

3 Highlight the syllables and stress in each month (e.g. *Jan-u-ry*). Next, ask the students to say each month correctly. Then, in pairs, the students say the months in order.

Answers

January, February, March, April, May, June, July, August, September, October, November, December

07 **4** Ask 'What's the date today?' and write the date on the board using the ordinal number, e.g. *7th September*. Ask the students to repeat the date and draw their attention to the box which explains the difference between how we say dates and how we write them. Check that they can pronounce the ordinal numbers on the calendar correctly, especially *20th* (twentieth) and *30th* (thirtieth). Then, ask them to listen and write down the eight dates on the recording. In pairs, they then check their answers by asking and answering questions:

A: *What's 1?*
B: *It's the first of March. What's 2?*

Answers

1 1st March 2 12th October 3 8th May 4 25th February
5 22nd July 6 31st December 7 3rd April 8 11th August

» AUDIOSCRIPT TB PAGE 265

5 Encourage the students to say the complete questions first. (*When's your birthday? What's today's date? / What's the date today? When's your mum's / dad's birthday?*) If necessary, write them on the board. Then, in small groups, the students take turns to ask and answer the questions. Remind them to begin their answers with *It's* .... Point out that they need to write down the other students' dates.

FAST FINISHERS

Fast finishers write some new questions about dates, e.g. *When's the next holiday? What's tomorrow's date? What date is our national day?* When the others are ready, the fast finishers ask the class their questions.

Answers

Students' own answers

GRAMMAR *can*

1 Encourage the students to look at the photos first and try to say what the people are doing in each one before they read the words and match them to the photos.

Answers
A draw a car B swim under water C make a cake
D ride a bike E speak three languages F run 5km
G play tennis H stand on your head

2 Encourage the students to make a question with each of the words in Exercise 1 first. With a weaker class, you might want to do this together on the board. Allow them time to ask and answer the questions in pairs. Then, if appropriate, ask them to stand up and ask at least four other students the questions. If not, they can do this in groups of six. Point out that they should take notes as they will need to report back to the class. They might find this easier if they complete a chart in their notebooks like the one below.

Name	swim under water?	speak three languages?	ride a bike?
Jon	✓	×	✓

When they have finished, ask 'How many students can swim under water?' and encourage them to answer with either a number or with names, e.g. *Five students can swim under water / Ana and David can swim under water.*

Answers
Students' own answers

Present simple

3 Ask the students to read what the people say about themselves and answer the questions. Point out that they should use complete sentences. In Unit 1, the students will look at the present simple with adverbs of frequency.

Answers
1 Yes, he does.
2 He hasn't got any brothers.
3 She likes swimming.
4 He wants to go to China.
5 He plays football.
6 She goes shopping on Saturday.

4 Write the question prompts on the board and encourage the class to make complete questions. Demonstrate by getting volunteers to ask you the questions and give full answers. For example:

Student: *What kind of music do you like?*

Teacher: *I like pop and rock. I don't like classical music.*

Then, the students take turns to ask and answer the questions. Point out that they will need to take notes so that they can tell the class about their partner.

MIXED ABILITY

For weaker students, write the question prompts on the board, leaving a space for the missing words, e.g.

1 …… do sports every day?

2 What kind of music …… like?

Invite volunteers to complete the questions on the board. Then, as above, demonstrate the activity and then ask the students to ask and answer in pairs. If they need more help, suggest that they copy the questions into their notebook and write down the answers so they are true for them, before they ask and answer with a partner.

Answers
Students' own answers

» **GRAMMAR REFERENCE AND PRACTICE ANSWER KEY TB PAGE 247**

SPEAKING

1 Brainstorm the questions as a class first. Then, invite two stronger students to demonstrate the activity orally, giving complete answers. The students then write the questions individually before asking and answering in pairs. Point out that they need to listen to their partner carefully as they will need to write some sentences about them. Remind them that when they do this, they need to use the third person *he* or *she*.

Answers
Students' own answers

COOLER

Tell the class that you're going to read four sentences about yourself and that the information in two of them is incorrect. Encourage them to listen carefully and say or guess which two sentences are incorrect and, if possible, correct the information. For example:

My name's Mrs Brown. (correct)

I'm 18 years old. (incorrect: I'm 40 years old.)

I've got two brothers. (correct)

I like travelling and I love sweets. (incorrect: I don't like sweets.)

Then, ask the students to write four sentences about themselves and include two sentences with incorrect information. In small groups, the students read their sentences and the others have to guess the incorrect information. If the students enjoy competition, they can award a point for identifying each incorrect sentence and an extra point if they can correct it.

GRAMMAR *can*

1 **Match the photos A–H to the words in the box.**

draw a car	make a cake	play tennis
ride a bike	run 5 km	speak three languages
stand on your head	swim underwater	

A

B

C

D

E

F

G

H

2 **In pairs, ask and answer about the activities in Exercise 1.**

Can you play tennis?

Yes, I can.

Can you swim under water?

No, I can't.

Now ask around the class. How many people can …

- swim under water?
- speak three languages?
- ride a bike?
- play tennis?
- draw a car?

Present simple

3 **Read about the students and answer the questions. Use complete sentences.**

1 Does Tyler like music?
2 How many brothers has Jason got?
3 What sport does Millie like?
4 Where does Tyler want to go?
5 What does Jason do every day?
6 When does Millie go shopping?

Hi, my name's Tyler.

I've got a brother and a sister. I like music and I love travelling. I want to go to China.

Hello, I'm Jason.

I haven't got any brothers or sisters. I like all sports and I play football every day.

Hello, my name's Millie.

I like swimming and I often go shopping with my sister on Saturday. I love sweets but I don't like ice cream.

4 **Work with a partner. Ask and answer the questions.**

0 / do sports every day?
A: *Do you do sports every day?*
B: *Yes, I do. I play tennis after school every day.*
1 What kind of music / like?
2 / like travelling?
3 / play football at school?
4 / like swimming?
5 What / favourite food?

Now tell the class.

Manuela doesn't like swimming. She likes …

» **GRAMMAR REFERENCE AND PRACTICE PAGE 138**

SPEAKING

1 **Write questions to find out about your partner's …**

- age
- address
- phone number
- brothers and sisters
- favourite pop star
- favourite school subject

In pairs, ask and answer the questions. Then write sentences about your partner.

1 SPORTS AND GAMES

ABOUT YOU

Do you like basketball, football or tennis?
Which sport do you prefer?
Do you play any sports?

VOCABULARY AND READING

Sports

1 Match the pictures A–M to the words in the box.

EP

do athletics	play badminton
do gymnastics	play baseball
go cycling	play hockey
go sailing	play rugby
go skating	play table tennis
go snowboarding	play volleyball
go surfing	

08 Listen and check. Then repeat.

2 In pairs, ask and answer the questions.

1 Which of the sports do you do in teams (a group of people)? Which do you do alone (just one person)?
2 Which of the sports can you do both in teams and alone?
3 Which of these sports do *you* do?
4 Do you prefer team sports or sports you do alone? Why?

PRONUNCIATION /eɪ/ and /aɪ/

3 Put the words into the correct column.

baseball bike fly play riding skating

/eɪ/ sailing	/aɪ/ cycling

09 Listen and check. Then repeat.

4 Read Sophie's and Ben's blogs. Who does their sport every week? Who can't do their sport where they live?

5 Read about Sophie and Ben again and answer the questions.

1 How many women and girls do Sophie's sport?
2 What does Sophie do at the weekend?
3 What does Sophie want to do at Loughborough University?
4 Where does Ben prefer to be?
5 Why does Ben go snowboarding every day?
6 Ben says he's 'goofy-foot'. What does 'goofy-foot' mean?

TEENBLOG: SPORT

Post about you and your sport here.

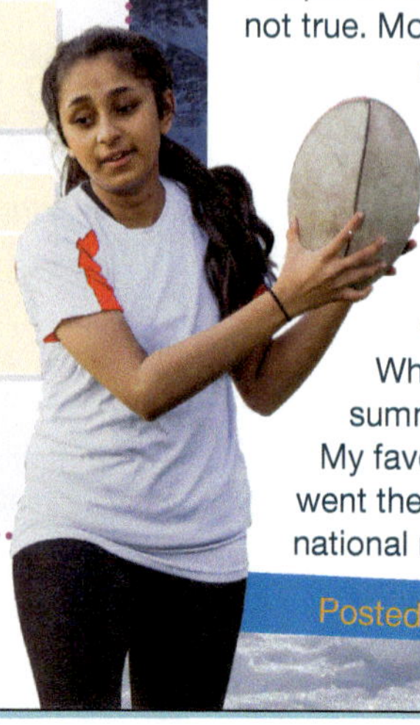

It's fun!

My sport is … rugby! That's me in the photo. People think that rugby is for boys, but that's not true. More than 18,000 women and girls play rugby in England. My team always plays a match on Saturday or Sunday, and I usually go to practice games three times a week. It's hard work, but it's never boring! I'm 14 and I play for the U15s. That's the team for players under the age of 15. When I'm older, I want to go to the rugby summer camp at Loughborough University. My favourite player, Fran Matthews, went there and now she plays for the England national rugby team.

Posted by **Sophie White**

1 SPORTS AND GAMES

Unit Overview

TOPIC	Common and unusual sports and games
VOCABULARY AND READING	Sports Teenblog: Sport
PRONUNCIATION	/eɪ/ and /aɪ/
GRAMMAR	Adverbs of frequency
READING	Try these sports!
VOCABULARY	Sports equipment
LISTENING	An interview about an unusual sport
SPEAKING	Talking about sports

Resources

GRAMMAR REFERENCE AND PRACTICE: SB page 138; TB page 247
WORKBOOK: pages 8–11
PHOTOCOPIABLE WORKSHEETS: Grammar worksheet Unit 1; Vocabulary worksheet Unit 1
TEST GENERATOR: Unit test 1

WARMER

Write _ _ _ _ _ _ / _ _ _ / _ _ _ _ _ on the board, with one space for every missing letter.

Encourage the students to take turns to guess the missing letters (*Sports and games*).

If the students say a wrong letter, write it on the board. Tell them that they can only guess five wrong letters.

ABOUT YOU

As a class, brainstorm a list of follow-up questions onto the board, e.g. *Why do you prefer it? How often do you play it? Who do you play it with? Where do you play it?* Encourage the student who is asking the questions to ask follow-up questions.

VOCABULARY AND READING

Sports

1 Ask students to try to name the sports in the pictures before they match them to the words in the box. Invite the students to say when we use *play* (*ball sports*), *go* (*sports ending in -ing*) and *do* (*all other sports*). Ask the students to make a table of sports you can *play*, *go* and *do* in their notebooks.

08

Answers

The answers are recorded for students to check and then repeat.
A go sailing B play volleyball C play table tennis
D go cycling E go snowboarding F play baseball
G do athletics H play rugby I play hockey J do gymnastics
K play badminton L go surfing M go skating

2 Ask students to read the first two questions and point out the explanations for *in teams* and *alone* given in brackets.

Answers

1 You play volleyball, baseball, rugby and hockey in teams. You go surfing, sailing and snowboarding alone.
2 You can do athletics and gymnastics in teams and alone. You can go cycling and skating in teams and alone. You can play badminton and table tennis in teams and alone.
3 and 4 Students' own answers

PRONUNCIATION /eɪ/ and /aɪ/

3 Write /eɪ/ *sailing* and /aɪ/ *cycling* on the board in two columns and model the pronunciation. Encourage the students to say the words in the box aloud and write them in the correct column.

09

Answers

The answers are recorded for students to check and then repeat.
/eɪ/ sailing, baseball, play, skating
/aɪ/ cycling, bike, fly, riding

4 Encourage the class to look at the photos first and say what sports Sophie and Ben do. Then, ask them to look at the two texts quickly and check their ideas. Finally, ask them to skim the texts to find the answers to both questions and to underline the answers in the text. Set a time limit (e.g. one minute) for this to discourage them from reading every word.

Answers

Sophie does her sport every week – four times a week (she plays one match and three practice games).
Ben can't go snowboarding in the city. He goes to the mountains.

5 Ask the students to try to answer the questions from memory before they read the texts again. If appropriate, remind them to underline the answers in the texts and write the question number next to the underlined answer. Check the answers as a class, encouraging students to say where they found the answers in the text.

Answers

1 More than 18,000 women and girls (play rugby).
2 She plays a rugby match.
3 She wants to go to a rugby summer camp.
4 He prefers to be in the mountains. (He feels at home there.)
5 He's good at snowboarding and wants to become a famous snowboarder.
6 'Goofy-foot' means Ben's right foot is in front on the board.

FAST FINISHERS

Encourage the fast finishers to compare their answers by using the phrases *What have you put (for number 1)? I've put … because here it says … .*

In a mixed ability class, encourage the fast finishers to help those who are struggling to find the answers.

10 The Reading text is recorded for students to listen and read.

GRAMMAR Adverbs of frequency

Books closed. Write these sentences on the board; don't rub out these sentences until after Exercise 2:

My team always plays a match on Saturday or Sunday.

It's never boring.

I sometimes go snowboarding with Mum.

Encourage the students to tell you whether the sentences refer to the present, past or future (*present*) and whether they are talking about something we are doing now or something we do often or every day (*often or every day*). Ask them to say what the underlined words are (*adverbs of frequency*).

1 Ask students to find the adverbs of frequency in the blogs. Copy the line onto the board and encourage volunteers to come to the board and write the adverbs in the correct place.

Answers

a never b sometimes c often d usually e always

2 Encourage students to look at the sentences on the board again (see above) before they answer the questions.

Answers

1 Present simple: My team always plays a match on Saturday or Sunday.
I often go with my little sister and other young people.
I sometimes go snowboarding with Mum.
2 *Be*: It's never boring.
It's usually quiet.

3 Encourage the students to look at the sentences on the board to help them complete the rules.

Answers

In sentences with the verb *be*, we put the adverb of frequency after the verb.
In sentences with the present simple, we put the adverb of frequency before the verb.

4 Write *I don't often play rugby* on the board. Check understanding of what a 'main' verb is by asking a volunteer to come up and underline the main verb (*play*). Then, students complete the rules.

Answers

In negatives and questions with the present simple, we put the adverb of frequency before the main verb.
In negatives and questions with the verb *be*, we put the adverb of frequency after the verb *be*.

» GRAMMAR REFERENCE AND PRACTICE ANSWER KEY TB PAGE 247

5 Encourage the students to underline the main verb in each sentence first (see answers below). Then ask them to say whether the adverb should go before or after the verb.

Answers

1 I usually play hockey at school on Fridays.
2 Sophie is often tired after rugby matches.
3 People don't always go sailing in teams.
4 My uncle and my dad never play table tennis.
5 Is gymnastics sometimes dangerous?
6 Do you often go cycling?

6 This icon indicates that the exercise has been informed by the Cambridge Learner Corpus. Encourage the students to look at each group of words first and say whether they need to make an affirmative sentence, a negative sentence or a question.

Answers

1 You are always welcome in our sports club.
2 We never do athletics on Mondays.
3 Does she usually go skating with her brother?
4 Students do not often play table tennis at school.
5 Lizzie and her sister sometimes go cycling at the weekend.

7 Highlight the use of *but* for a contrast (*I often … , but I never …*), *and* for in addition (*I often … and I usually …*) and also the use of adjectives (*It's great fun* and *It's never boring*). Encourage the students to ask questions with *How often do you …?* and to give full answers with adverbs of frequency and adjectives. Model a good answer with a strong student:

Student: *How often do you play badminton?*

Teacher: *I never play badminton, but I sometimes play tennis. It's great fun. How about you?*

Answers

Students' own answers

MIXED ABILITY

Put a stronger student with a weaker student. Ask the weaker students to ask some questions first so that the stronger student models some good answers.

8 Remind the students to use the follow-up questions from the beginning of the lesson (e.g. *Who do you play it with? Where do you play it?*). If time allows, encourage volunteers to report back to the class on their partner's answers.

Answers

Students' own answers

» GRAMMAR WORKSHEET UNIT 1

COOLER

Play Vocabulary Tennis. Divide the class into two teams and give each team the name of a famous tennis player. Team A says a sport and Team B scores a point if they make a correct sentence using *play*, *go* or *do* and an adverb of frequency. Team B then says a sport and so on. For example:

Team A: *badminton*

Team B: *I often play badminton with my friends.* (one point)

Team B: *skating*

Team A: *I go skating never.* (no points)

GRAMMAR Adverbs of frequency

We use the present simple to talk about things we do often or every day.
I go snowboarding every day.

1 **Look at these examples from the blogs. The adverbs of frequency are in purple.**

My team **always** plays a match on Saturday or Sunday. It's **never** boring.
It's **usually** quiet.
I **often** go with my little sister and other young people.
I **sometimes** go snowboarding with Mum.

Write the words in purple on the right place on the line.

0% 100%

a ______ b ______ c ______ d ______ e ______

2 **Answer the questions.**

1 Which sentences in Exercise 1 have a present simple verb?
2 Which sentences in Exercise 1 have the verb *be*?

3 **Choose the correct words to complete the rules.**

In sentences with the **verb *be***, we put the adverb of frequency *before* / *after* the **verb**.
In sentences with the **present simple**, we put the adverb of frequency *before* / *after* the **verb**.

Goofy-foot or regular?

I love the snow and the mountains. I feel at home there. I live in a city and there's no snow here, but in the holidays, I always go to the mountains with my family. I sometimes go snowboarding with Mum, but I often go with my little sister and other young people. Mum usually skis with my dad, and my sister and I like spending more time in the snow than they do. It's usually quiet. When we're in the mountains, I go snowboarding every day and I'm getting really good. I often think about the future – I want to be a famous snowboarder one day, like Max Parrot. Oh, and I'm *goofy-foot* – that means I put my right foot at the front of the board.

Posted by **Ben James**

4 **Read the examples and choose the correct words to complete the rules.**

People don't **always** play sport in teams.
Ben doesn't **usually** go snowboarding with his dad.
Do you **sometimes** play volleyball with friends?
Is rugby **often** dangerous?
Football isn't **always** boring!

In negatives and questions with the **present simple**, we put the adverb of frequency *before* / *after* the **main verb.**
In negatives and questions with the **verb *be***, we put the adverb of frequency *before* / *after* the verb *be*.

» GRAMMAR REFERENCE AND PRACTICE PAGE 138

5 **Put the adverbs in the right place to complete the sentences and questions.**

1 I play hockey at school on Fridays. (usually)
2 Sophie is tired after rugby matches. (often)
3 People don't go sailing in teams. (always)
4 My uncle and my dad play table tennis. (never)
5 Is gymnastics dangerous? (sometimes)
6 Do you go cycling? (often)

6 **Put the words in order to make sentences and questions and questions.**

0 often / school / plays / my friend / after / football
My friend often plays football after school.
1 welcome / sports / are / in / our / club / always / you
2 Mondays / do / on / athletics / never / we
3 skating / brother / she / go / her / usually / does / with / ?
4 table tennis / students / not / often / do / school / play / at
5 cycling / and / her sister / at / the weekend / sometimes / Lizzie / go /

7 **How often do you do the sports in Exercise 1 on page 14?**

I never play rugby, but I often play volleyball. It's great fun. How about you?

I sometimes play rugby, and I often go cycling. It's never boring.

8 **In pairs, ask and answer the questions.**

1 What sports do you do?
2 How often do you do them?
3 Do you play sports at school?
4 How often do you watch sports on TV?
5 How often do you go to watch sports?
6 Who are your favourite sports stars?

READING

1 Look at the photos of the sports and games. What can you see?

2 Read the three texts and match them to the photos.

11

TRY THESE SPORTS!

1 CYCLEBALL

This sport is like football on bikes. There are two teams. Each team has usually got two players. The bikes don't have any brakes to stop them. Players in each team try to hit the ball into the goal. They can use their bike or their heads to do this. The ball is quite heavy – it weighs half a kilogram. The winning team is the team with the most goals at the end of the game.

2 *GILLI-DANDA*

This is an ancient sport from India. The players use two things: one long stick, called a *danda* and a short egg-shaped bat, called a *gilli*. There are two teams. One player puts the *gilli* on the ground inside a small circle and hits it into the air with the *danda*. Then the player hits the *gilli* again and runs to touch a spot outside the circle to get a point.

3 OCTOPUSH

The sport is also called *underwater hockey*. There are two teams. Each team has got six players. Players swim underwater to play this game. They use small sticks and a puck. The puck is a little like a flat ball. It's heavy and weighs about a kilogram. Players try to push the puck along the bottom of a swimming pool into the other team's goal. The winning team is the team with the most goals at the end of the match.

3 Read the three texts again. Are the sentences right (✓) or wrong (✗)?

1. There are always two players in a cycleball team.
2. The ball in cycleball is small and light.
3. Players in cycleball can't hit the ball with their hands.
4. *Gilli-danda* comes from India.
5. The stick and the bat in *gilli-danda* are the same size.
6. Players use a small ball in *gilli-danda*.
7. People play octopush in teams.
8. Players in octopush hit the ball, or puck, with their hands.
9. Players in octopush swim underwater to play their game.

TALKING POINTS

Which of these sports do you want to try?

Do you have any sports like these in your country?

READING

WARMER

Before the class, write some of the sports from pages 14 and 15 on the board with the vowels missing, for example *b_dm_nt_n* and *v_ll_yb_ll*. Challenge teams to complete the words as quickly as they can.

BACKGROUND INFORMATION

These are three real sports.

Cycleball: People have been playing this sport since 1893 and there is an annual world championship which is governed by the International Cycling Union. However, because the bikes have no brakes, the gears are fixed and players can't put their feet on the ground, this sport is very difficult to play and crashes, falls and injuries are common.

Gilli-danda: This game is often played in rural areas between teams from different villages. Versions of this game are played in other parts of the world; for example *bilharda* in Galicia, Spain, *lippa* in Italy and *pee-wee* in the USA. Some people believe that sports like cricket, baseball and softball evolved from *gilli-danda*.

Octopush (or underwater hockey): This sport was invented in the UK in the early 1950s by divers who were bored of just swimming up and down the pool to get fit. It's now popular all over the world. As it is played underwater, it isn't easy for people to watch this sport.

1 Write these expressions on the board: *I can see … , I think it's a … , there's a … .* Encourage the students to say as much as they can about each photo by asking them to describe the players, their clothes and equipment, the place where the sport is played, and the sport itself. Encourage them to use full sentences. If necessary, pre-teach *stick* and *bat* by pointing to the stick bat in the photo (or drawing a picture on the board) and *underwater* by asking 'Where are the swimmers in photo B?'

Possible answers

A There are some people on bikes. They are trying to hit the ball with their bike.
B There are some swimmers underwater. They are pushing a small object.
C There is a boy with a stick. He's hitting something.

2 Set a time limit (e.g. three minutes) to encourage the students to skim read the text for gist. When they think they know the answer, ask them to underline the words or expressions in the text which suggest the answer, e.g. in the first text, *football on bikes, any brakes, hit the ball into the goal*, etc. During open class feedback, invite them to justify their answers, e.g. *A is cycleball because they are playing football on bikes.*

Answers

1 A 2 C 3 B

3 Ask the students to read the sentences in pairs and try to say if they are right or wrong before they read the texts again. If appropriate, encourage them to underline the answers in the texts and to correct the wrong sentences. Students may find question 6 a little more difficult because in *gilli-danda*, there isn't a ball as such – the short bat is used as a ball.

MIXED ABILITY

Divide the students into three groups: Group 1 reads the sentences about cycleball (1–3) and decides if they are right or wrong; Group 2 reads about *gilli-danda* (4–6); and Group 3 reads about octopush (7–9). All the students read the other sentences for homework and complete the exercise.

FAST FINISHERS

Fast finishers write three or more right or wrong sentences about the three sports for the rest of the class.

Answers

1 ✗ (There are usually two players.) 2 ✗ (The ball is quite heavy.) 3 ✗ (They can use their bike or their heads.) 4 ✓ 5 ✗ (There is one long stick called a danda and a short bat called a gilli.) 6 ✗ (Players use a short bat.) 7 ✓ 8 ✗ (Players hit the ball, or puck, with small sticks.) 9 ✓

11 The Reading text is recorded for students to listen and read.

TALKING POINTS

Encourage the students to explain why by using *because …* . With the second question, extend the conversation by encouraging the students to think of some sports in their country which visitors might find unusual. Ask them to think about how they would explain this sport. In the Speaking section at the end of the lesson, students will have an opportunity to talk about a sport they know.

VOCABULARY Sports equipment

1 Encourage the students to underline the sports equipment in the three Reading texts on page 16 (e.g. bike, ball, goal, stick, bat, puck). Then, ask them to try to find some of these underlined words in the photos before matching the words in the box.

12

Answers

The answers are recorded for students to check and then repeat.

A racket B stick C bat D ball E board

2 Books closed. Copy the table onto the board with the column headings and challenge the students to think of at least two sports for the first two columns and one sport for the last column (e.g. *surfing*, *snowboarding* and *skateboarding*). If appropriate, organise the students into teams and award points for sports with the correct spelling. Next, ask the students to complete the table in their books, but point out that some words don't go in the table, i.e. *sailing*, *skating*, *cycling*, *swimming* and *running*. Then, ask them to add any extra sports from the board.

13

Answers

The answers are recorded for students to check and then repeat.

Use a stick, a racket or a bat	Use a ball	Use a board
badminton (racket), baseball (bat), *gilli-danda* (sticks or one stick and one bat), hockey (stick), octopush (stick), table tennis (bat), tennis (racket)	baseball, basketball, cycleball, football, hockey, rugby, table tennis, tennis, volleyball	surfing snowboarding

3 Encourage the students to cover the words in Exercise 2 and try to complete the sentences from memory first. When they have finished, encourage them to test each other on these words in pairs by asking the question *What do you need to play [name of sport]?* and answering *You need ....*

Answers

1 bat 2 balls 3 bat 4 ball 5 racket 6 stick 7 ball

» VOCABULARY WORKSHEET UNIT 1

LISTENING

1 Encourage the students to look at the photos and predict how the sport is played, what equipment is needed, whether it is played in teams, and whether it is played inside or outside.

Answers

1 B 2 A

14 2 As they listen for the first time, students should also check their predictions in Exercise 1.

Answers

Pato

14 3 Encourage the students to read the sentences first and choose the correct words before they listen again. With a weaker class, play the recording for a third time and stop after each answer. With a stronger class, play the recording for a third time, stop after each of the interviewer's questions, and encourage the students to repeat the question with the correct intonation.

Answers

1 four 2 six 3 give 4 throw

» AUDIOSCRIPT TB PAGE 265

SPEAKING

1 Encourage the students to choose a sport quickly. Alternatively, write some sports on different slips of paper and give one slip to each student. Then, ask the students to read through the questions and make some notes on their sport. Check that the students can say each question with an interested intonation (rather than flat and bored) by asking them to listen to you and then repeat. Student A now asks Student B about their sport. Point out that Student B shouldn't use the name of the sport in their answer as Student A will need to guess the sport. Encourage Student B to use some of the new vocabulary and to use full sentences. Have Student A guess the sport before Student B confirms the answer. They then swap and Student B asks Student A about their sport.

Answers

Students' own answers

COOLER

Have a general knowledge sports quiz. On the board, write some questions based on the information in this unit (see below). Play in teams. Each team takes turns to answer a question and gets a point for a correct answer. If time allows, students write five questions for another general knowledge sports quiz. They can either use the information in the unit or they can look for new information on the internet. Finish the next class with this new quiz.

Sample questions (and answers)

1 What sport does Sophie White play? (rugby)
2 How often does she go to practice games? (three times a week)
3 Does Ben James live in the mountains? (no)
4 Does he go snowboarding with his friends? (no)
5 What's another name for octopush? (underwater hockey)
6 How many players are there on a cycleball team? (two)
7 Are *gilli-danda* sticks the same size? (no)
8 What's special about a Pato ball? (there are six handles)

VOCABULARY Sports equipment

1 **Match the photos A–E to the words in the box.**

EP

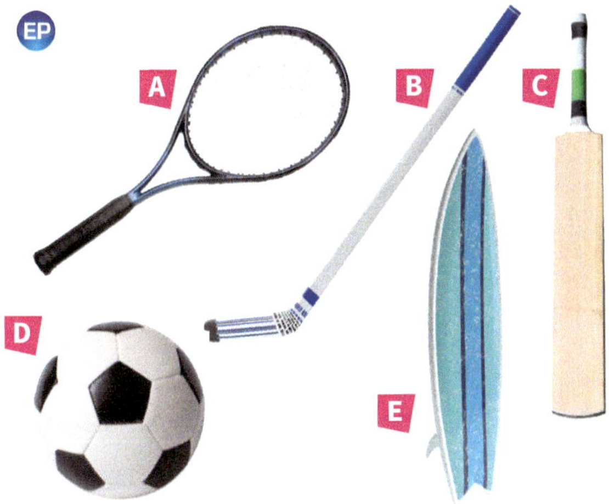

bat ball board racket stick

Listen and check. Then repeat. 12

2 **Complete the table with the sports in the box. Some sports can go in more than one column.**

badminton baseball basketball
cycleball cycling football
gilli-danda hockey octopush
rugby running sailing skating
snowboarding surfing swimming
table tennis tennis volleyball

 Use a stick, a racket or a bat	 Use a ball	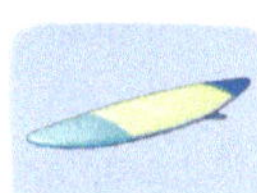 Use a board

Listen and check. Then repeat. 13

3 **Complete the information with the sports words in Exercise 1.**

TABLE TENNIS
1 One ________ for each player.
2 One small, light ________ for the game.

BASEBALL
3 One ________ for each team.
4 One small, hard ________ for the game.

BADMINTON
5 One ________ for each player.

OCTOPUSH
6 One small ________ for each player.
7 One heavy puck, like a flat ________ for the game.

LISTENING

1 **Look at the photo of the sport. Match the words 1–2 to A and B in the photo.**

1 handle **2** net

14 **2** **Listen to an interview with a boy about his unusual sport. What's the name of the sport?**

14 **3** **Listen again, and choose the correct words.**

1 There are *four* / *six* players in each team.
2 There are *six* / *eight* handles on the ball.
3 Players *throw* / *give* the ball to each other.
4 Players *throw* / *put* the ball in the net to score a goal.

SPEAKING

1 **Think of a sport. Choose one from this unit or another sport that you know. In pairs, take turns to ask and answer the questions.**

1 Do people do this sport inside or outside?
2 Is the sport on or under water?
3 Is this sport on snow?
4 What things do people need to do this sport?
5 Do people play this sport in your country?
6 What do you like about this sport?
7 Who are some of the famous players of this sport?

Try and guess the sport.

2 THIS IS MY DAY

ABOUT YOU

What time does your alarm go off on a school day?
What do you do in the morning before you go to school?

0:03 / 4:05

MY MORNING ROUTINE 11,345 views 1k Share

Maddie's mad life FOLLOW

A
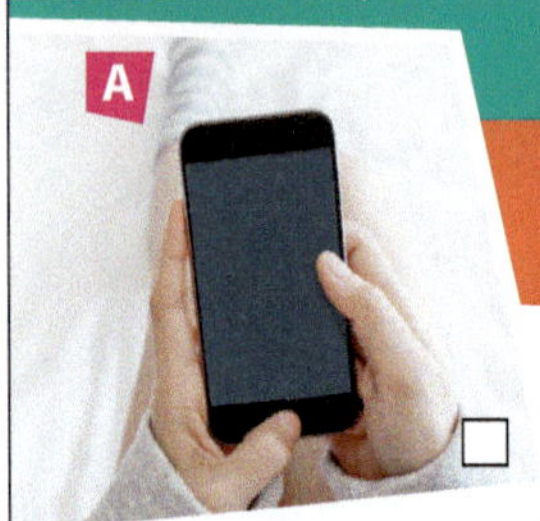

B

C

D

E
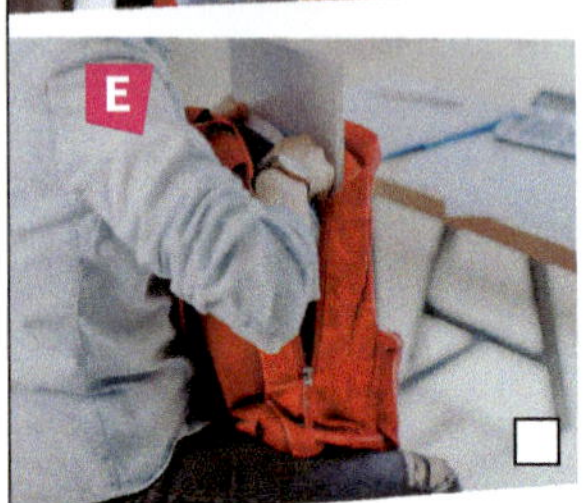

F

G

H

I

J

VOCABULARY AND LISTENING

Daily routines

1 Match the photos to the phrases in the box.

EP

brush your hair	check your messages	
clean your teeth	get dressed	have breakfast
leave the house	prepare your school bag	
put on your shoes	tidy your room	wake up

15 Listen and check. Then repeat.

16 **2** Listen to Maddie talking about her morning routine. Number the photos in the order that you hear them.

3 Can you remember Maddie's routine? Complete the sentences with the times in the box. You don't need to use all the times.

6.00	6.30	6.45	6.50	7.00	7.10
7.15	7.30	7.40	8.00	8.10	

1 My alarm goes off at ________.
2 I get up at ________.
3 I clean my teeth at ________.
4 I get dressed at ________.
5 I prepare my school bag at ________.
6 I put my shoes on and leave home at ________.

16 Listen again and check.

4 In pairs or small groups, talk about your morning routine.

I wake up at seven o'clock.

I get dressed and then I have breakfast.

2 THIS IS MY DAY

Unit Overview

TOPIC	Everyday routines
VOCABULARY AND LISTENING	Daily routines A description of a morning routine
GRAMMAR	Present continuous and present simple
READING	Tell us about your day ...
VOCABULARY	Food
PRONUNCIATION	The sound /ə/
LISTENING	Interviews about getting up in the morning
WRITING	A paragraph about your routine
EXAM TASKS	Reading Part 2

Resources

GRAMMAR REFERENCE AND PRACTICE: SB page 139; TB page 247
WORKBOOK: pages 12–15
PHOTOCOPIABLE WORKSHEETS: Grammar worksheet Unit 2; Vocabulary worksheet Unit 2
TEST GENERATOR: Unit test 2

WARMER

If appropriate, ask the students to close their eyes. Set off an alarm on a mobile phone or computer or make an appropriate noise or draw a picture on the board. Ask the class 'What happened?' and write on the board: *When my alarm goes off on a school day, I ...* . Brainstorm two or three activities from the class (e.g. *get up*, *have a shower*) and then challenge the students in small groups to write down as many activities as they can in two minutes. Write their ideas onto the board. Leave this list on the board so that the students can use it in the *About you* box and Exercise 1 below.

ABOUT YOU

Encourage the students to use the activities in the list on the board (see Warmer) to answer their partner's questions.

VOCABULARY AND LISTENING

Daily routines

1 Ask the students to match as many words on the board (see Warmer) to the photos in the book and to say what the person is doing in the remaining photos before looking at the words in the book.

15

Answers

The answers are recorded for students to check and then repeat.
A check your messages B tidy your room C get dressed
D have breakfast E prepare your school bag F leave home
G wake up H brush your hair I put on your shoes
J clean your teeth

16

2 Ask the students to look at the photos first and try to guess the order before they listen. With a weaker class, play the audio again stopping after each answer.

Answers

A 2 B 7 C 5 D 3 E 8 F 10 G 1 H 6 I 9 J 4

16

3 First, check that the students can say the times correctly, reminding them that there are often two ways of saying the same time, e.g. *six thirty* or *half past six* and *six forty-five* or *a quarter to seven*. With a weaker class, stop the audio after each answer.

Answers

1 6.30 2 6.45 3 7.00 4 7.15 5 7.30 6 7.40

» AUDIOSCRIPT TB PAGE 265

4 Ask the class to look at the sentences about Maddie in Exercise 3 and think of some questions to ask her, e.g. *What time does your alarm go off? Do you get up when your alarm goes off?* Write the questions on the board, practise the pronunciation and encourage the students to use these questions in their discussion.

Answers

Students' own answers

GRAMMAR Present continuous and present simple

1 Ask the students to look at the examples and say what the differences are between the first and second set (*the first are all be + -ing form and are talking about things happening today, at the moment or now; the second have adverbs of frequency because they talk about things we usually do*).

Answers

continuous
simple

2 Point out that the students should complete these rules with the underlined words in Exercise 1. Encourage stronger students to think of one or two more words for each one, e.g. present continuous: *right now*, *this week*; present simple: *often*, *normally*.

Answers

never, always, sometimes, usually
today, at the moment, now

» **GRAMMAR REFERENCE AND PRACTICE ANSWER KEY TB PAGE 247**

3 Before they complete the exercise, ask the students to look at the sentences again in Exercise 1 and say how to form the present simple (*I/you/we/they + verb, he/she/it + verb + s*) and present continuous (*I/you/he/she/it/we/they + be + verb + -ing*).

MIXED ABILITY

Ask stronger students to work through Exercises 3–6 at their own pace (see Fast finishers activity after Exercise 6). Ask the weaker students to work in pairs, find the adverb (*at the moment*, *always*, *today*, etc.) in each sentence and if appropriate underline it. Check their ideas. Pens down. Ask the whole group to say whether they should use the present continuous (PC) or present simple (PS) in each sentence and if appropriate, ask them to write *PS* or *PC* next to each one before they complete the exercise. With very weak students, read the complete sentence to them with the verb in the correct tense. Ask them to listen and say if the verb is in the present continuous (PC) or present simple (PS).

Answers

1 cooks 2 give 3 'm / am staying, 'm / am not going
4 'm / am watching 5 does, get up 6 not sleeping

4 Point out there is one mistake with the present continuous or present simple in every sentence. Encourage the students to find the words in sentence 1 which help them decide on the tense or the adverbs (*today*, *at the moment*, etc.) in sentences 2–5 to help them find the mistake.

Answers

1 How are you? **I'm writing** to you to give you some news.
2 What **are** you **doing** at the moment?
3 My brother and I **don't go** swimming every day.
4 My mum only **works** in the mornings.
5 We usually **eat** a big breakfast on Sunday.

5 Ask the students to look at the example sentence first (or write it on the board). Point out that *but* is used to connect the sentences and elicit whether the present simple or present continuous is used in each part. Do the first as an open class example to make sure everyone knows what to do.

Answers

1 I usually have a sandwich for lunch, but today I'm having spaghetti.
2 I usually watch TV after school, but today I'm doing my homework.
3 I usually play football on Saturday, but today I'm playing tennis.
4 I usually get up at seven o'clock, but today I'm getting up at eight o'clock.
5 I usually have a shower, but today I'm having a bath.

6 Elicit from the class how to form questions in the present continuous (*(Question word) + be + I/you/he/she/it/we/they + verb + -ing*) and the present simple (*(Question word) + do/does + I/you/he/she/it/we/they + verb*) and write these on the board. Then, ask the students to look at each set of words and underline the first word in each question first.

FAST FINISHERS

Ask the fast finishers to write some more questions using the present continuous and present simple. When the others have finished, put the students into small groups with a fast finisher, who asks the other students their new questions.

Answers

1 What is your friend doing at the moment?
2 What time do you usually go to bed?
3 How do you get home from school?
4 Is your teacher sitting down at the moment?
5 Is the sun shining today?
6 Do you get up at the same time every day?
1e 2b 3c 4d 5a 6f

7 Demonstrate this as a class first by miming one of the activities and asking the students to ask questions. If necessary, remind them to use the present continuous to ask their questions. Then give some more information about the activity in the present simple and elicit the tense from the class. If necessary, ask two stronger students to demonstrate the activity again to the class.

Answers

Students' own answers

» **GRAMMAR WORKSHEET UNIT 2**

COOLER

Ask the students to choose one of the activities in Exercise 7 and to write down some more information about it on a piece of paper, following the example in the book if necessary. Collect in the pieces of paper. Read out the information and award points to students or teams who guess which student wrote the information.

GRAMMAR Present continuous and present simple

1 **Look at the examples from the listening. Write *simple* or *continuous*.**

Present ______
Today, I'm talking about my morning routine.
I'm having cereal with fruit today.
At the moment, I'm wearing my favourite T-shirt.
I'm leaving the house now.
I'm not wearing my uniform today.

Present ______
I never have a shower in the morning.
I always check my messages in the morning.
I sometimes have toast and butter.
I usually wear my uniform.
I don't usually have a shower in the morning.

2 **Complete the rules with the underlined words.**

We often use the **present simple** with words like ______, ______, ______ and ______.
We often use the **present continuous** with words like ______, ______ and ______.

» GRAMMAR REFERENCE AND PRACTICE PAGE 139

3 **Complete the sentences with the correct tense of the verbs in brackets.**

0 I *'m shopping* (shop) at the moment. I can't talk.
1 My mum always ______ (cook) nice food.
2 The teachers usually ______ (give) us a lot of homework on Monday.
3 I ______ (stay) at home today. I ______ (not go) to school.
4 It's five o'clock now and I ______ (watch) TV with my sister.
5 What time ______ your dad usually ______ (get up) on a Sunday?
6 It's OK, Jack's ______ (not sleep) at the moment. You can go and talk to him.

4 **Correct the mistakes in the sentences.**

0 My cousin ~~gets~~ *is getting* married today.
1 How are you? I write to you to give you some news.
2 What do you do at the moment?
3 My brother and I are not going swimming every day.
4 My mum is only working in the mornings.
5 We usually are eating a big breakfast on Sunday.

5 **Make sentences with the present simple and present continuous. Use *usually* and *today* or *at the moment*.**

0 walk to school / go by bus.
I usually walk to school, but today I'm going by bus.
1 have a sandwich for lunch / spaghetti
2 watch TV after school / do my homework
3 play football on Saturday / play tennis
4 get up at seven o'clock / eight o'clock
5 have a shower / have a bath

6 **Put the words in order to make questions.**

1 your / the / moment / friend / what / doing / is / at?
2 bed / do / go / you / what / usually / to / time?
3 school / do / get / home / how / from / you?
4 sitting / is / teacher / at / down / your / the / moment?
5 sun / today / shining / is / the?
6 day / do / every / get / at / same / up / the / time / you?

Now match the questions to the correct answer.

a No, it isn't.
b 10 pm.
c I walk.
d Yes, he is.
e She's sleeping.
f Yes, I do.

In pairs, ask and answer the questions.

7 **Work in pairs. Student A, mime an activity in the box. Student B, guess what it is.**

catch a bus	check your messages
do some homework	go to sleep
paint a picture	play football
prepare lunch	put on your coat
take a photo	

Are you putting on your sunglasses?

No

Are you taking a photo?

Student A, when Student B guesses the activity, give more information:

I go to a photography club every Friday. It starts at 7 pm. I go there by bus.

Student B, ask more questions.

READING

1 Read the texts once. Who starts school the earliest?

Tell us about your day...

17

Three young people from around the world describe a typical school day

A Onni – Finland

I get up at 8.00 am. For breakfast I have cereal and milk, with orange **juice**. After breakfast, I meet my friend, and we go to school together on the metro. Some days school starts at 9.00 but on other days at 10.00. We don't wear a uniform, and we call our teachers by their first name. We all get a free lunch at school – meat or fish with vegetables for the **main course** and fruit for **dessert**. School usually finishes at 2.45, and after that I go to music lessons or drama club. I have a **snack** in the evening before bed.

B Diego – Mexico

I wake up at 6.00 am, have a shower and put on my uniform. My breakfast is coffee, with bread and cheese or avocado. At 7.00 am, it's time to go to school. Sometimes I walk, but often my mum drives me. Classes begin at 8.00 and finish at 2.30. After that, I have my art class. I have **lunch** at about 3.00, and then I do my homework. I do it till 6.00 or 7.00. After that, I go on the internet, or watch TV with my family. I have **dinner** at about 8.00.

C Aban – Ghana

My mother wakes me and my sister up at 5.00 am. I water the plants in the garden, and my sister prepares the food for the evening meal. Then we put on our school uniforms and brush our teeth. We leave the house at 6.30 and buy **breakfast** on our way to school. Lessons are from 7.30 to 2.30 pm. Lunch is at school – today, it's rice and tomatoes. I like it, but my sister doesn't! After school I have my football class, and in the evening I watch TV before bed.

2 Read the texts again. For each question, write *O* (Onni), *D* (Diego) or *A* (Aban).

1 Who says he uses the computer in the evening?
2 Who can choose what he wears to school?
3 Who doesn't have breakfast at home?
4 Who goes to school by car?
5 Who doesn't start school at the same time each day?
6 Who does sport after school?
7 Who has a hot drink in the morning?

TALKING POINTS

Whose school day is like yours? Whose is different?
Was any of the information surprising to you?

VOCABULARY Food

1 Look at the texts and find these words.

0 This is the first meal of the day. *breakfast*
1 This is sweet and you have it at the end of the meal.
2 You have this when you don't need a big meal.
3 You have this meal in the middle of the day.
4 This is a drink made from fruit.
5 This is the last meal of the day.
6 This is the largest or most important part of the meal.

2 Match the photos to the words in the box.

EP

avocado	bread	cabbage	cereal	
cheese	cucumber	fish	fruit	honey
hot chocolate	jam	mango	pasta	toast
tomatoes	rice	vegetables	yoghurt	

18 Listen and check. Then repeat.

READING

WARMER

Hold a geography quiz. Write the following table on the board and encourage the students in small groups to complete it. Set a time limit (e.g. five minutes). The answers are given below in *italics*.

	Finland	Mexico	Ghana
Continent	*Europe*	*North America*	*Africa*
Capital City	*Helsinki*	*Mexico City*	*Accra*
Official Language	*Finnish & Swedish*	*Spanish*	*English*
Currency	*Euro*	*Peso*	*Cedi*

Then, if possible, show the class where the three countries are on a map.

Finland, Mexico and Ghana appear in the reading text in this unit.

BACKGROUND INFORMATION

	Finland	Mexico	Ghana
Compulsory education	7–15	6–18	4–12[1]
Free	Yes[2]	Yes	Yes
Uniform	No	Most[3]	Yes
Homework	None	Yes	Yes (and lots of tests)

[1] some start later or can't afford to start at all because of cost of books, clothes, etc.

[2] includes university tuition fees

[3] compulsory in public (state) schools and most private schools

1 Books closed. Tell the class they are going to read about a typical school day of three people from Finland, Mexico and Ghana. Encourage a brief class discussion on what they think each day is like, who they think starts school the earliest and why. The students then read the texts and check their ideas.

Answers

Aban – Ghana

2 **A2 Key for Schools Reading Part 2.**

In this part of the exam, students read three texts about three different people, places, personal experiences, things, etc. and have to answer seven *Which person/ place/etc. … ?* type questions. Encourage the students to try to answer the questions before they read the texts again.

Answers

1 D 2 O 3 A 4 D 5 O 6 A 7 D

17 The Reading text is recorded for students to listen and read.

MIXED ABILITY

For Exercises 1 and 2, divide the class into three groups, A, B and C, making sure there is a mix of stronger and weaker students in each group. Group A reads about Onni, Group B Diego and Group C Aban. Ask them to read their text quickly to find what time each person starts school. Compare answers as a class and decide who starts the earliest. Then, ask them to read their text again and as a group try to answer as many questions in Exercise 2 as they can, encouraging the stronger students to help the weaker ones. Then, put the students into groups of three where each student has read a different text and ask them to share their answers. The students read the other two texts for homework.

FAST FINISHERS

Fast finishers write some more questions about the three texts for a class quiz, e.g. *Who has a cold drink in the morning? Who goes to school with a friend?* Organise the class into teams. The fast finishers come to the front of the class, ask each team some questions and give points for correct answers.

TALKING POINTS

Copy the table below onto the board and elicit some examples. Then, ask the students to copy the table and make notes before they start talking. Put the students into small groups for this activity; ask them to use their notes to answer the questions and also to say which of the people in the texts has the best and worst school day.

similar	different	surprising
e.g. Diego – I also start school at 8 am.	*e.g. Diego and Aban – I don't wear a uniform.*	*e.g. Onni's school starts late.*

VOCABULARY Food

1 Point out that the words are all in blue in the text. Make sure the students pronounce each word correctly.

Answers

1 dessert 2 snack 3 lunch 4 juice 5 dinner 6 main course

2 Encourage the students to cover the words and say what they can see in each photo first.

18 **Answers**

The answers are recorded for students to check and then repeat.

A mango B jam C fish D fruit E vegetables F bread
G honey H tomatoes I cabbage J cheese K cereal
L cucumber M rice N hot chocolate O pasta P avocado
Q toast R yoghurt

3 If the students are slow to think of more food words, encourage them to read the questions first, think about the food words they'll need to answer these questions and make a list. Model some good answers to the questions by encouraging the class to ask you the questions first.

Answers

Students' own answers

» **VOCABULARY WORKSHEET UNIT 2**

PRONUNCIATION | The sound /ə/

The sound /ə/ is also known as the schwa. In English it is mainly found where a vowel is unstressed, e.g. *butter*.

4 Encourage the students to say how each underlined sound is pronounced (/ə/). Check that students pronounce *vegetable* /ˈvedʒ.tə.bəl/ correctly and if necessary, point out that it has three syllables

19 **Audioscript**

The words are recorded for students to listen and repeat.

breakfast, dinner, vegetables

5 Encourage the students to try to find the sound /ə/ in each word before they listen, check and repeat. Point out that we say *chocolate* with two syllables. Ask the students to find some more words in this unit with the sound /ə/.

20 **Answers**

The answers are recorded for the students to listen and repeat.

banana chocolate cucumber pasta salad tomato yoghurt

LISTENING

1 Write some useful language on the board first so that the students can compare their ideas and say why, e.g. *I think (have a cold shower) is / isn't a good / great / bad tip because … ; I (don't) agree with this tip because … ; What do you think?; Do you agree?* Ask the students to look at the poster and say what it is about. Encourage them to guess what *tip* means from the context and then check understanding by asking them to think of synonyms, e.g. *idea, advice, help* or the word in their own language.

Answers

Students' own answers

21 2 This exercise is loosely based on A2 Key for Schools Listening Part 5, where students listen to someone talking about six people they know and choose one answer for each person out of eight possible answers (the first person is always an example). Point out that there is an extra tip that students do not need to use and that Student 1 has been done as an example. With a weaker class, stop after Student 1 and encourage the students to say what information on the recording tells them it's Tip C. Students listen to the recording again in Exercise 3.

Answers

Student 1 Tip C
Student 2 Tip E
Student 3 Tip G
Student 4 Tip D
Student 5 Tip A
Student 6 Tip F

21 3 Encourage the students to compare their answers in pairs before they listen again. If time allows, encourage the students to design a poster with tips for another part of the day, e.g. 'six tips to do your homework well' or 'six tips to get a good night's sleep'.

Answers

Students' own answers

» **AUDIOSCRIPT TB PAGES 265–266**

WRITING

PREPARE TO WRITE
A paragraph about your routine

Tell the students that they are going to write about their school day routine, similar to the paragraphs written by Onni, Diego and Aban.

GET READY Check the students understand the meaning of *and*, *but* and *or* by asking them for a translation. Encourage stronger students to rewrite the sentences so they are true for them.

Answers

2 but 3 and 4 but 5 or

PLAN If students are slow to start, encourage them to choose one of the three texts, e.g. Diego, think about which phrases they could use in their own paragraph and to write down complete sentences which are true for them, e.g. *I wake up at 7.30 am. My breakfast is biscuits and hot milk.*

WRITE Remind students to use *and*, *but* and *or* in their paragraph and to look at their notes and the texts for ideas.

REVIEW Encourage the students to look out for common mistakes. You will need to point these out to them or they won't know what to look for, e.g. writing 'i' instead of 'I' or putting the adverb after the verb, e.g. ~~*I have usually fish*~~.

COOLER

Organise the class into teams. Write a word from this unit on the board, e.g. *chocolate* and challenge the teams to think of a food or drink beginning with each letter, e.g. **c**abbage, **h**oney, **o**range, **c**urry, **o**nion, **l**emonade, **a**pple, **t**oast, **e**gg.

3 **Think of ten more food words. In pairs, compare your words. Then ask and answer these questions.**

1 What's your favourite food? What don't you like?
2 What do you have for breakfast?
3 What time do you have dinner? What do you have?
4 What snacks do you have every day?

PRONUNCIATION The sound /ə/

19 **4** **Listen and repeat.**

breakfast dinner vegetables

20 **5** **Listen and repeat. Circle the /ə/ sound in each word. One word has two /ə/ sounds. Which word is it?**

pasta chocolate banana salad
tomato yoghurt cucumber

LISTENING

1 **Read the poster. What do you think of these tips?**

21 **2** **Listen to the radio show. You will hear a woman asking six students about getting up in the morning. Match each student to the correct tip. There is one tip you do not need.**

Student 1	Tip A
Student 2	Tip B
Student 3	Tip C
Student 4	Tip D
Student 5	Tip E
Student 6	Tip F
	Tip G

21 **3** **Listen again and check. Then in small groups, discuss the questions.**

1 Which of the tips do you think are useful? Which are not useful?
2 Can you think of other tips for getting up in the morning?
3 Is getting up in the morning easy or difficult for you?

WRITING

PREPARE TO WRITE

A paragraph about your routine

GET READY Read the three texts in Exercise 1 on page 20 again and find all the examples of *and*, *but* and *or*.

Choose the correct words to complete the sentences.

1 We don't get chocolate ___or___ crisps at school. *or / but*
2 I walk to school ______ my brother gets the bus. *but / or*
3 I eat lots of fruit ______ drink lots of water. *and / or*
4 I like staying up late ______ I can't do that during the week. *but / and*
5 I don't like carrots ______ tomatoes. *or / but*

PLAN Make notes about what you do and eat on a typical school day.

WRITE Write a paragraph about it. Look at your notes and the reading texts for ideas. Use *and*, *but* and *or* in your paragraph.

REVIEW In pairs, read your own text and your partner's. Check for mistakes. Give your partner two ideas to make their text better.

CULTURE

THE PARALYMPIC GAMES

1 **In pairs, discuss the questions with your partner.**

1 Do you like doing sports? What sports do you do?
2 Do you like watching sports on TV? What sports do you watch?
3 Do you usually watch the Olympic Games and the Paralympic Games?

2 **Read the text in boxes 1–6 and match them to the sports in the photos. Write *SV* (sitting volleyball) or *WR* (wheelchair rugby).**

3 **Read the texts again and complete the table.**

	Sitting volleyball	Wheelchair rugby
Where do you play?	1	2 ....
What do they need?	a ball and a 3	wheelchairs and a 4 ....
How many players are there on a team?	5	6 ....
How many players from each team are on the court?	7	8 ....

4 **Find the words highlighted in the text and choose the correct meanings, a or b.**

1 medal
  a a type of ball
  b a prize in a sports competition
2 wheelchair
  a something people use when they can't walk
  b something people use to stand on
3 court
  a a place with seats
  b an indoor or outdoor area for games
4 player
  a a person in a wheelchair
  b a person playing a game or sport
5 goal line
  a a line you pass to get points
  b the number of players on a team

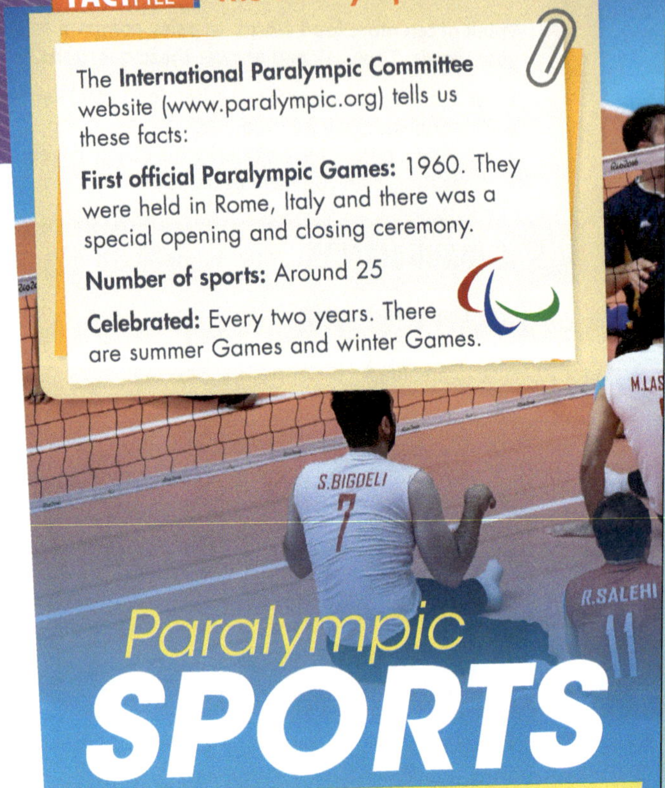

FACTFILE The Paralympic Games

The **International Paralympic Committee** website (www.paralympic.org) tells us these facts:

First official Paralympic Games: 1960. They were held in Rome, Italy and there was a special opening and closing ceremony.

Number of sports: Around 25

Celebrated: Every two years. There are summer Games and winter Games.

Paralympic SPORTS

The Paralympic Games take place every two years. There are winter Games and summer Games. Athletes with physical disabilities from different countries compete for gold, silver and bronze medals.

The Paralympic Games have a lot of different competitions for a lot of different sports. There are 22 sports in the summer Games and five sports in the winter Games.

Here's a description of two popular sports played in the Paralympic Games.

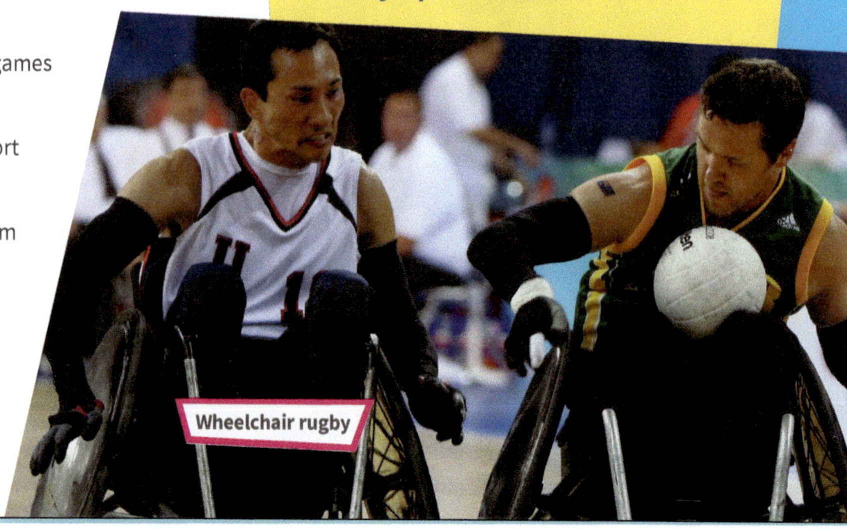

Wheelchair rugby

CULTURE

Learning Objectives

- The students learn about the Paralympic Games.
- In the project stage, they write interview questions for a Paralympic athlete and find the answers.

Vocabulary

medal wheelchair court player goal line

Resources

CULTURE VIDEO AND CULTURE VIDEO WORKSHEET: What is a Paralympic athlete?

BACKGROUND INFORMATION

The Olympic Games symbol is five interlaced rings (blue, yellow, black, green and red), which represent the five continents (Africa, America, Asia, Australasia and Europe). The Paralympic Games symbol is three red, blue and green 'agitos' (see illustration on unit page). An 'agito' (= 'I move' in Latin) is the symbol of movement. To compete in the Paralympic Games, each athlete is evaluated by a panel of judges. To avoid the least impaired athletes from winning all the competitions, each athlete is categorised according to their degree of impairment; this categorisation is sport specific. In the word Paralympics, 'Para' stands for *parallel* (= side by side with the Olympics) and not *paraplegic*.

WARMER

Draw the Olympic Games symbol (see Background information above) on the left-hand side of the board and ask the class what it is and what they know about these games. Write the class's ideas onto the left-hand side of the board. Next draw the Paralympic Games symbol (see Coursebook page and Background information above) on the right-hand side and ask what it is and what they know about these games. Write the class's ideas onto the right-hand side of the board. Then, ask them to read the factfile at the top of the page and the introduction to the six descriptions and check their ideas.

1 If necessary, ask the students to look at Vocabulary and Reading Exercise 1 on page 14 again to revise the names of sports before they do this exercise. Encourage them to answer in full sentences and ask follow-up questions where appropriate, e.g. *Where do you play football? Who do you play it with?*

Answers

Students' own answers

2 First, ask the students in pairs to look at the photos of the two different sports (sitting volleyball and wheelchair rugby), describe the sports and talk about how they think each one is played. Then, ask them to read the six texts (1–6) quickly to check their ideas before they write SV or WR.

MIXED ABILITY

For Exercises 2 and 3, weaker students read about sitting volleyball only (texts 2, 3 and 5). In Exercise 2 they complete the three texts with SV and in Exercise 3 they answer the questions for sitting volleyball only. Then, pair them up with a fast finisher who shares their information about wheelchair rugby, so that their weaker partner can complete the table.

Answers

1 WR 2 SV 3 SV 4 WR 5 SV 6 WR

3 Ask the students to try to complete the table before they read the texts again. Point out that they don't have to write complete sentences – they can write notes.

Answers

1 indoor court 2 indoor court 3 net 4 ball 5 six 6 twelve 7 six 8 four

22 The Reading text is recorded for students to listen and read.

4 Ask the students to find the five words in the texts first and try to understand the meaning of each one from context before they read the definitions.

FAST FINISHERS

In pairs, fast finishers take turns to say five sentences about one of the sports where some of the information is true and some is false. Their partners need to correct the false information.

Answers

1 b 2 a 3 b 4 b 5 a

TALKING POINTS

Ask the students to look at their completed tables in Exercise 3 again and decide on their own which of the two sports they'd like to play first and why. Then, ask them to compare their ideas with a partner. If appropriate, encourage the students to ask their sports teacher if they can try playing sitting volleyball.

23 **5** First, ask the students in pairs to describe the three pictures and to say how they think each one is played before they listen.

Answers

Wheelchair tennis

23 **6** Ask the students to try to answer the questions before they listen again. With a weaker class, it may be necessary to play the recording for a third time and pause it after each answer is given.

Answers

1 11 years old 2 near the/her school 3 the Paralympic Games 4 he has a lot of medals 5 the United States 6 no, she doesn't 7 no, she has competitions

» AUDIOSCRIPT TB PAGE 266

PROJECT *An interview*

Ask the students to read the instructions in bold. Check that they have understood them by asking 'Where do you work?' 'Who are you going to interview?' 'What do you need to write?'

Write the following table (with the title) on the board (without the example information about Martha):

A Paralympic Athlete

Name:	*e.g. Martha Dirksen*
Sport:	*e.g. wheelchair tennis*
Nationality:	
Medals:	
Questions:	1 2 3

As a class complete the table for Martha Dirksen (see example above), encouraging the students to think of three questions they would like to ask her. In pairs, ask the students to copy the table (with title) into their notebooks. Ask the students to find information about another athlete and complete the table with the information they find. Remind them that they need to write three of their own questions and also find the answers for these questions. With a less autonomous class, it may be a good idea to find the names of several Paralympic athletes and give one of these names to each group. Ask the pairs to give a short presentation to the class on their athlete.

PROJECT EXTENSION

Tell the pairs they are going to record an interview (either voice or video) for the radio, where one of them is the radio journalist and the other is the athlete. Encourage them to use some of the questions they wrote for their project above and their answers and where appropriate, to write some new questions. Point out they will also need to write an introduction to the interview where the journalist introduces the athlete. Tell the pairs they can either write out the full interview first or write some notes. They should rehearse their interview before they record it. When the pairs are ready, play the interviews back to the class and vote on the best three.

CULTURE VIDEO 01: What is a Paralympic athlete?

When students have completed the lesson, they can watch the video and complete the worksheet.

COOLER

Tell the students you are thinking of a sport (e.g. tennis). The students have to guess the sport, but they can only ask a maximum of five *Yes/No* questions, e.g. *Is it a ball sport?* (Yes, it is.) *Do you kick the ball?* (No, you don't.) Invite a student to come to the front of the class and to think of a sport. The students now ask their five questions and try to guess which sport it is.

1 WR You play this sport on an indoor court. Players are in wheelchairs. They need a ball. They pass the ball from one person to another.

2 ________ You play this sport on a court inside. Players sit on the floor. They need a net and a ball. Teams need to hit the ball over the net in three turns using their arms.

3 ________ Each team has six players on the court. Each team is on a different side of the net.

4 ________ There are 12 players on a team, but there are only four players on the court for each team at one time. For a goal, the team carries the ball over the opposite team's line and two wheels need to cross the line.

5 ________ The net is lower than in the Olympic version. In the Olympic version, the players stand.

6 ________ The indoor court is smaller than in the game played outside. It is the same size as a basketball court. The goal lines are at the far ends of the court.

TALKING POINTS

Which sport do you like best – sitting volleyball or wheelchair rugby. Why?

23 **5** **Listen to an interview with Martha Dirksen about a Paralympic sport. What sport does she do?**

23 **6** **Listen again and answer the questions.**

1. How old is Martha?
2. Where is the court?
3. What does she want to be in one day?
4. What has her sports hero got?
5. Where is David Wagner from?
6. Does Martha play tennis on Tuesdays?
7. Does Martha rest at weekends?

PROJECT *An interview*

Imagine you work for a radio station. In pairs, write interview questions to ask a Paralympic athlete.

- Find out:
  - Their name.
  - What sport they do.
  - Where they are from.
  - How many medals they have.
- Write three questions you can ask the athlete.
- Find information on a Paralympic athlete. Answer the questions.
- Tell the class what you found out.

01 NOW WATCH THE CULTURE VIDEO

3 GREAT SOUNDS

ABOUT YOU

02 Watch the video then ask and answer the questions.

When do you listen to music?
Where do you listen to music?
Do you listen to music alone or with friends?
Can you play any musical instruments? Which one(s)?

VOCABULARY AND LISTENING

Music

1 **Look at the words in the box. Complete the table.**

EP

classical music   drums   electric guitar
hip-hop   jazz   keyboard   opera
piano   pop   rap   rock   saxophone
soul   violin

Types of music	Musical instruments

2 **Match the photos A–F to the musical instruments in Exercise 1.**

24 **Listen and check. Then repeat.**

25 **3** **Listen to the different types of music. Match them to the types of music in Exercise 1.**

4 **What types of music do you think the people are playing in the photos?**

5 **Choose the correct word to complete the sentences.**

1 You usually need a lot of different instruments for *classical music / pop* and the pieces of music are often quite long.
2 People sometimes use sticks when they play the *keyboard / drums*.
3 There are different singers in *jazz / an opera*. It's a bit like a play with music and singing.
4 In *rap / rock*, the artists don't really sing the words; they speak them.
5 You put the *saxophone / violin* to your mouth to play it.
6 *A piano / an electric guitar* is quite easy to carry around.

3 GREAT SOUNDS

Unit Overview

TOPIC	Music
VOCABULARY AND LISTENING	Music A conversation about music and musical instruments
GRAMMAR	*like, don't like, hate, love + -ing*
READING	Starting in the music business
VOCABULARY	Music phrases
PRONUNCIATION	Email addresses, phone numbers and names
LISTENING	A conversation about a music school
SPEAKING	Giving opinions about music and musical instruments
EXAM TASKS	Speaking Parts 1 and 2

Resources

GRAMMAR REFERENCE AND PRACTICE: SB page 140; TB page 247
WORKBOOK: pages 16–19
VIDEO AND VIDEO WORKSHEET: Great sounds
PHOTOCOPIABLE WORKSHEETS: Grammar worksheet Unit 3; Vocabulary worksheet Unit 3
TEST GENERATOR: Unit test 3

BACKGROUND INFORMATION

There are several photos of famous musicians in this unit.

Page 24

A: Bruno Mars is an American singer, whose music has a variety of styles, including hip-hop, pop, reggae and soul.

B: Vanessa Mae is a British violinist born in 1978. She has sold several million albums.

C: Kyle J Simmons is the keyboardist with British band Bastille. Bastille were formed in 2010.

D: Cindy Blackman is an American jazz and rock drummer. She is famous for touring and recording with American singer Lenny Kravitz, but has also recorded solo albums.

E: Lady Gaga is an American singer, songwriter and actress, born in 1986 in New York City.

F: Jaleel Shaw is an American jazz saxophonist. He has degrees in Music Education and Performance, and Jazz Performance.

Page 26

Shawn Mendes is a Canadian singer-songwriter. He became famous after uploading covers of songs on a video sharing app.

Rihanna is a singer, songwriter and actress from Barbados born in 1988.

WARMER

Write the unit title on the board and ask the students to say what they think the unit is about. Ask the students to look at the photos at the top of the page for 15 seconds and then close their books. Challenge them to tell you as much as they can about each photo.

ABOUT YOU

02 You can begin the class and introduce the topic of the unit by showing the video and asking students to complete the video worksheet. Then, read the questions in the box and ask students to discuss them in pairs.

VOCABULARY AND LISTENING

Music

1 Books closed. Copy the table onto the board. As a class, brainstorm as many words as possible onto the board. Books open, students complete the table and then copy any extra words on the board into their table.

Answers

Types of music: classical music, hip-hop, jazz, opera, pop, rap, rock, soul
Musical instruments: drums, electric guitar, keyboard, piano, saxophone, violin

2 Ask the students to say who is playing what, e.g. *Lady Gaga is playing the piano.*

24 **Answers**

The answers are recorded for the students to check and then repeat.
A (electric) guitar B violin C keyboard D drums E piano F saxophone

25 3 Check that the students pronounce the types of music correctly. Then, stop the recording after each type and ask the students to work in pairs and say: *What do you think it is? I think it's [rap]. I agree / don't agree.*

Answers

1 hip-hop 2 rock 3 classical 4 pop 5 jazz 6 soul 7 rap 8 opera

4 Put the students in pairs to ask and answer questions about each photo.

Possible answers

A pop / rock B classical C pop D rock E pop / classical F jazz

5 Remind the students to read the complete sentence before choosing the correct answer.

Answers

1 classical music 2 drums 3 an opera 4 rap 5 saxophone 6 an electric guitar

26 **6** Ask the students to look at the photos first and predict who can play what before they listen. With a weaker class, point out that they play two instruments each.

Answers
1 Mia 2 Jason 3 Jason 4 Mia

26 **7** Ask the students try to say if the sentences are right or wrong before they listen again. With a stronger class, ask the students to correct the wrong sentences. With a weaker class, play the recording for a third time and stop after each answer.

Answers
1 ✓ 2 × (Jason doesn't like listening to opera.) 3 ✓
4 × (Jason tried to play the violin but it was difficult.)
5 × (She hates listening to the drums. They're too loud.)

» AUDIOSCRIPT TB PAGE 266

GRAMMAR *like, don't like, hate, love + -ing*

1 Books closed. Write the four sentences on the board and elicit who said what (Mia or Jason). Underline the verbs in bold and ask 'What do the expressions have in common?' (*They express a preference.*) Books open. Ask the students to say what the two emoticons mean in the exercise before they complete the table. Do not rub out the sentences as they'll be used again in Exercise 2.

27 **Answers**
The answers are recorded for students to check and then repeat.
a I hate playing the violin.
b I don't like listening to opera.
c She likes playing classical music.
d I love listening to rap.

» GRAMMAR REFERENCE AND PRACTICE ANSWER KEY TB PAGE 247

2 Rub out *listening* and *playing* from the four sentences on the board (used in Exercise 1). Ask the students to say what is missing in each sentence, write the missing word (*listening* or *playing*) in a different colour and highlight the *-ing* form. Ask the students to look at the table in their books and elicit the spelling rules by asking 'What happens with verbs that end in -e?' (*remove the 'e'*) 'And verbs with one syllable that end in consonant-vowel-consonant?' (*double the last consonant*) 'And all other verbs?' (*add '-ing'*)

Answers
help: learning, singing
write: choosing, driving, making, practising, riding
run: getting, sitting, swimming, winning

3 Encourage students to read the second sentence in each question first and decide whether they'll need to choose a positive or a negative word.

Answers
1 hate 2 doesn't like 3 loves 4 don't like

4 Point out that students often make mistakes with the *-ing* form after verbs such as *like*, *love*, *hate*, etc. and they should check their spelling carefully.

Answers
1 reading 2 playing 3 going 4 learning 5 listening

FAST FINISHERS
Ask fast finishers to write questions for each of the answers, e.g. *What do you like doing on Sundays? What does your dad like reading?* Then, they ask and answer the questions together.

5 A2 Key for Schools Speaking Parts 1 and 2.

In Part 1 Phase 2 of the exam, the examiner will ask each candidate some general questions about themselves on two different topics. One of the topics could be music, for example. In Part 2 of the exam, candidates talk about a different topic to Part 1. They discuss their likes and dislikes on a topic. It is possible that a topic such as music could appear in either Part 1 Phase 2 or Part 2. It will not appear in both. First practise saying the questions with the correct intonation by asking the students to copy your intonation. Remind them to give full answers and to ask follow-up questions.

MIXED ABILITY
With weaker students and more reluctant speakers, use a disappearing board conversation:

1 Write the questions with sample answers (see below) on the board.
2 Divide the weaker students into As and Bs. As a class, As read the questions and Bs read the answers, then change roles.
3 Students continue to do this in pairs. As they do this, begin to rub out words from the answers until the students are saying the answers from memory.
4 Encourage the students to read the questions (still on the board) and give their own answers.

Sample answers
1 I usually listen to music in my bedroom.
2 I love pop music. That's my favourite.
3 My favourite musician is Ed Sheeran. He sings and he plays the guitar.
4 I love listening to the piano but I can't play it.
5 Yes, they can. Students learn to play the recorder at my school.

Answers
Students' own answers

» GRAMMAR WORKSHEET UNIT 3

COOLER
Play track 25 again and ask the students to identify both the types of music and the musical instruments and also to express their opinion, e.g. *I hate this because I don't like jazz.*

6 Listen to Jason and Mia talking about music and musical instruments. Who can play: (26)

1 the saxophone?
2 the electric guitar?
3 the keyboard?
4 the piano?

7 Listen again. Are the sentences right (✓) or wrong (✗)? (26)

0 Mia likes the new album a lot. ✓
1 Mia often listens to jazz at home.
2 Jason likes opera.
3 Jason's sister plays in a rock group.
4 Jason thinks the violin is easy to play.
5 Mia likes the drums.

GRAMMAR *like, don't like, hate, love + -ing*

1 Put the words in bold on the correct place (a–d).

1 I **don't like** listening to opera.
2 She **likes** playing classical music.
3 I **hate** playing the violin.
4 I **love** listening to rap.

a ______ b ______ c ______ d ______

Listen and check. Then repeat. (27)

» GRAMMAR REFERENCE AND PRACTICE PAGE 140

2 Look at the examples in the table. How does the verb change in the *-ing* form?

help → helping	write → writing	run → running

Now complete the table with the *-ing* form of these verbs in the correct columns.

choose	drive	get	learn	make	
practise	ride	sing	sit	swim	win

3 Choose the correct words to complete the sentences.

1 I *like* / *hate* rock. It's too loud.
2 She *doesn't like* / *loves* playing the piano. She prefers the saxophone.
3 My mum *loves* / *hates* listening to opera. She often goes to watch it.
4 Lots of people *like* / *don't like* hip-hop, but I think it's great.

4 Complete the sentences with the correct form of the verbs.

0 On Sundays, I like *having* lunch with my family. (have)
1 My dad likes ______ the news online. (read)
2 I really love ______ football with my brother. (play)
3 I love ______ to my friends' houses to play computer games. (go)
4 Everyone in our class likes ______ English. (learn)
5 Do you like ______ to music when you are doing your homework? (listen)

5 In pairs, ask and answer the questions.

1 Do you listen to music?
2 What's your favourite type of music?
3 Who are your favourite musicians and what instruments do they play?
4 What's your favorite instrument?
5 Can students learn to play instruments at your school? Which ones?

READING

1 **Look at the photos. In pairs, ask and answer the questions.**

1. Is it easy to become a famous musician?
2. How do people start in the music business?
3. How can the internet help people to become musicians?

2 **Read the article quickly and match the teenagers' questions 1–3 to the advice A–C.**

28

STARTING IN THE MUSIC BUSINESS

DO YOU WANT TO PLAY IN A BAND, OR BECOME A FAMOUS SINGER OR SONGWRITER?

Read on to find out how!

Pete

1 I'm a singer-songwriter. I give concerts at a local club. Everyone likes listening to my music and wants to buy a CD. What can I do next?'

Shona

2 Hi, I play in a band with some friends from school. The others aren't serious about music, but I am. Help! Do I stay with the band or find other musicians to play with?

Spark

3 I'm 15 and a rapper. I record my songs and put them online. I get lots of hits! But I live in the countryside and there are no gigs here. It's too far for me to travel to the city. What can I do to become famous?

A Why not make a music video too? Then it doesn't matter where you live. Ask your parents or someone from school if it's okay, and they can show you how to do it. Then you can upload the video to a social network like YouTube or Instagram. That's how Shawn Mendes became famous!

B You already write and perform your own songs. Great! Next step: record an album using computer software and post it online. You don't need a record deal. College courses are a really useful way to learn how to do this, and can give you other ideas too. Ask at your school.

C Music is an important part of your life. Stay with your friends for the moment but think about going to a music school. These schools teach music and everything you need to know about becoming a musician. Talk to your parents about it. Good luck!

3 **Are the sentences right (✓) or wrong (✗)?**

1. Pete sells CDs of his songs at his concerts.
2. Pete needs to make an album with a record company.
3. Shona is more interested in music than her friends are.
4. Shona needs to change school as soon as possible.
5. Spark lives a long way from the city.
6. Spark doesn't need to perform live for people to hear his music.

TALKING POINTS

Are any of your friends musicians?

Do any of your friends upload their music to the internet?

Do you like listening to music on the internet?

Which sites do you prefer?

READING

WARMER

Play this dice game. (You'll need one dice for each group of six students.)

- Write this on the board:

1 love	1 listen (to)
2 like	2 play
3 quite like	3 watch
4 don't like	4 read
5 hate	5 sing
6 really hate	6 go

- Demonstrate the activity to the class. Roll the dice. This number (e.g. 2) gives you the first verb (*like*). Roll the dice again. This number (e.g. 6) gives you the second verb (*go*). Make a complete sentence (*I like going to the beach when the weather is good*). Encourage the students to ask follow-up questions, e.g. *Who do you go with? What do you do there?*
- Organise the students into groups of six and give each group one dice. Allow them to play the game for three or four minutes, reminding them to give full answers and to ask follow-up questions.

1 Pre-teach *music business* by asking the students to look at the photos and to say what the two people have in common (*they both work in the music business*). Check understanding by asking for some more examples (*e.g. Bruno Mars, Lady Gaga*) and also asking if there are other types of jobs (*e.g. songwriter, producer, sound engineer*).

Answers

Students' own answers

2 First, ask the students to find the three questions (1–3) and to underline what the three people want to know. Then, encourage them to match the three pieces of advice (A–C) quickly and to underline the information which gives them the correct answer.

28

Answers

The Reading text is recorded for students to listen, read and check their answers.

1 B 2 C 3 A

3 Encourage the students to try to answer the questions before they read the article again. Point out that the students will need to read both the questions and suggestions to find the answers. With a stronger class, encourage the students to correct the wrong answers.

Answers

1 × (Everyone wants to buy his CDs.) 2 × (He can make an album using computer software and post it online.) 3 ✓ 4 × (She should stay with her friends at the moment.) 5 ✓ 6 ✓

MIXED ABILITY

Whilst the other students are doing Exercise 3, ask the weaker students to decide if sentences 1 and 2 are right or wrong. Check their answers. If time allows, encourage them to try sentences 3 and 4.

TALKING POINTS

Remind the class that a *yes* or *no* answer isn't enough and they should always try to give full answers by using words like *and, so, because*, etc. Also remind them to ask follow-up questions. If necessary, set a minimum time limit for this exercise.

VOCABULARY Music phrases

1 Before the students complete the sentences, point out that they might have to add *-(e)s* to the verb for the third person.

FAST FINISHERS

Pairs take turns to be Student A and B. Student A reads out the sentences in Vocabulary Exercise 1 but says *banana* where there are missing words, e.g. *1 My dad can help me BANANA BANANA BANANA BANANA. Then I can upload it to Youtube.* With their book closed, Student B repeats the sentence but with the correct words.

Answers

1 make a music video 2 gives a concert 3 become a singer
4 plays in a band 5 record an album 6 become famous
7 teaches music 8 go on tour

2 Read the example question from Pete and ask a volunteer to read the advice. Then, ask pairs to think of advice for the other two questions. After they finish, if time allows, pairs can role play a conversation between one of the teenagers and someone in the music business giving advice.

Possible answers

1 I think you can stay with the band at the moment, but ask your parents about music schools. These schools help people become musicians.
2 I think you can make a music video and then ask adults to help you post it online. You don't need to give concerts. People can see you playing online.

» VOCABULARY WORKSHEET UNIT 3

LISTENING

PRONUNCIATION

Email addresses, phone numbers and names

1 Books closed. Write the examples on the board and highlight the pronunciation of @ ('at'), . ('dot'), two numbers or two letters ('double') and the number 0 ('oh' – like the letter o). If appropriate, point out that in American English we say *zero*. If necessary, revise the pronunciation of letters.

29 **Answers**

The answers are recorded for the students to check and then repeat.

1 school at musicpopcloud dot com
2 oh four five one, two five six, double three seven
3 J-o-a-double n-a

2 If they wish, students can write down their email address, phone number and mother or father's first name first. Encourage the students to ask and answer appropriate questions for this (e.g. *What's your email address?*) and to write down their partner's answer so that they can check it with their partner.

30 3 This exercise is loosely based on A2 Key for Schools Listening Part 2 where students need to complete information with words, numbers or dates. If the word is spelled on the recording, the spelling must be correct. Encourage the students to read the note first and to say what kinds of words are missing in each space (e.g. 1 & 2 part of the day, 3 a name, 4 a number, 5 a name, 6 an email address). Play the recording a second time for students to check their answers.

Answers

1 morning 2 afternoon 3 The Clarke School (C-L-A-R-K-E)
4 01572 399687 5 Phillips 6 info@clarke4music.com

» AUDIOSCRIPT TB PAGES 266–267

SPEAKING

1 **A2 Key for Schools Speaking Parts 1 and 2.**

In Part 1 Phase 2 of the exam, the examiner will ask each candidate some general questions and in Part 2 of the exam they will ask about their opinions. It is possible that a topic such as music could appear in either Part 1 Phase 2 or Part 2. It will not appear in both. Ask the class to ask you the questions and model good answers. Then, invite a confident student to the front to be the candidate. Ask them two or three questions; the rest of the class listen and say whether the candidate answers the questions well and why.

COOLER

Each pair writes sentences about a famous musician using some of the words from Vocabulary Exercise 1. Then, they read their sentences to the class without saying their name. The other students guess who it is.

VOCABULARY Music phrases

1 **Complete the sentences with the correct form of the words in the box.**

EP

become a singer	become famous
give a concert	go on tour
make a music video	play in a band
record an album	teach music

1 My dad can help me ______. Then I can upload it to Youtube.
2 My sister is a famous classical musician. She ______ in our town every summer.
3 Amy can't play an instrument, but she has a very good voice. She wants to ______.
4 Andy plays the drums well. He ______ with his friends on Saturdays at the music club.
5 We've got ten new songs and they're really good. Let's ______.
6 I really want to ______ one day and be on TV and play at big festivals.
7 My mum plays lots of instruments, and she ______ at our school.
8 When bands ______, they play concerts almost every night in lots of different places.

2 **Read the article again. In pairs, answer the questions in your own words using information from the article.**

0 Pete: 'What can I do next?'
I think you can record an album and play it to your friends.
1 Shona: 'Do I stay with the band or find other musicians to play with?'
2 Spark: 'How can I become famous?'

LISTENING

ə PRONUNCIATION

Email addresses, phone numbers and names

For @ we say 'at'. For . we say 'dot'.
For two numbers (77) we say 'double (seven)'.
For two letters (bb) we say 'double (b)'.
For the number 0 we say 'oh'.

1 **In pairs, practise.**

1 Say this email address: *school@musicpopcloud.com*
2 Say this phone number: *0451 256 337*
3 Spell this name: Joanna

29 **Listen and check. Then repeat.**

2 **In pairs, take it in turns.**

1 Say your email address.
2 Say your phone number.
3 Spell your mother's or your father's first name.

30 **3** **Listen to the conversation. Shona is talking to her friend Emma about the music school. Complete the notes.**

Music lessons are in the [1] ______
School lessons are in the [2] ______
Name of Music School: [3] ______
Phone number: [4] ______
Head's name: Ms [5] ______
Email address: [6] ______

30 **Listen again and check.**

SPEAKING

1 **In pairs, take turns to ask and answer the questions.**

1 Do you like different kinds of music? What are they?
2 Do you like different musical instruments? Which ones?
3 Do you think …
jazz is interesting?
opera is exciting?
classical music is boring?
the saxophone is difficult to play?
musical instruments are expensive?
4 Which of these different types of music do you like best?
5 Do you prefer listening to music at home or going to concerts? Why?
6 Which instrument would you like to play?

4 IT WAS AWESOME!

ABOUT YOU

What do you do to have fun with family and friends? Share your ideas with your classmates.

VOCABULARY AND LISTENING

Adjectives

1 Look at the photos. Where are the people and what are they doing?

31 **2** Listen and match the conversations to the photos.

Conversation 1 ___ Conversation 2 ___ Conversation 3 ___
Conversation 4 ___ Conversation 5 ___ Conversation 6 ___

31 **3** Listen again. How did the speakers feel about their experiences? Complete row A of the table with the conversation numbers.

4 Now complete row B of the table with the adjectives in the box.

EP

~~amazing~~ awesome brilliant fantastic
fine great horrible lovely OK
perfect really good terrible wonderful

		😫	😐	☺️	😃
A	Conversation				*1*
B	Adjectives	___ ___	___ ___	___ ___ ___	*amazing* ___ ___ ___ ___

32 Listen and check. Then repeat.

5 Choose the correct words to complete the conversations.

0 **A:** I'm not in the basketball team any more.
B: Oh no! That's *terrible* / *fantastic*!

1 **A:** I've got a new mobile phone.
B: Wow! That's *fine* / *brilliant*!

2 **A:** My sister's getting married.
B: That's *great* / *OK*!

3 **A:** Look at my lunch!
B: That's *horrible* / *excellent* – don't eat it!

4 **A:** Are you enjoying the film?
B: It's *OK* / *lovely*. It's not great.

5 **A:** I got top marks in my test.
B: That's *wonderful* / *terrible*, well done.

6 In pairs, practise the conversations. Then make some new conversations together.

4 IT WAS AWESOME!

Unit Overview

TOPIC	Feelings and emotions
VOCABULARY AND LISTENING	Adjectives Conversations about experiences
GRAMMAR	Past simple of *be*
PRONUNCIATION	*was/were*
READING	Activity days – latest reviews
VOCABULARY	Emotions
LISTENING	Five short conversations
WRITING	A description of a party
EXAM TASKS	Listening Part 1

Resources

GRAMMAR REFERENCE AND PRACTICE: SB page 141; TB page 247
WORKBOOK: pages 20–23
PHOTOCOPIABLE WORKSHEETS: Grammar worksheet Unit 4; Vocabulary worksheet Unit 4
TEST GENERATOR: Unit test 4

WARMER

Brainstorm a list of activities onto the board and then write the following: *love like don't like hate*

Ask the students to copy the table into their notebooks, then write each activity from the board into the column of the table that corresponds to how they feel about it. Then, ask the students to discuss the activities in small groups, e.g. **A:** *Do you like playing computer games?* **B:** *I love it!*

ABOUT YOU

At the end of the activity, ask the students if they have talked about any activities which are not on the board. If so, ask them to add the new activities to their table.

VOCABULARY AND LISTENING

Adjectives

1 Ask the students to look at the six photos first and to say if they think the people are having fun and why. Students then take turns to answer the question about each photo.

Answers

A The people are at a festival. They are listening to music and they are taking photos.
B The people are at a party having fun.
C They are at a funfair on a ride.
D The player is running in front of the goal.
E The people are at a wedding reception. One man is taking a photo.
F The people are at a barbecue. They are cooking.

31 2 Encourage the students to listen for words which tell them where the people are.

Answers

Conversation 1 C
Conversation 2 F
Conversation 3 A
Conversation 4 E
Conversation 5 D
Conversation 6 B

31 3 Ask the students to look at the table in Exercise 4 and say what each emoticon means: bad, OK, good, very good. Stop after each conversation to allow students to complete the table.

MIXED ABILITY

Pair up a weaker with a stronger student. Photocopy the audioscript on TB page 267 and allow the weaker student to read it as they listen. Then, stop the recording after each conversation and ask the students to complete the table in pairs. The weaker student can help their stronger partner by showing them the adjectives in the script.

Answers

1 Conversation 5
2 Conversation 2
3 Conversation 4 and 6
4 Conversations 1 and 3

» AUDIOSCRIPT TB PAGE 267

4 Point out that there is a space in each column for every missing word.

32 **Answers**

The answers are recorded for the students to check and then repeat.
Conversation 1 amazing, awesome
Conversation 2 fine, OK
Conversation 3 brilliant, perfect, fantastic
Conversation 4 wonderful, lovely, really good
Conversation 5 horrible, terrible
Conversation 6 great

5 Encourage the students to read the whole conversation and consider how happy the speaker is feeling first.

Answers

1 brilliant 2 great 3 horrible 4 OK 5 wonderful

6 Ask the students to say the adjectives again with the correct intonation before they practise the complete conversation. Encourage the students to write new conversations of at least two lines. When they are ready, invite volunteers to perform them in front of the class.

Answers

Students' own answers

GRAMMAR Past simple of *be*

1 The students look at the examples and complete the rules. Point out that the missing words are given in the box.

Answers

1 was 2 were 3 n't 4 was/were

» GRAMMAR REFERENCE AND PRACTICE ANSWER KEY TB PAGE 247

2 With a weaker class, ask the students to find the subject first and check whether it goes with *was* or *were* by looking at the rules in Exercise 1.

Answers

1 was 2 were 3 wasn't 4 weren't 5 was 6 were

3 Point out that there is a mistake with *be* in every sentence. Refer the students back to the rules in Exercise 1 if necessary.

Answers

1 All my friends **were** here on Saturday.
2 I like your new shoes! **Were** they expensive?
3 Yesterday I **was** at a friend's house.
4 The players **were** good and the weather was fine.
5 That **was** an awesome party last night!

4 Encourage the students to read the whole conversation first before they complete it. The students will practise the conversation in Exercise 5.

Answers

1 weren't 2 wasn't 3 was 4 Was 5 was 6 was 7 was 8 Were 9 weren't 10 were 11 was 12 was

FAST FINISHERS

Ask fast finishers to continue the conversation with Max asking Suzy 'Where were you after school yesterday?' and Suzy answering. If time allows, in Exercise 5 they can practise the whole conversation with the new part and then perform it to the class.

» GRAMMAR WORKSHEET UNIT 4

PRONUNCIATION *was/were*

5 Stop the audio after each sentence so that the students can repeat. With weaker classes, have them keep their books open so that they can read the sentences in the conversation in Exercise 4. With a stronger class, with books closed, ask them to listen and write down the complete sentence. Then, they listen again and underline the stressed words. Finally, they repeat the sentences with the correct sentence stress.

Audioscript 33

The sentences are recorded for the students to listen and repeat.

1 Where were you yesterday afternoon?
2 You weren't at school.
3 No, I wasn't. I was at a big athletics competition.
4 Was it fun?
5 Yes, it was. It was amazing!
6 I was the winner of the 800 m race!
7 Were your parents there?
8 No, they weren't. They were at work.
9 My brother was there with his video camera.

6 Point out that the students need to put a different word from the box in each gap. Check that the students say the questions correctly before they ask and answer them. Encourage them to give full answers. When they write their own questions, point out that they should use some of the sentence beginnings in the box.

Answers

1 What was 2 Was 3 Who were 4 Where were 5 What were 6 Were 7 When was
Students' own answers

COOLER

Books closed. Write the seven question beginnings from the box in Exercise 6 on the board. Tell the class that they are going to interview their teacher. Invite a volunteer to sit on a chair at the front of the class. Ask the students to ask original questions using the question beginnings for the volunteer to answer as if they were the teacher.

GRAMMAR Past simple of *be*

1 **Look at the examples.**

Positive
I was at my sister's wedding.
We were at a barbecue near the beach.
All the bands were fantastic.

Negative
The weather wasn't great.
You weren't in class.

Questions and short answers
Where were you last night?
How was the food?
Were you at the football match? Yes, I was.
Was it fun? No, it wasn't.

Now choose the correct words in the box to complete the rules about the past simple of *be*.

was	were	n't

1 We use ________ with *I/he/she/it*.
2 We use ________ with *you/we/they*.
3 We add ________ to *was/were* to make negative sentences.
4 We put ________ / ________ before the subject to make questions.

» GRAMMAR REFERENCE AND PRACTICE PAGE 141

2 **Choose the correct words to complete the sentences.**

1 My school lunch *was / were* really nice yesterday.
2 My brothers *was / were* late home this evening.
3 That TV programme *wasn't / weren't* very good!
4 We *wasn't / weren't* too tired after our walk.
5 What *was / were* the time when you got home?
6 How many people *was / were* on the school trip?

3 **Correct the mistakes in the sentences.**

0 The weather ~~is~~ *was* good yesterday.
1 All my friends was here on Saturday.
2 I like your new shoes! Are they expensive?
3 Yesterday I were at a friend's house.
4 The players was good and the weather was fine.
5 That is an awesome party last night!

4 **Complete the conversation with *was/wasn't, were/weren't*.**

Suzy: Hi Max. Where [0] *were* you yesterday afternoon? You [1] ________ at school.
Max: Oh hi Suzy. No, I [2] ________. I [3] ________ at a big athletics competition at the city sports club.
Suzy: Really? [4] ________ it fun?
Max: Yes, it [5] ________. It [6] ________ amazing! I [7] ________ the winner of the 800 m race!
Suzy: Fantastic! [8] ________ your parents there?
Max: No, they [9] ________. They [10] ________ at work. But my brother [11] ________ there with his video camera, so it [12] ________ fine!

ə PRONUNCIATION *was/were*

5 (33) **Listen to some sentences from the conversation and repeat them.**

Now practise the conversation with your partner. Take turns to close your book and see if you can remember it.

6 **Complete the questions with the words in the box. Then ask and answer the questions with a partner.**

Was	Were	What was	What were
When was	Where were	Who were	

1 ________ your dinner like last night?
2 ________ your friend late this morning?
3 ________ your teachers when you were six?
4 ________ you on Saturday morning?
5 ________ your favourite TV shows when you were little?
6 ________ you in this class last year?
7 ________ your last haircut?

Write three more questions to ask your partner. Tell the rest of the class the answers.

READING

1 Read the reviews of the activity days. Three of the reviews have four stars and one has five stars. Which one do you think has five stars?

ACTIVITY DAYS

34

LATEST REVIEWS

Fun day!

I was very surprised to get this activity day for my birthday, but indoor skydiving was awesome! I can't wait to go again. Before the activity, there are lots of hand signals to learn, so you can communicate when you're flying in the wind tunnel. You can't speak in there! At first, I was worried about forgetting them, but it was fine. **Jade**

Fantastic!

I'm really interested in cars, so this was an amazing day for me. I still can't believe that my first driving experience was in a Lamborghini and an Aston Martin! I've got a video of the whole thing. I'm glad about that, because on the day there's no time to look at the cars properly. As soon as you finish, the next driver gets in. I was a bit upset about that.
Liam

Amazing trip!

This was my first time in a helicopter, and I was quite nervous. I wasn't sure I wanted to do it. But there was no need to be afraid – in fact, I was sorry when it was over! I was in the front seat and the view was fantastic. The only problem was that we were back on the ground after only ten minutes. **Mia**

Really special!

What a brilliant afternoon! First, there was a talk about the history of chocolate. Then it was time for the best bit – making and decorating our own chocolates! The teachers were lovely and happy to help with any problems. There were photos to buy afterwards, but they were really expensive. I was angry about that. **Ethan**

2 Read the texts again and answer the questions with a phrase or short answer.

1 What does Liam like a lot?
2 What wasn't Liam able to do on his activity day?
3 Was Jade's activity day a present?
4 What wasn't possible in the wind tunnel?
5 What was Ethan's favourite part of the day?
6 Were the photos cheap?
7 Was Mia nervous after flying in a helicopter?
8 Was Mia's helicopter trip long or short?

TALKING POINTS

Would you like to do an activity day?
Which of these looks most fun?
What sort of presents do you get for your birthday?
What do you give other people?

VOCABULARY Emotions

1 EP Look at the texts. Find and underline the words in the box. Match some of them to the emojis.

afraid	angry	glad	happy	interested
nervous	sorry	surprised	upset	worried

2 Choose the correct words to complete the sentences.

1 I'm so *sorry* / *afraid* you're not feeling well!
2 I'm *angry* / *nervous* about my piano exam tomorrow! I don't feel ready.
3 My little brother's crying. He's *upset* / *glad* because my mum isn't there.
4 I'm painting a picture at the moment, and I'm really *happy* / *surprised* with it.
5 My mum's *worried* / *interested* about my school work, but my teacher says it's fine.
6 I'm really *glad* / *angry* you're here at last! Why are you so late?

READING

WARMER

Write the adjectives from Student's Book page 28 Exercise 4 on the board. Next draw four emoticons in four columns on the board to represent bad, OK, good and very good. Ask the students to put the adjectives in the correct column. Next, encourage the students to ask questions with *How was your … ?* with *evening*, *weekend*, *maths test*, *birthday*, *match*, *music lesson*, etc. and answer using the adjectives, e.g. *How was your weekend? It was amazing. How was your maths test? It was … .*

BACKGROUND INFORMATION

Several companies sell 'Activity Days' where you can buy an experience like flying, sailing or painting lessons or even circus skills and give it to someone as a present. Some companies such as Virgin Experience Days offer experiences like paintballing and bungee-jumping which are specially designed for teenagers.

Review sites like TripAdvisor encourage their own members to write reviews of activities and award a rating between 1 and 5. This is called User-Generated Content (UGC).

1 Ask the students to look at the title of the text, the four photos and headings (but not to read the text) and to answer these questions: *What's an activity day?* (a day when you can try something) *What's a review?* (an opinion about something). Ask the students to look at the photos again and say what activity each reviewer did (if necessary, use the photos to pre-teach *indoor skydiving* and *helicopter*). Point out that reviewers often give points or stars and briefly discuss the difference between a 4- and a 5-star review before they do the exercise. Ask the students to say why three of the reviews only got 4 stars (each one had a minor complaint).

Answers

5 stars – Jade's (no complaints)

2 Encourage the students to try to answer the questions before they read the texts again. Point out that they only need to write a short answer but they should say where they found the answer in the text. If necessary, do the first question as an example.

Answers

1 cars/driving 2 look at the cars 3 Yes, it was. 4 talking
5 making and decorating the chocolates 6 No, they weren't.
7 No, she wasn't. 8 It was short.

34 The Reading text is recorded for students to listen and read.

FAST FINISHERS

Ask fast finishers to think of another idea for an activity day. When the others are ready, the fast finishers present their ideas to the class.

TALKING POINTS

Point out that these activity days were given to the four young people for their birthdays (see Background information). Discuss whether they would like to receive an activity day for their birthday. Encourage the students to ask and answer the questions in small groups and then to appoint a spokesperson to report back to the class on their answers.

VOCABULARY Emotions

1 First, ask the students to look at the texts and find as many adjectives as they can. Then, ask them to look at the words in the box to check that they have found these ones in the text. Check that the students pronounce the words correctly by asking them to repeat the words and to underline the stressed syllables (*surprised* /səˈpraɪzd/ and *worried* /ˈwʌrid/ are two syllables and *interested* /ˈɪntrəstɪd/ is three). Next, ask the students to look at each image and to say which adjective they represent. If time allows, ask them to draw (or if appropriate, find on their phone) images for the other four adjectives.

Answers

A afraid B angry C surprised D upset E nervous
F glad/happy

2 Remind the students that they need to read the whole sentence before they choose the correct adjective. When they have finished, encourage the students to test each other. Student A reads out the sentences saying *banana* instead of the adjective and Student B says the missing adjective. Then they change roles.

Answers

1 sorry 2 nervous 3 upset 4 happy 5 worried 6 glad

» VOCABULARY WORKSHEET UNIT 4

LISTENING

1 Read the questions as a class before asking students to work in pairs to describe the pictures in as much detail as possible.

Answers

Students' own answers

35 2 **A2 Key for Schools Listening Part 1.**

In this part of the exam, students listen to five short conversations and answer a question by choosing the correct picture, A, B or C. They listen to each conversation twice. Before they listen, ask the students to read each question again and say how each of the three pictures answers it. Do the first as an example: *What was Bella happy with at the party? In A Bella was happy about the people, in B she was happy about the food and in C she was happy about the music.* The students then listen to the three conversations and choose the right picture for each one. After they listen for the first time, encourage them to compare their answers with a partner and to say why they think their answer is correct. Play the recording for a second time for the students to check their ideas. With a weaker class, play the recording for a third time and stop it after the correct answer is given. With a stronger class, ask the students to say why the other pictures are not correct, e.g. *In 1 Bella says the music wasn't great and there weren't many people there.* They can do this by listening again.

Answers

1 B 2 C 3 C 4 A 5 B

» AUDIOSCRIPT TB PAGE 267

WRITING

PREPARE TO WRITE
A description of a party

GET READY Before the students read the text, invite a short class discussion on parties by asking 'Do you ever go to birthday parties? What do you do? What do you eat and drink?' If the students don't go to parties, invite a discussion on the other ways they celebrate special days like birthdays. After the students have underlined the adjectives, encourage them to say where adjectives go in the sentence: either after subject + *be* (*we were excited*) or before the noun (*a really big party*).With a stronger class, encourage them to find words we can use to describe the adjective (modifiers), e.g. *really* and *so* and remind them that we can use *very* too. Then, ask the students to complete the sentences with the adjectives in brackets. Remind them that we never put an *-s* on an adjective even if the noun is plural, i.e. *big parties* not ~~*bigs*~~ *parties.*

Answers

It was Isabella's party.
It was at Isabella's home.
It was from 6 pm to 9 pm.
The food was pizza, salad and cake.

party/food – big, nice, brilliant
people's feelings – excited, nervous, fine

1 There was some nice food at the party.
2 There were lots of happy people at the party.
3 This is terrible music.
4 Jake is a brilliant dancer.
5 I like going to big parties.

PLAN Encourage the students to ask and answer the four questions in *Get ready* orally in pairs before they make notes. If the students don't go to birthday parties, encourage them to write about a special day or meal with their family.

WRITE Ask the students to use the model to help them (see Mixed ability below).

IMPROVE Encourage the students to check that they have included enough adjectives, that they have put them before the noun, spelled them correctly and have not added an *-(e)s* to make the adjective plural. They should also check that they have used *was/were* correctly. Then, ask them to check their partner's paragraph for these things.

MIXED ABILITY

Ask the stronger students to work though this section at their own pace. With weaker students, write the model text on the board. Ask the students to say which words are information words, rub these out and leave the paragraph structure, e.g.:

I was at .... birthday party last .... name's .... and the party was at .... on ...., from .... to ....

Next, complete the text together on the board with appropriate information. Then, rub out the information words again. Ask them in pairs to complete the text again with new words.

If appropriate, for homework, ask the stronger students to write at least 80 words about a different special day (e.g. a family celebration) and weaker students to write at least 40 words about a birthday party.

COOLER

In pairs, the students take turns to mime one of the words in Vocabulary Exercise 1 page 30 and guess the emotion.

LISTENING

1 **Read questions 1–5 and look at the pictures. What can you see in each picture?**

35 **2** **Listen to five short conversations. For each question, choose the correct picture (A, B or C).**

1 What was Bella happy with at the party?

2 Where is Kyle's ticket?

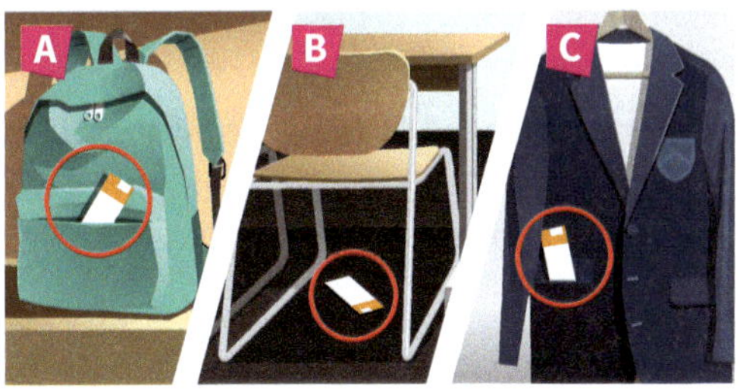

3 What was the weather like?

4 How much was the boy's T-shirt?

5 Where was the girl on Saturday?

WRITING

PREPARE TO WRITE

A description of a party

GET READY Read the text and answer these questions. Whose party was it? Where was it? What time was it? What food was at the party?

> I was at my best friend's birthday party last month. Her name's Isabella and the party was at her house on 12th May, from 6 pm to 9 pm. It was a really big party. All her friends and family were there, and we were so excited about it. There was lots of food – pizza, salad and of course cake! It was all really nice. Isabella was nervous before the party, but she was fine when everyone was there. It was a really brilliant evening!

Now underline all the adjectives. Which describe the party and the food, and which describe how the people felt?

Put the adjectives in the correct place in the sentences.

1 There was some food at the party. (nice)
2 There were lots of people at the party. (happy)
3 This is music! (terrible)
4 Jake is a dancer. (brilliant)
5 I like going to parties. (big)

PLAN Make notes about a party you were at. Use the questions in *Get ready* to help you.

WRITE Write a paragraph about the party.

IMPROVE In pairs, read each other's paragraphs. Check for mistakes with *was/were* and adjectives. Give your partner two ideas to make their paragraph better. Use your partner's advice and rewrite your paragraph.

LIFE SKILLS COLLABORATION

REACHING AGREEMENT

LIFE SKILLS

Reaching agreement

For two people to agree, you need to:

- listen carefully
- give your opinions calmly and clearly
- try to understand the other person's ideas before you decide what to do.

1 Read the sentences. Answer the questions.

Let's agree to disagree.

We can find a 'win-win' solution.

1 What do you think the sentences mean?
2 Which sentence do you prefer? Why?
3 When do you need to make decisions? For example, think about doing a class project, going to an event or watching TV.

2 Do you ever disagree with friends about these things? How do you reach an agreement?

What to do at the weekend
What to buy a friend for their birthday
What topic to choose for a school project

3 Read the problems on Danny's page quickly and write the names on the correct replies. Do you have any problems like these in your life?

4 Read the texts again. Which person/people has/have these problems?

Which person/people …

1 has/have a problem with a friend?
2 has/have a problem with a family member?
3 has/have a problem at school?
4 hasn't/haven't got a lot of time?
5 wants/want to go to the cinema?
6 maybe needs/need to agree to disagree?

5 Complete the sentences with the highlighted words from the texts.

1 I don't ______ with the things my friend does in class. She doesn't listen to the teacher.
2 Do you agree or ______ with the idea of going to the cinema?
3 I hope you ______ the film.
4 Can you give me some ______? I don't know what to do.
5 I'm ______. I can't go to the cinema with my friends. My mum and dad want me to stay at home with my little brother.
6 Maybe you don't agree. In that ______, you can make your own plans.

37 **6 Listen to Lola, Oscar and Daisy talking. What are they planning?**

a They are making plans to go the cinema.
b They are making plans to study for their maths exam together.
c They are making plans for a surprise party.

37 **7 Listen again and choose the correct words to complete the sentences.**

1 First, they need to decide on a ______ for the party.
   a present b day
2 They decide to meet on ______.
   a Sunday night b Saturday afternoon
3 Lola thinks it's a good idea to get a ______.
   a basketball shirt b notebook
4 Oscar thinks it's a better idea to get a ______.
   a T-shirt b CD
5 Michael loves ______.
   a listening to music b going to the cinema
6 They decide to ______.
   a get nothing b get a CD and a book
7 Oscar wants to ______.
   a buy a cake at the shop b make a cake
8 Lola needs to ______.
   a study b help her mum

8 Are the sentences in the *Useful language* box used for agreeing (A), disagreeing (D) or making suggestions (S)?

USEFUL LANGUAGE

I disagree *D*
How about a basketball shirt?
I have a better idea.
I agree.
I think a CD is a better idea than a book.
That's an awesome idea!

32 LIFE SKILLS

LIFE SKILLS

Learning Objectives

- The students learn how to reach agreement.
- In the project stage, they plan a party, design an invitation and present their ideas to the class.

Vocabulary

agree disagree enjoy advice unhappy case

BACKGROUND INFORMATION

Advice columns or agony columns are a part of a British newspaper or magazine where letters from readers asking for advice are printed. An agony aunt (or uncle if male) answers these letters giving some advice on how to deal with the situation. Originally, it was generally an older woman who gave the advice (hence *aunt*). The readers' letters are generally anonymous and are often signed using an emotion and the location, e.g. *Miserable, Brighton* or *Confused, Norwich*.

WARMER

Books closed. Do a running dictation with the two sentences in Exercise 1.

- Copy the sentences onto three or four pieces of paper and put them on the classroom walls. Make sure the writing is small enough so that the students can't read it from their desks.
- In pairs, students decide who will be the secretary and the messenger. Give the students enough time to reach an agreement. (The class will discuss this stage at the end of this activity.)
- Tell the messengers they need to stand up and walk to a sentence, memorise it and then walk back to their secretary, who will write it down.
- Allow the pairs enough time to do this and then ask them to check their sentences with the book.
- Ask 'How did you decide on the secretary and the messenger?' 'Did you agree easily?' 'Did one of you have to give in?'

LIFE SKILLS
Reaching agreement

Ask the students to read the information in the box, decide which points they agree with, and compare with a partner.

1 First, ask the students to ask and answer the questions in pairs and then if appropriate, encourage the students to discuss their ideas as a class.

Possible answers

1 Let's agree to disagree: Let's accept that we see things differently.
We can find a 'win-win' solution: We can find an answer that is good for everyone.
2 and 3 Students' own answers

2 Ask the students to read the instructions and the things. Then, allow them some time to think about their own answers before they compare their ideas with a partner.

Answers

Students' own answers

3 Ask the class to look at the text title, the introduction and the photos and ask 'What are you going to read?' (*letters asking for advice and the replies*) Point out that all the letters are about problems with friends. Next, ask the students to read the three letters (1–3) quickly and look at the names of the people who have written the letters (*Bored Best Friend*, *Unhappy Friend*, *Birthday Brother*) and ask 'Why don't they write their real names?' (*so no one knows they wrote it*) Then, ask them to match each letter to its reply and write in the sender's name in the space.

MIXED ABILITY

Ask weaker students to read one letter only and then match it to its reply. Then, for Exercises 4 and 5, pair them up with a stronger student who has read all three letters and can help them with the answers.

Answers

A Birthday Brother B Bored Best Friend C Unhappy Friend

4 Ask the students in pairs to try to answer the questions before they read the letters again. Point out that the question asks *Which person/people …*, so there may be more than one person in each answer.

FAST FINISHERS

In pairs, encourage fast finishers to talk together about whether they agree with Danny's advice and why.

Answers

1 Bored Best Friend / Unhappy Friend 2 Birthday Brother
3 Unhappy Friend 4 Birthday Brother 5 Bored Best Friend
6 Bored Best Friend

36 The Reading text is recorded for students to listen and read.

5 Encourage the students to read through the sentences and try to complete them with a suitable word first. Then, ask them to look at the highlighted words and try to work out the meaning from context before they complete the sentences. If necessary, point out that *agree* is a verb, so we say *I agree* (not *I am agree*), the negative form is *I don't agree* or *I disagree* (not *I'm not agree*) and the question is *Do you agree?* (not *Are you agree?*).

Answers

1 agree 2 disagree 3 enjoy 4 advice 5 unhappy 6 case

Continued on page 62.

37 **6** Before the students listen, ask them to read through the three situations (a–c) in pairs and talk about what the three friends will need to agree on (plans for an event).

Answers

c They are making plans for a surprise party.

37 **7** Ask the students to try to complete the sentences before they listen again. With a weaker class, it may be necessary to play the recording for a third time and pause it after each answer is given.

Answers

1 b 2 b 3 a 4 b 5 a 6 b 7 b 8 b

» **AUDIOSCRIPT TB PAGE 268**

8 When the students have completed the activity, check that the students say the useful language with the correct intonation by asking them to listen and repeat. If time allows, ask the students to copy the table below into their notebooks and complete it with the useful expressions, e.g.:

Making suggestions	Agreeing	Disagreeing
How about a basketball shirt?	*I agree.*	*I disagree.*

Answers

How about a basketball shirt? S
I have a better idea. D
What do you think? S
I agree. A
I think a CD is a better than a book. S
That's an awesome idea! A

TALKING POINTS

Encourage the students to think of their own answers first before they take turns to ask and answer the questions in small groups.

PROJECT ***Planning a surprise party***

Ask the class to read the instructions in bold and ask 'Do you like parties?' 'Have you ever planned a party?' 'Have you ever planned a surprise party?' Ask the students to read through the Think about points first on their own and make notes. Next, organise the students into small groups and ask them to compare their ideas. Encourage them to reach an agreement on each of the points using the language in the *Useful language* box. If necessary, ask them to read the points in the *Life skills* box at the top of page 32 again.

When they have reached an agreement, ask them to design an invitation which includes the necessary information. Remind the students that they will have to reach an agreement here too, e.g. *Who will do the artwork? Who will write the content?* Encourage them to look at each other's invitations, give feedback and make suggestions for improvement.

PROJECT EXTENSION

Tell the class that as a whole, they are going to plan a party or a small event for some of the other classes in the school (for example this could be other classes using the same book). Ask them to read through the Think about points again, decide whether they are going to plan a party or a small event, and to reach an agreement as a class. They will also need to negotiate their party or event with you. If time allows, ask them to design the invitation. If appropriate, allow them to hold the party or event for the other classes.

COOLER

Ask each student to write a problem on a piece of paper. Collect in the problems and hand them out so that each student has a different problem. Organise the students into groups of six and ask them to take turns to share their problems and also to listen and give advice. Encourage the students to use the useful language in Exercise 8 on page 32. At the end of the activity, ask them to talk together about whether the other students are good listeners and whether they give good advice.

Help me, Danny!

Send me your problems and I can give my advice.

36

1

Dear Danny,

I want to go to see a film tonight, but my best friend wants to play basketball. We always play basketball and I'm bored! What can I do?

Regards,
Bored Best Friend

2

Dear Danny,

I have a problem. My best friend is often not nice to our maths teacher. She doesn't listen, she never does her homework and she says bad things about the teacher. I tell her to stop, but she gets angry with me. What can I do? Thanks for your help.

Unhappy Friend

A

Dear ________,

It's important for you and your sister to agree because you haven't got a lot of time. Make a list of good things about each present to help you decide. Then go shopping and choose the present together. Try to find a win–win solution.

Enjoy shopping and happy birthday to your brother! *Danny*

B

Dear ________,

This is often a problem with friends and family. You can talk to your friend and ask to do something different, or you can talk to your friend about how you feel. Maybe agree to disagree. In that case, go to the cinema alone or with another friend.

Good luck! *Danny*

3

Dear Danny,

It's my brother's birthday at the weekend. My sister wants to buy him a T-shirt, but I want to buy him a book. We have only £15 and only one day to go shopping. What do you think?

Birthday Brother

C

Dear ________,

I think it's a good idea to talk to your friend and tell her to stop. You can tell her that it's important to be good in class and that you don't like what she's doing. Is she finding maths difficult? Does your friend need help studying? Listen carefully to your friend to help her.

Enjoy your lessons at school!

Good luck! *Danny*

PROJECT

Planning a surprise party

In small groups, plan a party to surprise a friend.

- Think about:
  - who the party is for
  - when the party is
  - where the party is
  - what food and drink you want
  - what you need to do
  - what you need to buy
  - what music to play
  - what activities you can do at the party
- Design an invitation for your party.
- Present your invitation to the class.

TALKING POINTS

How about YOU? Are you organising a party for someone? Do you normally buy presents for your friends? Do you and your friends always agree? What do you do then?

REACHING AGREEMENT 33

REVIEW 1 UNITS 1–4

VOCABULARY

1 **Match the sports equipment words to the photos.**

ball   bat   racket   stick

Now match the equipment to these sports.

baseball   basketball   hockey   rugby
table tennis   tennis   volleyball

2 **Put the words into the correct column.**

athletics   cereal   cheese
classical music   cold meat   cycling
dessert   dinner   drums   fish
fruit   gymnastics   keyboard
hip-hop   jazz   juice   opera
piano   pop   rap   rice   rock
sailing   saxophone   snowboarding
soul   tomatoes   vegetables   violin

Food	Music	Sport

3 **Complete the missing word in each sentence.**

1 Please can you p________ your school bag after breakfast?
2 I want to m________ a music video with my brother.
3 He likes cooking a________. He doesn't like cooking with other people.
4 That's a f________ idea. I think it's really good.
5 Do you always t________ your bedroom at weekends?
6 My sister is u________ because she can't come to the party.
7 Bands usually go on t________ when they make a new album.
8 That's b________ news about the tennis match. Well done!
9 I always get d________ before breakfast.
10 My brother doesn't like exams. He always gets very n________.

GRAMMAR

1 **Choose the correct words to complete the sentences.**

1 I love *talk* / *talking* to my friend and I love *go* / *going* shopping with her too.
2 I *sing* / *am singing* in the school hall on Fridays.
3 The film *was* / *were* very exciting.
4 In my free time, I *usually stay* / *stay usually* at home.
5 That *is* / *was* a very good barbecue last Sunday.

Correct the mistakes in the sentences.

6 I go often with my friends to the cinema.
7 How are you? I write to you to give you some news.
8 The weather amazing last month.
9 I like go to school because I like my teachers.
10 Yesterday is my birthday.

2 **Put the words in order to make questions.**

0 your brothers / what / wake up / do / time / usually / ?
What time do your brothers usually wake up?
1 making / what / you / are / ?
2 mum / the / does / play / guitar / your / ?
3 play / you / Tuesday / do / tennis / every / ?
4 your / you / at the moment / are / doing / homework / ?
5 your / brother / playing / this morning / football / is / ?

3 **Now match the questions to the answers. Then complete the answers with the verb in the correct tense.**

a Yes, she ________ (play) it really well. She ________ (learn) a new song at the moment. It sounds great! ☐
b They *are sleeping* (sleep) at the moment but they usually *wake up* (wake up) at seven. *0*
c Yes, I am. I ________ (do) my maths. It's really difficult! ☐
d No, he's with his friends. They ________ (watch) a film at Tom's house. ☐
e Yes, I do, and I often ________ (play) on Saturdays as well. ☐
f I ________ (make) my breakfast. I usually ________ (have) bread, but today I ________ (have) a bowl of cereal with fruit. ☐

REVIEW 1 UNITS 1–4

Overview

VOCABULARY	Sports; Sports equipment; Daily routines; Food; Music; Music phrases; Adjectives; Emotions
GRAMMAR	Adverbs of frequency; Present continuous and present simple; *like, don't like, hate, love + -ing*; Past simple of *be*
LISTENING	Five short conversations
READING	Tamburello
SPEAKING	Asking questions; talking about music
EXAM TASKS	Listening Part 1; Speaking Part 1

Resources

PHOTOCOPIABLE WORKSHEETS: Grammar worksheets Units 1-4; Vocabulary worksheets Units 1-4; Review Game Units 1-4; Literature worksheet; Speaking worksheet; Writing worksheet

WARMER

Play Pictionary. Begin to draw one of the pieces of equipment from Unit 1 (*bat, ball, board, racket* or *stick*) on the board and encourage the class to guess what it is by asking Is *it a ...?* Do the same with all five words and, if time allows, some of the sports. If appropriate, organise the class into teams and award points for the correct answers. If possible, leave the pictures of the sports equipment on the board for Exercise 1.

VOCABULARY

1 Ask the students either to look at the pictures of sports equipment on the board (see Warmer) or in the book and say what they are again before they match them to the words. Also encourage them to say which sports use each piece of equipment before they match them. When they have finished, challenge them to think of some more sports for each sports equipment word.

Answers

A bat B stick C ball D racket
ball: baseball, basketball, hockey, rugby, table tennis, tennis, volleyball
bat: baseball, table tennis
racket: tennis
stick: hockey

2 First, check that the students can pronounce these words correctly by asking them to listen and repeat. Next, do the first two words as a class by asking:

Teacher: *Where does 'athletics' go?*
Student: *It goes with 'Sport'.*
Teacher: *Where does 'cereal' go?*

Encourage the students to continue in pairs by asking and answering questions about each word.

FAST FINISHERS

Invite fast finishers in pairs to play Pictionary with some of the words in this exercise.

Answers

Food: cereal, cheese, cold meat, dessert, dinner, fish, fruit, juice, rice, tomatoes, vegetables
Music: classical music, drums, keyboard, hip-hop, jazz, opera, piano, pop, rap, rock, saxophone, soul, violin
Sport: athletics, cycling, gymnastics, sailing, snowboarding

3 Ask the students to read the whole sentence first and try to think of the missing word before they complete it. Encourage the students to complete as many of the sentences as they can and then allow them to look back at the vocabulary sections in Units 1–4 and find the words.

Answers

1 prepare 2 make 3 alone 4 fantastic 5 tidy 6 upset
7 tour 8 brilliant 9 dressed 10 nervous

GRAMMAR

1 For questions 1–5, encourage the students to read the complete sentence first before they choose the correct answer. In questions 2 and 5, ask them to look at the time expression before they decide on the correct word. For questions 6–10, point out that there is a problem with the verbs in each of these sentences.

Answers

1 talking, going 2 sing 3 was 4 usually stay 5 was
6 I **often go** with my friends to the cinema.
7 How are you? **I'm writing** to you to give you some news.
8 The weather **was** amazing last month.
9 I like **going** to school because I like my teachers.
10 Yesterday **was** my birthday.

2 With a weaker class, it may be necessary to give the students the first word in each question. Correct the questions before the students move on to Exercise 3.

Answers

1 What are you making?
2 Does your mum play the guitar?
3 Do you play tennis every Tuesday?
4 Are you doing your homework at the moment?
5 Is your brother playing football this morning?

3 Ask the students to read the questions in Exercise 2 again and try to think of a suitable answer before they match them to the correct answer (a–f). Remind the students to read through the complete answer first looking at the time expressions before they write the verb.

Answers

a plays, is / 's learning 2 c 'm / am doing 4
d 're /are watching 5 e play 3
f 'm / am making, have, 'm / am having 1

MIXED ABILITY

With very weak students, write the complete questions on the left hand side of the board and the complete answers on the right hand side of the board first and ask them to match them. Next, rub out the questions on the board and ask the students to do the first part of the exercise. Then, invite volunteers to come to the board and write the question next to its correct answer.

LISTENING

38

1 A2 Key for Schools Listening Part 1.

In this part of the exam, the students listen to five short unrelated conversations. They have to read a question for each one and choose the correct picture. Each conversation is repeated after the students hear it for the first time. First, ask the students to read the questions and underline the key words. Then, ask them to look at three pictures and say what is the difference between each one (e.g. 1 A it's 1.30, B it's 2.00 and C it's 2.30) before they listen to the recording. Allow them to listen to each conversation at least twice.

Answers

1 A 2 A 3 C 4 B 5 C

» **AUDIOSCRIPT TB PAGE 268**

READING

1 First, ask the students in pairs to look at the text title and look at the photo and to predict how you play Tamburello. Pre-teach *tambourine* by asking them to find a picture of a musical instrument near the text and asking 'What is it?' Next, ask them to read the text and check their ideas. Then, ask them to try to answer the questions before they read it again. If time allows, challenge each pair to make up a new sport using a musical instrument.

Answers

1 Italy 2 500 years old 3 six 4 a tambourine 5 13 6 the ball and the points

SPEAKING

1 A2 Key for Schools Speaking Part 1.

In this part of the exam, both candidates are first asked the following questions *What's your name?, How old are you?* and *Where do you live?* Then, in Part 1 Phase 2, candidates are asked questions on two different topics, e.g. fashion, shopping, hobbies, etc. For each topic, the candidates are asked two different questions (*what/ where/who/when*, etc.). Then, one candidate is asked to give a longer response to a question that always begins 'Tell me something about …'

With a weaker class, encourage the students to find the question word first, i.e. *1 What's, 2 Where* and tell them that this is the first word in each question.

Answers

1 What's your name?
2 Where do you live?
3 How old are you?
4 What's your favourite sport?

2 In Phase 2 of the exam, one of the topics might be 'sports' and then the examiner will ask each candidate in turn two questions related to the topic, e.g. *Which sports do you do?* or *How often do you do them?* One of the candidates is then asked another question like *Please tell me something about your favourite sports team* and encouraged to give a longer answer. The examiner then repeats this phase with another topic (e.g. school, music) and the other candidate is asked the second extended response question.

First, encourage the students to look back at Unit 3 and make some notes about music before they speak to their partner.

Answers

Students' own answers

COOLER

Reverse pictionary

Tell the students to take a piece of paper and divide it into four equal parts by folding it into quarters (and then unfolding it again). Ask them to label each part with one of these words: *sport*, *food*, *music* and *emotions* (i.e the vocab areas from Units 1–4). Next, choose some words from Units 1–4, say each word and encourage the students to draw a picture of it under the heading. At the end of the activity, ask the students to compare their drawings in small groups and try to guess what each other has drawn.

Tamburello

Tamburello is a sport from the north of Italy. It is a very old sport. The first games were in the 16th century. Players can play the game inside or outside.

It's a team sport and there are usually three players in each team. Players hit the small tennis ball to players in the other team. But they don't use bats or rackets to hit the ball. They use tambourines. Have a look at the photo. Yes, the players have got tambourines in their hands. The Italian word for tambourine is *tamburello*. That's how the sport gets its name.

A player in one team hits the ball over the line to players in the other team. A player in the other team hits it back. When a player doesn't hit the ball or when the ball goes too far, the other team wins a point. There are four points in each game. That's the same as the points in tennis. When players play a match, they usually play 13 games.

LISTENING

1 Listen to five short conversations. For each question, choose the correct picture.

1 What time do they agree to meet?

A 
B 
C 

2 Which instrument does Mona need to practise tonight?

A 
B 
C 

3 What is Finley's brother doing?

A 
B 
C 

4 Where were they in the morning?

A 
B 
C 

5 What does the girl want to have for dinner?

A 
B 
C 

READING

1 Read the text and answer the questions.

1. Which country does the game come from?
2. How old is the game?
3. How many players are there in a game of *tamburello*?
4. What do the players hit the ball with?
5. How many games are there in a *tamburello* match?
6. What two things in *tamburello* are like the game of tennis?

SPEAKING

1 Put the words in order to make questions.

1. name / your / what's / ?
2. you / where / live / do / ?
3. old / you / how / are / ?
4. favourite / what's / sport / your / ?

Ask and answer the questions with your partner. Take turns to speak.

2 In pairs, talk about music. Take turns to speak.

- Let's talk about music. What kind of music do you listen to?
- When do you listen to music?
- Do you listen to music on your phone?
- Who is your favourite singer / favourite band?
- Tell me something about your singer / band.

5 MOMENTS IN HISTORY

VOCABULARY AND READING

Historical events

1 Look at the photos in the quiz. Can you name any of these people? Do you know, or can you guess, why they are famous?

2 Match the photos to the quiz questions.

3 Complete the quiz questions with the words in the box.

EP

climbed	crossed	died	opened
painted	played	published	received
recorded	travelled		

ABOUT YOU

What famous people do you know from history?
Why are they still famous today?
When and where were they born?

4 In pairs, do the quiz. Choose A, B or C.

40 Listen and check.

5 In pairs, Student A, name a photo. Student B, say what happened.

Student A: *Photo J*
Student B: *Cleopatra died.*

Women in history

A

B

C

D

1 **Cleopatra, Queen of Egypt and the last pharaoh, ________**
A in 180 BCE.
B in 70 BCE.
C in 30 BCE.

2 **Marie Curie ________ the Nobel Prize in chemistry**
A in December 1911.
B in December 1925.
C in December 1950.

3 **Valentina Tereshkova ________ into space**
A on 12th August 1961.
B on 3rd April 1962.
C on 16th June 1963.

4 **Amelia Earhart ________ the Atlantic Ocean, alone, by plane**
A in 1932.
B in 1941.
C in 1950.

5 **Coco Chanel ________ her first shop in Deauville, France**
A in the 18th century.
B in the 19th century.
C in the 20th century.

6 **Frida Kahlo ________ her self-portrait with parrots**
A in 1920.
B in 1935.
C in 1941.

7 **Serena Williams ________ her first match at Wimbledon**
A in 1996.
B in 1998.
C in 2000.

8 **Junko Tabei ________ Mount Everest**
A on 16th May 1975.
B on 5th April 1977.
C on 12th May 1980.

9 **J. K. Rowling ________ her first Harry Potter book**
A in March 1985.
B in June 1997.
C in July 2004.

10 **Ella Fitzgerald ________ her first song**
A in 1928.
B in 1930.
C in 1936.

J

I

H

G

F

E

36 UNIT 5

5 MOMENTS IN HISTORY

Unit Overview

TOPIC	Famous events in history
VOCABULARY AND READING	Historical events Women in history
GRAMMAR	Dates with *in* and *on*; Past simple: regular verbs
PRONUNCIATION	Past simple *-ed*
READING	The Great Fire
VOCABULARY	Buildings
LISTENING	An interview about a moment in history
SPEAKING	Giving a presentation about a moment in history

Resources

GRAMMAR REFERENCE AND PRACTICE: SB page 142; TB page 248
WORKBOOK: pages 24–27
PHOTOCOPIABLE WORKSHEETS: Grammar worksheet Unit 5; Vocabulary worksheet Unit 5
TEST GENERATOR: Unit test 5

BACKGROUND INFORMATION

The years BC (Before Christ) and AD (Anno Domini) are often referred to as BCE (Before Common or Current Era) and CE (Common or Current Era).

Valentina Tereshkova is a Russian astronaut who became the first woman and first civilian to fly in space. In 2013 (at the age of 77), she offered to go on a one-way trip to Mars.

Frida Kahlo (1907–1954) was a Mexican painter. Due to a childhood illness and accident, she had medical problems for the rest of her life. Her portraits and self-portraits often depict her suffering.

Junko Tabei (died 2016 aged 77) was a Japanese mountaineer. She was the first woman to reach the top of Everest and the first woman to climb the 'Seven Summits' (the highest mountains in each of the seven continents).

Ella Fitzgerald (1917–1996) was an American jazz singer. She wanted to be a dancer but began to earn money by singing on the streets in Harlem, New York. She then won first prize ($25) at an amateur singing night at the Apollo Theatre, Harlem and went on to become the 'Queen of Jazz'.

WARMER

If necessary, first remind the students how to say dates correctly by writing some dates on the board and asking them to listen and repeat.

Do a date quiz: Choose five important years and dates in history and dictate them to the class. Check pronunciation by saying them and having students repeat.

Organise the class into teams. Ask each team why the date is important. Award points for the best answers (i.e. those closest to the truth).

ABOUT YOU

Brainstorm a list of famous people from history onto the board. Then, in pairs, encourage the students to ask and answer the questions about the people.

VOCABULARY AND READING

Historical events

1 Ask the class to look at the photos and say what they have in common (*They are all famous women in history*). If the class enjoy competitions, do Exercises 1, 2 and 4 as a class quiz by organising the students into teams of four. Begin by asking the teams to identify the famous people or things in the photos and say what they know about them. Award points for every correct piece of information but do not worry too much about correct sentences in the past tense for now.

Answers
A Coco Chanel B Ella Fitzgerald C Junko Tabei
D Frida Kahlo E Valentina Tereshkova F Amelia Earhart
G J. K. Rowling H Serena Williams I Marie Curie J Cleopatra
Students' own answers

2 Point out that the students should not choose the options A, B, C yet. If appropriate (see Exercise 1), award the teams a point for every correct answer.

Answers
1 J 2 I 3 E 4 F 5 A 6 D 7 H 8 C 9 G 10 B

3 Encourage the students to work in pairs and find the object in sentences 2–10. Then they should think of a suitable verb for each one (e.g. 2 *win* + *the Nobel Prize*) before they look at the words in the box.

Answers
1 died 2 received 3 travelled 4 crossed 5 opened
6 painted 7 played 8 climbed 9 published 10 recorded

40
4 Invite pairs to read out their answers. Record these on the board. Then, play the recording for students to hear the correct answers. If appropriate, award one point for each correct answer.

Answers
1 C 2 A 3 C 4 A 5 C 6 C 7 B 8 A 9 B 10 C

» AUDIOSCRIPT TB PAGE 268

5 Demonstrate this activity first by asking the students to turn over their books. Say a photo and its letter and encourage the students to give you the correct past event. (See exercise for example.)

Answers
Students' own answers

GRAMMAR Dates with *in* and *on*

1 Books closed. Elicit the sentence about Valentina Tereshkova from the quiz and write it on the board: *Valentina Tereshkova travelled into space on 12th August 1961.*

Ask the students which preposition we use with dates and then to complete the exercise in the book by looking back at the quiz.

Answers

on: on 12th August 1961, on Tuesday
in: in January, in 2004, in the 20th century

2 Put the students in pairs. Student A (book open) reads out a date or a year from the quiz and Student B (book closed) says the event. Then they change roles.

Answers

Students' own answers

Past simple: regular verbs

3 Ask 'Did these events happen now or in the past?' (*in the past*) 'How does the verb change when we use it to talk about the past?' (*verb + -(e)d*). Point out that we call these verbs *regular* verbs because they all end in the same way (verb + *-(e)d*).

Answers

-d and *-ed*

4 Point out that there are spelling rules for the regular verbs and ask the students to tell you the rules: verbs ending in …

consonant → + *-ed*

-e → + *-d*

consonant + *y* → *-ied*

vowel + *y* → + *-ed*

Ask the students to copy the table into their notebooks and complete it.

Answers

climbed: cleaned, cooked, finished, helped, joined, painted, wanted
changed: completed, invited, phoned
carried: copied, studied
stayed: enjoyed, played
stopped: planned, preferred

» GRAMMAR REFERENCE AND PRACTICE ANSWER KEY TB PAGE 248

5 Point out that students also need to write *in* or *on*. Remind them to check their spelling by looking at the table in Exercise 4.

FAST FINISHERS

Fast finishers rewrite the sentences so that they are true for them, e.g. *I joined the school swimming team in May.*

Answers

1 cooked, on 2 studied, in 3 played, in 4 invited, on

» GRAMMAR WORKSHEET UNIT 5

PRONUNCIATION Past simple *-ed*

41
6 Demonstrate the difference in sound, e.g. *crossed* /ˈkrɒst/ (one syllable) and *recorded* /rɪˈkɔːdɪd/ before the students listen. After they have listened to the answers, ask the students 'When is there an extra syllable?' (*When the final sound is* /t/ *or* /d/.) With a stronger class, show them the three different ways to pronounce the *-ed* ending: /d/ after a voiced sound, /t/ after an unvoiced sound and /ɪd/ after /t/ and /d/.

42
Answers

The answers are recorded for the students to check and then repeat.
No extra syllable: cleaned, cooked, copied, enjoyed, finished, helped, joined, phoned, planned, played, preferred, studied
Extra syllable: completed, invited, painted, wanted

7 Ask the students to read each sentence first and decide whether it is in the present or the past. After checking answers, point out that according to the corpus, one of the most common mistakes made by students at this level is writing the verb in the present instead of the past.

Answers

1 watches 2 wanted 3 started 4 enjoyed 5 liked 6 need

8 Point out that the students should write at least six grammatically correct sentences, some of which are false. They should also include the date (*on*), the year (*in*), the month (*on*) or the day (*on*).

Answers

Students' own answers

MIXED ABILITY

Write some sentences together as a class on the board. Erase the verbs and encourage the students to complete the sentences with the correct past simple verb . Finally, ask them to copy and change three to six sentences (depending on ability) so that they are true for them. Either ask a stronger student to check the sentences for grammatical mistakes or check the sentences yourself.

COOLER

Play noughts and crosses. Organise the class into two teams: 0s (noughts) and Xs (crosses). Make sure everyone knows how to play and draw this grid on the board:

dance	play	join
finish	climb	cross
visit	paint	open

In order to win a square, the team needs to pronounce and spell the past simple form of each verb correctly.

GRAMMAR Dates with *in* and *on*

1 **Look at the answers to the quiz again. Complete the rules for *in* and *on*.**

We use *in* / *on* for the date and the day.
________ *12th August 1961* / ________ *Tuesday.*

We use *in* / *on* for months, years and centuries.
________ *January* / ________ *2004* /
________ *the 20th century.*

2 **In pairs, test your partner.**

In 1998 — Serena Williams played her first match at Wimbledon.

Past simple: regular verbs

3 **Read the sentences. Look at the letters in purple. What do we add to the verbs to make the past tense?**

Ada Lovelace complet**ed** the first computer program in 1842.
NASA's Curiosity Mars Rover land**ed** on Mars on 6th August 2012.

4 **Look at the verbs in the table. Write the past simple forms of the verbs in the box in the correct column.**

~~clean~~ complete cook copy enjoy finish help invite join paint
phone plan play prefer study want

climb → climb**ed**	change → change**d**	carry → carr**ied**	stay → stay**ed**	stop → stop**ped**
cleaned				

» GRAMMAR REFERENCE AND PRACTICE PAGE 142

5 **Now complete the sentences with the past simple form of the verbs and *in* or *on*.**

1 I ________ (cook) dinner ________ Sunday.
2 My mum ________ (study) history at university ________ 2001.
3 My dad ________ (play) for Manchester United ________ September 1988.
4 She ________ (invite) us to her 14th birthday party ________ 8th June.

PRONUNCIATION Past simple *-ed*

41 **6** **Listen to the *-ed* sounds. Sometimes we add another syllable when we say the *-ed* and sometimes we don't.**

Put the verbs from the box in Exercise 4 into the correct column.

finished: *ed* is NOT an extra syllable	waited: *ed* IS an extra syllable

42 **Listen and check. Then repeat.**

7 **Choose the correct verb forms.**

0 I ~~*like*~~ / *liked* the competition because my sister was in the team.
1 She *watches* / *watched* TV and likes playing on the computer.
2 We really *want* / *wanted* to go to skiing last week, but there wasn't any snow.
3 It *starts* / *started* to rain in the night. It was very noisy.
4 I really *enjoy* / *enjoyed* the weekend. I don't want to go home tomorrow.
5 The film was really great yesterday. I *like* / *liked* it.
6 I *need* / *needed* a new coat. Can we go shopping this afternoon?

8 **Make six sentences about you using the past simple and *in* or *on*. Use the words in the box to help you.**

climb complete cross dance
finish join open paint play
record reveal start visit

This year we started school on 4th September.
I visited China with my family in 2013.

READING

1 Look at the photos.

What do you know about London today? How was it different in the 17th century? Discuss your ideas with your partner.

2 Read the article and check your ideas from Exercise 1. Match the four photos A–D to paragraphs 1–4.

3 Choose the correct word to complete the sentences about the Great Fire of London.

1 London is *bigger* / *smaller* today than it was in the 17th century.
2 The fire started in a bread shop early on *Saturday morning* / *Sunday morning*.
3 A lot of people lived in houses made of *wood* / *stone*.
4 The houses burned *quickly* / *slowly*.
5 5th September was the *first* / *last* day of the fire.
6 The Tower of London is *more than* / *less than* 350 years old.
7 St Paul's Cathedral is a(n) *new* / *old* stone building.

The Great Fire

1 Saturday 1st September 1666 was a normal day in London. The city was smaller than it is today, but the little shops were busy and there were lots of people in the streets.

2 Just after midnight that night, something happened in a bread shop in Pudding Lane to change everything. A small fire started in the building. Most people lived in small houses in those days. These houses were very close to each other. The floors at the bottom of the houses were made of stone, but the rest of the houses were made of wood. The fire moved first to the houses and shops on each side of the bread shop, jumping from roof to roof. The buildings started to burn, and the fire travelled quickly from house to house, from shop to shop and from street to street. The fire moved very fast through the buildings and burned for three days, from Sunday 2nd until Wednesday 5th September.

3 After the fire, the buildings made of wood were not there anymore, but many churches and the famous castle, the Tower of London, were still there because they were made of stone.

4 So the people of London decided to make new buildings of stone. You can still see many of those stone buildings from after the fire in London today. One of the most famous is a church. It's called St Paul's Cathedral.

READING

WARMER

Hand out twelve strips of coloured card to groups of three. Ask each group to write one verb from Exercise 8 on page 37 of the Student's Book (*climb*, *complete*, etc.) on the front of each card in large, clear letters, and the past simple of the verb on the back.

Ask them to mix the cards and take four each. They take turns to test the other group members, as follows: *What's the past of climb?* (climbed)

How do you spell it? (c-l-i-m-b-e-d)

Give me a sentence with it! (I climbed a mountain in May.)

NB: Encourage the students to continue to make past simple verb cards as they learn more (and the irregular verbs). This activity can be used to start or finish any class and also given to fast finishers.

1 Books closed. Find out if anyone in the class has been to London and encourage the other students to ask them questions about the city, e.g. *Is it big? What can you see and do there?* Then, ask the students to copy the following table into their notebooks:

	London today	London in the 17th century
Size	*big*	*smaller*
People		
Building		

As a class, begin to complete it together (see examples above). Books open. In groups ask the students to say what they can see in each photo: A St Paul's Cathedral, B an area of London in the past, C the Tower of London, D a fire in London in the past. Then, ask the students to continue completing the table by using the photos to help them.

Answers
Students' own answers

2 Ask the students to read the article title and look at the photos again and say what they think it will be about (*a large fire which destroyed parts of London in 1666*). Point out that the four paragraphs of the text are in order. Ask them to read the four paragraphs quickly and to underline the words that tell them the answer, i.e. 1 1st September 1666, 2 a small fire started, 3 the Tower of London, 4 St Paul's Cathedral.

MIXED ABILITY

Encourage stronger students to work though Exercises 2 and 3 at their own pace. Check their answers. With weaker students ask them to read parts of the text only, e.g. weaker students could read paragraph 2 and very weak students one or two of the shorter paragraphs (1, 3 or 4). Then, ask them to match their text to its photo in Exercise 2, answer the questions they can in Exercise 3, and then share their answers with students who have read different parts.

Answers
1 B 2 D 3 C 4 A

3 If necessary pre-teach *wood* and *stone* by asking the students 'What's the Tower of London made of?' (*stone*) and 'What are trees made of?' or 'What material do we get from trees?' (*wood*) Ask the students to choose the correct word and then find the answers in the article.

Answers
1 bigger 2 Sunday morning 3 wood 4 quickly 5 last
6 more than 7 old

43 The Reading text is recorded for students to listen and read.

VOCABULARY Buildings

1 Check that the students can pronounce each word correctly by asking them to listen and repeat. Then, ask them to say what the words have in common before they do the exercise, i.e. buildings or parts of buildings.

Answers
1 roof 2 palace 3 statue 4 church 5 stairs 6 cathedral
7 square 8 floor 9 castle 10 ceiling

2 Do *castle* and *ceiling* as an open class example.

FAST FINISHERS

Fast finishers play Pictionary where Student A draws a picture of one the words in Exercise 1 and Student B has to say what it is. Then they change roles.

Answers
Places/things in a city: castle, cathedral, church, palace, square, statue
Parts of buildings: ceiling, floor, roof, stairs

3 Students work in small groups, making sure there are stronger students in each group. Encourage the students to ask *How do you say X in English?* and *How do you spell it?* As a class, write the words from each group onto the board in a table and ask the students to copy them into their notebooks.

Answers
Students' own answers

» VOCABULARY WORKSHEET UNIT 5

TALKING POINTS

Encourage the students to take turns to ask and answer the questions giving full answers. Also encourage them to talk about their favourite buildings in their town, to say why they like them, how often they go there, etc.

LISTENING

44 1 Before the students listen, encourage them to look at the photo on the page and ask 'What do you think Janet is going to talk about?' Then, ask them to listen to the interview and check their ideas.

Answers
getting a colour TV

44 2 Encourage the students to read the sentences first and say if they are right or wrong in pairs before they listen again. Ask stronger students to correct the wrong sentences.

Answers
1 ✗ (Janet lived in a flat.) 2 ✗ (There were no computers or mobile phones.) 3 ✓ 4 ✗ (Janet's dad went to the shop to buy a colour television.) 5 ✓ 6 ✓

» AUDIOSCRIPT TB PAGES 268–269

SPEAKING

1 Explain that each pair is going to give a presentation to the class on a moment in history. Brainstorm a list of historical events from the students' country onto the board. Encourage the students to say which have been the most important and elicit some key information about each one.

Encourage each pair of students to choose one moment in history. Ask them to read through the four questions and prepare to give a short presentation to the class about their event. They could prepare either by writing notes, or by answering the questions in full sentences. With a stronger class, encourage the students to prepare a presentation using a program (PowerPoint, Prezi, Google Slides, etc.) to illustrate their talk.

Answers
Students' own answers

2 Students give their talks to the class. Encourage the class to listen to the presentations and answer the questions in Exercise 1.

Answers
Students' own answers

3 Draw a timeline on the board and invite some students to put the events of the Great Fire on it (see below). They should then draw a similar timeline for their event. They could use an age appropriate program to create an online timeline (search for 'online timeline').

1st Sept 1666	2nd Sept 1666	5th Sept 1666	1677
Normal Day	The GF started	The GF ended	New buildings made of stone

Answers
Students' own answers

COOLER

Read out four sentences about the events in this unit but include some false information in each one (see below). Ask the students to listen carefully and to correct the sentences.

In small groups, the students write some more sentences (with some false information) about the facts in this unit.

Reorganise the groups. Group members take turns to read out their sentences and the others have to correct them. For example:

Cleopatra won the Nobel Prize in Chemistry. (Marie Curie)

Amelia Earhart crossed the Atlantic by ship. (plane)

The Great Fire started in Manchester in 1666. (London)

After the fire, the people of London decided to make St Paul's Cathedral out of wood. (stone)

VOCABULARY Buildings

1 **Match the words in the box to the meanings.**

EP

castle cathedral ceiling
church floor palace roof
square stairs statue

1 This is on the top of a building and keeps out the sun and the rain.
2 Someone important or rich, like a king or queen, lives in this very large house.
3 This is a model of a person or an animal, made of wood or stone.
4 This is a building that Christians use.
5 You use these to go up or down to another part of a building.
6 This is a very large building that Christians use.
7 This is an open space in the centre of a town .
8 We walk on this part of a room.
9 This old stone building has large walls and towers.
10 This part of a room is above our heads.

2 **Complete the table with the words from Exercise 1.**

Places / things in a city	Parts of buildings

3 **Add other words that you know to the table.**

TALKING POINTS

Which of the places or things in a city in Exercise 1 are in your town?
Which buildings are made of stone?
Which buildings are made of wood?
Which do you think is better, a building made of stone or a building made of wood? Why?

LISTENING

44 **1** **Listen to the radio programme *Living History – I was there!***

Dave Brown is talking to Janet about a moment in history she remembers. What moment does Janet remember?

44 **2** **Listen again. Are the sentences right (✓) or wrong (x)?**

1 Janet lived with her family in a house in Manchester.
2 There were computers but no mobile phones in the 1960s.
3 Black and white televisions only show black and white pictures.
4 Janet's dad telephoned the shop to buy a colour television.
5 Her dad and uncle carried it to the flat.
6 The first programme they watched in colour was sport.

SPEAKING

1 **Work in small groups. The Great Fire of London was an important moment in British history. Think of/find out about an important moment in the history of your country.**

Talk about it and prepare a presentation. Use these questions to help you.

- What's the important moment?
- When was it?
- What happened?
- Why was it important?

2 **Tell the class about your moment in history.**

Our important moment from history is ______.

It happened on (date) in (place).

These are some of the things that happened. There was … and then …

It was an important moment because …

3 **In your groups, draw a timeline and put your events on the timeline.**

6 WHAT A GREAT JOB!

ABOUT YOU

03 **Watch the video and answer the questions about you.**

What job do you want to do when you're older? Why?
What job don't you want to do? Why not?

VOCABULARY AND READING

Jobs

1 **Match the photos A–P to the words in the box.**

EP

actor artist cook dentist
engineer factory worker farmer
manager mechanic model nurse
photographer pilot police officer
shop assistant sports coach

45 **Listen and check. Then repeat.**

2 **Choose five of the jobs and write what the person does. Then work in small groups. Say your sentences and see if the other students can guess the job.**

A: *This person helps you when you want to buy something.*
B: *Is it a shop assistant?*

3 **In groups, look at the adjectives in the box and discuss which jobs they apply to.**

boring difficult easy fun interesting

PRONUNCIATION | Three-syllable words

46 **4** **Listen and repeat the words. Then put them into the correct column in the table.**

~~afternoon~~ ~~assistant~~ difficult
engineer expensive interesting
manager mechanic understand

Ooo	oOo	ooO
	assistant	*afternoon*

5 **Look at the title of the article and the photo. What do you think the article is about? Read it once to check your ideas.**

50 weeks, states, different jobs

When Daniel Seddiqui was 26, he travelled around the USA for a year. He visited all 50 states and worked for a week in each one. He didn't use buses or planes – he travelled by car from job to job. He earned money for every job he did, but hotels were too expensive for him. He usually stayed in his boss's home, or with one of the other workers. 'People were very good to me,' says Daniel. 'They looked after me really well.'

But why did Daniel do this? And did he enjoy it? 'Yes, I did! I wanted to travel and learn about my country,' he says. 'And I wanted to try lots of different jobs.' Things weren't always easy for Daniel. In week 7, he worked as a farmer in Nebraska. 'The days were long, and I got really dirty,' he says. In week 38, he was a cook in a fish restaurant in Maryland. 'That was really hard! Often I didn't even have time to get a drink of water.'

Other jobs were fun. He worked in a theme park in Florida and as a model in North Carolina. He was a football coach in Alabama. In Alaska, he was a photographer. 'That was great. Alaska is a very beautiful place,' says Daniel.

6 **In pairs, answer the questions.**

Which jobs from Exercise 1 did Daniel do?
Where did he do them?
Why do you think he chose those jobs?
Would you like to do any of these jobs?

6 WHAT A GREAT JOB!

Unit Overview

TOPIC	Work and work experience
VOCABULARY AND READING	Jobs 50 weeks, 50 states, 50 different jobs
PRONUNCIATION	Three-syllable words
GRAMMAR	Past simple: negatives and questions
READING	Students at work!
VOCABULARY	Work
LISTENING	A conversation about work experience
WRITING	A paragraph about work
EXAM TASKS	Reading Part 3

Resources

GRAMMAR REFERENCE AND PRACTICE: SB page 143; TB page 248
WORKBOOK: pages 28–31
VIDEO AND VIDEO WORKSHEET: Jobs
PHOTOCOPIABLE WORKSHEETS: Grammar worksheet Unit 6; Vocabulary worksheet Unit 6
TEST GENERATOR: Unit test 6

WARMER

Write the unit title *What a great job!* on the board. Challenge the students in small groups to think of a job beginning with each of the letters in the title. Write the jobs onto the board and leave this list on the board for Exercise 1.

ABOUT YOU

03 You can begin the class and introduce the topic of the unit by showing the video and asking students to complete the video worksheet. After the students have completed the video activities they can answer the questions.

VOCABULARY AND READING

Jobs

1 Ask the students to look at the photos first and see how many they can match to the words on the board (see Warmer).

45 **Answers**

The answers are recorded for the students to check and then repeat.
A photographer B cook C factory worker D actor
E police officer F dentist G sports coach H artist I engineer
J farmer K shop assistant L mechanic M manager N nurse
O pilot P model

2 Books closed. Demonstrate this exercise as a class first: read out the example A in the book (*This person helps you when you want to buy something*) and ask the students to guess who it is by asking an appropriate question (e.g *Is it a shop assistant?*).

Answers

Students' own answers

3 Demonstrate the activity with a stronger student first. If necessary, write the dialogue on the board for students to use as a model.

Answers

Students' own answers

PRONUNCIATION | Three-syllable words

4 Ask the students to listen and repeat first. Then, ask them to look at the columns and ask 'What do the column headings mean?' (*the larger O shows the stressed syllable in each word*). With a weaker class, point out that there are three words in each column. With a stronger class, ask them to find silent letters in two of the words, i.e. the *e* in *interesting* and the *h* in *mechanic*.

46 **Audioscript**

The words are recorded for the students to listen and repeat.
afternoon, assistant, difficult, engineer, expensive, interesting, manager, mechanic, understand

Answers

Ooo	oOo	ooO
difficult interesting manager	assistant expensive mechanic	afternoon engineer understand

5 If the class is slow to come up with ideas, ask them to also read the first line of the article and ask 'How long was Daniel in the USA?' (*a year = approx 50 weeks*); 'How many states are there in the USA?' (*50*); and 'How many different jobs do you think he did?' (*50*). Then ask the students to read the text and underline the jobs he did.

Answers

Students' own answers

6 Ask the students to check their answers to the first two questions by reading the text again. Ask them to add any new jobs to the box in Exercise 1, e.g. *wedding planner*.

Answers

farmer (Nebraska), cook (Maryland), model (North Carolina), sports coach (Alabama), photographer (Alaska), mechanic (Detroit), factory worker (Pennsylvania), (oil) engineer (Texas)
Students' own answers

47 The Reading text is recorded for students to listen and read.

GRAMMAR Past simple: negatives and questions

1 Ask the students to look at the table and say what it shows. Ask them to find more examples of these forms in the text. Elicit how we form the negative, question and short answers. Check understanding, e.g. 'Do we use *did* for *he/she/it*?' 'What form of the verb do we use after *did*?'

Answers

didn't
did
did, didn't

» GRAMMAR REFERENCE AND PRACTICE ANSWER KEY TB PAGE 248

2 Ask the students to read the questions first and think about a suitable answer before they match them to the answers (a–f). Encourage stronger students to write complete answers, e.g. c *He visited 50 states.*

Answers

1 c 2 d 3 a 4 e 5 f 6 b

3 Ask the students to read the sentences quickly and put a tick next to the true ones first. Then, point out that they need to follow the example, i.e. a sentence in the negative followed by a sentence in the affirmative. Make sure they use the infinitive after *didn't* and not the past simple. Remind them to check their spelling.

Possible answers

1 I didn't finish my homework at 6 pm. I finished it at 7 pm.
2 I didn't cook the dinner on Saturday. My dad cooked it.
3 I didn't text ten friends yesterday. I texted five.
4 I didn't paint a picture last week. I painted a picture last month.
5 I didn't climb a mountain during my last holiday. I rode a horse.
6 I didn't watch a film on TV last night. I played football.

4 Point out all the sentences are in the past simple and that they need to find one mistake with the verb in each sentence.

Answers

1 Did you **enjoy** yourself on holiday?
2 Tom **didn't** talk to me for very long at the party.
3 I didn't **finish** the history homework before the lesson.
4 I really **didn't** want to go to my dancing class yesterday.
5 Did you **remember** my birthday?

5 Encourage the students to give full answers (with verbs in the past). With a stronger class, ask them to ask follow-up questions, e.g. *Did you enjoy the lesson? Did you do your homework?*

MIXED ABILITY

Make the questions together as a class by nominating stronger students to come to the board and write up the questions. Pair up a stronger student with a weaker student. Ask the weaker students to ask the questions first so that the stronger student models some good answers.

FAST FINISHERS

Ask the fast finishers to write some more questions. When the others have finished, put the students into small groups with a fast finisher in each group. The fast finisher asks their new questions.

Answers

1 Did you play any sport last week?
2 Did you visit anywhere interesting last month?
3 Which school clubs did you join last year?
4 Did you answer a question in your last lesson?
5 What date did you start school this year?
6 When did you last travel to another country?

» GRAMMAR WORKSHEET UNIT 6

COOLER

The students play *What's my job?* in small groups. Demonstrate this activity: choose one of the jobs on pages 40–41 and tell the students they have to guess your job. They do this by asking a maximum of eight questions where the answer is *yes* or *no*, e.g. *Do you work in an office? Do you get dirty?*

47

Some more of Daniel's jobs

- Wedding planner, Las Vegas
- Mechanic, Detroit
- Factory worker, Pennsylvania
- Oil engineer, Texas
- Cheesemaker, Wisconsin
- Sugar maker, Vermont
- Fisherman, Maine

GRAMMAR Past simple: negatives and questions

1 **Look at the examples in the table and complete the rules with *did* and *didn't*.**

Negatives	Questions	Short answers
He didn't use buses or planes. I didn't even have time to get a drink of water.	Why did Daniel do this? Did he enjoy it?	Yes, he did No, he didn't.

We use ________ and the main verb in the infinitive in negative sentences.
We use ________ and the main verb in the infinitive in questions.
We use ________ or ________ and leave out the main verb in short answers.

» GRAMMAR REFERENCE AND PRACTICE PAGE 143

2 **Match the questions to the answers.**

1 How many states did Daniel visit?
2 How did Daniel travel from job to job?
3 Why did Daniel stay in people's homes?
4 Did Daniel like being a farmer in Nebraska?
5 Did Daniel work at a theme park in Florida?
6 What did Daniel do in Alaska?

a Because hotels were too expensive.
b He worked as a photographer.
c 50
d By car.
e No, he didn't.
f Yes, he did.

3 **Tick (✓) the sentences that are true for you. Correct the ones that are wrong.**

0 I travelled to school by bus today.
I didn't travel to school by bus today. I walked to school.
1 I finished my homework at 6 pm last night.
2 I cooked the dinner on Saturday.
3 I texted ten friends yesterday.
4 I painted a picture last week.
5 I climbed a mountain during my last holiday.
6 I watched a film on TV last night.

4 **Find and correct the mistakes with the past simple.**

1 Did you enjoyed yourself on holiday?
2 Tom don't talk to me for very long at the party.
3 I didn't finished the history homework before the lesson.
4 I really don't want to go to my dancing class yesterday.
5 Did you remembered my birthday?

5 **Make questions. Then ask and answer with a partner.**

0 What / learn about in the last lesson?
What did you learn about in the last lesson?
1 /play any sport last week?
2 /visit anywhere interesting last month?
3 Which school clubs / join last year?
4 /answer a question in your last lesson?
5 What date / start school this year?
6 When / last travel to another country?

READING

1 Read the article quickly. Where did Nina and Julia do work experience?

STUDENTS AT WORK!

Nina and Julia are 14 years old and go to school in London. But they weren't at school last week – they were doing work experience. This is when young people spend a few days doing a job. They don't earn money, but they work hard and learn about the world of work. Nina's job was in a café and Julia worked for a TV company. We asked them to tell us all about it.

Nina: I was really happy about working in a café, because I'd like to be a cook one day. But I didn't do any cooking at all. Instead I served food and drinks to the customers, cleaned the tables and washed the floor. The café opened at 7 am and closed at 6 pm, but my working hours were 6 am to 2 pm. The staff were friendly, but we didn't have much time for talking. We were all really busy!

Julia: I worked in the office of a TV company. At first, I was upset about that. My plan was to work in a TV studio, not in an office. But the staff were all very nice to me, and I learned a lot about the business. I started at 10 am and finished at 6 pm. In the morning, I opened all the letters. Then I helped my boss with different jobs. Sometimes I answered the phone. Other times he asked me to use the computer to look for information he needed. I was often so busy that I only had ten minutes for lunch!

48

2 **For each question, choose the correct answer.**

1 From the introduction we learn that Nina and Julia
   A enjoyed their jobs.
   B worked in different places.
   C were sorry to go back to school.

2 What kind of work did Nina want to do at the café?
   A cleaning
   B cooking
   C serving food

3 What does Nina say about her working day?
   A It was very long.
   B It started too early.
   C There was a lot for her to do.

4 Why was Julia upset in the beginning?
   A She didn't want to work in an office.
   B She didn't like the people she worked with.
   C She didn't know anything about the TV business.

5 Julia often didn't have much time to
   A eat her midday meal.
   B answer the phone.
   C speak to her boss.

TALKING POINTS

What do you think about students doing work experience? Is it a good idea? Why? / Why not?
What sort of work experience would you like to do?

READING

WARMER

Challenge the students to tell you as much as they can remember about Daniel Seddiqui (page 40). If appropriate, award points for correct information in the past. Then, write the following on the board (Exercise 2 page 41) and ask the students to make full questions in the past simple:

1 How many states / Daniel visit?
2 How / Daniel travel from job to job?
3 Why / Daniel / stay in people's homes?
4 Daniel / like being a farmer in Nebraska?
5 Daniel / work at a theme park in Florida?
6 What / Daniel do in Alaska?

Then, ask the students to ask and answer the questions in pairs. If necessary, allow them to look at the text again.

BACKGROUND INFORMATION

In the UK, students in their fourth year of secondary school (aged 14–15 years old) often do work experience for one or two weeks. In some schools, they are expected to find their own placements so that they take on some responsibility, they choose something they want to do, and they gain experience in looking for and applying for a job. In some schools, younger students spend one or two days at the workplace of a parent or family friend.

1 First, ask the class to look at the photos of Nina and Julia (*without* reading the text) and say how old they are and what they are doing. Tell the students that Nina and Julia are doing work experience (see Background information). Invite a brief discussion by asking 'Do students do work experience in your country?' 'Do you know anyone who has done work experience?' ('Where did they work?' 'What did they do?' 'Did they enjoy it?') 'What are the good (and bad) things about doing it?' Then, ask them to read the text quickly to find out where they did their work experience.

48

Answers

The Reading text is recorded for students to listen and check their answers.
Nina – a café
Julia – an office of a TV company

2 **A2 Key for Schools Reading Part 3.**

In this part of the exam, students will need to read a text and choose the correct answer (A, B or C) for five questions. These five questions may be questions (*What kind of work did …?*) or the first part of a sentence (*We learn that Nina and Julia …*).

Tell the students to read the question or sentence beginning first and underline the key words. Next, they should look for the answers in the text without reading the options (A–C). Then, they should read the options (A–C) and decide which one best matches the answer. Do the first question as an open class example. If the students struggle to find the correct answer, ask 'After reading the introduction, do you know if they enjoyed their jobs?' (*no*) 'Do you know if they were sorry to go back to school?' (*no*) 'Do you know if they did different jobs?' (*yes*)

MIXED ABILITY

Allow the stronger students to find the answers for themselves. Give weaker students a few minutes to read the text and help them with any vocabulary. Then, pair up a stronger student (who has finished) with a weaker student. Ask the stronger student to give their weaker partner two options only, e.g. 1 A or B, 2 B or C. They then help their partner to find the words in the text which give each answer.

Answers

1 B 2 B 3 C 4 A 5 A

TALKING POINTS

As a class, first invite a brief class discussion on whether the students would prefer to work in a café like Nina or work in an office like Julia. Encourage them to say why. Next, ask them to ask and answer the questions in small groups.

VOCABULARY Work

1 Ask the students to find and underline the words in the box in the text, decide whether each one is a verb, noun or adjective, and try to work out the meaning from context before they read the sentences.

Answers

1 busy 2 customers 3 boss 4 staff 5 office 6 earn

FAST FINISHERS

Ask fast finishers to continue onto Exercise 2. When they have finished Exercise 2, they write a sentence with each of the words in the box. When the others are ready, they read their sentence to the class without the word and the others have to guess the word, e.g. *I'm ..., because I'm helping my mum today.* (busy)

2 Remind the students to write their sentences in the past simple.

Answers

Students' own answers

» VOCABULARY WORKSHEET UNIT 6

LISTENING

49 1 This exercise has a similar format to A2 Key for Schools Listening Part 1, where students hear five short conversations and have to choose the correct picture to answer the question for each conversation. In this exercise, however, students answer questions about one longer conversation.

Ask the students to read the task, look at the example (0) and say where Joe worked last week (in a museum shop). Encourage them to say what the other two pictures represent. Next, ask the students to look at the three pictures (A, B and C) for each question (1–4) and try to say what the possible options are. For example:

1 He ... **A** helped customers **B** cleaned **C** put things on the shelves

Play the recording at least twice.

Answers

1 A 2 B 3 B 4 C

» AUDIOSCRIPT TB PAGE 269

2 Elicit when we use the expressions in the box (to react to news). Ask the students to say which we use to react to positive news, which we use to react to negative news, and which we use to show surprise.

50 **Audioscript**

The phrases are recorded for students to listen and repeat.

That's brilliant. Congratulations! Wow! Oh no! That sounds boring. Really?

3 Point out that the students can use the phrases in Exercise 1 but should replace *he* with *you* for their conversation. Demonstrate with a strong student first by continuing the example.

Answers

Students' own answers

WRITING

PREPARE TO WRITE
A paragraph about work

GET READY Ask the students to circle three examples of full stops, capital letters and apostrophes in the article about Nina and Julia. Before they read the rules in the box, ask them to say when we use each one. Then, ask them to say in what ways punctuation is different in English from their own language.

Advise the students to separate the paragraph into separate sentences with full stops and capital letters before they try to add the rest of the punctuation.

Answers

My friend Sarah's got a job in a café in the centre of town. The café's called The Silver Fish and the manager's name is Bill. On Saturday, Sarah started at 9.00 am. She cleaned the floors and served customers. After that she helped the cook make soup. It was really busy but Sarah enjoyed the day.

PLAN With a weaker class, brainstorm some questions as a class onto the board (see below) and ask them to copy them into their notebooks; e.g.

Where did you work?

How did you travel to work?

What time did you start?

What time did you finish?

Who did you do it with?

Did you enjoy it?

Encourage the students to interview somebody who works in the school, at home, in their sports or music club, etc. and to make notes.

WRITE Remind the students to use the past simple to describe the day. Encourage stronger students to write more words.

IMPROVE Remind students to check that the paragraph is written in the past and that the use of full stops, capital letters and apostrophes is correct.

COOLER

Read out three sentences about yourself to the class and encourage the students to react using the phrases in Listening Exercise 2. For example:

Teacher: *I cleaned the house yesterday.*

Class: *Oh no! That sounds boring.*

Now ask the students to write three true or made up sentences in the past simple about what they did recently. In groups, they read them to each other and react appropriately.

VOCABULARY Work

1 **Look at the article and find the words in the box. Then match them to sentences 1–6.**

EP

boss	busy	customers	earn
office	staff		

1 This means you're working hard and have lots to do.
2 These people buy things in shops or cafés.
3 When you have a job, this person tells you what to do.
4 These people work for a business.
5 There are usually desks, phones and computers in this place.
6 This means 'get money for doing work'.

2 **Write five sentences about Julia and Nina using the words in Exercise 1. In pairs, read your sentences. Say *Right*, *Wrong* or *We don't know!* to your partner's sentences.**

Julia and Nina earned lots of money. — Wrong

Julia's boss was friendly. — We don't know!

LISTENING

49 **1** **Listen to Joe talking about the job he did last week. Tick (✓) the correct picture (A, B or C).**

0 Where did he work?

1 What did he do?

2 What time did he start?

3 How did he travel to work?

4 How did he get the job?

50 **2** **Listen and repeat.**

That's brilliant!	Congratulations!	Wow!
Oh no! That sounds boring.	Really?	

3 **Work with a partner. One of you is Joe and the other is Joe's friend. Use phrases in Exercise 2 to make a conversation.**

Where did you work?

I worked in the museum.

Wow! That's brilliant.

WRITING

PREPARE TO WRITE

A paragraph about work

GET READY Look at the article about Nina and Julia's work experience on page 42. Find examples of full stops (.), capital letters (A, B, C) and apostrophes (').

Full stops – These are at the end of a sentence.

Capital letters – Use these after a full stop. Also use them for names, days of the week and months, and for the word 'I'.

Apostrophes – These are for contractions (*I've got*) and for possessives (*Jane's dog*).

Read the paragraph about a teenager's day at work. Add full stops, capital letters and apostrophes.

> My friend sarahs got a job in a café in the centre of town the cafés called the silver fish and the managers name is bill on saturday, sarah started at 9.00 am she cleaned the floors and served customers after that she helped the cook make soup it was really busy but sarah enjoyed the day

PLAN Talk to someone you know who has a job. Ask them about what they did one day last week. Make notes using some or all of these verbs:

close	enjoy	finish	open	start
stop	travel	use	work	

WRITE Write a paragraph about the person's day. Write about 50 words.

IMPROVE In pairs, read your paragraph and your partner's. Check for mistakes with punctuation.

CULTURE

SATURDAY JOBS

A

FACTFILE Saturday jobs

In English-speaking countries, many teenagers have Saturday jobs.
Having a Saturday job helps teenagers:
- ★ plan their time
- ★ meet new people
- ★ make some pocket money
- ★ learn new skills
- ★ learn the value of money

1

JOB OFFER – Saturday mornings

Do you like animals? Do you like nature? Do you like walking? Do you want to earn some pocket money? Well, dog-walking is your dream job. And we pay well.

A small, family company is looking for young people to help walk dogs.

WHEN: 2 hours on Saturday mornings
THE JOB: Walk 2–3 small dogs
WHERE: Local parks

For more information, visit our *Doggie Walks* website.

B

1 **Look at the photos. In pairs, discuss the questions.**

1. What are the two jobs in the photos?
2. Do teenagers work for pocket money where you live? What jobs do they do?
3. What are some good things about being a dog-walker or doing a paper round?

2 **Read the job offers. In pairs, discuss which one you think is the best.**

3 **Match the photos A and B to two of the job offers 1–3.**

4 **Read the job offers in Exercise 2 again. Answer the questions.**

1. How many hours a week is the dog-walking job?
2. Is the dog-walking job for a company?
3. Where is the Saturday afternoon job?
4. How can you get more information about the Saturday afternoon job?
5. When is the paper round job?
6. Where do you take the newspapers on the paper round?

5 **Complete the sentences with the highlighted words in the job offers in Exercise 2.**

JOB OFFER – Saturday mornings	You can earn some [1] ________ . You need to [2] ________ 2–3 small dogs.
Help Wanted – Saturday afternoons	You are [3] ________ for plants, pets and small jobs. You need to [4] ________ the cats.
Extra pocket money?	The job is doing a [5] ________ . You need to be [6] ________ .

CULTURE

Learning Objectives

- The students learn about Saturday jobs for teenagers.
- In the project stage, they design their own job offer, apply for one of the jobs and choose the best person.

Vocabulary

pocket money walk responsible feed paper round healthy

Resources

CULTURE VIDEO AND CULTURE VIDEO WORKSHEET: Summer camp

BACKGROUND INFORMATION

The Universal Declaration of Human Rights states that children should be protected from doing any work which prevents them from receiving free primary education and that every country should establish an appropriate minimum age and regulate the hours and conditions. In the USA, you need to be 14 and you may not work more than three hours a day and 18 hours a week during the school year. In Europe, the minimum age is 13 and the work cannot be harmful to the safety, health or development of the child, nor should it prevent them from attending school and participating actively. In the UK, research has shown that people who do not have part-time jobs as teenagers may not be well-prepared to take on full-time work; however, the number of teenagers taking on part-time jobs is falling. Some experts suggest this is because of the pressure to do well at school in order to get a good job in the future. Others say this is also due to a change in our habits; more people read the news online so there is less demand for children to do paper rounds.

WARMER

Revise the jobs from Unit 6 by writing these anagrams on the board (answers given in brackets). The first letter of each word is a capital: cAtro (actor), rttiAs (artist), kCoo (cook), heraPootgprh (photographer), cChoa (coach), leMdo (model), hSop ssttanAsi (shop assistant), eNrus (nurse)

Then, say 'A student in your country wants to earn some extra money while they are studying. Which of these jobs can they do?' Invite a brief classroom discussion and then ask 'Can you think of any more jobs they can do?' (e.g. *look after children, work in a café, bar or restaurant*)

1 Pre-teach *pocket money* by asking 'What do you call the money your parents give to you?' Next, ask the pairs to describe what they can see in each photo. If necessary, point out that A is a dog-walker (someone who walks dogs) and B is doing a paper round (delivering newspapers to houses). Then, ask the students to take turns to ask and answer the questions.

Answers

1 dog walking and delivering newspapers
2 Students' own answers
3 You can earn money and get exercise.

2 Ask the students to read the three offers, decide which they like best and then quickly discuss their choice with a partner. In *Talking points*, the students will talk in small groups about which job they prefer.

MIXED ABILITY

Ask very weak students to read the dog-walking job offer only (Text 1). In Exercise 3, ask them to find the photo which goes with the offer they read and in Exercise 4, encourage them to answer questions 1 and 2 only.

Answers

Students' own answers

3 Point out that there are three job offers but only two photos of jobs.

Answers

1 A dog walking 3 B a paper round

4 Ask the students to try to answer the questions before they read the job offers again.

Answers

1 two hours 2 yes 3 in a house 4 by emailing the small company 5 Monday–Saturday mornings 6 to people's homes and offices

5 First, ask the students in pairs to read through the sentences and try to complete them with a suitable word. Next, ask the students to look at the highlighted words in the job offers again and try to guess the meaning of each one from context. Then, ask them to complete the sentences with these words.

FAST FINISHERS

Allow fast finishers to work through Exercises 2–5 at their own pace. Then, in pairs, encourage them to take turns to choose a job offer and persuade their partner that they are the best person for the job.

Answers

1 pocket money 2 walk 3 responsible 4 feed
5 paper round 6 healthy

52 **6** First, ask the students in pairs to describe what they can see in each photo. Next, before the students listen, make sure they understand what they have to do, i.e. choose the correct photo for each sentence (1 and 2).

Answers

1 dog walking 2 piano class

52 **7** Ask the students to try to decide if the sentences are right or wrong before they listen again. Encourage stronger students to correct the wrong sentences. If necessary play the recording for a third time for weaker students.

Answers

1 ✗ (She has piano lessons on Saturday mornings.)
2 ✗ (Mrs Wilson needs someone to help in the garden.) 3 ✓
4 ✓ 5 ✗ (Daniel's son walks dogs in the park.) 6 ✓

» **AUDIOSCRIPT TB PAGE 269**

TALKING POINTS

Ask the students to look at the choice they made in Exercise 2 and the reasons they wrote down. Point out that they can change their mind if they want, but they may need to rewrite their reasons. Then, in small groups, encourage them to compare their ideas and give their reasons why they'd like (and wouldn't like) to do the jobs on offer.

Alternatively, organise the students into groups of three, where Student A has to argue that job offer 1 is the best, Student B argues for job offer 2 and Student C argues for job offer 3. Give the students a little time to prepare their arguments and then encourage them to discuss their ideas.

PROJECT *A job offer*

Ask the students to look again at the three job offers in this lesson in pairs, think about what other information they'd like to know about each one, and write down some questions, e.g. *Doggie Walks – What do I do if the weather is bad? Help wanted – What are the other small jobs? Paper Round – Do I need to do the paper round by bike?*

Next, ask the students to read the instructions in bold. Check that they have understood them by asking 'What do you need to think of?' 'What do you need to write?' If you did the Warmer activity, ask 'Which of those jobs would be suitable for a Saturday job for a teenager?' and/or 'Can you think of any more suitable jobs?' Write a list on the board.

In small groups, ask the students to choose one of the jobs on the board and make notes under the headings (what the job is, experience, etc.) in their notebooks. Encourage the students to produce a neat copy of their job offer. They could either do this by hand or as a slide for a presentation program. Point out that they can look at the three job offers in this unit for ideas.

Tell the groups they are going to need to find a person to do their job, so they should write four or five interview questions. Display the job offers (either on the classroom walls or use a presentation program to project them). Ask the students to look at each offer and write down one or two questions they'd like to ask about each one. Encourage them to look at the questions they wrote in preparation for this project to help them.

Reorganise the students into new groups so that they are working with people who wrote different adverts. Encourage them to take turns to interview each other for their jobs. The interviewee should also ask the questions they wrote to ask for more information.

Ask the students to return to their original groups, talk about who they interviewed for the job, their answers and then decide who the best person for the job is and why. Encourage the groups to report back to the class.

PROJECT EXTENSION

Extend the project before the stage where students write interview questions: ask the students to choose one of the class job offers, write a brief CV (Curriculum Vitae) and also write an email to apply for the job. Give the students a model CV to copy from and also a model email which applies for the job and asks for more information. Then, ask the groups to interview those students who have applied for their job.

CULTURE VIDEO 02: Summer camp

When students have completed the lesson, they can watch the video and complete the worksheet.

COOLER

Write *Advantages* and *Disadvantages* in two columns on the board and encourage the students to make a list of advantages and disadvantages of young people working part-time. For example, *advantages: you have money to buy things; disadvantages: no time to study.*

2 HELP WANTED – Saturday afternoons

Are you free on Saturday afternoons over the school holidays? Do you want to earn some pocket money?

We are looking for a responsible person to help us at home on Saturday afternoons.

WHEN: 3–4 hours on Saturday afternoons

THE JOB:

- water house plants
- do simple garden jobs
- feed two cats
- clean bird cage
- help with small jobs around the house

For more information, send an email and tell us about you.

3 EXTRA POCKET MONEY? DO A PAPER ROUND!

A small company is looking for young people aged 13–14 to do paper rounds.

WHEN: Monday to Saturdays. 1–2 hours in the morning.

THE JOB:

- you need to take newspapers to people's homes and offices
- you need to be healthy
- it helps to have a bicycle
- you need to get up early in the morning
- you need to be responsible and leave newspapers on time

For more information about the job and the pay, send us an email and tell us about you and your experience.

51

52 **6 Listen to Olivia and her dad talking about Saturday jobs. Tick the correct answers.**

1 Olivia has experience doing ________.

dog-walking

a paper round

2 Olivia has a ________ on Saturday mornings.

piano class

guitar class

52 **7 Listen again. Are the sentences right (✓) or wrong (✗)?**

1 Olivia wants a job on Saturday mornings.
2 Mrs Wilson hasn't got a garden.
3 Olivia sees a job offer in the newspaper.
4 The paper round job is in the centre of the town.
5 Mrs Wilson's son is a dog-walker.
6 Olivia walks the family dog.

TALKING POINTS

Which job would you prefer? Why?

PROJECT *A job offer*

Work in small groups. Think of Saturday jobs. Write an offer for a job on Saturday mornings or Saturday afternoons.

- Think about the following:
  - what the job is
  - experience
  - morning or afternoon
  - number of hours
  - times
  - what you need to do
- Ask other groups questions about their job offers.
- Try to find someone from the other group for your Saturday job. Is anyone in the group a good person for the job? Why? / Why not?
- Tell the class about your job and who is/are a good person

04 NOW WATCH THE CULTURE VIDEO

SATURDAY JOBS 45

7 AN EXCITING TRIP

ABOUT YOU

Where do people in your country like to go on holiday?
Do you like busy holidays or quiet ones?

VOCABULARY AND LISTENING

Holidays

1 (EP) **Look at the photos. Match the activities to the words in the box.**

buy presents	do water sports
go camping	go sightseeing
lie on the beach	ride a bike
stay at a hotel	take photos

(53) **Listen and check. Then repeat.**

2 (54) **Listen to Callum and Lottie talking about their holidays. Answer the questions.**

1 Where did Lottie go?
2 Where did Callum go?
3 Did they enjoy their holidays?

3 (54) **Listen again and look at the photos in Exercise 1. What activities did Callum and Lottie do? Write *C* or *L* for each picture.**

4 **Work in groups. Say what you like and don't like doing on holiday.**

GRAMMAR Past simple: irregular verbs

1 **Read the sentences from Callum and Lottie's conversation and look at the irregular past simple forms. What verbs do they come from?**

1 My friend Annabel came with us. *come*
2 We swam in the sea every day.
3 We lay on the beach.
4 We did lots of water sports.
5 We rode our bikes.
6 We got up late every day.
7 We had a really good time.
8 My parents gave me a new phone.
9 I took hundreds of photos.
10 I went to Istanbul, in Turkey.
11 I saw some interesting places.
12 I bought you a present.
13 I only ate one sweet.
14 We could walk to the beach in five minutes.

» GRAMMAR REFERENCE AND PRACTICE PAGE 144

7 AN EXCITING TRIP

Unit Overview

TOPIC	Holidays and trips
VOCABULARY AND LISTENING	Holidays (1) A conversation about holidays
GRAMMAR	Past simple: irregular verbs
READING	Crossing the world on a rickshaw to see the Olympics
VOCABULARY	Holidays (2)
PRONUNCIATION	Sounds and spelling
LISTENING	A description of a journey
SPEAKING	Telling a travel story

Resources

GRAMMAR REFERENCE AND PRACTICE: SB page 144; TB page 248
WORKBOOK: pages 32–35
VIDEO AND VIDEO WORKSHEET: Holidays
PHOTOCOPIABLE WORKSHEETS: Grammar worksheet Unit 7; Vocabulary worksheet Unit 7
TEST GENERATOR: Unit test 7; Term test 1

WARMER

Write some question words (*What? Where? When? Who … with? How?*) on the board. Tell the class that you had a fantastic holiday and encourage them to ask you questions about it using the words on the board. At the end of this lesson, the students will have the opportunity to talk about their own holiday.

ABOUT YOU

Ask the students to look at the unit title and the photos on the page and to tell you what the unit is about. Ask them to ask and answer the questions in pairs. Also encourage them to ask and answer the questions *Where do you like to go on holiday? Who do you go with?*

VOCABULARY AND LISTENING

Holidays

1 Ask the students to look at the photos first, say what they can see in each one, and say what they have in common. (*They are all things you do on holiday.*) Then, ask them to match them to the activities. Check that they can pronounce each activity correctly by asking them to listen and repeat.

53

Answers

The answers are recorded for students to check and then repeat.
A ride a bike B buy presents C go sightseeing D take photos E stay at a hotel F go camping G lie on a beach H do water sports

54

2 Before the students listen, ask them to look at the photo and ask them 'What are Callum and Lottie doing?' (*talking about their holidays and showing each other their photos on their phones*) Pre-teach *Turkish Delight** by pointing at the photo and asking the students to say where either Callum or Lottie went (*Turkey*).

*Turkish Delight is small cubes of jelly which may taste of roses, oranges or lemons. It is often served in Turkey and the Middle East with coffee or tea.

Answers

1 (to a campsite in) France
2 (to a hotel in) Istanbul, Turkey
3 Yes, they both enjoyed their holidays.

54

3 Ask the students to work in pairs and talk about which activities Callum and Lottie did before they listen again.

Answers

Photo A L (ride a bike) Photo B C (buy souvenirs) Photo C C (go sightseeing) Photo D L (take photos) Photo E C (stay in a hotel) Photo F L (go camping) Photo G L (lie on a beach) Photo H L (do water sports)

» AUDIOSCRIPT TB PAGES 269–270

4 Ask the students to read the task first and think of suitable questions to ask each other, e.g. *What do you like doing on holiday? What don't you like doing*? Ask them to think of some follow-up questions too, e.g. *Where? When? Why?* Encourage them to use the activities in Exercise 1 during their conversations.

Answers

Students' own answers

GRAMMAR Past simple: irregular verbs

1 Ask the students to read the sentences and say who said which one, i.e. Callum or Lottie. If necessary play the recording again so that they can check their answers. Then, ask them to look at the verbs and ask 'Why are these verbs different from the regular past simple verbs?' (*because we don't add '-ed' to the verb, each irregular past verb is different and these have to be learned*). With a weaker class write the infinitives on the board in a different order for the students to match.

Answers

1 come 2 swim 3 lie 4 do 5 ride 6 get up 7 have 8 give 9 take 10 go 11 see 12 buy 13 eat 14 can

» GRAMMAR REFERENCE AND PRACTICE ANSWER KEY TB PAGE 248

55 2 Tell the class that they will hear the past tense form and that they need to say the verb it comes from (i.e. the infinitive). Do the first as an example to make sure that everyone knows what to do.

Audioscript

swam, got, rode, gave, bought, took, ate, came, had, saw, went

Answers

swim get ride give buy take eat come have see go

3 Encourage the students to read the whole conversation before they fill the gaps. Point out that the negative and question form of past simple irregular verbs is the same as regular verbs. Point out that we can also use *Of course!* and *Of course not!* to say *Yes, I did* or *No, I didn't*. After checking answers, pairs role play the conversation.

MIXED ABILITY

With a mixed ability class, with pens down, read the completed conversation to the class and encourage the students to listen for the missing words. Then ask them, in pairs, to fill the gaps.

FAST FINISHERS

Encourage fast finishers to continue Callum and Lottie's conversation for at least four more lines.

Answers

Callum: *How was your summer holiday, Lottie?*
Lottie: *It was brilliant! I* ***didn't*** *want to leave!*
Callum: ***Did*** *you* ***get up*** *early every day?*
Lottie: *Of course not! We* ***got up*** *late and we* ***went*** *to bed late.*
Callum: ***Did*** *you* ***take*** *any photos?*
Lottie: ***Yes, I did***. *I took hundreds of them!*

4 Ask the students to read the complete conversation in each question first. Point out that the first answer is a short answer, i.e. *Yes, I/we did* or *No, I/we didn't* and that the students should use the same verb in brackets (*go*, *swim*, *buy*, *eat* and *have*) in the answer. Do the first as an open class example on the board.

Answers

1 Did, go
didn't, went
2 Did, swim
did, swam
3 Did, buy
didn't, bought
4 Did, eat
did, ate
5 Did, have
did, had

5 Begin this activity as a class. Elicit a verb from the class, e.g. *ride*. Next, elicit a question, e.g. *Did you ride a bike on holiday*? and then a suitable answer beginning *Yes, of course! / Yes, I did* or *Of course not! / No, I didn't*. Finally, ask the students to write three new holiday conversations. Invite pairs of students to read their conversations to the class.

Answers

Students' own answers

6 Point out that students often make mistakes with past simple irregular verbs and ask the students to find one mistake in each sentence with the verb.

Answers

1 Yesterday I **went** with my father to a football competition.
2 I went shopping and **bought** lots of presents.
3 I had a party and all my friends **came** to my house.
4 I was happy because I **got** a bag and a T-shirt for only £10!
5 My friend **gave** me some money to buy an ice cream.

7 Ask the students to look at the photo and guess where Lee went on holiday. Then, ask them to read the email to check their ideas (but they should not write in the verbs yet). With a weaker class elicit the past form of each of the verbs before they complete the email.

Answers

1 had 2 stayed 3 could 4 ate 5 visited 6 went 7 saw 8 loved 9 bought 10 took

8 As a class, look at Lee's email again in Exercise 7 and discuss how it is organised before students write their own. There are 4 paragraphs: 1 introduction (*Hi guys! I hope your holidays were good*); 2 the place, the hotel and the view; 3 the food and; 4 activities (sightseeing, shopping and taking photos).

Answers

Students' own answers

» **GRAMMAR WORKSHEET UNIT 7**

COOLER

Chain drill: Say to the class 'I went on holiday and I took hundreds of photos'. Ask a student to repeat what you said and to add another activity, e.g. *I went on holiday and I took hundreds of photos and I went to the beach.* Then, invite another student to repeat this and to add a further activity. Organise the students into small groups to continue the activity.

2 (55) Close your book and listen. You will hear the irregular past tense. Say the verb it comes from.

3 Complete Callum and Lottie's conversation. Use the words and phrases in the box.

Did x2	didn't	get up	take
Yes, I did	got up	went	

Callum: How was your summer holiday, Lottie?
Lottie: It was brilliant! I ________ want to leave!
Callum: ________ you ________ early every day?
Lottie: Of course not! We ________ late and we ________ to bed late.
Callum: ________ you ________ any photos?
Lottie: ________. I took hundreds of them!

4 Make conversations. Use the verbs in brackets.

1
________ you ________ to the mountains for your holiday? (go)
No, we ________. We ________ to the beach.

2
________ you ________ in the sea every day? (swim)
Yes, we ________, and we also ________ in the pool.

3
________ you ________ any clothes? (buy)
No, I ________. But I ________ a lot of presents.

4
________ you ________ a lot of ice cream? (eat)
Yes, we ________! And we ________ a lot of sweets.

5
________ you ________ a good time? (have)
Yes, we ________. We ________ a great time.

5 Write a holiday conversation. Use the conversations in Exercises 3 and 4 for ideas.

6 Correct the mistakes with the past simple.

0 My family and friends were there and they ~~gived~~ *gave* me a lot of presents.
1 Yesterday, I go with my dad to a football competition.
2 I went shopping and bough lots of presents.
3 I had a party and all my friends come to my house.
4 I was happy because I get a bag and a T-shirt for only £10!
5 My friend gaves me some money to buy an ice cream.

7 Complete the email. Use the verbs in the box in the correct form.

be	buy	can	eat	go	have
love	see	stay	take	visit	

To: Su
From: Lee
Subject: Holiday Plans
Reply Forward

Hi guys!

I hope your holidays [0] *were* good.

I [1] ________ a great time in New York. It was a special holiday for my dad's 50th birthday. We [2] ________ at a nice hotel called Alberto's. We [3] ________ see lots of famous places from our bedroom window.

The food in New York was great. We [4] ________ in a different restaurant every night. My favourite restaurant was Chinese.

We did lots of sightseeing and [5] ________ some interesting museums. We [6] ________ to the Statue of Liberty and the Empire State Building. We also [7] ________ a show on Broadway. Of course, my mum [8] ________ the large shops. She [9] ________ new clothes for all of us. I [10] ________ lots of photos. They're all online now – have a look!

8 Write an email to a friend about your last holiday. Look at the text in Exercise 7 for ideas.

CROSSING THE WORLD ON A RICKSHAW TO SEE THE OLYMPICS

56

When Chen Guan Ming was a young man, he never travelled far from his farm in a small village in China. But now he is famous for following the Olympic Games around the world in his three-wheeled rickshaw. The story **began** in 2001, when he **heard** that the games were coming to Beijing. He **left** his village and cycled 90,000 km all over China, visiting 1,764 cities before finally arriving at the famous Bird's Nest Stadium.

Then, he decided to travel to London for the 2012 Olympics. In 2010, he packed his things into his rickshaw and began his journey. He **slept** in his rickshaw and sometimes worked for food and money. Finally, he got to France, and **caught** a ferry to Britain. He only travels by boat or plane when there's no other choice.

When he arrived in London, he **met** lots of tourists and **told** them his story. Some people didn't believe him. Then he showed them the stamps in his passport, and the photos of himself at places like the Eiffel Tower in Paris and Petronas Towers in Kuala Lumpur.

After the London Olympics, Chen left his rickshaw in the UK and caught a flight home to plan his next trip – to the Rio Olympics. In 2013, he **flew** back to London. He **put** his rickshaw on a ship to Canada, and he **took** a plane there. A friend **paid** for his flight ticket. Then, he **got on** his rickshaw and **rode** to Brazil through the US, Mexico and Central America. The journey took three years. He **had** an amazing time in Rio and **made** lots more friends.

READING

1 **Look at the title of the article and the photos. Which countries do you think the man visited? Read the article quickly and check your ideas.**

2 **Read the article about Chen Guan Ming and answer the questions.**

1 What was Chen's job when he was young?
2 How far did he cycle to get to Beijing?
3 When did Chen leave home to go to London?
4 Did Chen go sightseeing during his journey?
5 Where did Chen go after the London Olympics?
6 Did Chen travel with his rickshaw to Canada?

3 **Look at the irregular past tenses in purple in the article. Write the infinitives.**

4 **Do you know about any other long journeys? Would you like to do a journey like this?**

VOCABULARY Holidays

1 **Match the photos A–I to the words in the box.**

EP

airport	coach	ferry	flight
guidebook	map	passport	station
suitcase	ticket	tour guide	tourist

57 **Listen and check. Then repeat.**

A

B

C

G

H

I

READING

WARMER

Either project some pictures of people doing things on holiday onto the board or ask the students to look at the photos again in Exercise 1 page 46. Describe one of the pictures: 'Last year, I went on holiday. I had a fantastic time and I did lots of watersports' and ask the students to guess which photo you're describing, e.g. *Is it photo H?* Then, ask the students to continue in pairs.

BACKGROUND INFORMATION

This article is based on a true story. Chen Guan Ming was a Chinese farmer from eastern China who travelled to three Olympics Games on his rickshaw to promote the 'Olympic spirit'. In 2017, he was on his way to the 2020 Tokyo Games when he died in a traffic accident. Chen Guan Ming thought he had achieved three Guinness Records: 1 he rode his tricycle up a mountain to 7,600 metres; 2 he rode his tricycle for the longest distance (over 150,000 kilometres) and; 3 he rode the smallest 'home on wheels'.

1 Tell the students that they are going to read about the journey of a Chinese man called Chen Guan Ming. Ask the students to look at the title and the photos and pre-teach *rickshaw* /ˈrɪkʃɔː/ by asking 'How did Chen Guan Ming travel?' Then, ask them to look at the map and guess which countries he visited. Ask the students to read the article quickly and underline the countries.

Answers

Students' own answers
The article mentions Britain, France, Kuala Lumpur (Malaysia), Canada, Brazil, the US, Mexico and Central America.

56 The Reading text is recorded for students to listen and read.

2 Ask the students to read the questions and try to answer them before they read the text again.

MIXED ABILITY

With a mixed ability class, ask stronger students to read the complete text but ask weaker students to read only one or two paragraphs. Students A read paragraph 1 and answer questions 1 and 2, Students B read paragraph 2 and 3 and answer questions 3 and 4 and Students C read paragraph 4 and answer questions 5 and 6. Then, they form groups of A, B and C and share their answers.

Answers

1 He was a farmer.
2 90,000 km
3 in 2010
4 Yes, he did.
5 He went home. Then he went to the Olympic Games in Rio via Canada and the USA.
6 No, he didn't.

3 Ask the students to look at the verbs first and say whether they are regular or irregular. Check that they can pronounce each one correctly by asking them to listen and repeat. Encourage them to take turns to ask and answer questions about these verbs in pairs, e.g.

Student A: *What's the infinitive of 'began'?*
Student B: *It's 'begin'. What's the infinitive of 'heard'?*

FAST FINISHERS

Fast finishers take turns to test each other on past simple irregular verbs:

Student A (book open): *What's the past of 'begin'?*
Student B (book closed): *It's 'began'.*

Answers

begin hear leave sleep catch meet tell fly put take pay get on ride have make

4 Put the students into small groups to answer these questions. If time allows, encourage them to use the map in the article to talk about a long journey they would like to go on.

Answers

Students' own answers

VOCABULARY Holidays

1 Encourage the students to identify the things in the photos before they match them to the words. If time allows, ask them to organise the words into four groups and to add more words to each one, e.g.

Transport	Place	Things to take	People
coach	airport	map	tourist
ferry	station	passport	

Answers

A map B guidebook C passport D ferry E coach F airport G ticket H station I suitcase J tourist K flight L tour guide

2 Do the first one together as an open class example by asking the students to find two examples of *catch* in the article and saying which words go with it (*a ferry and a flight*). Then, ask them to find the group of words with *ferry* and *flight* (*number 6*). Ask stronger students to add more words to the groups if they can.

Answers

1 take 2 pack 3 get on/off 4 travel by 5 arrive 6 catch

3 Demonstrate good full answers by asking the students to ask you or a stronger student the questions first. Remind them to answer in the past and to ask follow-up questions. If time allows, ask the students to change groups and do the activity again but this time giving even longer answers.

Answers

Students' own answers

» VOCABULARY WORKSHEET UNIT 7

PRONUNCIATION | Sounds and spelling

4 Encourage the students to say the words aloud. Monitor their pronunciation carefully and, if necessary, correct it. Point out that in English, different letter combinations, for example <u>augh</u>t and <u>ough</u>t, may be pronounced in the same way: /ɔː/.

58 **Answers**

The answers are recorded for the students to listen and check.

met – slept /e/	coach – phone /əʊ/
caught – bought /ɔː/	map – catch /æ/
plane – station /eɪ/	journey – work /ɜː/
flew – group /uː/	passport – car /ɑː/

LISTENING

59 1 Pre-teach *island* by drawing a picture on the board. Ask the students to say how you can get to an island (*by boat, ship, plane, swimming*). Then, ask them to identify the types of transport in the pictures (*A boat, B train, C taxi, D(aero)plane, E coach, F bus*) before they listen. Point out that there is an extra means of transport which isn't mentioned on the recording. Don't give the students the answers yet as they will compare their answers in Exercise 2.

Answers

Students are given the answers in Exercise 2 after they have compared their answers.

59 2 Ask the students to compare their answers to Exercise 1 in pairs and then allow them to listen again to check. With a weaker class, it may be necessary to stop the recording after each means of transport is mentioned. Check the answers as a class, pointing out that she didn't travel by plane. Invite a brief class discussion on why Marion says *It's funny …* and encourage the students to talk about the advantages and disadvantages of flying and taking lots of different means of transport.

Answers

Marion travelled by taxi, train, coach, boat and bus.
1 C 2 B 3 E 4 A 5 F Not needed: D (plane)
Because they didn't need to do such a long journey with so many different ways of travelling. It's possible to fly straight to the island.

» AUDIOSCRIPT TB PAGE 270

TALKING POINTS

05 Ask the students to watch the video and complete the activities first. Then, ask them to read the questions, think about their own answers and to make notes. Encourage them to use some of the holiday activities in Exercise 1 page 46 to do this. If students have not been on holiday recently, encourage them to make up a holiday in the past.

SPEAKING

1 Encourage the students to write some notes about a real or imaginary journey by writing down when they went, where they went, who they went with, etc. Then ask them, in pairs, to take turns to tell their story including all the information and using the expressions in the useful words box. If time allows, encourage the students to create a presentation with real or found photos or drawn pictures and a map for homework and then to present it to the class.

Answers

Students' own answers

COOLER

Ask the students to look at the article again on page 48. Tell them they are going to mime sentences from the text for their classmates to guess. Ask them to copy two sentences from the text into their notebooks. Demonstrate the activity first by saying: 'Watch me carefully. What sentence is this?' Mime the sentence *He heard that the games were coming to Beijing* and invite suggestions from the class.

When a student guesses the correct answer, ask him or her to come to the front of the class and to mime one of the sentences they have written down. Then, ask the students to continue in small groups.

2 Look at the verbs in the box and find them in the article. Then complete the phrases using each verb once only.

EP

arrive catch get on / off pack
take travel by

1 ________: a photo, a long time, a train, a bus

2 ________: your things, a suitcase

3 ________: a bus, a train, a bicycle, a plane

4 ________: car, bicycle, train, bus

5 ________: at the airport, in the city

6 ________: a train, a ferry, a flight, a bus

3 In small groups, ask and answer the questions.

1 Do you have a passport?
2 What do you always pack when you go on holiday?
3 Are guidebooks useful?
4 How do you travel to school/the shops/your friend's house?
5 When did you last travel on a ferry/coach/plane/train?

PRONUNCIATION | Sounds and spelling

4 Match the words with the same vowel sound.

met	group
caught	car
plane	catch
flew	work
coach	phone
map	station
journey	bought
passport	slept

58 Listen and check.

LISTENING

59 **1** Listen to Marion talking about a journey. How did she travel? Number the photos in the order you hear them. There is one extra photo that you don't need.

59 **2** Work in pairs, compare your answers. Then listen again and check. Why does Marion say *It's funny …* at the end of her story?

TALKING POINTS

05 Watch the video. Ask and answer the questions with a partner.

Where did you go on your last holiday?
What did you do there?
What did you see?
What did you eat?

SPEAKING

1 Work in pairs. Tell your partner a travel story.

Include this information in your story:

- When you went
- Where you went
- Who you went with
- How you travelled
- How long your journey took

Useful words
This happened … months/years ago.
First, we …
Then we …
We took a … / We caught a … / We went by bus/car.
Anyway …

8 FAVOURITE PLACES

ABOUT YOU

What is your bedroom like?
What do you do there?

VOCABULARY AND READING

Bedroom furniture

1 Match the photos A–K to the words in the box.

EP

armchair blanket bookshelf carpet
chest of drawers cupboard curtains
cushion lamp mirror photographs

60 Listen and check. Then repeat.

PRONUNCIATION /ɜː/ and /ɔː/

61 **2** Listen to the sounds /ɜː/ and /ɔː/.

Look at the words in the box and put them in the correct column in the table.

bought curtains drawers
first floor furniture saw
wall were work

/ɜː/ bird	/ɔː/ board
curtains	*bought*

62 Listen and check. Then repeat.

3 What do you have in your bedroom?

4 Read the article. Which of the things from Exercise 1 are NOT mentioned in Rebecca's article?

Everyone needs a FAVOURITE PLACE

by Rebecca Grant

Today, I want to write about my favourite place. It's by the window in my bedroom. I've got a dark red armchair and a blanket. My grandma made the blanket for me when I was little. Next to the chair is a bookshelf with my favourite books, and there's also a little chest of drawers. On top of it, there are some stones I collected from the beach. I've got a few photographs on one side of the window and a mirror on the other side. I've got curtains on my window, too.

Do you have a favourite place at home? Is it in your bedroom, or in the sitting room, or somewhere else? Maybe you don't have one, but you want to make somewhere you like special. Then here are a few ideas to help you create your special place.

1. Light is important in a room. Is there natural light or do you need a lamp?
2. You don't need a lot of furniture. A chair or an armchair is enough. Or you can put a few large cushions on the carpet in a corner. You don't really need anything else.
3. What colours do you like around you? Use something like cushions to give colour to your bed. Posters and blankets work well for colour too.
4. Now you can collect some favourite things to put in your special place.

63 Remember, no one is the same, so everyone's favourite place is different. Anyone can make their place special.

8 FAVOURITE PLACES

Unit Overview

TOPIC	My favourite place and activities
VOCABULARY	Bedroom furniture
AND READING	Everyone needs a favourite place
PRONUNCIATION	/ɜː/ and /ɔː/
GRAMMAR	*someone*, *anyone*, etc.
READING	Artists' favourite places to work
VOCABULARY	Free-time activities
LISTENING	Descriptions of favourite places
WRITING	A description of a favourite place
EXAM TASKS	Reading Part 1

Resources

GRAMMAR REFERENCE AND PRACTICE: SB page 145; TB page 248
WORKBOOK: pages 36–39
PHOTOCOPIABLE WORKSHEETS: Grammar worksheet Unit 8; Vocabulary worksheet Unit 8
TEST GENERATOR: Unit test 8

WARMER

Ask the students to imagine they're at home in their bedroom; if appropriate, ask them to close their eyes to do this. Ask them the following questions in a soft voice; tell them not to speak, but to think about their answers. 'Are you sitting or lying down? Where?' 'What can you see around you?' 'Is your room tidy or messy?' 'Have you got a table or a desk? What's on it?' 'Have you got a TV or a computer? Where?' 'What's on the walls? Have you got posters or pictures?' Now ask them to look at the *About you* box.

ABOUT YOU

If you did the Warmer, ask the students in pairs to compare their answers to your questions above. If you didn't do the Warmer, ask the students in pairs to ask and answer the questions in the book. Then, ask the pairs to look at the title of the unit and encourage them to ask and answer the question *What's your favourite place in your house? Why?*

VOCABULARY AND READING

Bedroom furniture

1 Before the students do this exercise, ask them to cover the words in the box and look at the photo again. Challenge them, in small groups, to name as many things as they can in three minutes. Begin the activity as a class, e.g. *lamp, mirror* . . . . Then, ask them to find the words in the box in the photo.

60

Answers

The answers are recorded for the students to check and then repeat.

A carpet B armchair C lamp D cushion E chest of drawers F cupboard G photographs H blanket I curtains J bookshelf K mirror

PRONUNCIATION /ɜː/ and /ɔː/

61

2 Ask the students to listen and repeat *bird* and *board* with the correct pronunciation before they put the words in the correct column.

62

Answers

The answers are recorded for students to check and then repeat.

/ɜː/ bird: curtains first furniture were work
/ɔː/ board: bought drawers floor saw wall

3 Ask the students to work in pairs and discuss what they have in their bedroom. Encourage them to use as many words from Exercise 1 as possible.

4 Ask the students to look at the title of the article, the photo of Rebecca and to read the first two sentences. Then, ask them to try to guess which of the things in Exercise 1 are not in her bedroom. As the students read, encourage them to underline the words and also tick them off either in the box in Exercise 1 or in their tables in Exercise 2.

MIXED ABILITY

Encourage stronger students to read the article and complete Exercises 4 and 5 (on page 51) at their own pace. Ask very weak students to read the first paragraph only and find the bedroom furniture vocabulary. Then, ask them to tick off the words in their table in Exercise 2. Point out that they need to find six words (*armchair*, *blanket*, *bookshelf*, *chest of drawers*, *mirror* and *curtains*). If time allows, ask them to read the rest of the article.

Answers

cupboard

5 Encourage the students to try to answer the questions before they read the article again. Ask stronger students to correct the wrong sentences. After checking the answers, encourage the students to react to the text by asking 'Do you agree with her ideas?' 'Would you add anything to her list?' If time allows, invite a class discussion on room design principles, in particular *feng shui* (see Background information below) and whether the students think these principles are important.

Answers

1 ✓ 2 × (I've got a few photographs on one side of the window.) 3 × (She doesn't say this, she says 'Light is important.') 4 ✓ 5 ✓ 6 × (Everyone's favourite place is different.)

63 The Reading text is recorded for students to listen and read.

BACKGROUND INFORMATION

Feng shui is a Chinese belief that the way spaces are organised bring happiness, health and success to the people who live there. It was developed in China over 3,000 years ago. In room design, to achieve good *feng shui*, the room should be cleared of clutter, which means getting rid of all unnecessary objects. There should also be natural air (open the window often) and light. The walls should not be painted in a dark colour, and any photos should be of happy people.

GRAMMAR *someone, anyone, etc.*

1 Instead of asking the students to do the matching immediately, you could first ask them to cover a–c and to look at 1–3 and say what each group has in common: 1 they are talking about people; 2 they are talking about places; and 3 they are talking about things or objects.

Answers

1 c 2 a 3 b

» GRAMMAR REFERENCE AND PRACTICE ANSWER KEY TB PAGE 248

2 If necessary, point out that there are seven examples in the article (Exercise 4, page 50) and none of them begin with *no-*.

Answers

1 **Everyone** needs a favourite place
2 Is it in your bedroom, or in the sitting room, or **somewhere** else?
3 Remember, no one is the same, so **everyone**'s favourite place is different.
4 **Anyone** can make their place special.
5 You don't really need **anything** else.
6 Use **something** like cushions to give colour to your bed.
7 Maybe you don't have one, but you want to make **somewhere** you like special.

3 Encourage the students to look at each sentence first and decide whether it is talking about a place, a thing or a person. Point out that we write *no one* as two words but all the others (*someone*, *anyone*, etc.) as one word.

Answers

1 one 2 thing 3 where 4 thing 5 where 6 one 7 thing 8 one 9 where

4 Point out that in sentences 2 and 3, the students will need to look at the verb. If it is negative, they should use *anything*.

Answers

1 anything 2 nothing 3 anything 4 something 5 everything

5 Point out that in A2 Key for Schools, students often make mistakes with *someone*, *anyone*, etc. and that they should look for one mistake with these words in each of these sentences. It may be necessary to remind students with verbs in the negative (sentences 1, 2 and 4), we use *any-* and not *no-*.

Answers

1 I don't have **anything** to do next weekend.
2 You don't need to bring **anything** else.
3 You can write **anything** you like.
4 I can't see **anyone**.
5 I want to buy **something** at the supermarket.

FAST FINISHERS

Encourage fast finishers to work through Exercises 3–5 at their own pace. Then, ask them to choose some of the questions and sentences from these exercises and, in pairs, turn them into mini conversations. When the others are ready, they can perform their conversations to the class. For example:

A: *Did anyone come to your party? (Exercise 3 question 0)*

B: *Yes, lots of people came to my party.*

6 **A2 Key for Schools Reading Part 1.**

In this part of the exam, students will need to read six short texts (short emails, text messages, web messages or notices) and then choose the correct answer (A–C) for each one.

Pens down. Ask the students to look at each text quickly and say what type of text each one is (1 shop advertisement, 2 email, 3 text message, 4 personal ad). Do the first one together. Ask them to read the advertisement carefully and ask 'What's Bright's?' (*a shop*) 'Is it expensive?' (*No, it's cheaper than other shops.*) 'What can you buy there?' (*cushions*) 'What do you get if you buy two?' (*another one for free*) 'Can you get this every day?' (*No, only today.*) Next, read the sentences together as a class, decide whether each one (A–C) is true or false and which one is the correct answer (B). Then, encourage the students to do questions 2–4 on their own, looking at each option carefully to decide if it is true or false before they choose the correct answer.

Answers

1 B 2 C 3 C 4 B

» GRAMMAR WORKSHEET UNIT 8

COOLER

Organise the students into new pairs. Ask them to take turns to ask and answer the questions in the *About you* box at the top of page 50, but this time they should try to use as much of the new bedroom furniture vocabulary as they can. If they enjoy competition, they should listen carefully to each other and award points for every new word their partner uses correctly.

5 Read the article again. Are the sentences right (✓) or wrong (✗)?

1 Rebecca has got three pieces of furniture in her favourite place.
2 Rebecca's photographs are next to the mirror.
3 She says it's nicer to have light from a window.
4 She has ideas for a favourite corner without any furniture.
5 She tells us the colour of one thing in her favourite place.
6 She says most people's favourite places are the same.

GRAMMAR *someone, anyone, etc.*

1 Look at the table. Match the words in 1–3 to a–c.

1	everyone someone	anyone no one	These words are about …
2	everywhere somewhere	anywhere nowhere	a a place. b a thing. c a person.
3	everything something	anything nothing	

» GRAMMAR REFERENCE AND PRACTICE PAGE 145

2 Look at the article again. Find seven sentences or questions with the words in Exercise 1.

3 Complete the pronouns with *-thing*, *-one* or *-where*.

0 Did any*one* come to your party?
1 Some________ gave me these shoes. Do you like them?
2 There was ________ on the bookshelf. I looked.
3 Can you think of any________ to go this afternoon?
4 I'm hungry but there's no________ in the fridge!
5 She went some________ hot for her holidays.
6 No________ told me that you wrote stories!
7 I'd like some________ to eat, please.
8 Every________ in the class, except me, likes the colour blue.
9 No________ in my house is a special place.

4 Complete the sentences with *anything*, *everything*, *nothing* or *something*.

1 Do you remember ________ about the film?
2 The bookshelf is empty. There is ________ on it.
3 It's very dark. I can't see ________.
4 I learn ________ new in English every day.
5 I don't need any help thanks. I can carry ________.

5 Correct the mistakes in these sentences.

0 Please tell me ~~anything~~ *something* about your holiday.
1 I don't have something to do next weekend.
2 You don't need to bring nothing else.
3 You can write everything you like.
4 I can't see no one.
5 I want to buy anything at the supermarket.

6 For each question, choose the correct answer.

1

A One cushion costs the same as two.
B Other shops are more expensive than Bright's.
C The shop is not open today.

2

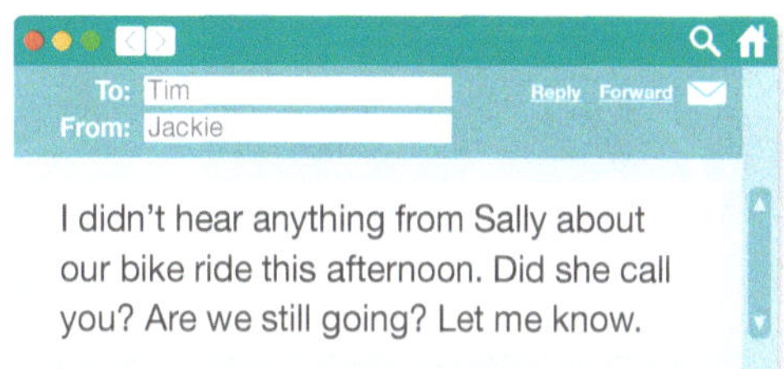

Why did Jackie write this email?
A to invite Tim on a bike ride
B to find out where Tim is today
C to ask Tim what's happening later

3

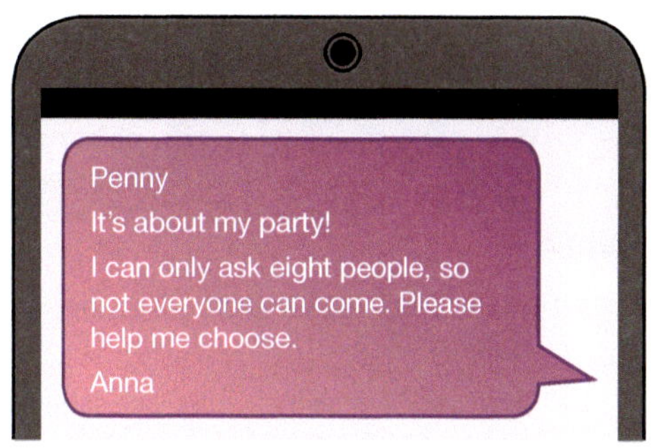

A Anna only wants eight friends to come to her party.
B All Anna's friends can come to her party.
C Anna wants Penny to help her decide who to ask.

4

A Jo doesn't need her desk lamp anymore.
B Jo would like to buy a desk lamp from someone.
C Jo can answer calls about her desk lamp during the day.

FAVOURITE PLACES 51

READING

1 Look at the photos. In pairs, discuss the questions. What do you think these three people do? What do you think their favourite places are?

2 Read the article. Match the photos A–C to the artists in the article. What is each artist's favourite place?

B
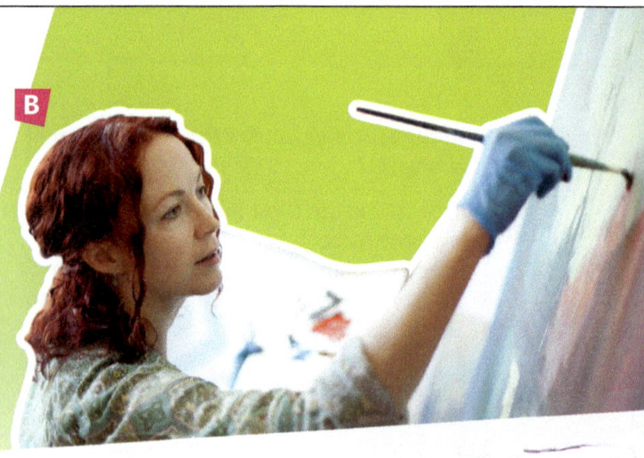

Artists' FAVOURITE PLACES

64

1 Gemma Blake, *painter*

Last summer, I spent four weeks on the north-west coast of Scotland in a little house by the sea. In the evenings, I sat by the open window and listened to the sound of the wind and the waves. It was wonderful. After breakfast, when I went out to paint and draw, I always had lots of ideas for pictures. Most days, I didn't see anyone except my neighbour. He was a fisherman. He really liked my work, and I sold him a drawing for his wall.

C

2 Susie Grey, *singer-songwriter*

I grew up in a small town in Canada. My grandma took me for walks and told me everything about the animals and plants there. When I was 19, I went to music school in Toronto. At first, I loved the big city. Then I started writing my own songs about, guess what, nature in and around my home town. So, five years ago, I moved back, and now I don't want to live anywhere else.

A

3 Paul Davidson, *dancer*

I started dancing when I was very young. It was hard work, but I was good, and I danced with famous companies in Russia, the USA and Europe. I didn't really have a home, so when I had enough money I bought a tiny flat in London. I love it there. The world of dance is busy and tiring, and it's great to be able to get back to my flat. I close the door, lie on my bed and listen to music.

3 Read the article again and answer the questions.

1 What did Gemma hear when she sat next to the open window?
2 What did she do in the mornings?
3 What did the fisherman buy from her?
4 What did Susie learn from her grandma?
5 Why and when did she move away from home?
6 What does she write songs about?
7 Why did Paul travel to so many countries?
8 What did he spend his money on?
9 What does he do when he gets home?

TALKING POINTS

Where is your favourite place? Why? Describe it to your partner.

VOCABULARY Free-time activities

1 Match the verbs in box A to the words and phrases in box B. The verbs can be used more than once.

EP

A
draw listen to paint play
read write

B
a blog computer games a diary
the drums the guitar magazines
music pictures songs stories

2 Write eight sentences using words from box A and box B in Exercise 1.

Give your sentences to your partner and check each other's.

Everyone came to my place last night and we played computer games and listened to music.

READING

WARMER

Books closed. Write *My favourite place is …* on the board. Ask the students 'What do you remember about Rebecca's favourite place?' Now encourage the students to complete the sentence with their own special place. Brainstorm possibilities onto the board, e.g. *my room, a park, my grandparents' house, a small village*. Ask the students 'Why are these places special?' and 'What do you like to do in these places?'

1 Encourage the students to look at the three photos and to say what the three people have in common (*they are all artists*). Next, in pairs, ask them to look at the photos and to describe the people and the place before they answer the questions. Alternatively, the pairs take turns to describe one of the photos for their partner to guess which one it is.

Answers

Students' own answers

2 Ask the students to read the title and the three headings and try to match the photos (A–C) to the artists (1–3). Then, they read the article and check their ideas about each person's favourite place.

Answers

1 B 2 A 3 C
Gemma's favourite place is the north-west coast of Scotland; Susie's favourite place is her home town in Canada; Paul's favourite place is his tiny flat in London

64 The Reading text is recorded for students to listen and read.

3 Encourage the students to try to answer the questions before they read the article again. Point out that their answers need to be full sentences.

Answers

1 Gemma heard the sound of the wind and the waves.
2 She went out to paint pictures and to draw.
3 He bought one of her drawings.
4 Susie learned about the animals and plants that lived near her home town.
5 Because she went to music school in Toronto. When she was 19.
6 She writes songs about nature in and near her home town.
7 Because he danced with different international dance companies.
8 He bought a tiny flat in London.
9 He lies on his bed and listens to music.

FAST FINISHERS

In pairs or small groups, fast finishers imagine that they are journalists and they are interviewing these three artists for a radio programme. They take turns to be the interviewer, who asks questions from Exercise 3 and/or new questions, and to be one of the artists, who answers the questions using the information in the article and their imagination.

TALKING POINTS

Encourage each student to think about their own answer and to write down two reasons to support their opinion, e.g. *My favourite place is … because I think it's … and also I think it's …* . Then, ask them to work in pairs and describe it to their partner.

VOCABULARY Free-time activities

1 Encourage the students to look at the words and phrases in Box B first, and in pairs to try to think of a suitable verb for each one. Then, they compare their ideas with the verbs in Box A.

Answers

draw: pictures
listen to: the drums, the guitar, music, songs, stories
paint: pictures
play: computer games, the drums, the guitar, music, songs
read: a blog, a diary, magazines, stories
write: a blog, computer games, a diary, music, songs, stories

2 Ask the students to read the example sentence first and find two of the free-time activities from Exercise 1 (*play computer games* and *listen to music*). If students enjoy guessing competitions, encourage each student to write some true and some false sentences. Then, they take turns to read out their sentences, check they are correct and also say whether they are true or false. With a strong class, encourage the students to write interesting questions with the words.

Answers

Students' own answers

» VOCABULARY WORKSHEET UNIT 8

LISTENING

65 1 Before they listen, ask the students in pairs to look at the three photos of places A–C, to describe what they can see, and to say what teenagers can do in each one. Encourage them to use the vocabulary from the Vocabulary section. Point out that they need to write a letter only next to each name in the *Place* column.

Answers

George – B
Abby – C
Jo – A

65 2 Ask the students to try to complete the *What they like doing there* column before they listen again. Point that they need to write the activity here (and not a letter).

Answers

George – lying on his bed, on the cushions, reading
Abby – sitting under a tree, writing her diary
Jo – playing the guitar and writing songs

» AUDIOSCRIPT TB PAGE 270

WRITING

PREPARE TO WRITE
A description of a favourite place

GET READY Ask the students to try to predict the answer from the photo before they read.

Answers

Tom's favourite place is the beach. He likes walking along the beach without his shoes on.

Ask the students to find *because* and *so* in the text and underline them. Then, ask them to say which word is followed by a reason (*because*) and which word is followed by a consequence (*so*). Ask them to say which word comes after a comma (*so*). If appropriate, ask them to translate the words into their own language.

Answers

1 because 2 so 3 so 4 because

PLAN Ask the class to choose a favourite place. They should now make notes about it using the ideas they discussed in both the Warmer and Listening Exercise 3. This does not need to be a true answer.

Answers

Students' own answers

WRITE Encourage the students to use Tom's description as a framework for their own writing.

MIXED ABILITY

Encourage stronger students to write more words on their own. With weaker students, write Tom's description on the board. Ask them to come to the board and underline expressions they can use in their own paragraph, e.g. *My favourite place is .... I like going there ... because .... I like ....* Then, rub out all the other words and encourage these students to think of words to complete the paragraph, e.g. *My favourite place is* ***the park****. I like going there* ***on Saturday afternoon*** *because ....* Finally, rub out these new words again and ask these students to write at least 30 words about their favourite place using the words on the board.

IMPROVE Tell the students to check each other's spelling and punctuation and that they have correctly used *because* and *so* (as well as *and, but, or*). Ask them if they can give each other ideas to help them improve their final version.

COOLER

Copy this table onto the board. Organise the students into small groups and challenge them to write as many correct sentences in the present or past as they can, using one word from each column, e.g. *I often draw pictures when I go to the beach.* Allow them about five minutes.

1	2	3
draw	a blog	beach
listen to	the drums	room
paint	pictures	garage
play	magazines	park
read	stories	school
write	songs	mountain

LISTENING

65 **1** Listen to three teenagers, George, Abby and Jo, talking about their favourite places. Look at the photos A–C. Match the teenagers to their favourite places. Write the letters in column 1 of the table.

65 **2** Listen again. What do they like doing in their special places? Write the answers in column 2 of the table.

	1 Place	**2** What they like doing there
George	....	....
Abby	....	....
Jo	....	....

WRITING

PREPARE TO WRITE

A description of a favourite place

GET READY Read about Tom's favourite place.

- Where is it?
- What does he like doing there?

Read the text again and underline *because* and *so*. Think about how Tom uses these words to join ideas in a sentence.

My favourite place is the beach. I like going there in the afternoons because all my friends go there then. I like feeling the sand under my feet, so I take off my shoes and walk along the beach. I love the sound of the birds and the sound of the sea. It's amazing!

Now join these sentences using *so* or *because*.

1. I'm wearing my coat ________ it's very cold.
2. The bus didn't come on time, ________ we were late for school.
3. I was tired, ________ I went to bed.
4. Sorry, I can't come this evening ________ I've got lots of homework.

PLAN Make notes about your favourite place.

- Where is it?
- Why is it special for you?
- What do you have there?
- What do you like doing there?

WRITE Write a paragraph of about 50 words about your favourite place. Include ***because*** and ***so*** in your writing.

IMPROVE In pairs, read your own paragraph and your partner's. Check for mistakes.

Give your partner two ideas to make their text better. Use your partner's advice and rewrite your paragraph.

LIFE SKILLS PHYSICAL WELL-BEING

SAFETY AT HOME

LIFE SKILLS
Safety at home
What is safety at home?
- Being careful with hot drinks or hot food
- Taking care with broken glass
- Never leaving things on stairs

1 Look at the signs and answer the questions.

1 What do you think each sign means?
2 Where can you see each sign?
3 What does a fire extinguisher do?

2 Look at the photos. Match the photos A–G to the words 1–7.

1 lighter	4 heater	6 stairs
2 rug	5 iron	7 matches
3 knives		

Talk about the things you have in your home. How can these things be dangerous?

3 Read the text quickly. Match the words in the box to the paragraphs. Do you follow these tips at home?

Burns Cuts Falls

TIPS TO BE SAFE AT HOME

Homes are wonderful places. We can rest, study, play games and spend time with our friends and family in our homes, but there are dangers there too.

Here are some ideas to help keep safe and happy at home.

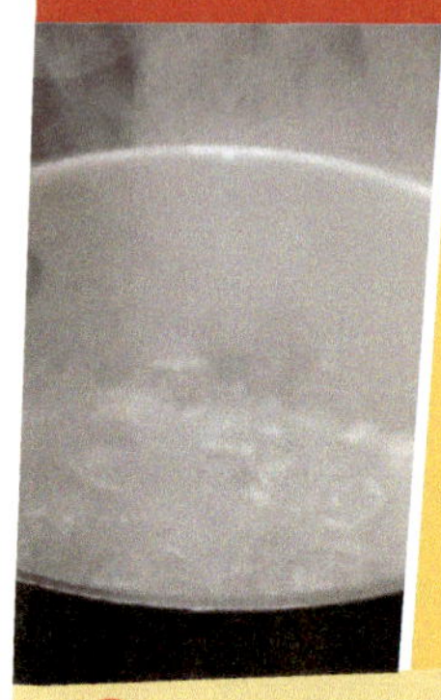

1 ____________

- Be careful in the kitchen – hot food and hot drinks can burn you.
- Cookers can be dangerous – take care.
- Don't touch a hot iron or heater.
- Be careful with matches and lighters.
- It is a good idea to keep a fire extinguisher at home.

2 ____________

- Don't leave books, bags, shoes or other things on the stairs.
- Turn the light on when you use the stairs.
- Don't run upstairs or downstairs.
- Make sure rugs don't move.
- Be careful when the floor is wet.
- Don't stand on chairs or tables.

3 ____________

- Use scissors and knives carefully.
- Be careful with broken glass or mirrors.
- Don't touch sharp, metal objects.

66

WHAT TO DO IN AN EMERGENCY

Keep a list of emergency telephone numbers in a special place at home or on your mobile phone. Are you hurt? Ask a parent or teacher for help, or call the emergency services.

LIFE SKILLS

Learning Objectives

- The students learn about safety in the home.
- In the project stage, they write a leaflet about safety at home and present it to another group.

Vocabulary

iron heater rug sharp mirror fire extinguisher

BACKGROUND INFORMATION

According to the website of the British charity ROSPA (Royal Society for the Prevention of Accidents), more accidents happen at home in Britain than anywhere else, most commonly in the living room. There are around 6,000 deaths a year because of these accidents at home. The most common accidents are falls; while over 65s can fall anywhere in the house, children tend to fall on stairs or from windows. Accidental poisoning and burning are common, especially among young children.

WARMER

Books closed. Write the words below on the board and ask the students to put them in order to make three sentences (these are the sentences from the *Life skills* box at the top of page 54).

- with / Being careful / or / hot drinks / hot food
- with / broken glass / Taking care
- on / Never / leaving things / stairs

Next ask 'What do you think the unit title is?' If necessary, write the following on the board to help them: S_ _ _ _ _ at h_ _ _ .

LIFE SKILLS

Safety at home

Invite a class discussion on why the students should do these things. With a strong class, ask students to suggest other things you can do to be safe at home.

1 If appropriate, draw or project the signs onto the board and invite a class discussion on what each one means. Then, encourage the students to answer questions 2 and 3 in pairs.

Possible answers

1 (from left to right) Be careful, hot water is dangerous; There is a fire extinguisher here; Be careful of electricity; Be careful on stairs
2 building sites; schools, offices
3 It puts out/stops a fire.

2 Ask the students to look at the photos in pairs and try to name each one before they match them to the words. If necessary, point out that *knives* is the plural of *knife*. Check that the students say each word correctly by asking them to listen and repeat, in particular iron /aɪən/ (British English) or /aɪrn/ (US English). Next, encourage the students in pairs to talk about these things and say how they can be dangerous.

Answers

1 D 2 F 3 C 4 B 5 A 6 E 7 G
Students' own answers

3 Ask the class to read the text title and the introduction and ask 'What is a tip, do you think?' (*a piece of useful advice*) Next, ask them to look at each photo, describe what they can see in pairs, and say what they think each tip is about (without reading it for now). Then, ask them to read the tip, check their ideas and think of a suitable heading for each one before they look at the words in the box. Finally, ask them to share their opinions on the tips with their partner.

MIXED ABILITY

Ask weaker students to read one paragraph only and match it to one of the words. In Exercise 4, they will need to work with students who have read the other paragraphs.

66 **Answers**

The Reading text is recorded for students to listen, read and check their answers.
1 Burns 2 Falls 3 Cuts

4 Ask the students in pairs to try to complete the sentences before they read the tips again.

Answers
1 b 2 b 3 c 4 b 5 c 6 a

5 Encourage stronger students to look at the meanings (and cover the words 1–6) and try to think of a suitable word for each one before they look at the words.

FAST FINISHERS

Encourage fast finishers to choose some words from the text and write two definitions for each one; a correct and an incorrect one. When the others are ready, organise the class into groups. The fast finishers take turns to say their word and the two definitions and the groups have to say which one is true.

Answers
1 b 2 c 3 f 4 a 5 d 6 e

TALKING POINTS

As a class brainstorm some ways the students' school might be dangerous (*e.g. wet floors*) and write these on the left-hand side of the board. Next, ask the students to think of some ways they could make these things safer on the right (*e.g. put up a 'wet floor' sign*).

Encourage the students to take turns to ask and answer these questions in small groups and also share their opinions on some of the things on the board, e.g. do they agree with the tips?

67 6 Ask the students to look at the photo of the man at the bottom of page 55 and ask 'What's his job?' (*a firefighter*) Next, ask them to read the questions and try to guess what they think the answers will be before they listen. Then, encourage them to compare their answers with a partner before they listen again.

Answers
1 b 2 b

67 7 In pairs, encourage the students to try to answer the questions before they listen again.

Answers
1 not using them correctly can start house fires
2 to stop fires
3 Yes, it can burn you.
4 They can get hot.
5 No, this can start a house fire.
6 emergency numbers

67 8 Encourage the students to try to choose the correct words in the *Useful language* box before they listen again.

Answers
1 good 2 be careful with 3 can burn you 4 It's good to have

» AUDIOSCRIPT TB PAGES 270–271

PROJECT ***A safety leaflet***

Ask the class to read the instructions in bold and ask 'What do you need to write?' 'What about?' Next, draw a picture of a house with its rooms onto the board and elicit the names of the rooms (include *kitchen*, *living room*, *hall*, *stairs*, *bedroom*, *bathroom*, *garage* and *garden*). Organise the students into small groups and ask them to copy the house onto an A4 piece of paper. Encourage them to think of possible dangers in each of the rooms in the house and write them down. Ask the groups for their ideas and write them in the appropriate room in the house in the board.

Ask the groups to either choose one room or the whole house, to choose four or five dangers and also possible ways we can prevent the danger. Ask the groups to read the points in the *Project* box and to put together a leaflet. Remind the students that they will have to reach an agreement here on both the content and also who will do what, e.g. *What title will we choose? Which ways to stay safe shall we include? Who will find the pictures?* Encourage them to use the expressions for reaching agreement in the *Useful language* box in Exercise 8 on page 32.

Encourage the students to present their leaflet to another group, give feedback and make suggestions for improvement.

PROJECT EXTENSION

Tell the class that as a whole, there are going to design some signs for their school and also a leaflet to give to students, staff and parents. First, draw a plan of the school (or ask a student) on the board and invite suggestions on where the possible dangers are. Then, as class, ask them to decide which group of students will ...

- design the signs
- create the content of the leaflet
- design the leaflet
- produce the leaflet
- distribute the leaflet.

COOLER

Write some dangers on the board and encourage the students to draw a sign for at least three of these (or they can use their own ideas), e.g. rocks falling, weak bridge, dangerous chemicals, wet paint, broken window, construction area, wet floor, dangerous animals. When they have finished, in pairs encourage them to take turns to show each other their signs and say what they think each one means.

4 **Look at the text again. Then choose the correct answers to complete the sentences.**

1 It's dangerous to _____ lighters and matches wrongly.
  a touch **b** use **c** have
2 Cookers get _____. You can burn yourself.
  a cold **b** hot **c** fire
3 It's a good idea to keep a _____ at home for emergencies.
  a lighter **b** heater **c** fire extinguisher
4 It's not a good idea to leave _____ on the stairs.
  a a rug **b** shoes and books **c** a desk
5 Be careful! You can _____ down the stairs.
  a burn yourself **b** cut yourself **c** fall
6 It's dangerous to play with _____ and scissors.
  a knives **b** rugs **c** glasses

5 **Match the highlighted words in the text to the meanings.**

1 iron	a this cuts things easily
2 heater	b you use this on clothes
3 rug	c this warms the air
4 sharp	d you can see yourself in this
5 mirror	e this stops fires
6 fire extinguisher	f a soft piece of material that covers the floor

TALKING POINTS

Do you think safety is important at home and at school? How can you make schools and homes safer?

67 **6** **Listen to someone talking to a class at school and choose the correct answers.**

1 Who is visiting the class?
  a a police officer **b** a firefighter
2 What are the students learning to use?
  a the internet **b** a fire extinguisher

7 **In pairs, try to remember the answers to these questions.**

1 Why is it dangerous to use matches and lighters?
2 What can you do with a fire extinguisher?
3 Can hot soup be dangerous?
4 Why do you need to be careful with cookers, irons and heaters?
5 Is it a good idea to dry your clothes on heaters? Why / Why not?
6 What can you leave next to the phone or on your smartphone?

67 **Listen again and check.**

67 **8** **Now listen again and choose the correct words.**

USEFUL LANGUAGE

1 It's not a *good* / *bad* idea to use lighters and matches without adults around.
2 You need to *use wrongly* / *be careful with* hot irons.
3 Some heaters and cookers *can burn you* / *put out fires*.
4 *It's good to have* / *Don't keep* emergency numbers next to the phone.

PROJECT

A safety leaflet

In small groups, write a leaflet about safety at home.

- Choose a title for your leaflet.
- Think of some ways to stay safe at home.
- Find some pictures.
- Choose a good design.
- Put it all together.
- Present your leaflet to another group. Take turns.

REVIEW 2 UNITS 5–8

VOCABULARY

1 **Choose the correct word to complete the sentences.**

0 The *ferry* / *plane* arrived at the airport at ten thirty.
1 It's dark in here. Can you turn on the *lamp* / *pillow*?
2 Don't walk on the *ceiling* / *floor*. The paint is wet.
3 My dad's a *mechanic* / *farmer*. He keeps sheep and cows.
4 That's a beautiful *palace* / *statue* of two children.
5 I keep my *diary* / *passport* in my bag. I like to write in it every day.
6 It's very cold in here. Can you lend me a *carpet* / *blanket*?
7 There are lots of *bosses* / *customers* in the shop today. It's very busy.
8 We usually travel to London by *staff* / *coach*. It's cheaper than the train.

2 **Match the verbs to the nouns.**

1 ride	**a** a blog
2 cross	**b** pictures
3 join	**c** a bike
4 stay	**d** a club
5 play	**e** a match
6 write	**f** a river
7 draw	**g** at a hotel

3 **Match the words in the box to the sentences.**

blanket	building	cook	cupboard
map	office	~~shop assistants~~	square
stairs	suitcase	tourists	

0 These people help you in a shop. *shop assistants*
1 You can keep things in here.
2 You can find places in a city on this.
3 These are people on holiday.
4 Your school and your house are examples of this.
5 People work in this place.
6 This person does a job preparing food.
7 You can go up and down these.
8 You can pack your clothes in this.
9 This keeps you warm.
10 This is an open space in a town or city.

GRAMMAR

1 **Choose the correct words to complete the sentences.**

1 Your birthday party was great. *Do* / *Did* everyone have a good time?
2 I went with my friends to the mountains and we *climb* / *climbed* the hill.
3 Yesterday was my birthday and I *had* / *got* a computer.
4 Please, can you bring *something* / *somewhere* to the picnic?

Correct the mistakes in the sentences.

5 Last summer, I went to the United States. Some days it was hot but on others it rain.
6 Today, we watched a football game but my sister don't like it very much.
7 At my party, I danced, singed and ate and drank a lot of things.
8 I didn't do nothing special.

2 **Write the past simple of the verbs.**

0 come *came*
1 begin ....
2 buy ....
3 catch ....
4 fly ....
5 give ....
6 meet ....
7 sleep ....
8 swim ....
9 ride ....
10 take ....

3 **Make sentences or questions about the past.**

0 they / come / yesterday?
Did they come yesterday?
1 I / not / see / that film / last night.
2 They / can / cycle / 50 km / in a day.
3 you / get / an email / this morning?
4 She / not / sleep / in a tent / on her holiday.
5 they / clean / their classroom / last week?
6 He / travel / to India / last winter.
7 We / not / stay / in a hotel / in London.
8 she / have / a computer / in her room?

REVIEW 2 UNITS 5–8

Overview

VOCABULARY	Historical events; Buildings; Jobs; Work; Holidays; Bedroom furniture; Free-time activities
GRAMMAR	Dates with *in* and *on*; Past simple: regular verbs; Past simple: negatives and questions; Past simple: irregular verbs; *someone*, *anyone*, etc.
READING	Six short messages
SPEAKING	Asking questions; talking about your room
EXAM TASKS	Reading Part 1; Speaking Part 1 Phase 2

Resources

PHOTOCOPIABLE WORKSHEETS: Grammar worksheets Units 5–8; Vocabulary worksheets Units 5–8; Review Game Units 5–8; Literature worksheet; Speaking worksheet; Writing worksheet

WARMER

Write the titles for Units 5–8 at the top of the board in four columns (*Moments in history*, *What a great job*, *An exciting trip* and *Favourite places*). Next, ask the students to look back at Units 5–8 in their Student's Book or notebook and in small groups write down at least three new words for each unit. Then, ask each group to take turns to say one of their words. The other groups say which column the word goes in, e.g.:

Group 1: *Our first word is 'plane'.*

Group 3: *Does it go in Unit 7 An exciting trip?*

Group 1: *Yes, that's right.*

If appropriate, award points for correct answers.

VOCABULARY

1 Ask the students read the complete sentence first before they say what the correct word is. Encourage stronger students to either change parts of the sentence to make it correct for the other word, e.g *The **ferry** arrived at the **port** at ten thirty*, or, if more appropriate, write a new sentence for the other word.

Answers

1 lamp 2 floor 3 farmer 4 statue 5 diary 6 blanket
7 customers 8 coach

2 Encourage the students to look at the nouns first and try to think of at least two suitable verbs before they match them to the correct verbs.

Answers

1c 2f 3d 4g 5e 6a 7b

3 Ask the students to read the sentences first and try to think of a suitable word before they look at the words in the box. Ask students in pairs to look back at Units 5–8 to check their ideas before you check their answers as a class.

Answers

1 cupboard 2 map 3 tourists 4 building 5 office 6 cook
7 stairs 8 suitcase 9 blanket 10 square

GRAMMAR

1 For questions 1–4, encourage the students to read the complete sentence first before they choose the correct answer. If necessary, point out that sentences 1–3 are in the past. For questions 5–8, point out that there is a problem with the verbs in 5–7 but in question 8 there is a different kind of mistake.

Answers

1 Did
2 climbed
3 got
4 something
5 Last summer, I went to the United States. Some days it was hot but on others it **rained**.
6 Today, we watched a football game but my sister **didn't** like it very much.
7 At my party, I danced, **sang** and ate and drank a lot of things.
8 I didn't do **anything** special.

2 Ask the students to do this exercise quickly on their own and then check their answers with the irregular verb list on SB page 158.

Answers

1 began 2 bought 3 caught 4 flew 5 gave 6 met 7 slept
8 swam 9 rode 10 took

3 Point out that students need to write complete sentences or questions in this exercise and not order the words.

MIXED ABILITY

With very weak students, write the complete questions or sentences on the board and ask them to listen and repeat at least twice. Next, rub out verbs and ask the students to repeat the sentences or questions again with the correct verbs. Then, ask them to do the exercise.

Answers

1 I didn't see that film last night.
2 They could cycle 50 km in a day.
3 Did you get an email this morning?
4 She didn't sleep in a tent on her holiday.
5 Did they clean their classroom last week?
6 He travelled to India last winter.
7 We didn't stay in a hotel in London.
8 Did she have a computer in her room?

READING

1 A2 Key for Schools Reading Part 1.

In this part of the exam, the students need to read six short unrelated texts (short emails, text messages, web messages or notices) and choose the correct answer (A–C) for each one. First, ask the students to look quickly at each text and say what each one is (*1 a postcard, 2 a notice, 3 a text message, 4 probably a banner on the hotel's website, 5 a notice and 6 a text message*). Then, ask them to read each text carefully first before they read and answer each question. Encourage stronger students to say why the other options are incorrect.

Answers

1 A 2 C 3 B 4 C 5 A 6 A

68 The Reading texts are recorded for students to listen and read.

SPEAKING

1 With a weaker class, help the students by giving them the first word or words of each question. Then, remind them to give full answers when they ask and answer the questions in pairs.

Answers

1 Do you live in a flat or a house? / Do you live in a house or a flat?
2 How many rooms are there in your home?
3 How many brothers and sisters do you have?
4 Is your bedroom big or small? / Is your bedroom small or big?

2 A2 Key for Schools Speaking Part 1 Phase 2.

In this part of the exam, both candidates are first asked the following questions *What's your name?, How old are you?* and *Where do you live?* Then, candidates are asked questions on two different topics e.g. their home, school, hobbies, etc.

In Phase 2 of the exam, the examiner begins by saying *Now let's talk about …* . One of the topics might be 'your home' and then the examiner will ask each candidate in turn two questions related to the topic, e.g. *Who do you live with?* or *Where do you watch TV at home?* One of the candidates is then asked another question like *Please tell me something about what you like doing at home* and encouraged to give a longer answer. The examiner then repeats this phase with another topic (e.g. school, sports) and the other candidate is asked the second extended response question.

First, encourage the students to look back at Unit 8 Vocabulary and Reading Bedroom furniture page 50 and make some notes about their own room before they speak to their partner. If time allows, ask all the students to do the fast finisher activity below.

FAST FINISHERS

Ask fast finishers to ask their partner some more 'Tell me about your …' questions using some of the topics from Units 5–8, e.g. *Tell me about your last weekend / last holiday / favourite kind of holiday / favourite building or place.*

Answers

Students' own answers

COOLER

Write the titles from Units 5–8 in four columns on the board again (see Warmer). Then, say one of the words from the Vocabulary section in this Review section and invite a student to write it in the correct place on the board. Continue with more words. If appropriate, organise the students into teams and award points for correctly spelled words in the right column. If time allows, then ask the students to play the game in small groups. Each student writes the unit titles in four columns in their notebook. Then, they take turns to call out the words and write them down in the correct column.

READING

1 **For each question, choose the correct answer.**

1

What did Bella do first?

A sightseeing
B water sports
C shopping

2

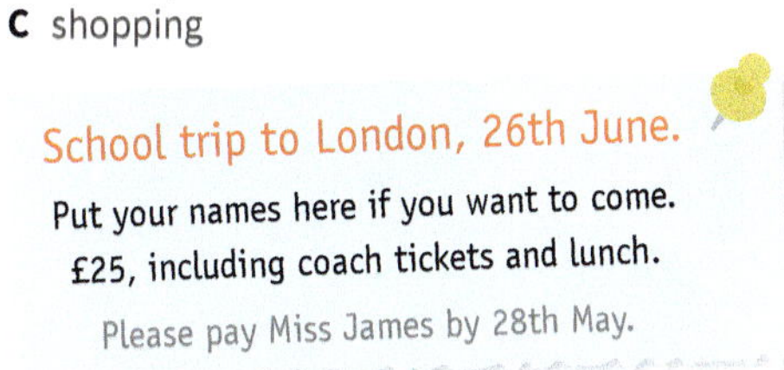

A Students need to ask Miss James for information about the trip.
B Students need to bring something for lunch on 26th June.
C Students don't need to pay for the school trip until 28th May.

3

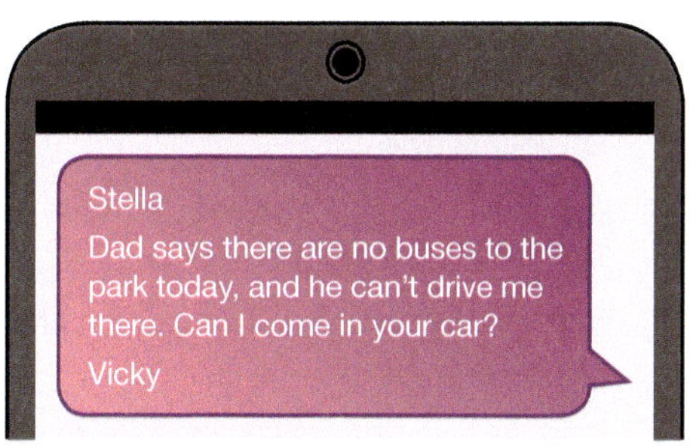

Why did Vicky write this message?

A to say where Stella can catch the bus
B to ask Stella for some help
C to tell Stella how to get to the park

4

A Everyone who wants to swim needs to pay £5.00.
B Only hotel guests can use the swimming pool.
C People staying here don't need to pay to swim.

5

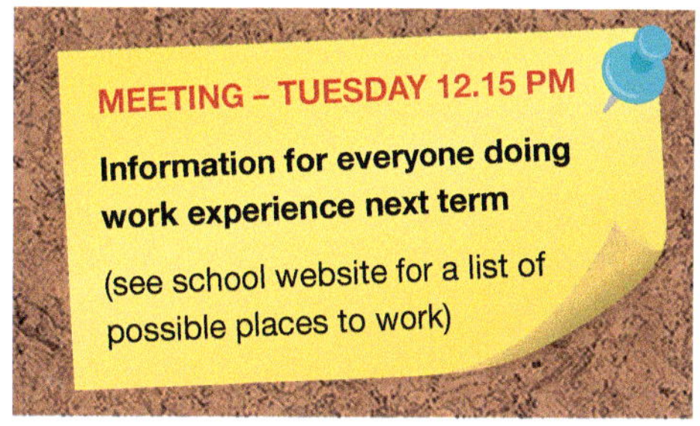

This notice tells students

A when they can find out about doing work experience.
B about a change in the time of an important meeting.
C to let the school know about their work experience plans.

6

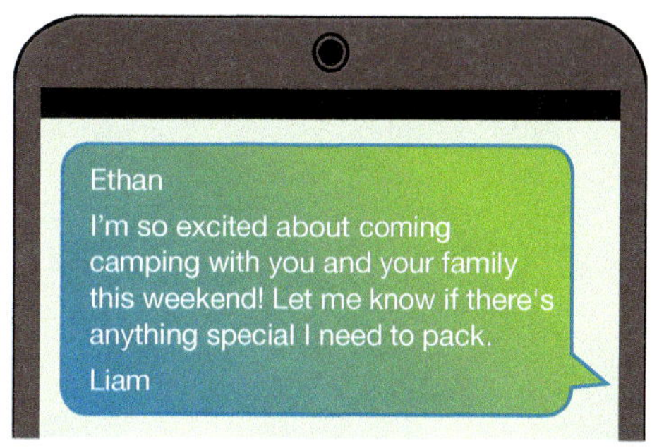

What does Liam want to know?

68

A what he should bring.
B where they are going.
C who is coming camping.

SPEAKING

1 **Put the words in order to make questions.**

1 live / you / flat / house / or / a / do / in / a / ?
2 rooms / home / how / your / there / many / are / in / ?
3 you / do / brothers / sisters / and / have / how many / ?
4 big / bedroom / or / your / is / small / ?

In pairs, ask and answer the questions. Take turns to speak.

2 **In pairs, talk about your room. Take turns to speak.**

Tell me about your room.

The walls are white and the carpet is blue. There are some shelves with …

9 CLOTHES AND FASHION

ABOUT YOU

What clothes do you like wearing in summer and in winter?
What are your favourite clothes? Why?
What colour are they?

VOCABULARY AND READING

Clothes

1 EP **Match the photos of clothes A–L to the words in the box.**

boots cap gloves jumper
scarf socks suit
sunglasses swimming costume
swimming shorts tie trainers

69 **Listen and check. Then repeat.**

2 EP **Look at the photos. Who is wearing pale yellow clothes and who is wearing bright yellow clothes?**

3 **Which clothes in Exercise 1 are:**

bright red? pale blue? bright blue?
pale grey? black and purple? black?
pink? pale green?

4 **Find pale and bright things in the classroom. Tell your partner.**

5 **Read the blog and match the clothes A–L in Exercise 1 to the people.**

6 **What are their best buys? Who doesn't have a best buy?**

7 **Read the blog again and answer the questions.**

1 When did Samuel get his boots?
2 Did Megan need the jumper for her holiday?
3 Why did Ed get a suit and tie?
4 How is Isaac's holiday different from Megan's?
5 Amelia bought a swimming costume. Who else got one?

8 **Think back over the last few months. What was your best buy? Tell your partner.**

9 CLOTHES AND FASHION

Unit Overview

TOPIC	Clothes and their materials
VOCABULARY	Clothes
AND READING	What's your best buy?
GRAMMAR	Pronouns and determiners
READING	They're made of … what?
VOCABULARY	Materials
PRONUNCIATION	Words beginning with /s/, /ʃ/, /tʃ/
LISTENING	Descriptions of unusual things to use to make clothes
SPEAKING	Describing what someone is wearing

Resources

GRAMMAR REFERENCE AND PRACTICE: SB page 146; TB page 248
WORKBOOK: pages 40–43
PHOTOCOPIABLE WORKSHEETS: Grammar worksheet Unit 9; Vocabulary worksheet Unit 9
TEST GENERATOR: Unit test 9

WARMER
Ask the students to look at each other and name as many clothes as they can. Ask them to draw a Venn diagram with the headings 'winter' and 'summer' and to complete it with as many clothes as possible.

ABOUT YOU
Ask the students to use the words in their Venn diagram (see Warmer) to ask and answer the questions in groups.

VOCABULARY AND READING

Clothes

1 Ask the students in pairs to name the clothes in the photos before they look at the words in the box. Then, ask them to add any new words to their Venn diagrams (see Warmer).

69

Answers
The answers are recorded for the students to check and then repeat.
A socks B jumper C sunglasses D cap E swimming shorts F trainers G scarf H gloves I suit J swimming costume K boots L tie

2 Ask the students to name the clothes in the photos first and then say what the difference in colour is.

Answers
girl: pale yellow clothes; boy: bright yellow clothes

3 Ask the students to choose one item of clothing for each colour. Remind them that we use *bright* and *pale* before the colour, e.g. *pale green* (not *green pale*). Also point out that *light* is a near synonym of *pale*.

Answers

bright red boots	black and purple jumper
pale blue swimming shorts	black trainers
bright blue cap	pink swimming costume
pale grey suit	pale green tie

4 With a stronger class, increase the challenge by setting a time limit, e.g. find as many pale things as possible in 30 seconds.

Answers
Students' own answers

5 Pre-teach *best buy* by asking 'Is an expensive T-shirt, which gets smaller in the washing machine, a best buy?' (*no*).

Answers
Samuel: K boots
Megan: A socks, H gloves, G scarf, B jumper
Ed: I suit, L tie
Isaac: D cap, E swimming shorts, C sunglasses, F trainers
Amelia: J swimming costumes

6 Ask the students to read each person's post again and to find the words or expressions which say whether they like the clothes they have bought (= *a best buy*) or not.

Answers

Best buys	Ed: no best buy
Samuel: boots	Isaac: cap
Megan: jumper	Amelia: swimming costume

7 Encourage the students to try to answer the questions before they read the blog again. Point out that they need to write full sentences.

Answers
1 He got them last year.
2 No. She bought it because she liked it.
3 Because his dad bought it for Ed to wear at a wedding.
4 Megan is going skiing and Isaac is going swimming.
5 Her sister bought one too (and Isaac bought swimming shorts).

70 The Reading text is recorded for students to listen and read.

8 If the students are slow to start, write these questions on the board: *What's your favourite item of clothing? Where did you buy it? Why are you happy with it?*

FAST FINISHERS
Encourage the fast finishers to work through Exercises 6–8 at their own pace and then to write their own post for the *What's your best buy?* blog.

Answers
Students' own answers

GRAMMAR Pronouns and determiners

1 Books closed. Copy the table onto the board with the gaps in the Pronouns column. Write the determiners (*my*, *your*, *his*, etc.) in a different colour and circle the determiner + object (e.g. *my trainers*, *your swimming shorts*). Invite students to come to the board and write a word in each gap which replaces the circled determiner + object (e.g. *mine* replaces *my trainers*). Rub off the answers and ask the students to complete the table in their book.

Answers

Are they yours?
It's his.
Are they hers?
It's ours.
They're theirs.

» **GRAMMAR REFERENCE AND PRACTICE ANSWER KEY TB PAGE 248**

2 With a weaker class, point out that they should look for *mine*, *yours*, *his*, etc. and that there are pronouns in the blog.

Answers

Samuel's text: His, mine; Ed's text: Mine, his; Amelia's text: mine, hers

3 Ask the students to identify the subject of each sentence before they complete it with the correct pronoun.

MIXED ABILITY

With a mixed ability class, copy these sentences onto separate strips of paper with the numbers:

1 I'm sure those gloves are mine.
2 I bought them yesterday.
1 Hey you two, are those caps yours?
2 I found them under the table.
1 Ed doesn't like jackets with pockets on them.
2 But most jackets have them.
1 Samuel bought red boots not green ones.
2 I don't think those green boots are his.
1 Megan and Isaac both love the colour grey.
2 I'm sure those grey scarves are theirs.
1 Are all these clothes ours?
2 We've got so many clothes.
1 Excuse me. Are these sunglasses yours?
2 I think you dropped them.

Make enough sets of strips for groups of four (stronger and weaker students) to have one set each. Ask the groups to match each Sentence 1 to a Sentence 2. Then, ask them to find the pronoun and to say why it is used, e.g. *We use 'yours' with 'you'.*

If you don't have time to make the strips, do the exercise orally with the weaker students first. Then, ask the students to complete the sentences.

Answers

1 yours 2 his 3 his 4 theirs 5 ours 6 yours

4 Point out that there is one mistake with either the determiner or the pronoun in each sentence. You could also point out that *mine* is always singular; we never say *Those shoes aren't mines.*

Answers

1 You can borrow **my** book.
2 I think you can buy a pair of trainers like **mine**.
3 I like it because **its** colour is bright blue.
4 The cap isn't **mine**. It's my brother's.
5 The clothes on the bed are all **yours**.

5 Put the students into small groups with a desk or a table in the middle. Ask them to put three or four of their smaller possessions (pen, pencil, pencil case, rubber, etc. but not something valuable) onto the desk or the table. Ask the students to read the words in the box and then demonstrate an example with a stronger student:

Teacher: *(picks up a rubber) Ana, is this yours?*
Student: *No, it isn't mine. It's his. (points at a male student) Mine is long and thin.*

Answers

Students' own answers

» **GRAMMAR WORKSHEET UNIT 9**

COOLER

Repeat Exercise 5 as a whole class. Collect one object from each member of the class and put them on a table at the front of the class. Invite students to take turns to come to the front and ask questions about the objects on the table. With stronger students, encourage them to ask follow-up questions: *Where did you get it? When did you get it? Do you like it? Why? Was it a best buy?*

WHAT'S YOUR BEST BUY?

70 Tell us about your cool clothes!

Samuel08 March 22 at 11.06

I just love clothes! My best buy last year was a pair of bright red boots. Cool! I wanted to get some like my brother's. His are green, but now I like mine best. I'm wearing them right now.

Megan33 March 22 at 12.30

I got my best buy yesterday! My parents bought me warm things for my skiing holiday – socks, gloves and a scarf. Then I saw an amazing black and purple jumper with pockets. I don't really need it, but I bought it anyway.

Ed14 March 22 at 13.13

Your clothes sound amazing! Mine are all so boring! Dad takes me shopping, and he buys me what *he* likes. Yuk. Last week he bought me a pale grey suit and a pale green tie for my cousin's wedding! They're just like his! Can you believe it! You're both so lucky.

Isaac60 March 22 at 13.25

Tell your dad it's great he wants to buy your clothes for you, but say *you* want to choose them sometimes. I got things for a holiday. I got pale blue swimming shorts and sunglasses. Oh, and black trainers – the best thing is a bright blue cap!

Amelia55 March 22 at 14.20

What great clothes – except the suit (sorry, Ed!). My sister and I always like the same clothes and our best buys last summer were swimming costumes! Mine is pink and hers is green. They look great!

GRAMMAR Pronouns and determiners

1 **Complete the sentences with the pronouns below.**

hers his ~~mine~~ ours theirs yours

Determiners	Pronouns
They're **my** trainers.	They're *mine*.
Are they **your** swimming shorts?	Are they ______ ?
It's **his** jumper.	It's ______ .
Are they **her** gloves?	Are they ______ .
It's **its** blanket.	-
It's **our** clothes blog.	It's ______ .
They're **their** swimming costumes.	They're ______ .

» GRAMMAR REFERENCE AND PRACTICE PAGE 146

2 **Find all the pronouns in the blog in Exercise 5.**

3 **Complete the sentences with pronouns.**

0 I'm sure those gloves are *mine*. I bought them yesterday.
1 Hey you two, are these caps ______? I found them under the table.
2 I hate going shopping for jackets with Ed. He doesn't like pockets on ______, but most jackets have them.
3 Samuel bought red boots not green ones, so I don't think those green boots are ______.
4 Megan and Isaac both love the colour grey, so I'm sure those grey scarves are ______.
5 Are all these ______? We've got so many clothes!
6 Excuse me. Are these sunglasses ______? I think you dropped them.

4 **Correct the mistakes in the sentences.**

1 You can borrow me book.
2 I think you can buy a pair of trainers like my.
3 I like it because it colour is bright blue.
4 The cap isn't my. It's my brother's.
5 The clothes on the bed are all your.

5 **Work in small groups. Ask and answer questions about the things you have on your desk. Use these words to help you.**

Is this yours?
Yes, it's mine.
No, it isn't mine. It's his / hers / yours / theirs.
It's long and thin and it's bright green. It's a crayon and you use it to draw and colour in.

Is this your textbook?
Yes, it's mine.
Are these pens yours?
No, they're not mine. They're hers.

READING

1 Look at the photos A–E. Which item of clothing do you like the best? Why?

2 Read the article and match the photos A–E to the paragraphs 1–5.

THEY'RE MADE OF ... WHAT?

Are you wearing a pair of leather boots? Is your jumper made of wool? Are your shorts made of cotton? Sorry, that's not cool! You need to wear clothes made of something else.

71

1 What do you do with your old tin cans? Do you recycle them? What happens to them next? Well, some people use them to make clothes. This dress is made of metal from old food cans. It looks good, but maybe it's a bit noisy when you move.

2 Cork comes from the outside of some trees in countries like Portugal and Spain. We usually find corks in the top of bottles, but you can use cork for other things too. Did you know you can use it to make clothes, handbags, hats and shoes? It's very popular in the big fashion houses.

3 What do you do with your plastic knives and forks after your picnic? Do you recycle them? Do you collect them? Some people do. In fact, they make jewellery out of them. Can you believe it? This designer has made hers into an amazing hat.

4 This dress won a prize in the yearly Toilet Paper Wedding Dress contest! You need a lot of toilet paper and, of course, you don't want to go out in the rain when you're wearing it.

5 Everyone needs shoes and lots of people drive cars. When you change your car tyres, why not use the old ones to make ... shoes! They are easy and cheap to make, and they don't look bad.

3 Read the article again and choose the correct answer.

The article is about:

a what to do with old clothes and jewellery.
b making things to wear out of unusual things.
c how to make cheap clothes and jewellery.

4 Now answer these questions.

1 What is the dress in photo B made of?
2 What can you make with cork?
3 What is the hat in photo A made of?
4 Why should you be careful when you wear the dress in photo C?
5 What are tyres usually used for?

TALKING POINTS

Would you like to wear any of the clothes and jewellery from the article? Why? / Why not?

What do you do with your old clothes when you don't wear them anymore?

READING

WARMER

Play Pictionary. Begin to draw one of the items of clothing from Exercise 1 page 58 and encourage the students to put up their hands and guess what it is by asking *Is it a ... ?* Next, invite a student to come to the board and draw a picture for the class to guess. Then, encourage the students to continue in small groups.

BACKGROUND INFORMATION

When producing clothes, **sustainable fashion** (or **eco-fashion**) takes into account the impact the process might have on both the environment (e.g. the chemicals used and their effects) and also on the people who work for the clothes manufacturer (e.g. over 1,000 people died after a fire in a clothes factory in Bangladesh. The building had too many floors and couldn't support the heavy machinery).

Recycling: According to the Environmental Protection Agency in the USA, people throw away over 30 kg of clothes a year, even though most of these could be recycled. Recycling helps in different ways. It reduces our use of natural resources such as water, which is used to grow cotton. It also reduces our need to use chemicals, which are needed to make new clothes.

Upcycling (or **creative reuse**) is turning unwanted products into something useful. In fashion, upcycling might mean turning a pair of curtains with an attractive design into a fashionable dress, or even turning old electrical wire into jewellery.

1 Ask the students to describe the clothes in each photo first before they say which one they like best.

Answers

Students' own answers

2 Read the introduction first as a class, encouraging the students to answer the questions for themselves, i.e. *Are you wearing a pair of leather boots?* Vocabulary Exercise 1 page 61 presents these materials through a matching activity.

MIXED ABILITY

Tell the stronger students that there may be some words they don't understand, but they should try to match the texts (1–5) to the photos (A–E) by looking at the key words they do understand (e.g. text 2 mentions *hats*, so it must go with photo E).

With the weaker students, pre-teach the more difficult words, e.g. *cans*, *cork*, *plastic*, *knives*, *forks and spoons*, *jewellery*, *toilet paper* and *car tyres*. Do this by asking the students to find these things in the photos (A–E) before they match the texts (1–5).

Answers

1 B 2 E 3 A 4 C 5 D

3 Ask the students to try to answer this question before they read the article again. Stronger students may not need to read it again.

Answers

b

4 Point out that the students may not find the answers by just looking at the photos. They may need to read the accompanying texts (1–5) again.

Answers

1 old food cans
2 clothes, handbags, hats and shoes
3 knives, forks and spoons (cutlery)
4 you don't want to go out in the rain when you're wearing it
5 shoes

71 The Reading text is recorded for students to listen and read.

TALKING POINTS

Take a class vote first on the clothes by asking the students to vote for their favourite photo (A–E). Then, organise the students into small groups to discuss the questions. If appropriate, encourage a class discussion on sustainable fashion (see Background information above), e.g. *Don't throw away your clothes. Buy secondhand clothes or from eco-friendly shops.*

VOCABULARY Materials

1 Ask students to try to name the materials in the photos before they match them. Check pronunciation by asking them to listen and repeat.

72

Answers

The answers are recorded for students to check and then repeat.
A wool B cotton C cork D metal E plastic F leather

2 With a weaker class, point out that they only need to read the introduction and the first three texts to find the words.

Answers

Introduction: … leather boots, … made of wool, … made of cotton
Paragraph 1: … made of metal
Paragraph 2: Cork comes from …, … use cork
Paragraph 3: … your plastic knives

3 Write the example sentences on the board and highlight the difference in the prepositions: *we can make shoes from plastic* (focuses on the process) but *my jeans are made of cotton* (focuses on the final product). Next, brainstorm a list of unusual materials onto the board and encourage the students to make as many sentences as they can using *made from* and *made of*.

FAST FINISHERS

Encourage fast finishers to work through this section at their own pace. When they have finished Exercise 3, they challenge each other to find objects made of the materials in Exercise 1 in the classroom.

Possible answers

Paper cups, coconut fibre and coffee grounds can all be used to make clothes.
Students' own answers

» **VOCABULARY WORKSHEET UNIT 9**

PRONUNCIATION

Words beginning with /s/, /ʃ/, /tʃ/

4 Read *sick*, *shower* and *chair* together and make sure the students can hear the difference between the three sounds. Point out that they need to classify the words by their first sound.

73

Answers

The answers are recorded for the students to check and then repeat.
/s/ – sick, sea, socks, suit
/ʃ/ – shower, shirt, shoes, shorts
/tʃ/ – chair, change, cheese, chilli

5 If the students struggle to say the sentence correctly, break it down into short sections for them to repeat. Start at the end of the sentence and slowly build it up, e.g.:

suit shop
in the suit shop
seven shirts in the suit shop
six socks and seven shirts in the suit shop
She sees six socks and seven shirts in the suit shop.

Next, say the whole sentence together as a class, getting faster each time. Then, invite volunteers to say the sentence as fast as they can.

Answers

Students' own answers

LISTENING

74

1 Play the recording for the first time and ask the students to complete the first column. Then, play the recording again and ask the students to complete the second column.

Answers

	What is it?	What is it made of?
Henry	jacket	newspapers and magazines
Molly	necklace	chocolate
Lauren	shorts	money – notes

74

2 First, encourage the students to read Henry's sentence, to say whether he talks about clothes or jewellery, and to circle the correct one. Next, they should try to fill the three gaps with the correct word. Ask them to do the same for Molly and Lauren before they listen again and check their ideas.

Answers

Henry: It's a really good idea to make clothes out of newspapers and magazines because you've got something to read when you're bored.
Molly: It's a really good idea to make jewellery out of chocolate because you've got something to eat when you're hungry.
Lauren: It's a really good idea to make clothes out of money because you've got something to spend when you need it.

» **AUDIOSCRIPT TB PAGE 271**

3 Ask the class to dictate Henry's sentence back to you. Next, ask them to write their own sentence in their notebooks, using some of the materials you brainstormed in Vocabulary Exercise 3 on this page. Organise the students into pairs, then ask them to compare their sentences and vote for the best one.

Answers

Students' own answers

SPEAKING

1 Read the example aloud as a class first. Invite a volunteer to come to the front and walk around as if in a fashion show. While they are doing this, ask the class to describe him or her. The students then continue in pairs.

Answers

Students' own answers

COOLER

Describe what one of the students in the class is wearing (the clothes, the colour and the material) but don't say who it is. The class have to guess who it is. Ask the students to continue in small groups.

VOCABULARY Materials

1 Match the photos A–F to the words in the box.

EP

cork	cotton	leather
metal	plastic	wool

72 Listen and check. Then repeat.

2 Read the article on page 60 again. Find the words in exercise 1 and underline them.

3 What other unusual things can we use to make clothes, shoes or jewellery? What are your clothes and shoes made of?

We can make shoes from plastic.
My jeans and socks are made of cotton, my shoes are made of leather and my jumper is made of wool.

ə PRONUNCIATION

Words beginning with /s/, /ʃ/, /tʃ/

4 Look at the words and think about the first sound. Put the words into the correct columns.

change cheese chilli
sea shirt shoes shorts
socks suit

/s/ **s**ick	/ʃ/ **sh**ower	/tʃ/ **ch**air

73 Listen and check. Then repeat.

5 Now say this!

She sees six socks and seven shirts in the suit shop.

LISTENING

74 **1** Listen to three people talking about their ideas for unusual things to use to make clothes or jewellery. Complete the table.

	What is it?	What is it made of?
Henry		
Molly		
Lauren		

74 **2** Listen again. Complete the sentence three times: once for Henry, once for Molly and once for Lauren. Choose *clothes* or *jewellery*.

Henry: It's a really good idea to make *clothes* / *jewellery* out of ________ because you've got ________ when you ________.

Molly: It's a really good idea to make *clothes* / *jewellery* out of ________ because you've got ________ when you ________.

Lauren: It's a really good idea to make *clothes* / *jewellery* out of ________ because you've got ________ when you ________.

3 In pairs, describe your idea for clothes made of unusual things.

It's a really good idea to … .

SPEAKING

1 Work in pairs. You are at a fashion show. Take turns to describe what your partner is wearing, what colour the clothes are and what they are made of.

And this is Richard. Today he's wearing dark blue cotton trousers, bright red cotton socks and pale blue sandals made of cork. His shirt is … .

10 BUYING THINGS

ABOUT YOU

Where do you do most of your shopping: online or in the shops? Which is better?

What do you buy online and what do you buy in shops? Why?

VOCABULARY AND READING

Buying and selling

1 Match photos A–H to the words in the box.

EP

bill	cash	discount	price
purse	receipt	sale	wallet

75 Listen and check. Then repeat.

2 Do the shopping quiz. Do you agree with the statements? Choose *yes* or *no* for each sentence.

3 Now check your answers on page 124.

4 In pairs, discuss your answers. Which of you:

1 buys more online than in the shops?
2 sometimes checks the bill?
3 usually shops in the sales?
4 carries cash in their purse or wallet?
5 never asks shop assistants anything?
6 spends more on clothes than their friends?

5 Put the words from Exercise 1 into the correct columns.

Countable nouns (C)	Uncountable nouns (U)

What kind of shopper are you?

Choose *yes* or *no* and find out.

1	I look at the price before I buy expensive things, like some shoes.	Yes / No
2	I'm not interested in any discounts. I want to buy the best.	Yes / No
3	I make sure I keep a few receipts from my shopping.	Yes / No
4	I don't buy much in the shops, only a few things a month.	Yes / No
5	I usually buy a lot of T-shirts and tops in the sales.	Yes / No
6	I often ask the shop assistant for some advice on what to buy.	Yes / No
7	I always check the bills when I eat in cafés or restaurants.	Yes / No
8	I never have any cash in my wallet or purse. I spend money quickly.	Yes / No
9	I don't buy CDs, but I share a lot of music with my friends.	Yes / No
10	I spend a bit of time every week looking at clothes online.	Yes / No

76

10 BUYING THINGS

Unit Overview

TOPIC	Buying and selling things
VOCABULARY AND READING	Buying and selling What kind of shopper are you?
GRAMMAR	*some, any, a lot of, a few, a bit of*
PRONUNCIATION	Weak forms: /ə/
READING	Two young entrepreneurs to watch
VOCABULARY	Phrases with *for*
LISTENING	Five short conversations
WRITING	A story about a problem buying something online
EXAM TASKS	Listening Part 4

Resources

GRAMMAR REFERENCE AND PRACTICE: SB page 147; TB page 248
WORKBOOK: pages 44–47
PHOTOCOPIABLE WORKSHEETS: Grammar worksheet Unit 10; Vocabulary worksheet Unit 10
TEST GENERATOR: Unit test 10

WARMER

Brainstorm a list of shops onto the board, e.g. *sports shop, clothes shop, bookshop*, etc. Say to the class 'I bought something in a clothes shop last week. What are they?' Encourage them to ask you *Yes/No* questions and try to guess what they are. For example: *Are you wearing them now?* (*Yes, I am.*) *Are they made of cotton?* (*No, they aren't.*) *Are they made of leather?* (*Yes, they are.*) *Are they your shoes?* (*Yes, they are.*) Allow the students three or four minutes to do the same activity in small groups, encouraging them to talk about things they bought in some of the other shops on the board.

ABOUT YOU

Ask the students to look at the unit title and the photos and to say what they think this unit is about (*buying and selling, shopping*). Then, ask them to ask and answer the questions in small groups.

VOCABULARY AND READING

Buying and selling

1 Ask the class to look at the photos first and in pairs describe what they can see. Invite a brief class discussion by asking 'Do you like shopping?' 'What sort of shops do you like?' 'Do you have a favourite shop?' 'What do you like buying?' Highlight the difference between *purse* and *wallet* by asking 'Is it usually for a man or a woman?' 'Do you put coins or notes in it?' If necessary, point out that the *p* in *receipt* is silent: /rɪˈsiːt/.

75

Answers

The answers are recorded for the students to check and then repeat.
A discount B receipt C bill D purse E wallet F cash G sale H price

2 Either do the quiz as a class or organise the students into small groups. Students take turns to read the sentences aloud. Point out that they need to circle *yes* if the sentence is true for them or *no* if the sentence is false for them.

Answers

Students' own answers

76 The Reading text is recorded for students to listen to for Exercise 2.

3 Ask the students to count how many *yes* and how many *no* answers they have. Then, they read the result on page 124 and say if they think it's true or false for them and why.

Answers

(Page 124 Student's Book)
More *Yes* than *No* answers.
You are careful with your money and want to buy things for a good price. You usually think and look before you buy.
More *No* than *Yes* answers.
You love clothes and shopping, and you like spending money. You don't always think before you buy and you spend a bit too much sometimes.

4 Remind the students that they should try to have a conversation by asking follow-up questions. Demonstrate this activity with a stronger student, e.g.:

Teacher: *Do you buy more online than in the shops?*
Student: *No I don't. I buy more in the shops than online.*
Teacher: *What do you buy online?*
Student: *I sometimes buy books for school.*
Teacher: *What do you buy in the shops?*

With a weaker class, it may be necessary to elicit a dialogue from the class and write it on the board for the students to use as a model.

Answers

Students' own answers

5 Ask the class to look at the table and elicit the difference between countable and uncountable nouns. After they have completed the table, ask them to think of some more examples of countable and uncountable nouns, e.g. *three eggs* and *five apples* are countable, but *some rice* and *some milk* are uncountable.

Answers

Countable: bill, discount, price, purse, receipt, sale, wallet
Uncountable: cash

GRAMMAR *some, any, a lot of, a few, a bit of*

1 Ask the students to read the sentences and say whether the noun following *some, any, a lot of, a few* or *a bit of* is countable or uncountable. Then, elicit which sentences are positive and negative before they complete the rules. Point out that we use some of the words with both countable and uncountable nouns.

Answers

1 countable and uncountable
2 countable and uncountable
3 countable and uncountable
4 countable
5 uncountable

» GRAMMAR REFERENCE AND PRACTICE ANSWER KEY TB PAGE 248

2 Ask the students to say what they can see in the photos before they match them to the sentences.

Answers

1 A 2 D 3 C 4 B

3 Ask the students to look at the photos and describe what they can see before they complete the sentences. Encourage stronger students to write their own sentences with *a bit of, a few* or *a lot of* before they look at the sentences.

Answers

1 a lot of 2 a bit of 3 a few 4 a few 5 a lot of 6 a bit of

FAST FINISHERS

Ask the fast finishers to rewrite the sentences with an opposite meaning, e.g. *1 There are a few socks on the bed. 2 There's a lot of cake left.*

» GRAMMAR WORKSHEET UNIT 10

PRONUNCIATION Weak forms: /ə/

4 English is stress-timed. This means that the stressed syllables are said at regular intervals, e.g. *Da- Da-Da.* In order to maintain this pattern, some of the other syllables are reduced to the /ə/ sound so that they can fit in between. Point out that the /ə/ sounds in each sentence (*a bit of your burger, a few* and *A lot of*) are highlighted in a different colour.

Audioscript 77

The sentences are recorded for students to listen and repeat.

1 Can I have a bit of your burger?
2 He took a few photos.
3 A lot of people came.

5 Tell the students to underline the stressed syllables and circle the /ə/ sound first in each sentence in Exercise 3. Then, Student A taps a regular rhythm while Student B says the sentence and then they swap roles.

Answers

Students' own answers

6 Point out that there is one mistake in each sentence. In most of them, the article *a* is incorrect.

Answers

1 Please can you bring **some** pencils for drawing.
2 I want to buy **some** clothes. Can you help me?
3 I'm phoning to tell you **some / the / a bit of** good news.
4 You only need to bring **some** shorts and a T-shirt.
5 I'm sorry, but I haven't got **any** cash.

7 Brainstorm some ideas onto the board by asking:

'Do you prefer shopping in department stores or small shops?'

'Do you prefer the town centre or the shopping centre?'

'What sorts of things do you usually buy?'

'Do you prefer to go shopping with your family or your friends?'

'Do you ever buy things online? What? Why?'

'When are there usually sales? Do you usually buy things then?'

Then, allow the students five minutes to make notes on their own answers. Encourage them to use *some, any, a bit of, a few* and *a lot of.*

They discuss their answers in pairs or small groups checking that the other members of the group have used *some, any, a lot of, a few* or *a bit of* correctly.

MIXED ABILITY

Pair up a stronger student with a weaker student. Ask the weaker student to interview the stronger student first using the questions above. Encourage the stronger student to use *some, any, a lot of, a few* or *a bit of* in their answers. Next, ask them to write down six sentences together using the stronger student's answer. Then, ask each pair to work with another pair (now a group of four) and to compare their answers as above. You could ask each pair to write some true and some false sentences for the other pair to guess which are true and which are false.

Answers

Students' own answers

COOLER

Organise the class into teams. Say an object from Unit 9 or 10 and ask each team to make a sentence with *some, any, a lot of, a few* or *a bit of* and the word. Give a point to the team with the longest sentence. For example:

Teacher: *leather boots*

Team A: *There are a lot of leather boots in the department store.* (11 words > 1 point)

Team B: *My mum hasn't got any leather boots.* (8 words)

GRAMMAR *some, any, a lot of, a few, a bit of*

1 **Read the sentences from the quiz. Then complete the rules with *countable*, *uncountable* or *countable and uncountable*.**

I look at the price before I buy expensive things, like some shoes.
I often ask the shop assistant for some advice on what to buy.
I'm not interested in any discounts.
I never have any cash in my wallet or purse.
I usually buy a lot of clothes, like T-shirts and tops, in the sales.
I share a lot of music with my friends.
I make sure I keep a few receipts from my shopping.
I spend a bit of time looking at clothes online.

1 We use **some** in positive sentences with ________ nouns.
2 We use **any** in negative sentences with ________ nouns.
3 We use **a lot of** in positive sentences with ________ nouns.
4 We use **a few** in positive sentences with ________ nouns.
5 We use **a bit of** in positive sentences with ________ nouns.

» GRAMMAR REFERENCE AND PRACTICE PAGE 147

2 **Match the photos A–D to the sentences.**

1 He's got a bit of pizza.
2 He's got a few books.
3 He's got a lot of pizza.
4 He's got a lot of books.

3 **Look at the photos. Complete the sentences with *a bit of*, *a few* or *a lot of*.**

1 There are ________ socks on the bed.
2 There's ________ cake left.
3 There are ________ eggs in the fridge.
4 There are ________ books on the shelf.
5 He's got ________ money in his wallet.
6 I only ate ________ breakfast this morning.

ə PRONUNCIATION | Weak forms: /ə/

77 **4** **Listen and repeat.**

1 Can I have a bit of your burger?
2 He took a few photos.
3 A lot of people came.

5 **In pairs, take it in turns to read the answers from Exercise 3.**

6 **Correct the mistakes in the sentences.**

1 Please can you bring a pencils for drawing.
2 I want to buy a clothes. Can you help me?
3 I'm phoning to tell you a few good news.
4 You only need to bring a shorts and a T-shirt.
5 I'm sorry, but I haven't got some cash.

7 **Write six sentences about your shopping habits using *some*, *any*, *a lot of*, *a few* or *a bit of*.**

In pairs, compare your sentences and check you are using the grammar correctly. Are any of your partner's statements true for you?

READING

1 What ideas can you think of for an online business? Discuss your ideas with a partner.

2 Look at the photos of the two young business people. Read and complete the information:

1

NAME: ....

COUNTRY: ....

NAME OF BUSINESS: ....

TYPE OF BUSINESS: ....

2

NAME: ....

COUNTRY: ....

NAME OF BUSINESS: ....

TYPE OF BUSINESS: ....

TWO YOUNG ENTREPRENEURS TO WATCH

Cory Nieves, or Mr Cory, is from the United States. He started his business when he was six years old because he was tired of getting the bus to school. He wanted to make some money to help his mum, Lisa, buy a car. First, Mr Cory sold hot chocolate in front of his home in New Jersey. He did well, and he began to sell other things too, like lemonade and cookies. Mr Cory and his mum tried a lot of different recipes for cookies. Then, one day they baked some perfect chocolate chip cookies. Now they bake a lot of different cookies and sell them on his website mrcoryscookies.com. You can also buy them from shops. The cookies are all natural, and Mr Cory and his mum still try the recipes at home before they sell them to customers. Mr Cory also works with organisations that help young people in the United States.

Bella Tipping is Australian. She got the idea for her website while she was on holiday with her family in the US, when she was 12 years old. Bella and her mum talked about their experience. Her mum said the vacation was great. When Bella didn't agree her mum was really surprised. Bella said a lot of things in the hotels and restaurants were for adults not children. The places didn't think about what children wanted or needed. So, Bella started her website called Kidzcationz, where children can post their reviews of hotels and restaurants. Now, when families are planning their holidays and looking for places to stay and eat, they can look at the Kidzcationz website first to see which places are best for children.

78

3 Read the articles again and answer the questions.

1 Why did Cory want his mum to buy a car?
2 What did Cory sell before he sold the cookies?
3 What kind of cookies did they make first?
4 What do Cory and his mum still do?
5 How old was Bella when she had the idea for Kidzcationz?
6 What surprised Bella's mum after the holiday?
7 What was the problem with the hotels and restaurants?
8 How can families use Kidzcationz?

TALKING POINTS

Which do you think is a better idea: Mr Cory's Cookies or Kidzcationz? Tell your partner.

READING

WARMER

Write *Buying and selling online* on the board. Organise the class into teams and challenge the teams to write a list of things that the students often buy online and a list of things they *don't* usually buy online. Allow them two or three minutes to do this. If appropriate, award points for each thing. Write the ideas on the board in two columns. Then, invite a brief class discussion on the advantages and disadvantages of buying online.

BACKGROUND INFORMATION

Both Cory Nieves (Mr Cory's Cookies) and Bella Tipping (Kidzcationz) are real young entrepreneurs with real websites. Cory now works with several other companies and brands including department stores (e.g. Macy's) and supermarkets (Whole Foods). Part of his company has been bought by an American businessman. He donates part of his profits to local children charities. On the website, his single mother Lisa has written a letter of support and encouragement to other single mothers. On her Kidzcationz website, Bella Tipping takes internet security very seriously: reviewers' identities are protected and cannot be contacted directly. She also encourages reviewers to highlight places that support adults or children with special needs.

Other child entrepreneurs include Gabrielle Goodwin (hair accessories), Sebastian and Brandon Martinez (socks), Amber Kelley (Cook with Amber YouTube Channel), Ryan Kelly (dog treats) and Mikaila Ulmer (Life Skills on page 98 in this book includes an article about Mikaila's lemonade company).

1 Encourage the pairs to imagine that they would like to start their own online business and ask them to answer these questions: *What would you sell? How would you do it? Would you use a website like eBay or would you create your own online store?* Then, invite a brief class discussion on people they know (including family members) or local shops or businesses who have sold things online (*What do they sell? Are they successful?*).

Answers

Students' own answers

2 Ask the students to look at the photos, the profiles and the title and try to guess what *entrepreneur* means (/ˌɒn.trə.prəˈnɜːr/ *someone who starts their own business, especially when they see a new opportunity*). Then, ask them to read the article quickly and complete the information on the profiles.

MIXED ABILITY

For Exercises 2 and 3, divide the students into two groups. Students in group A read about Cory Nieves and those in group B read about Bella Tipping. Pair up a stronger student with a weaker one in their group and ask them to complete the information about either Cory or Bella in Exercise 2 and answer the questions about their entrepreneur in Exercise 3. Then, ask each pair in group A to sit next to a pair in group B and to share their information.

Answers

1
Cory Nieves
The United States
Mr Cory's Cookies
It sells cookies
2
Bella Tipping
Australia
Kidzcationz
It gives information

3 Encourage the students to try to answer the questions before they read the texts again. Remind them to answer the questions in full sentences.

Answers

1 Because he was tired of getting the bus to school.
2 He sold hot chocolate and lemonade.
3 They made chocolate chip cookies first.
4 Cory and his mum still try out the recipes themselves at home.
5 Bella was 12.
6 She was surprised that Bella did not think the holiday was great.
7 They didn't think about what young people wanted or needed on holiday.
8 They can look at reviews from young people about hotels and restaurants.

78 The Reading text is recorded for students to listen and read.

TALKING POINTS

Allow the students time to think about some reasons for their choice before they tell their partner. If time allows, take a class vote on the most popular idea.

VOCABULARY Phrases with *for*

1 Write the sentences with *for* on the board and ask the students to replace the phrases with something similar (e.g. *for just over a dollar/a euro/75p*, *for parties/picnics/lunch*). Encourage them to think about the different uses of *for* before they look at the meanings in the exercise.

Answers

1 for the next day
2 for 'cookies'
3 for just over a dollar each
4 for parties
5 for his website

2 Encourage stronger students to read the sentence beginnings first and try to complete them with *for* (1–5) and an expression before they read the endings (a–e). Alternatively, with books closed, dictate the sentence beginnings to the class and then ask them to try to complete them in pairs.

Answers

1d 2c 3e 4a 5b

3 Encourage the students to think about what sort of word is missing using the meanings in Exercise 1 (*e.g. 1 payment, 2 occasion, etc.*) before they look at the words and phrases in the box.

FAST FINISHERS

In pairs, ask fast finishers to write some true sentences about themselves on strips of paper using the different phrases with *for*. Then, they cut their sentences in halves where the second half begins with *for* (see Exercise 2). When the others are ready, they pass their strips to groups of students to match the sentence halves.

Answers

1 two pounds
2 her birthday
3 its tasty cookies
4 tomorrow
5 entrepreneur

» VOCABULARY WORKSHEET UNIT 10

LISTENING

79 1 A2 Key for Schools Listening Part 4.

In this part of the exam, students listen to five short conversations or monologues and answer a question about each one by choosing the correct answer (A, B or C). Ask the students to read each question carefully and if appropriate, underline the key words. Point out that the students will probably hear information about all three answers, but only one is correct. Play the recording at least twice. If the students find this exercise difficult, photocopy the audioscript on TB page 271. Ask them to read it and both find the answer and also find where the other options are mentioned and why they are not correct.

Answers

1 B 2 C 3 A 4 B 5 C

» AUDIOSCRIPT TB PAGE 271

WRITING

PREPARE TO WRITE
A story

GET READY With a stronger class, write the time expressions *after that*, *after two weeks*, *six days later* and *finally* on the board and ask these students to retell the story from memory after they have read it. With a mixed ability class, after they have read the story, pair up a stronger student with a weaker student. The stronger student retells the story with their book closed; the weaker student provides clues with their book open, e.g. *After that he waited …, Six days later, it … .*

PLAN Remind the students (especially the weaker ones) that they can use the story about the jacket as a model to answer these questions, but that they should change the information, e.g. they didn't want to buy a *jacket*, they wanted to buy a *T-shirt*. With a mixed ability class, pair up a weaker student (A) with a stronger student (B). Student A reads out the questions, Student B answers the questions, and Student A writes down the answer. With a very weak class, brainstorm answers to these questions together and write notes on the board.

WRITE If you brainstormed the notes together as a class on the board, now ask the students to link the notes together. Remind them to begin with *I wanted to buy …* etc., use the time expressions and write about 50 words.

IMPROVE Remind the students of their most common mistakes, e.g. with the past simple, the position of adjectives, the use of possessive pronouns.

Answers

Students' own answers

COOLER

Write sentence 1 in Exercise 1 on the board. Challenge the students in groups to write as many new sentences as they can using the *for* expression within a time limit (about two minutes), e.g.:

Cory sells his cookies for just over a dollar each.

Burger King sells hamburgers for just over two euros each.

My brother is selling his bike for just under 80 euros.

Then, write sentence 2 on the board and set a time limit. Continue in the same way with the remaining sentences.

VOCABULARY Phrases with *for*

1 **Look at the sentences with *for*.**

EP Cory sells his cookies for just over a dollar each.
People often buy cookies for parties.
People can order cookies online for the next day.
Cory is well-known for his website Mr Cory's Cookies.
What's British English for 'cookies'?

Match the phrases with *for* to the meanings:

1 time
2 the meaning of
3 payment
4 occasion
5 reason

2 **Now match the two halves of the sentences.**

1 People don't pay
2 Australia is famous
3 Let's book a table
4 What's another word
5 Bella went out with friends

a for 'vacation'?
b for her 14th birthday.
c for its beaches and amazing countryside.
d for the information on Bella's website.
e for lunch.

3 **Complete the sentences. Use the words and phrases in the box.**

entrepreneur	its tasty cookies	her birthday
tomorrow	two pounds	

1 How many oranges can I buy for ______?
2 I want to buy my sister some jewellery for ______.
3 This shop is famous for ______.
4 You need to do your English homework for ______, please.
5 What's the word in your language for ______?

LISTENING

79 **1** **For each question, choose the correct answer.**

1 Two friends are talking at the shopping centre. Why is the boy at the shopping centre?
A His computer's not working.
B He wants to visit a new shop.
C He always gets his shopping there.

2 A boy, Adam, is talking about shopping. What did he buy?
A some fruit
B a dog
C some bread

3 A woman is talking to her daughter about a present for her son, Matt. What is the present?
A something for Matt to wear
B something that Matt asked for
C something Matt needs for school

4 Two friends are talking at one of the friend's houses. What is the boy doing?
A He's reading his homework diary.
B He's looking at websites.
C He's doing his homework.

5 A teacher is talking to the class about a school trip. What is he telling them to do?
A get to school early
B bring T-shirts
C wear warm clothes

WRITING

PREPARE TO WRITE

A story

GET READY You're going to write a story about a problem you had buying something online, beginning with this sentence: *I wanted to buy a ______, so I looked on the internet. I found one on this fantastic website and ….* Read the story about Chris and his jacket on page 124. Find and underline these words in the story: *after that*, *after (two weeks)*, *(six days) later* and *finally*.

PLAN In your story, you tried to buy something online and there was a problem. Read the questions and make notes.

1 What did you want to buy? Describe it and say why you liked it.
2 How did you buy it? Did you use cash?
3 How long did it take to arrive?
4 What happened when it arrived? What was wrong with it?
5 What did you do?
6 What happened at the end of the story?

WRITE Write your story in about 50 words. Try to link the events in your story with the words *after that*, *after*, *later* and *finally*. Start with the sentence in *Get ready*.

IMPROVE In pairs, read your own story and your partner's. Check for mistakes. Give your partner two ideas to make their story better. Use your partner's advice and rewrite your story.

CULTURE

SHOPPING

FACTFILE Shopping

Shopping is an important part of people's lives. People often want to buy different things at good prices. In English-speaking countries, these types of shops are popular:

- **Charity shops:** People give these shops clothes, books and other things they don't use or want anymore. These shops then sell these things to other people. Charity shops give the money they make to help others.
- **Farmers' markets:** In these markets, farmers sell fruit, vegetables, cheese, honey and other local items.
- **Shopping centres:** These are big, modern buildings with lots of shops and places to eat. In the United States, shopping centres are called 'malls'.

1 In pairs, discuss the questions with your partner.

1. Is your home or school near a shopping centre, farmers' market or charity shop?
2. How are small shops and shopping centres different?

2 Read about shopping in different countries. Where do *you* do your shopping?

SHOPPING SURVEY

We asked three teens in three different countries 'Where do you do your shopping?' Here are their answers.

1 Mark, age 14
Seattle, USA

Where: Northgate Mall, near Seattle

Why? I shop at Northgate Mall because there are lots of different stores and places to eat. I like listening to music and there is an excellent choice of technology stores in the mall. I also like Northgate Mall because it is near my house and I can walk or cycle there. I don't have a lot of pocket money, but I don't mind because I can look at things in different shops and go window shopping!

2 Karen, age 13
Dublin, Ireland

Where: Charity shops on Camden Street, Dublin

Why? I haven't got a lot of pocket money, so I need to shop carefully. Every penny counts! One way I save money is shopping at charity shops. I love going shopping in Dublin and I really love Camden Street. Some of the charity shops only have clothes people donate, but others have jewellery, other accessories and furniture.

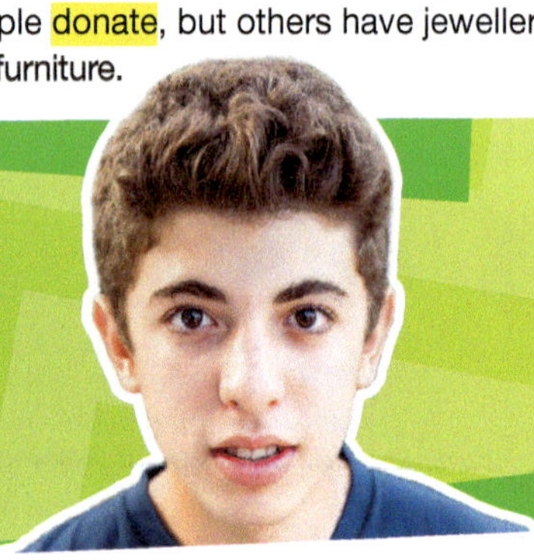

3 Darren, age 13
Ta' Qali, Malta

Where: Farmers' Market near Mdina

Why? I love cooking and sometimes I go with my mum and dad to the Ta' Qali Farmers' Market to get fresh fruit and vegetables. The food at the market is from local farms and my parents say the prices are great. We buy special Maltese honey at the Farmers' Market for making sweets. I have yoghurt, fruit and honey for breakfast every morning.

80

66 CULTURE

CULTURE

Learning Objectives

- The students learn about different types of places to go shopping.
- In the project stage, they prepare and carry out a survey and then present their findings to the class.

Vocabulary

window shopping local donate accessories penny technology

Resources

CULTURE VIDEO AND CULTURE VIDEO WORKSHEET: Street fairs everywhere

BACKGROUND INFORMATION

Charity Shops: In the 19th century, the Salvation Army used to sell secondhand clothes. (The Salvation Army is an organisation which helps the poor.) Oxfam (**Ox**ford **Fam**ine Relief) opened the first charity shop in Oxford in 1947–8 to raise money to reduce famine in Greece. There are now around 10,500 charity shops in the UK. Even the department store Harrods, a luxury department store in London, opened a temporary charity shop for a month called 'Fashion Re-told'. It sold designer clothes and accessories donated by customers, employees and brands to raise money for the UK children's charity NSPCC (National Society for the Prevention of Cruelty to Children).

Farmers' markets: While public markets tend to take place in a permanent structure often on a daily or weekly basis, farmers' markets take place less frequently. In a farmers' market, you buy directly from a local producer and most of the profit from the sale goes directly to them. Modern farmers' markets started to appear in the 2000s when people began to look for fresher, more seasonal products and also for homemade cakes, jam, bread, cheese, etc.

Shopping centres / malls: Most of the biggest shopping centres in the world are in Asia where land is cheapest. The Dubai Mall, for example, is the size of 50 soccer pitches and has over 1,200 shops, 22 cinema screens, 120 restaurants and cafés, an aquarium, an ice rink and a hotel.

WARMER

Write on the board *In our shopping centre there's a ....* Check that the class understand *shopping centre* by asking 'What's the name of the shopping centre in [name of place]?' Next, begin the activity by saying 'In our shopping centre there's a sports shop and ... .' Encourage a stronger student to continue, e.g. *In our shopping centre there's a sports shop, a clothes shop and ....* Then, encourage other students to continue adding more shops to the sentence. Continue this activity either as a whole class or in small groups.

1 Books closed. Write *charity shop*, *farmers' market* and *shopping centre* on the board in three columns. Ask the students in small groups to try to write at least three things they can buy in each one. If they don't know the meaning of the places, they should make a guess. Books open. The students read the factfile at the top of the page and check their ideas. Next, ask them to take turns to ask and answer the questions in Exercise 1.

Answers

1 Students' own answers
2 Small shops: sell one sort of thing, such as clothes or books; help you choose your shopping; are often in villages, towns, cities; Shopping centres: have lots of different shops and different things for sale in one place; are often found outside city centres.

2 If necessary, pre-teach *shopping survey* by encouraging the students to read the introduction to the text and asking 'What do you think a survey is?' (*asking different people about their habits or opinions*) Next, ask them to look at the photos (without reading the answers) and try to predict where the people do their shopping and why. Then, ask them to read the three answers and check their ideas. The students will talk more about where they do their shopping in *Talking points* and also in the *Project* box.

Answers

Students' own answers

80 The Reading text is recorded for students to listen and read.

3 Ask the students in pairs to describe what they can see in each photo before they match them to the texts.

Answers
A2 B3 C1

4 Ask the students in pairs to read the sentences and try to say if they are right or wrong before they read the texts again.

MIXED ABILITY

Encourage the stronger students to correct the wrong sentences. Fast finishers can write some right or wrong sentences. When the others are ready, the fast finishers read out their sentences. With weaker students, first ask them to read the sentences and decide which text each sentence refers to (Text 1 – sentences 1 and 2, Text 2 – 3 and 4, Text 3 – 5 and 6). Next, do the exercise as a group by highlighting the sentence in each text which gives the answer and asking the students to say whether the sentence in the exercise is right or wrong.

Answers
1 × (There is an excellent choice of technology stores.) 2 ✓
3 ✓ 4 × (Others have furniture, jewellery and other accessories.) 5 ✓ 6 ✓

5 First, ask the students in pairs to read through the sentences and try to complete them with a suitable word. Next, ask the students to look at the highlighted words in the text and try to guess the meaning of each one from context. Then, ask them to complete the sentences with these words.

Answers
1 window shopping 2 local 3 donate 4 accessories
5 penny 6 technology

TALKING POINTS

As a class, brainstorm some reasons why people shop at the three places in the survey. Then, organise them into small groups and ask them to take turns to ask and answer the questions. Remind them to say why.

81 6 Ask the students to read through the questions first before they listen. Point out that they'll need to listen for information about Leo in 1 and Gemma's mum in 2.

Answers
1c 2b

81 7 As a class, ask the students to match sentence 1 to its half (1e) and then ask them to try to match the rest of the sentence halves individually before they listen again. If necessary, play the recording for a third time for weaker students.

Answers
1e 2a 3h 4d 5b 6g 7c 8f

» AUDIOSCRIPT TB PAGES 271–272

PROJECT ***A survey***

Ask the students to read the project instructions in bold and ask 'What are you going to do for this project?' (*a shopping survey*) Brainstorm some questions as a class and write them on the board. Then, organise the students into small groups and ask them to think of five or six questions they'd like to ask.

Ask the students to draw a table on a piece of paper and to write their questions in the left-hand column. They should include six columns to write different people's answers.

Reorganise the class into new groups where each member has a different set of questions. Ask them to take turns to ask and answer their questions, but point out that they need to write down the answers in note form. Encourage the students to think of at least two people outside the class they can ask these questions.

If appropriate, encourage the students to present their results using graphs, pie charts, etc.

FAST FINISHERS

Encourage fast finishers to write more questions and to try to use some of the new grammar from Units 1–10, in particular the past simple. Also ask them to help those groups which are struggling to write five questions.

PROJECT EXTENSION

Ask the students to look at the three texts again and encourage them to produce a profile about themselves using these as a model. In their profile they should include their name, their age, where they are from and they should answer the questions: *Where do you usually do your shopping?* and *Why?* These profiles can either be handwritten and displayed on the walls or presented together on a program like PowerPoint or put on a class or school blog.

CULTURE VIDEO 03: Street fairs everywhere

When students have completed the lesson, they can watch the video and complete the worksheet.

COOLER

Describe your favourite shop to the students, but don't tell them the name. When you have finished your description, ask 'What's my favourite shop?' Then, encourage the students to continue the activity in small groups.

3 **Match the texts (1–3) in Exercise 2 to the photos (A–C).**

4 **Read the texts again. Are the sentences right (✓) or wrong (✗)?**

1 There are not a lot of technology stores at the mall.
2 Mark walks or cycles to the mall.
3 Karen likes shopping in Camden Street in Dublin.
4 Charity shops only sell clothes.
5 The Farmers' Market in Ta' Qali sells food from local farms.
6 Darren likes eating honey and yoghurt in the morning.

5 **Complete the sentences with the highlighted words in the texts.**

1 When I go to the centre of town, I love going ________. I don't buy anything but I look at lots of products.
2 I like buying ________ fruit and vegetables at the Farmers' Market. That way, I help small businesses and farmers from the area.
3 I'm taking some clothes to the charity shop to ________ them.
4 I love shopping for hats, scarves, sunglasses and other ________.
5 I need to save every ________ of my pocket money to buy a concert ticket next month.
6 I need a new phone. This afternoon my mum is taking me to a ________ store to see some different phones.

TALKING POINTS

Do you ever shop at any of the places in the survey?
Where is your favourite place to do your shopping? Why?

81 **6** **Listen to Gemma talking to two people about shopping. Tick the correct answers.**

1 Leo likes shopping …
  a at charity shops.
  b at the Farmers' Market.
  c at the shopping centre.
2 Gemma's mum likes shopping …
  a at charity shops.
  b at the Farmers' Market.
  c at the shopping centre.

81 **7** **Listen again and match the two halves of the sentences.**

1 Leo is …
2 Leo likes …
3 Leo goes shopping …
4 Leo sometimes buys
5 Gemma's mum goes shopping …
6 She likes …
7 She always buys …
8 Gemma and her dad love …

a window shopping at the shopping centre.
b three times a week.
c fruit and vegetables.
d music magazines.
e 13 years old.
f cheese.
g the local products and the prices.
h at weekends.

PROJECT *A survey*

In small groups, prepare and carry out a shopping survey.

- Think of five or six questions for your shopping survey.
  Ask questions about:
  - Where people shop
  - Why they shop there
  - When they shop
  - What they buy
- Write down the shopping survey questions.
- Compare your questions with another group's questions.
- Ask members of a different group your questions and record the results.
- After school, ask two friends in another class or family members about where they shop.
- Tell the class what you found out.

06 NOW WATCH THE CULTURE VIDEO

11 EATING OUT

VOCABULARY AND READING

Food

ABOUT YOU

How often do you eat out?
Which do you prefer – restaurant food or home-cooked food?
What is 'fast food'? Do you ever eat it?

1 Look at the restaurant advertisements. Match the things in the photos A–M to the words in the box.

EP

burger chicken legs cola cream fresh vegetables grapes lemonade mineral water pasta with tomato sauce mushroom salad soft drinks strawberry

2 Complete the phrases with one or two food words from the food in the menus in Exercise 1.

a bowl of ....
a glass of ....
a bottle of ....
a piece of ....
a slice of ....
a plate of ....

3 Look at the menus in Exercise 1 again. In pairs, say which foods you like and don't like. Then say what you'd like to eat or drink right now!

I like salad.

Me too.

I want to eat a bowl of fruit salad now.

4 Read the advertisements again. Are the sentences right (✓) or wrong (✗)?

1 The party room at Pizza Palace is smaller than the one at Easy Burgers.
2 You can watch something while you eat at Easy Burgers.
3 The food at Easy Burgers looks healthier.
4 Pizza Palace is more expensive than Easy Burgers.
5 The menu at Easy Burgers is longer than the one at Pizza Palace.
6 Easy Burgers and Pizza Palace are both popular.

11 EATING OUT

Unit Overview

TOPIC	Food and drink, restaurants and street food
VOCABULARY AND READING	Food (1) Menus
GRAMMAR	*as … as*; Comparative adjectives
READING	Street food around the world
VOCABULARY	Food (2)
PRONUNICATION	/ʌ/ and /ɒ/
LISTENING	A conversation about a street food festival
SPEAKING	Ordering food

Resources

GRAMMAR REFERENCE AND PRACTICE: SB page 148; TB page 248
WORKBOOK: pages 48–51
VIDEO AND VIDEO WORKSHEET: Street foods
PHOTOCOPIABLE WORKSHEETS: Grammar worksheet Unit 11; Vocabulary worksheet Unit 11
TEST GENERATOR: Unit test 11

WARMER
Write *food and drink* on the board and play the alphabet game. Challenge the class to think of a type of food or drink for as many letters of the alphabet as they can.

ABOUT YOU

Pre-teach *eat out*: have the class look at the photos and text titles in this unit and ask 'Are the people in this unit eating at home?' (*no*) 'Where are they eating?' (*in restaurants or at a food market; they're eating out*). Point out that *eating out* is eating in a restaurant, a café or at a stall and not eating outside. If necessary, also pre-teach *fast food* by asking 'What do we call the food in places like McDonalds, Burger King, [fast food places in the students' country], etc.?' (*fast food*) Then, ask the students to take turns to ask and answer the questions in pairs.

VOCABULARY AND READING

Food

1 Ask the students to look at the photos first and try to name as much of the food as possible before they look at the words. As the students repeat the words, check that they pronounce the following correctly: *chicken* /ˈtʃɪk.ɪn/ (*kitchen* /ˈkɪtʃ.ən/ is where we cook), *vegetable* /ˈvedʒ.tə.bəl/ (with three syllables), *tomato* /təˈmɑː.təʊ/ (the *a* is pronounced /ɑː/ in British English), and *strawberry* /ˈstrɔː.br.i/ (the e is often silent). Check students understand the meaning of *main course* and *dessert* (/dɪˈzɜːt/) by asking for examples of each one. If time allows, ask the students to divide a page in their notebook into a menu, using the headings *Main course* and *Dessert* and *Drinks*. Ask them to add the words in the box to their menu.

Answers
A mushroom B pasta with tomato sauce C strawberry D cream E soft drinks F cola G chicken legs H burger I grapes J fresh vegetables K salad L mineral water M lemonade

2 Encourage the students to do this exercise in pairs leaving out the words they don't know. Point out they can use the words in both the box and also in the advertisements. Then, go over the answers as a class and encourage a volunteer to come to the board and draw a picture of each recipient (a bowl, a glass, etc.).

Answers
a bowl of ice cream/rice/salad/pasta/fruit salad
a glass of (mineral) water/cola/juice/lemonade/soft drink
a bottle of (mineral) water/cola/juice/lemonade/soft drink
a piece of cake/cheesecake/pizza
a slice of cake/cheesecake/pizza
a plate of chips/pasta with tomato sauce/chicken legs

3 Ask the students to read the example first and use it as a model for their own conversation. With a stronger class, brainstorm a list of appropriate questions onto the board, e.g. *What's your favourite food? What's your least favourite? Which food do you like on the menu? Which food don't you like? Are you hungry now? Do you want to eat or drink anything on the menus right now?* Then, encourage them to take turns to ask and answer these questions.

Answers
Students' own answers

4 Pre-teach *healthy* by asking the students to say which of the food and drink in Exercise 1 is healthy and which is less healthy. Explain that *popular* means that a lot of people like it.

Ask the students to read the sentences first and then look for the answers in the advertisements. Encourage stronger students to correct the wrong sentences.

Answers
1 ✗ (The party rooms are the same size – they both hold thirty people.) 2 ✓ (*We play all your favourite music videos while you eat.*) 3 ✓ (There are fresh vegetables, salad, fruit salad and fruit juice.) 4 ✗ (Pizza Palace is cheaper than Easy Burgers.) 5 ✓ (There is more variety.) 6 ✓

GRAMMAR *as … as*

1 First, ask the students to look at the photo and say what the girl, Nicky, is thinking about. Ask them to read what she says and say if they agree or disagree with her. Then, ask them to find and, if appropriate, underline *as … as* in the speech bubbles. Elicit what word Nicky uses between *as … as* (*an adjective*).

Answers

1 the same 2 different

2 Point out that the students need to write two sentences about each pair of things, one using the first adjective and the other using the second. (Cristiano Ronaldo and Marcus Rashford are both professional footballers.)

MIXED ABILITY

Encourage stronger students to work at their own pace. When they have finished, ask the students to write some more sentences using *(not) as … as* and the two advertisements, e.g. *Pizza Palace is as big as Easy Burgers* (there's space for 30 guests in each), *Pizza Palace isn't as healthy as Easy Burgers*. With the weaker students, write the following on the board and encourage them to make *(not) as … as* sentences as a class before they write some sentences for themselves. If necessary, point out that *maths* is a singular noun.

Oranges		healthy/sweet		lemons.
Trains		comfortable/slow		buses.
Maths	is / are	easy/interesting		English.
Cats	(not) as	friendly/noisy	as	dogs.
My country		hot/big		the UK.
Ronaldo		young/famous		Marcus Rashford.

Answers

Students' own answers

Comparative adjectives

3 Write the following on the board and ask the students to complete the sentences with *Pizza Palace* or *Easy Burgers*:

______ *is cheaper than* ______.

(Pizza Palace; Easy Burgers)

______ *is more expensive than* ______.

(Easy Burgers; Pizza Palace)

Ask the class to say which words compare one thing with another (*cheaper than and more expensive than*). Point out that these are examples of comparative adjectives and ask the class to say how we form these (short adjective + *er* + *than* or *more* + long adjective + *than*). If appropriate, ask the students to underline all the examples of comparative adjectives in Vocabulary and Reading Exercise 4 page 68. Check that the students understand the meaning of the adjectives in the box by asking them to give you a sentence with each of them, e.g. *I can't go out because I'm* ***busy****. I've got a lot of homework.* Then, ask them to copy the table into their notebooks and write the adjectives and their comparatives in the correct column.

Answers

short adjectives				long adjectives
one syllable	one syllable ending in *e*	two syllables ending in *y*	one syllable ending in vowel consonant	use *more* + adjective
short – shorter colder harder longer newer taller	nice – nicer larger later	healthy – healthier busier dirtier funnier	big – bigger fatter hotter thinner	expensive – more expensive more beautiful more exciting more popular

» GRAMMAR REFERENCE AND PRACTICE ANSWER KEY TB PAGE 248

4 Point out that there is one mistake with the comparative form of the adjective or *as … as* in each sentence.

Answers

1 The tickets for adults cost £25, but the tickets for students **are cheaper**.
2 The concert is very **big** and has lots of famous singers.
3 This bag is not **as** big as my last one.
4 It's cold here so bring some **warm** clothes.
5 I **was** luckier than my friends.
6 My drink was not **as** expensive as yours.

5 As a class, brainstorm some things for each category first and encourage the students to choose two for each and write them down. Then, ask the students to write some comparative sentences. Encourage them to check that they have spelled the comparative form correctly by looking at the table in their notebook (see Exercise 3). In groups they check each other's sentences.

FAST FINISHERS

For this exercise fast finishers work together in a group. When they have checked each other's sentences, they choose three or four of their sentences and discuss whether they agree or disagree with each one.

Answers

Students' own answers

» GRAMMAR WORKSHEET UNIT 11

COOLER

Put the students into small groups. Tell them that they are going to organise an end of term party for the class and that some of them want to go to Pizza Palace and the others want to go to Easy Burgers. Encourage them to have a discussion using comparative sentences where possible. Begin as a class, e.g.:

Teacher: *I think we should go to Easy Burger because it is healthier.*

Student: *I disagree because Pizza Palace is cheaper and we don't have a lot of money.*

Teacher: *Yes, but the menu is longer and …*

GRAMMAR *as … as*

1 **Read what Nicky thinks and complete the sentences with *the same* or *different*.**

1 We use *as … as* to say that two things are ________.
2 We use *not as … as* to say that two things are ________.

2 **Compare the pairs of things using *as … as* or *not as … as*.**

0 oranges … lemons
Oranges are as healthy as lemons. / Lemons are not as sweet as oranges.
1 trains … buses — *comfortable / slow*
2 maths … English — *easy / interesting*
3 cats … dogs — *friendly / noisy*
4 your country … the UK — *hot / big*
5 Cristiano Ronaldo (born 1985) … Marcus Rashford (born 1997) — *young / famous*

Comparative adjectives

3 **Read the rules. Write the comparative forms of the adjectives in the box and then complete the table.**

beautiful busy cold dirty exciting fat funny hard hot large late long new popular tall thin

Short adjectives				Long adjectives
one syllable	one syllable ending in *e*	two syllables ending in *y*	one syllable ending in vowel consonant	
add *-er*	add *-r*	change *y* to *-ier*	double the last letter and add *-er*	use *more* + adjective
short – shorter	nice – nicer	healthy – healthier	big – bigger	expensive – more expensive

» GRAMMAR REFERENCE AND PRACTICE PAGE 148

4 **Correct the mistakes in the sentences.**

1 The tickets for adults cost £25, but the tickets for students are more cheaper.
2 The concert is very bigger and has lots of famous singers.
3 This bag is not big as my last one.
4 It's cold here so bring some warmer clothes.
5 I was more luckier than my friends.
6 My drink was not expensive as yours.

5 **Think of two different things for each category.**

1 sports *football, tennis*
2 foods
3 ways of travelling
4 jobs
5 things you wear
6 restaurants you go to

In pairs, write sentences to compare the two things. Use adjectives from Exercise 3 and any other adjectives you know. Work in groups and check each other's sentences.

Football is more exciting than tennis. Tennis is harder to learn than football.

READING

1 **Look at the title of the article and the photos. Where do you think the food in the photos comes from? Read the article quickly and compare your ideas with your partner's.**

STREET FOOD AROUND THE WORLD

1 In lots of countries around the world street food is very popular. In India, you can get different kinds of **curry** made with meat or with vegetables and lots of **chilli**. On the streets of Thailand, you can get fish soup, **omelettes**, rice or **noodles** and **grilled meat**. For dessert, you can have fried bananas, fresh fruit **pancakes** or Thai **sweets**. Mexico is famous for its wonderful tacos served with salsa made of green onions, cucumber and tomatoes. In Germany and Denmark, you can have meat served with bread and **fried onions**, and in France they serve lovely pancakes called crêpes. At the seaside in many countries, people eat **chips**, ice cream or **seafood**.

2 In many ways, street food is better than restaurant food. It's much cheaper, and you know it's fresh because you watch the chef prepare and cook it in front of you. It's also more fun to eat – you can use your hands and not worry about what the waiter thinks of you! People often buy and eat food outside at music festivals and at sports events like football matches. There are also street food festivals in many cities. People can try new food from around the world at these festivals.

82

2 **Read the article again and answer the questions.**

1. Which countries are famous for street food? What kind of street food do they have?
2. What three things does the writer like about street food?
3. At what sort of events do people eat street food?
4. What happens at street food festivals?

3 **Do you agree with the writer that street food is better than restaurant food? Why / Why not?**

TALKING POINTS

07 **Watch the video. Ask and answer the questions with a partner.**

Would you like to try any of the street food in the photos? Why / Why not?

Which street foods do you have in your country?

What's your favourite street food?

VOCABULARY Food

1 **Match the photos A–J to the words in paragraph 1 in the article.**

EP

A 
B 
C 
D 
E 
F 
G 
H 
I 
J 

READING

WARMER

Play the dice game. Write the following on the board:

1 football	1 interesting
2 pizza	2 enjoyable
3 dog	3 popular
4 English	4 easy
5 buses	5 expensive
6 trainers	6 exciting

Shake a dice (use a real dice or find an online dice program); this number gives you the noun (e.g. a 3 is *dog*) and then shake the dice again and this gives you an adjective (e.g. a 2 is *enjoyable*). The aim is to make a comparative sentence with these two words which makes sense, e.g. *Being with my dog is more enjoyable than doing homework.* Do a couple of examples as a class. Then, organise the students into groups to play. If you don't have enough dice for each group, ask the students to write the numbers 1–6 on small pieces of paper and the player takes a piece of paper twice from the pile.

1 If necessary, pre-teach *street food* by asking the students to look at the photos first and say what they think it is (*food you buy from stalls in the street and then eat in the street*). The students follow the instructions and then if they have written the new food and drink vocabulary in their notebooks in a menu (Vocabulary and Reading Exercise 1 page 68), encourage them to add the new vocabulary from this article.

Answers

Students' own answers

2 Encourage the students to try to answer these questions before they read the article again. Point out that they need to write their answers in full sentences.

Answers

1 India – curry made from meat or vegetables and lots of chilli; Thailand – fish soup, omelettes, rice or noodles and grilled meat; fried bananas, fresh fruit pancakes or Thai sweets; Mexico – tacos served with salsa made of green onions, cucumber and tomato; Germany and Denmark – meat served with bread and fried onions; France – pancakes called crêpes.
2 It's cheap, it's fresh and it's fun to eat.
3 music festivals and sports events, like football matches
4 People try new food from around the world.

82 The Reading text is recorded for students to listen and read.

3 Invite a brief class discussion here, but students will have more information about street food after watching the video in *Talking points* below.

Answers

Students' own answers

TALKING POINTS

07 After the students have completed the video activities, encourage them to take turns to ask and answer the questions in pairs. Point out that things like ice cream stalls, hot dogs and 'churros' (fried dough sold in Spain) are also examples of street food.

MIXED ABILITY

With a mixed ability class, pair up stronger students with weaker ones. Encourage the weaker ones to read out the questions and allow them to give shorter answers. Encourage stronger students to give fuller answers.

VOCABULARY Food

1 Ask the students to look at the food in the photos and try to name it before they match them to the words in blue in the text. Check that the students can pronounce these words correctly by asking them to listen and repeat.

Answers

A noodles B chilli C fried onions D omelette E seafood F pancakes G sweets H grilled meat I curry J chips

» VOCABULARY WORKSHEET UNIT 11

ə PRONUNCIATION /ʌ/ and /ɒ/

2 Tell the students to listen carefully for the difference between the two sounds as they listen and repeat the words.

83 **Audioscript**

The words are recorded for students to listen and repeat.

coffee, cup, horrible, lovely, much, mushroom, omelette, one, onion, want, what

84 **Answers**

The answers are recorded for students to check and then repeat.

/ʌ/: cup, lovely, much, mushroom, one, onion
/ɒ/: coffee, horrible, omelette, want, what

LISTENING

85 1 Ask the students to read the question and look at the notes, and ask 'What do you think the boy and his friend Nadia are talking about?' (*the details – dates, times, address and transport – of a street food festival*) Encourage them to predict what the boy wants Nadia to do before they listen.

Answers

He wants Nadia to go to a street food festival.

2 Read the dates, prices, numbers and times to the students and ask them to repeat. Ask them to write at least two dates, two prices, two numbers and two times each to test their partner.

Answers

Students' own answers

FAST FINISHERS

Fast finishers write some questions which require a price, date, time or number as the answer. When the others are ready, they ask the class their questions.

Then, organise the class into small groups, each with a fast finisher. The fast finishers ask their questions and the others answer.

85 3 Ask the students to read the notes first and say what kind of information is missing in each question (*1 dates, 2 website name, 3 price, 4 time, 5 name, 6 number*).

Remind them that they may hear two possible answers, but only one of them answers the question correctly.

Answers

1 June 2 foodzone 3 8.50 4 9.30 5 Green 6 74, 89

» AUDIOSCRIPT TB PAGE 272

SPEAKING

BACKGROUND INFORMATION

Paella is a regional rice dish from Valencia in the South of Spain. The word *paella* actually refers to the large flat pan that this dish is cooked in.

Aloo Tikki comes from North India, Pakistan and Bangladesh. It's made of potatoes, onions and spices.

Turkish **Shish** (or Seekh) **Kebab** are skewers of meat, normally lamb, which are grilled.

Yakisoba are Japanese stir-fried noodles with pork and vegetables.

Zapiekanka comes from Poland. It's half a baguette with mushrooms and melted cheese on top.

Ponchiki (or Donut Holes). These Russian Donuts are made with cottage or ricotta cheese, and fried in oil.

86 1 Pre-teach *seafood* by pointing to it in the photo. Ask the students to cover the conversation in Exercise 2 before they listen.

Answers

a small plate of paella

86 2 Encourage the students to try to complete the conversation before they listen again. With a weaker class, it may be necessary to play the recording for a third time and pause it after each answer so that the students can write down the missing word. Then, ask the students to practise the conversation with a partner.

Answers

1 Spain 2 rice 3 chicken 4 wonderful 5 much 6 6.00
7 are 8 enjoy

» AUDIOSCRIPT TB PAGE 272

3 Ask the class to look at the photos first; use the Background information (see above) to answer any questions about the food shown. Next, in A and B pairs, the students take turns to order food using the conversation in Exercise 2 as a model. They should turn to the relevant page at the back of the book (page 125 or 126) to answer questions about their partner's order.

Answers

Students' own answers

COOLER

Board race. Write two menu frameworks on the board:

<u>Team A</u>	<u>Team B</u>
MENU	MENU
Main course	Main course
Dessert	Dessert
Drinks	Drinks

Divide the class into two teams (A and B); each team member has a number. Say one of the food or drink words from this unit and a number, e.g. 'Chicken legs! Number 3!' The number 3 from each team comes to the board and writes the word in the correct space on their menu. Award one point for a correct answer with the correct spelling.

ə PRONUNCIATION | /ʌ/ and /ɒ/

83 **2** **Listen to the words in the box and repeat them. Listen to the sound of the underlined letters. Then put the words in the correct columns – /ʌ/ or /ɒ/.**

~~coffee~~ ~~cup~~ horrible
lovely much mushroom
omelette one onion
want what

/ʌ/	/ɒ/
cup	*coffee*

84 **Listen and check. Then repeat.**

LISTENING

85 **1** **Listen to a boy speaking to his friend Nadia. What does he want Nadia to do?**

2 **In pairs, practise saying these dates, prices, numbers and times. Write some more and test your partner.**

3rd July 28th June £8.50 £2.50
74 89 2 o'clock 11.30 am

85 **3** **Listen again and complete the notes.**

SPEAKING

86 **1** **Listen to a girl talking to a food seller at the street food festival. What does she order?**

2 **Complete the conversation from Exercise 1.**

Girl: Excuse me, what are you selling?
Seller: It's called paella. It's from [1] ________. It's made with seafood, [2] ________, vegetables and [3] ________.
Girl: Oh. What's it like?
Seller: It's [4] ________! Would you like to try some?
Girl: Yes, please. How [5] ________ is it?
Seller: It's £4.50 for a small plate or [6] £ ________ for a large plate.
Girl: I'll have a small plate, please.
Seller: That's £4.50, please.
Girl: Here you [7] ________.
Seller: Thanks. I hope you [8] ________ it!

86 **Listen again and check. Then in pairs, practise the conversation.**

3 **Work in pairs. Imagine you are at the street food festival. Student A, ask about and order the food in photos A–C. Student B, answer Student A's questions. Then swap roles and ask and answer about the food in photos D–F. Student A see page 126. Student B see page 125.**

12 THE LATEST TECHNOLOGY

ABOUT YOU

08 **Watch the video, then ask and answer the questions in pairs.**

What technology do you use?
How many hours a day do you spend online?
How often do you chat to your friends online?

VOCABULARY AND READING

Technology

1 **Match the photos A–L to the words in the box.**

EP

> e-reader fitness tracker games console
> headphones keyboard laptop mouse
> printer screen smartphone speaker tablet

87 **Listen and check. Then repeat.**

2 **In small groups, ask and answer these questions.**

1 How many things with screens are there in your home?
2 What are they, and whose are they?
3 How many printers/speakers/games consoles are there? Where are they in your house?
4 Have you got a smartphone? If so, what kind?

3 **Read the facts about technology. Write *K* if you *knew* the information already, *S* if the information *surprises* you and *W* if it *worries* you. Then compare your answers with a partner.**

4 **In pairs, ask and answer the questions.**

1 Which of the facts surprises you the most?
2 Which of the facts worries you the most?

DID YOU KNOW ...?

The most popular games console of all time is the PlayStation 2.

Having problems falling asleep? Looking at the screen on your smartphone, laptop or tablet before bed is one of the worst things you can do. The blue light keeps you awake.

South Korea has the fastest internet in the world. That means it's the best place to watch a movie on your smartphone!

The world's earliest mouse was made of wood and had two wheels. You moved it with your hand.

IMDb is probably the oldest website on the internet. It began in 1990 and now has information on about 3.5 million movies.

Your keyboard is one of the dirtiest things in your home. Clean it often and wash your hands before you start typing!

Today, almost all of us have a smartphone for calling people or sending texts, and even the smallest ones are more powerful than the computers used to send Apollo 11 to the moon.

The world's largest and widest screen can show pictures up to 12 metres high and 50 metres across!

88

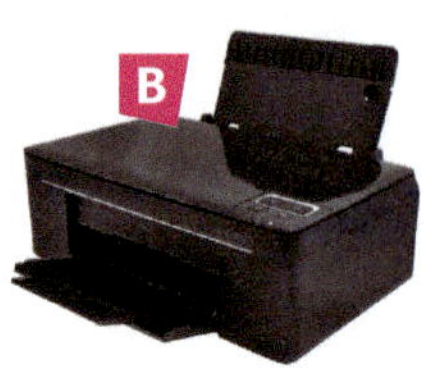

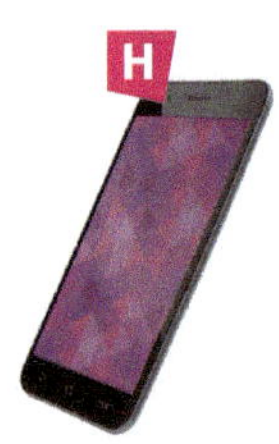

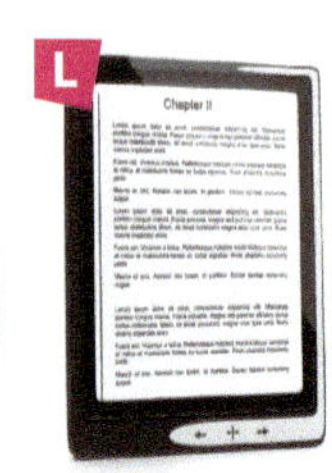

12 THE LATEST TECHNOLOGY

Unit Overview

TOPIC	Electronic gadgets
VOCABULARY AND READING	Technology Did you know ...?
GRAMMAR	Superlative adjectives
PRONUNCIATION	Stress in superlatives
READING	The history of computers
VOCABULARY	Computers and the internet
LISTENING	A conversation about a new computer
WRITING	An email to a friend
EXAM TASKS	Listening Part 3; Writing Part 6

Resources

GRAMMAR REFERENCE AND PRACTICE: SB page 149; TB page 248
WORKBOOK: pages 52–55
VIDEO AND VIDEO WORKSHEET: Technology
PHOTOCOPIABLE WORKSHEETS: Grammar worksheet Unit 12; Vocabulary worksheet Unit 12
TEST GENERATOR: Unit test 12

WARMER

Write the unit title *The latest technology* on the board and brainstorm a list of modern technology onto the board. Include *smartphone* and *laptop*. Ask the students to decide which of the things they could and couldn't live without. Encourage them to use comparative adjectives, e.g. *A smartphone is more useful than a laptop because you can phone people and take photos with it.*

ABOUT YOU

08 You can begin the class and introduce the topic of the unit by showing the video and asking students to complete the video worksheet. After they have completed the video activities, ask them to take turns to ask and answer the questions in pairs.

VOCABULARY AND READING

Technology

1 If you have brainstormed a list of modern technology onto the board (see Warmer), ask the students to match these words to the photos (A–L) before they look at the words in the box.

87 **Answers**

The answers are recorded for the students to check and then repeat.
A laptop B printer C tablet D keyboard E mouse
F speaker G screen H smartphone I fitness tracker
J games console K headphones L e-reader

2 Organise the students into small groups. Encourage them to give full answers and ask follow-up questions where appropriate by asking a pair of students to demonstrate this activity with you (for variety, encourage a less confident one to ask the questions), e.g.:

Student A: *How many things with screens are there in your home?*
Student B: *Um, I think we've got about seven.*
Teacher: *What are they? Where are they?*
Student B: *Well, we've got two TVs, one in the living room and ...*

Answers

Students' own answers

3 First, ask the students to read the sentences and find the words in Exercise 1. If necessary, pre-teach *surprise* and *worry* by asking the class to say things that surprise them (*e.g. a loud noise, a present or an exam they weren't expecting*) and things that worry them (*e.g. the news or a test*). Next, ask them to read each sentence more carefully on their own and write *K*, *S* or *W*. Point out that there are no right or wrong answers to this exercise and they can write more than one letter next to each fact. If necessary, do the first two as open class examples so everyone knows what they have to do. Then in pairs, encourage them to say why some of the facts surprise or worry them.

Answers

Students' own answers

88 The Reading text is recorded for students to listen and read.

4 Allow the students some time to decide on their own which fact surprises or worries them the most before they compare with a partner. Encourage them to ask the question *Which of the facts surprise you the most? And which worry you the most?* and to justify their answer using *because ...* .

Answers

Students' own answers

GRAMMAR Superlative adjectives

1 Books closed. Write the following on the board and ask the students to say what these are all examples of (superlative adjectives). If necessary, accept answers in the students' L1:

the fastest

the smallest mobile phone in the world

the most expensive

Books open. Ask the students to find the superlative adjectives in the article.

Answers

… is one of the worst things you can do.
it's the best place to watch a movie …
The world's earliest mouse …
IMDb is probably the oldest website …
Your keyboard is one of the dirtiest things in your home.
… even the smallest ones …
The world's largest and widest screen …

» GRAMMAR REFERENCE AND PRACTICE ANSWER KEY TB PAGE 248

2 Invite three volunteers to stand at the front. Ask the students to compare two of them, e.g. *Daniel is taller than Sonia.* Then, ask them to say something about the third student, e.g. *Jon is the tallest.* Next, ask the students to look at the superlative adjectives they found in the article and say how we form them. Point out that the spelling rules are the same as for comparative adjectives. Also point out that there are some irregular adjectives, e.g. *good, bad* and *far*.

Answers

Adjective	Comparative	Superlative
Regular		
big	bigger	the biggest
famous	more famous	the most famous
early	earlier	the earliest
thin	thinner	the thinnest
beautiful	more beautiful	the most beautiful
young	younger	the youngest
Irregular		
good	better	the best
bad	worse	the worst

3 Ask the students to think about how to write the superlative form of each adjective first. Check spelling by writing the answers on the board.

FAST FINISHERS

Fast finishers rewrite the sentences so that they are true for them. Then, in pairs, they ask and answer questions, e.g. *Who has got the best computer in your house?*

Answers

1 best 2 lightest 3 most popular 4 biggest 5 worst 6 oldest

4 Point out that there is one mistake with the superlative form in each of these sentences.

Answers

1 Football is the **most** famous game in the world.
2 The **best** time to come to my house is 5.30.
3 The **easiest** way to travel there is by bus.
4 Wear the **oldest** clothes you've got to do this job.
5 My room is the **biggest** in the house.

» GRAMMAR WORKSHEET UNIT 12

PRONUNCIATION Stress in superlatives

5 Play the recording and ask the students to repeat each superlative adjective. Point out that we don't stress *most*.

89

Answers

The answers are recorded for students to listen and repeat and then listen and check.

oO	oOo	oOoo	oooOo
the worst	the biggest the nicest the quickest	the cleverest the friendliest	the most exciting the most expensive

6 Pre-teach *size, weight* and *battery.* Point out that when we talk about sizes, the first number is height, the second number is width and the last number is thickness. Also point out that the phone with the most stars is the best.

MIXED ABILITY

Pair up a stronger student with a weaker student and ask them to match the adjectives to the categories first: *cheap/expensive* – price; *big/small* and *thick/thin* – size; *heavy/light* – weight. Ask them to write two sentences with each pair of adjective, one comparative and the other superlative, e.g.:

Cloud 7 is more expensive than Bluebird.

High Star is the cheapest.

Possible answers

Cloud 7 is the most expensive. High Star is the cheapest.
High Star is the smallest. Cloud 7 is the biggest.
High Star is the thinnest. Cloud 7 is the thickest.
High Star is the easiest to use.
Bluebird has the best camera. High Star has the worst camera.

7 Ask students to turn to page 124 and write at least one sentence about each of the things, i.e. a school subject, a computer game they play, etc. The sentences should be true for them. They can use the adjectives given or their own ideas.

Answers

Students' own answers

COOLER

Prepare some true and false sentences about yourself using superlative adjectives (for example *I'm the youngest teacher in this school. I've got the newest car in the school.*). Organise the students into teams. Read the sentences to the class and ask each team to write if they think each sentence is true or false. Next, the students ask you and other students questions to find out, e.g. *Who's the youngest teacher in this school? How old is your car?*

GRAMMAR Superlative adjectives

1 **Look at the examples of superlative adjectives. Read *Did you know … ?* on page 72 again and find all the superlatives.**

the fastest internet in the world   the most popular games console

Short adjectives				Long adjectives
one syllable	one syllable ending in *e*	two syllables ending in *y*	one syllable ending in vowel consonant	use *the most*
add *-est*	add *-st*	change y to *-iest*	double the last letter and add *-est*	use *the most* + adjective
quiet - quietest	nice - nicest	dirty - dirtiest	big - biggest	expensive – the most expensive

» GRAMMAR REFERENCE AND PRACTICE PAGE 149

2 **Read the rules above and complete the table with comparatives and superlatives.**

Adjective	Comparative	Superlative
Regular		
big	*bigger*	*the biggest*
famous	*more famous*	*the most famous*
early		
thin		
beautiful		
young		
Irregular		
good		
bad		

3 **Complete the sentences with the superlative form of the adjectives.**

1 My dad has the ________ (good) computer in our house.
2 My laptop is the ________ (light) one you can buy.
3 The ________ (popular) website among my friends is YouTube.
4 This smartphone has the ________ (big) screen of all the ones in the shop. Do you like it?
5 The ________ (bad) thing about my computer is the mouse. It doesn't work properly.
6 My mum's phone is the ________ (old) one in our family.

4 **Correct the mistakes in the sentences.**

1 Football is the famous game in the world.
2 The better time to come to my house is 5.30.
3 The easier way to travel there is by bus.
4 Wear the older clothes you've got to do this job.
5 My room is the bigger in the house.

ə PRONUNCIATION Stress in superlatives

89 **5** **Listen and repeat the words. Then put them into the correct column of the table.**

the biggest   the cleverest
the friendliest   the most exciting
the most expensive   the nicest
the quickest   the worst

oO	oOo	oOoo	oooOo
	the biggest		

89 **Listen again and check.**

6 **Look at the three mobile phones. In pairs, compare them. Use some of the adjectives in the box.**

big/small   cheap/expensive   good/bad
heavy/light   thick/thin

A: *The High Star's battery is better than the Cloud 7's battery.*
B: *The Bluebird's battery is the worst.*

	 High Star	 Bluebird	 Cloud 7
Price	£299	£355	£450
Size	115 x 58 x 9 mm	116 x 61 x 12 mm	135 x 67 x 17 mm
Weight	130 g	142 g	155 g
Easy to use	★★★★	★★★	★
Camera	★★	★★★★	★★★
Battery	★★	★	★★★

7 » **Work with a partner. Go to page 124.**

The history OF COMPUTERS

205BCE

The Antikythera Mechanism

In 1900, a group of people diving near the Greek island of Antikythera found this machine on the sea floor. For many years, no one understood what it was or how it worked. Scientists now say it was used to find out the positions of the sun, moon and stars. Many people call it the world's earliest 'computer'.

around 2,700 BCE to today

The abacus

People still use abacuses today in many parts of the world, especially to teach maths to children. Of course, they are very different from modern computers, but the idea is the same – to answer difficult maths questions much more quickly than a human can.

1791–1871 and 1815–1852

Charles Babbage and Ada Lovelace

The modern computer was Charles Babbage's idea. The machine he wanted to build, called a 'difference engine', was special because it had all the parts that a modern computer has. It could save information and was also a kind of printer. Ada Lovelace was the first computer programmer. She had the idea for 'software' – a way of telling a computer to do different things.

90

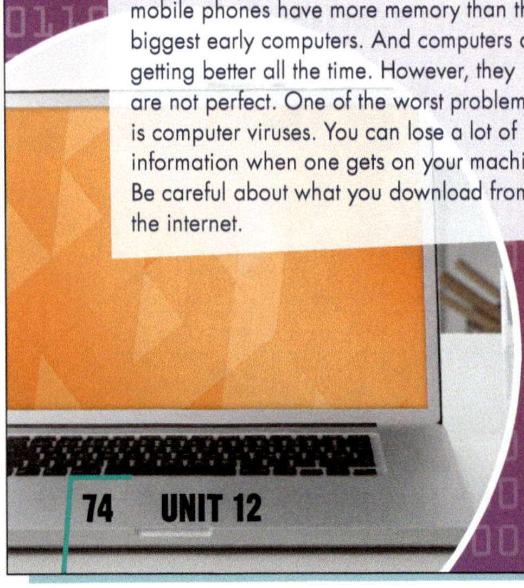

1940s

Alan Turing

Alan Turing wasn't well known when he was alive, but he's now one of the most famous scientists of the 20th century. His ideas on computer science changed the world. He worked on the first digital computer – it was called Colossus, weighed 30 tonnes, and was as big as a large living room.

From the 1950s

Modern computers

From the 1950s, computers got smaller, faster and cheaper. Today, the smallest mobile phones have more memory than the biggest early computers. And computers are getting better all the time. However, they are not perfect. One of the worst problems is computer viruses. You can lose a lot of information when one gets on your machine. Be careful about what you download from the internet.

READING

1 **Do you know the names of any early computers? Read the article once and check your ideas.**

2 **Complete the sentences with one or two words from the article.**

1 Some children use an abacus to learn how to do ________.
2 Charles Babbage's computer had several different ________.
3 The first person to program a computer was ________.
4 Colossus was as big as a ________.
5 Modern ________ are small but can do more than the biggest computers of the past.

TALKING POINTS

Computers can now do a lot of clever things. But are they more intelligent than us? Why / Why not?

74 UNIT 12

READING

WARMER

Challenge the students in small groups to draw a picture of a computer with its accessories (mouse, keyboard, screen, printer, etc.) and to label as many of the different parts as they can, using some of the words from Vocabulary and Reading Exercise 1 page 72, as well as their own ideas. If appropriate, award points for correct words and spelling. Then, invite a brief class discussion on what they know about the history of computers by asking: 'When was the computer invented?' 'Who invented it?' 'What was the first computer like?' 'What is one of the worst things about modern computers?'

1 First, ask the students to look at the photos and describe what they can see in each one. Ask them to find the photo of the first computer (the photo of Colossus is above the heading *Alan Turing*). Ask them if they know anything about it, e.g. do they know its name? Then, encourage the students to read the article once. If you have asked the questions in the Warmer, ask them to find the answers to these questions too (answers to questions in the Warmer: *1940s, Alan Turing, it weighed 30 tonnes and it was the size of a large living room, one of the worst things about modern computers are viruses*).

MIXED ABILITY

Encourage stronger students to do Exercises 1 and 2 at their own pace. There is a fast finisher activity after Exercise 2. With very weak students, write *Who invented the first computer?* and *What was it like?* on the board. Ask them to read the paragraph about Alan Turing and write down their answers to these two questions. Then, pair them up with a stronger student who has read the complete article and can help them with the answers in Exercise 2.

Answers

Abacus and Antikythera Mechanism. From reading, the students should find *difference engine* and Colossus.

2 Encourage the students to try to complete the sentences before they read the article again. Point out that they should write one or two words only.

FAST FINISHERS

Fast finishers work in pairs and write some quiz questions about the information in the text. When the others are ready, organise them into teams. The fast finishers come to the front of the class and ask the questions. If appropriate, award points for correct answers.

Answers

1 maths 2 parts 3 Ada Lovelace 4 living room
5 mobile phones

90 The Reading text is recorded for students to listen and read.

TALKING POINTS

As a class, brainstorm a list of the 'clever things' a computer can do (*solve problems, calculate answers, store and receive enormous amounts of data, display information, compare information, control other machines, etc.*) and then invite a class discussion on whether they are more intelligent than us (see Background information below).

BACKGROUND INFORMATION

Artificial Intelligence

In 2011, Watson, a 'question-answering' computer system, won the American quiz show *Jeopardy*. Watson can understand natural language (or human speech), process it and look for the answer within its own memory. However, unlike humans or animals, computers are still not completely successful at making intelligent or emotional decisions where they adjust their behaviour according to experience. For example when a human realises that their neighbour's dog bites, they take a different route to school or work, but a computer cannot successfully do this. In 1955, John McCarthy introduced the term *Artificial Intelligence* (AI) to distinguish the intelligence of a machine from *Natural Intelligence*, the intelligence of humans and animals. Work in this field is rapidly developing and in our lifetime, we may see robots as friends who can understand human emotions, develop their own emotions and also hold meaningful conversations.

VOCABULARY Computers and the internet

1 Ask the students to find the words in the box in the article, say if they are adjectives, verbs or nouns, and try to work out the meaning from context before matching them to the definition. Then, check pronunciation by asking them to listen and repeat.

Answers

1 machine 2 memory 3 virus 4 save 5 digital 6 download 7 software

2 Ask the students to look at the nouns first and try to think of a suitable verb for each one before they look at the verbs on the left-hand side.

Possible answers

buy clothes, games, music, videos
chat online
download games, music, videos
go online
play games, music
surf the internet, websites
visit websites
watch videos
Students' own answers

3 If necessary, pre-teach *survey*: either show an online survey program or ask what we call a list of questions which we use to find out people's opinions or habits. Encourage the students to work in pairs to write two new questions and to use some of the verb + nouns in Exercise 2. Next, ask the students to stand up, ask at least five other students and make a note of their answers.

Answers

Students' own answers

4 Brainstorm some useful expressions for this onto the board, e.g.:

All / Most / Some / A few members of the class …

Everybody / Some / Nobody …

A half / third / quarter of the class …

Ask the students to work in small groups to do this. They should share their answers first and then write some sentences together.

Answers

Students' own answers

» VOCABULARY WORKSHEET UNIT 12

LISTENING

91 1 **A2 Key for Schools Listening Part 3.**

In this part of the exam, students listen to a conversation and answer five multiple-choice questions. They should read the questions before they listen and underline the key words. First, tell the students to read question 0 and the options A, B, C and underline the key words, i.e. <u>When</u> and <u>new computer</u>. Play the first part of the recording only. Point out that in this part of the test, the students may hear all the words in all three options (A–C), but only one will answer the question correctly.

Answers

A is the right answer
B is when Dad agreed to buy it
C is when his old one broke

91 2 Ask the students to underline the key words in the questions (1–5) first, making sure that they underline key words only and not the whole question or sentence. Point out that on the recording the students might not hear exactly the same word as in the options A, B, C, but a different word which has a similar meaning. For example, in **1**, the answer is A *a website*, but on the recording they will hear *bought it online*. When checking the answers, encourage the students to say why the other two answers are wrong. If necessary, play the recording for a third time.

Answers

1 A 2 B 3 A 4 C 5 C

» AUDIOSCRIPT TB PAGE 272

WRITING

PREPARE TO WRITE
An email

GET READY When the students have read the email, ask 'Who wrote the email?' 'Who to?' 'Why did he write it?'

Answers

Morgan wants some information about his friend's computer.

PLAN Ask the students to underline the three questions first and, in small groups, brainstorm possible answers.

Possible answers

1 when – last weekend
2 cost – £200
3 best thing – really fast, great screen

WRITE **A2 Key for Schools Writing Part 6.**

In this part of the exam, students have to write a communicative note or email of 25 words or more. They are given three pieces of information which they must include. Remind the students that they should begin and end the email with a suitable expression and that they must answer all three of Morgan's questions.

IMPROVE Ask the students to check that the email begins and ends with a suitable expression, that it answers all three questions and that there are at least 25 words.

Model answer

Hi Morgan,
I got my new computer last weekend. It was only £200. I love it because it's really fast and has a great screen.
Best wishes,
Tomas

COOLER

Play Coffee Pot. Read out some sentences using the verb and nouns from Vocabulary Exercise 2 page 74 but instead of saying the verb, say 'coffee pot', e.g. *I often <u>coffee pot</u> to friends online*. Invite students to repeat your sentence with the correct verb (*chat*).

VOCABULARY Computers and the internet

1 EP **Look at the article again and find the words in the box. Match them to the definitions.**

digital download machine memory save software virus

1 This has moving parts and helps humans to do work.
2 This is a part of a computer – it holds information.
3 This is a dangerous computer program.
4 You do this to make sure the computer keeps your work.
5 This describes cameras, computers and clocks that record information as 0s or 1s.
6 This means to copy information from the internet onto your computer.
7 This is all the programs that make a computer do different things.

2 EP **Match the verbs to the nouns. Then make sentences.**

buy	friends
chat	clothes
download	games
go	the internet
play	music
surf	online
visit	videos
watch	websites

I often chat online with my cousins.

3 Read the survey. Choose three or four questions and write two more of your own. Walk around the class asking your questions.

COMPUTER SURVEY

- What sort of things do you download from the internet?
- Do you know how to stop a virus from getting onto your computer?
- How much memory has your phone got? Is it enough?
- Do you ever forget to save your work?
- How often do you chat to friends online?

4 Write some sentences about what you found out.

Everybody downloads music and half the class downloads games from the internet.
Four people sometimes forget to save their work.
Most people chat to friends online every day.

LISTENING

91 **1 Listen to and read the first part of the conversation and look at Question 0. Which is the correct answer: A, B or C? Why are the other two answers wrong?**

Ella: Nice new laptop Andy! When did you get it?
Andy: Yesterday. My old one broke a month ago, and last week Dad agreed to buy me this.

0 When did Andy get his new computer?
A yesterday **B** last week **C** a month ago

91 **2 Listen to the whole conversation. For each question, choose the correct answer.**

1 Andy's dad bought the computer from
A a website. **B** a shop. **C** a friend.
2 How much did it cost?
A £150 **B** £250 **C** £2,000
3 What does Andy want to buy for the computer?
A a camera **B** a mouse **C** a printer
4 Andy doesn't use his computer to
A do homework. **B** chat to friends.
C play games.
5 What does Andy like most about the computer?
A the keyboard **B** the screen **C** the speakers

91 **In pairs, compare your answers. Then listen again and check your answers.**

WRITING

PREPARE TO WRITE

An email

GET READY Read the email from your friend Morgan. Why did Morgan write the email?

My laptop broke yesterday, and I need to get a new one. Tell me about your new computer. When did you get it? How much did it cost? What's the best thing about it?

Best wishes,
Morgan

PLAN Think of an answer to each of Morgan's questions.

WRITE Write an email to Morgan with answers to all his questions. Begin your email with *Hi Morgan*, or *Dear Morgan*, and end it with *See you soon.* or *Best wishes*, and your name. Write 25 words or more.

IMPROVE In pairs, read your email and your partner's. Check that all three questions have an answer. Give your partner two ideas to make their email better. Use your partner's advice and rewrite your email.

LIFE SKILLS ICT LITERACY

WRITING A BLOG

LIFE SKILLS
Writing a blog
A blog can help you:
- improve your computer skills
- organise your ideas
- share opinions and views with other people.

1 **Look at the sentences and answer the questions.**

Great minds think alike.

We can learn a lot sharing our ideas, opinions and views.

There's a blog for everyone.

1 What do you think the sentences mean?
2 Do you agree with the sentences? Why? / Why not?
3 Do you have a blog? Do you know any bloggers?

2 **Look at the topics for blogs. Choose two topics you think are interesting. Share your ideas with a partner.**

activities animals fashion food life experiences music special days and holidays sports travel

3 **Read the text quickly. Complete the article with the headings in the box. Is it easy to start a blog?**

A Stay safe!
B Think about your readers
C Have one day for writing

4 **Answer the questions.**

1 What do you need to choose first?
2 Who do you need to think about?
3 What do platforms give you?
4 Before you put a blog post online, who looks at it?
5 Do you need to write posts every day?
6 What are some things we should not post online?

5 **Complete the sentences with the highlighted words from the text. There are some letters to help you.**

1 I __ o __ __ o __ a blog about sports.
2 Choose a topic you like and you find i __ __ e __ e __ __ i __ __.
3 To start a blog, you need to choose a p __ a __ __ o __ __.
4 It is a good idea to write a __ o __ __ once a week.
5 You need to decide on your topic and __ e __ i __ __, and think about your readers.
6 You need to be careful online. It is not safe to post p __ __ s __ __ a __ __ e __ __ i __ __ like your address or phone number.

TALKING POINTS
Do you think it's a good idea to start a blog? Why? / Why not?
Do you prefer reading a blog or reading a book?

93 **6** **Listen to Katie and David talking about blogs. Choose the correct answers to complete the sentences.**

1 They are at
a Katie's house.
b David's house.
c school.

2 Katie's blog is on
a dogs.
b cats.
c music.

93 **7** **Listen again. Are the sentences right (✓) or wrong (✗)?**

1 Katie's mum is at home.
2 Katie is in the living room.
3 Katie is studying for an exam.
4 Katie thinks starting a blog is difficult.
5 Katie likes music.
6 Katie wants to write a post about David's pets.

8 **Match the two halves of the sentences.**

USEFUL LANGUAGE
1 You're good at …
2 It isn't safe to …
3 Is your blog …
4 Ask people …
5 Do you want a lot of people …

a about music?
b to follow your blog?
c before you put photos of them online.
d put personal information online.
e using computers.

LIFE SKILLS

Learning Objectives

- The students learn how to write a blog.
- In the project stage, they write and design a blog post and share it with other students.

Vocabulary

follow interesting platform post design personal details

BACKGROUND INFORMATION

Weblogs, blogs or online journals first appeared in 1994. There are now over 1.5 billion blogs on the internet; most of them are in English. Most bloggers are between the ages of 21 and 35. Two popular blogging platforms are Wordpress and Blogger. An edublog is a blog which is used for educational purposes. The Edublog Awards give annual prizes to winners in categories including class, student and teacher blogs.

WARMER

Write *What can we use a computer for?* on the board and challenge the students in small groups to write a list, e.g. *to surf the internet, to write an email, to download films or music, to find information, to present information*. If appropriate, award points to the teams for their ideas and write a list on the board. Make sure you include *write a blog* on the list. Next, ask the students in their groups to take turns to ask and answer: *What do you use a computer for? What would you like to learn to do on a computer? Why?*

LIFE SKILLS

Writing a blog

Draw students' attention to the unit title *Writing a blog* and ask 'Why do people write blogs?' 'How can writing a blog help you?' and encourage a brief class discussion. Next, ask the students to read the *Life skills* box and compare their ideas.

1 In pairs, ask the students to ask and answer the questions about the sentences.

Answers

Students' own answers

2 First, ask the students to look at the third sentence again *There's a blog for everyone* and ask *What sort of blog would you like to read?* Encourage the students to think about their own answer and then share their ideas with their partner. Then, encourage them to look at the topics and choose two from the list.

Answers

Students' own answers

3 Ask the class to read the text title and the introduction and ask 'What is the text about?' 'Why do you think your parents need to agree?' (see information at the bottom of the article). Next, ask them to read the rest of the text and try to think of a suitable heading for paragraphs 2, 5 and 6 before they look at the words in the box. Encourage them to compare their answers with a partner and then talk together about whether it is easy to start a blog.

92

Answers

The Reading text is recorded for students to listen, read and check their answers.

2 B 5 C 6 A

4 Ask the students in pairs to try to answer the questions first before they read the text again.

Answers

1 a topic 2 your readers 3 a way to start a blog 4 friends and family 5 no, you don't 6 personal information (address, telephone number); some people don't want you to use their photos

5 If necessary, point out that there is one word missing in sentences 1–5 and two words in sentence 6. Some of the letters are given in these missing words and there is a space for every missing letter.

FAST FINISHERS

Encourage fast finishers in pairs to take turns to say one of the headings from the text and ask their partner to say as much as they can remember about that paragraph, e.g.:

Student A: *Tell me about 'Choose a topic'.*

Student B: *First, you have to choose your topic. You need to feel happy about it and …*

Answers

1 follow 2 interesting 3 platform 4 post 5 design 6 personal details

TALKING POINTS

Encourage the students to take turns to ask and answer these questions in small groups. Also encourage them to talk about other things they like to read (comics, magazines, etc.) and also things they like to write (messages or posts on social media, etc.).

93

6 Ask the students to read through the sentences and their options before they listen.

MIXED ABILITY

For Exercises 6 and 7, pair up a stronger student with a weaker student. After the students have listened to the recording for each exercise, ask the stronger student to share their answers and say why they think their answer is correct.

Answers

1 a 2 b

Continued on page 150.

93 **7** In pairs, encourage the students to try to say if the sentences are right or wrong before they listen again. Encourage stronger students to correct the wrong sentences.

Answers

1 ✓ 2 ✓ 3 × She is working on her blog. 4 × She thinks it is easy. 5 ✓ 6 × The blog is on cats and David doesn't have a cat, just a dog and a hamster.

» **AUDIOSCRIPT TB PAGES 272–273**

8 Point out that all these sentences come from the recording. If time allows, play the recording again so that the students can check their answers.

Answers

1 e 2 d 3 a 4 c 5 b

PROJECT ***Writing a blog***

Ask the class to read the instructions in bold and ask 'What do you need to do for this project?' Either for homework, or during classtime, ask the students to go online and find at least two blogs that a) they find interesting and b) they like the design of. Organise the students into small groups (maximum four students) and ask them to talk about the blogs they found which they like and why.

Encourage the groups to choose a blog topic and also to think about the design. Remind them that they need to reach an agreement and encourage them to use the useful language in Life skills page 32. Next, encourage them to write two short blog posts (the group could divide into pairs, with each pair writing a post each). Then, ask them to decide together how they will present their two posts.

Reorganise the students so that they are working with students in other groups. Encourage them to share their ideas, give feedback and make suggestions for improvement.

PROJECT EXTENSION

Set up a student blog challenge where each student (or pair of students) needs to set up their own blog for six weeks, write at least four posts and write comments on at least four of their classmates' blogs. At the end of six weeks, ask the students to evaluate their own work by answering some questions, for example:

- Was it easy to create your own blog?
- How many posts did you write? What were they about?
- How many other blogs did you visit? Did you leave comments?
- How could you improve your blog?
- Would you like to continue with your blog?

COOLER

Checking the blog for mistakes: A grammar auction

Choose ten sentences from the students' blog posts; five with mistakes (spelling, punctuation, grammar, etc.) and five very good sentences. Write them on the board. Organise the students into small teams who decide which sentences are correct and also find and correct the mistakes in the incorrect ones.

Next, tell each team you are going to 'sell' the sentences to the group who offers you the most points (or money if appropriate). Give each team 100 points (or €1,000). Hold a sentence auction where you ask each team to make a bid for each sentence; however, they should only bid for the correct sentences. The winner is the team with the most correct sentences. If there is a draw between teams, the team with the most points (or money) left is the winner.

At the end of the activity, correct the mistakes in the incorrect sentences as a class. Point out that the sentences are from the class's blog posts and encourage them to always check their work before they post anything on their blogs.

DO YOU WANT TO START A BLOG?

Do you read or follow any blogs? What topics do you like to read about?

How about you? Have you got a blog? Why not? Now is a good time to start if your parents agree!

Follow these quick and easy steps to start your own blog.

92

1 Choose a topic for your blog

The first thing you need to do is choose a topic. What do you want to blog about? Your favourite sport, music or video games? Choose a topic you feel happy to talk about and find interesting. You've got a topic? Now choose a title and a design for your blog.

2 ....

Who's going to read your blog? Is your blog for your friends and family? Is it on a special topic you and your friends like? What is interesting about it?

3 Decide on a platform

There are different free platforms to start your blog. Most platforms give easy instructions on how to start. Some popular platforms are Blogger, Medium and WordPress. Take a look and decide!

4 Write a blog post

It can sometimes be difficult to write your first blog post. It's a good plan to share your ideas with close friends and family before you put your post online. Don't worry if you don't like what you put online – you can always change it later. Remember, make sure people let you use their photos or information.

5 ....

At the beginning, you can choose a day of the week to write your blog posts. It's important to write a post every week.

6 ....

Blogs can be fun, but never put your personal details online. Never write your address or telephone number. Remember, you need to stay safe online.

Don't forget, **always** check with your parents before starting a blog. Parents can help young people under the age of 13 to set up a blog.

PROJECT Writing a blog

In small groups, write and design a blog post:

- Choose a blog topic and think about the design for the blog.
- Write two short blog posts about the topic.
- Decide what to include with each of the posts (a photo and a link? a video?)
- Look at the design of some other blogs on a platform.
- Design how you think the posts would look on a platform.
- Share your ideas for posts and design with another group.

REVIEW 3 UNITS 9–12

VOCABULARY

1 **Complete the sentences with the words in the box.**

bright	~~digital~~	discount
download	keyboard	pocket
tablet	wallet	wool

0 I really like that new *digital* camera.
1 This computer was £500 last week. Now it's £425. That's a big ________.
2 My jumper's made of ________. It's really warm!
3 My dad gave me a ________ for my birthday. And he put £20 in it!
4 I want to buy a new coat. I like that one, but it's only got one ________.
5 The trainers are all too ________. I prefer pale colours.
6 The ________ on that new computer is very small. It's difficult to see the letters.
7 Most people ________ music from the internet these days. They don't buy CDs or records.
8 At my new school, all the students have a ________ or a laptop. They don't have books.

2 **Put the words in the correct column.**

boots cap cola cream e-reader gloves grapes laptop lemonade mineral water memory mouse mushroom noodles omelette scarf screen socks software speaker suit swimming costume tie virus

Food and drink	Clothes	Technology

3 **Use the pictures to write sentences with *for*.**

I played tennis with my friend for two hours yesterday.

GRAMMAR

1 **Choose the correct words to complete the sentences.**

1 I bought a new T-shirt because *my* / *mine* is old.
2 Do you have *any* / *a* present for me?
3 I love my room because it's *bigger* / *biggest* than my old room.
4 You can find different bands and the *better* / *best* music at the festival.

Correct the mistakes in the sentences.

5 You can wear yours sports clothes.
6 I bought a new jeans and a shirt.
7 I bought them because they were more cheap – they cost only £5 each!
8 It was the great holiday ever.

REVIEW 3 UNITS 9–12

Overview

VOCABULARY	Clothes; Materials; Buying and selling; Phrases with *for*; Food; Technology; Computers and the internet
GRAMMAR	Pronouns and determiners; *some*, *any*, *a lot of*, *a few*, *a bit of*; *as … as*; Comparative adjectives; Superlative adjectives
READING	A short text about Tom and his sisters
LISTENING	Five short monologues or dialogues
SPEAKING	Asking questions; talking about your favourite things
EXAM TASKS	Listening Part 4; Speaking Part 1 Phase 2

Resources

PHOTOCOPIABLE WORKSHEETS: Grammar worksheets Units 9–12; Vocabulary worksheets Units 9–12; Review Game Units 9–12; Literature worksheet; Speaking worksheet; Writing worksheet

WARMER

Write the following on the board:

Unit 9:	scarf	boots	keyboard	cap
Unit 10:	bill	pancakes	cash	receipt
Unit 11:	tie	mushroom	grapes	salad
Unit 12:	printer	screen	tablet	purse

Ask the students 'Which word does not belong to the unit?' (*keyboard*, *pancakes*, *tie*, *purse*) Next, ask 'What words did we study in each unit?' (*9 clothes and materials*, *10 buying and selling*, *11 food*, *12 technology*) In pairs, ask the students to look at their books or notes and write four words for each unit (9–12) where one word does not belong. Then, ask each student to find a new partner. They take turns to read out their words and say which word does not belong to the unit.

VOCABULARY

1 If you did the Warmer activity, ask the students to look at the words in the box and say which unit each word belongs to. Then, ask them to complete the sentences.

Answers

1 discount 2 wool 3 wallet 4 pocket 5 bright 6 keyboard 7 download 8 tablet

2 Encourage the students to do this activity in pairs by asking and answering questions, e.g. *Where does 'boots' go? It goes with Clothes.* Then, encourage the students to check their ideas with the words in the units or with their notebooks before giving them the answer.

Answers

Food and drink: cola, cream, grapes, lemonade, mineral water, mushroom, noodles, omelette
Clothes: boots, cap, gloves, scarf, socks, suit, swimming costume, tie
Technology: e-reader, laptop, memory, mouse, screen, software, speaker, virus

3 Ask the students to first look at Vocabulary Phrases with *for* Exercise 1 on page 65 again to remind themselves of the expressions. Next, ask them to look at the pictures, read the example and find the phrase with *for*. Then, ask them to look at the four pictures and try to think of a sentence for each one.

Possible answers

1 I bought these for 30 euros.
2 I use my laptop for playing games.
3 He got a mobile phone for his birthday.
4 She got a prize for her painting.

MIXED ABILITY

With very weak students, write the answers on the board in a different order to the pictures. Ask the students to find the phrase with *for* in each one and then ask them to match them to the pictures. Rub the sentences off the board and ask the students to write a sentence for at least two pictures for themselves.

GRAMMAR

1 For questions 1–4, encourage the students to read the complete sentence first before they choose the correct answer. For questions 5–8, point out that there is one mistake in each sentence.

Answers

1 mine
2 a
3 bigger
4 best
5 You can wear **your** sports clothes.
6 I bought **some** new jeans and a shirt.
7 I bought them because they were **cheap** / **cheaper**; they cost only £5 each!
8 It was the **greatest** holiday ever.

2 First, ask the students to look at the noun after the space in each question. Then, encourage them to say whether it is countable or uncountable before they complete the sentences.

Answers

1 a bit of 2 a few 3 a few 4 a bit of 5 A few 6 a bit of
7 a bit of 8 a few

3 Ask the students to read the two examples first. Then, ask them to read each sentence and say whether it is a comparative or superlative before they complete it. During the feedback stage, make sure that the students spell the adjective correctly.

FAST FINISHERS

Ask fast finishers to work through this exercise at their own pace and check their answers. Next, ask them to do the Reading Exercise 1, check their answers and then ask them to write their own puzzle text using comparatives. When the others have finished the Reading exercise, ask the fast finishers to read out their puzzle text for the others to solve.

Answers

1 busier than 2 the best 3 the most popular
4 funnier than 5 thinner than 6 the worst
7 the most comfortable 8 cleverer than

READING

1 If the students need some help, encourage them to read the text quickly and find the youngest person first (Alice) and then work out the age of the next youngest (Beth), then the next (Tom) and finally the oldest (Mia). It might help if the students draw a picture of Tom and his family in age order.

Answers

Tom is 10; Beth is 7; Mia is 14

LISTENING

94 1 **A2 Key for Schools Listening Part 4.**

In this part of the exam, the students listen to five separate short monologues or dialogues and choose the correct answer (A–C) for each one. They need to identify the topic or main message. The students listen to each monologue or dialogue twice.

With a stronger class, do the exercise like an exam, i.e. the students listen to each monologue or dialogue twice and complete the answers. Then, ask them to say why the other options are incorrect.

Answers

1 C 2 B 3 A 4 B 5 A

» AUDIOSCRIPT TB PAGE 273

SPEAKING

1 **A2 Key for Schools Speaking Part 1 Phase 2.**

In this part of the exam, both candidates are asked some questions about their interests. Then, candidates are then asked questions on two different topics, e.g. fashion, shopping, hobbies, etc.

With a weaker class, help the students by giving them the first word or words of each question. Then, remind them to give full answers when they ask and answer the questions in pairs.

Answers

1 What are your favourite clothes?
2 Where do you like to go shopping?
3 What food do you like to eat?
4 How often do you use your smartphone?

2 In this part of the exam, the examiner will ask each candidate in turn two questions related to the topic, e.g. *What do you do in the evenings?* or *What activities do you do at the weekend?* One of the candidates is then asked another question like *Please tell me something about what you like doing at the weekend* and encouraged to give a longer answer. The examiner then repeats this phase with another topic (e.g. school, sports) and the other candidate is asked the second extended response question.

First, encourage the students to look back at Units 9–12 and make some notes about their favourite things before they speak to their partner.

Answers

Students' own answers

COOLER

Tell the students that a good way to learn new words and expressions is by using them. Ask the students in small groups of three or four to look at the words in the box in Vocabulary Exercise 2 on page 78 again and either write or draw a picture of each one on a small piece of paper (one piece per word). Next, ask them to put the pieces of paper on the table in two piles face down. The students take turns to turn over the top words and try to make a sentence comparing them. For example: *boots* and *cola. Boots are more expensive than cola but when I'm thirsty, cola is more useful than boots.* Point out that the students will need to be creative with their sentences.

2 Complete the sentences with *a bit of* or *a few.*

0 Would you like *a bit of* chocolate?
1 I wrote the number down on ________ paper and now I can't find it.
2 We saw ________ people on the train today.
3 There are ________ advertisements in the newspaper.
4 That cake looks nice. Can I have ________ it please?
5 ________ companies have only online shopping.
6 That pizza smells good. I want to try ________ it. Don't you?
7 I've got ________ time. I can help you with your project.
8 He was sick and he stayed in bed for ________ days.

3 Complete the sentences with the comparative or superlative form of the adjectives in brackets.

0 Oranges are *sweeter than* lemons. (sweet)
00 All these books are old but this one is *the oldest*. (old)
1 You are always ________ me! (busy)
2 All the students' work is good today, but yours is ________. (good)
3 Football is ________ sport in the UK. (popular)
4 I liked your story. It was ________ mine. (funny)
5 Our cat is ________ it was two years ago. (thin)
6 That café has ________ hot chocolate in town. (bad)
7 The chairs in this classroom are ________ (comfortable) in the school.
8 The new smartphones are ________ the old ones. (clever)

READING

1 Read the text and answer the question.

Tom has got three sisters – Beth, Mia and Alice. Beth is three years younger than Tom and seven years younger than Mia. Alice is the youngest. She's six years old. She's one year younger than Beth.

How old are Tom, Beth and Mia?

LISTENING

94 1 For each question, choose the correct answer.

1 Listen to two friends talking together in a shop. Why does Ruby want to buy the sunglasses?
A She's happy with the price.
B She likes the bright colour.
C They're the right size.

2 Listen to a man and a girl talking about what they want to eat. Where are they?
A in a café
B at a food festival
C in a supermarket

3 Listen to a boy talking to a girl about his laptop. What does the girl offer to do?
A lend him a laptop
B take his laptop to the repair shop
C return a laptop she borrowed

4 Listen to a message in a shopping centre. What change do customers need to know about?
A New discounts are available.
B There is a later closing time.
C New stores are opening soon.

5 Listen to a girl talking about a party. What did she like about it?
A the food
B the music
C the party room

SPEAKING

1 Put the words in order to make questions.

1 favourite / what / are / clothes / your / ?
2 where / like / you / do / shopping / go / to / ?
3 food /do / eat / you / what / to / like / ?
4 use / your / often / you / do / how / smartphone / ?

In pairs, ask and answer the questions. Take turns to speak.

2 In pairs, talk about some of your favourite things. Take turns to speak.

Tell me about some of your favourite things.

I've got a favourite pair of jeans. I like them very much because …

13 HEALTHY BODIES

ABOUT YOU

09 **Watch the video. Then ask and answer the questions in pairs.**

What was your last health problem?
When did it happen?
What did you do?

VOCABULARY AND LISTENING

Illness

1 Match the sentences to the photos.

EP
1 I've got a cold.
2 I hurt my leg.
3 I've got a broken arm.
4 My eye hurts.
5 I feel sick.
6 I've got a stomach ache.
7 I've got a temperature.
8 I've got toothache.
9 I've got a pain in my foot.
10 I've got a headache.

95 **Listen and check. Then repeat.**

96 **2 Listen to three conversations. Match the health problems to the people in the pictures.**

A B

1
2
3

96 **3 Listen again. Match the advice to the health problems in Exercise 2. Write *1*, *2* or *3*.**

don't do any sports ☐
eat fruit and vegetables ☐
don't watch TV late ☐
go to hospital ☐
don't walk ☐
rest ☐
go to sleep now ☐
drink a lot ☐

4 In pairs, discuss the questions.

1 Do you do anything that is bad for your health?
2 How do you want to change it?

I play computer games for three hours a day.
I'd like to play more sport.

80 UNIT 13

13 HEALTHY BODIES

Unit Overview

TOPIC	Health and illness
VOCABULARY AND LISTENING	Illness Conversations about health problems
GRAMMAR	*should / shouldn't*
PRONUNCIATION	Silent consonants
READING	What is so great about running?
VOCABULARY	Health
LISTENING	A conversation about a race
SPEAKING	Giving advice

Resources

GRAMMAR REFERENCE AND PRACTICE: SB page 150; TB page 249
WORKBOOK: pages 56–59
VIDEO AND VIDEO WORKSHEET: Health problems
PHOTOCOPIABLE WORKSHEETS: Grammar worksheet Unit 13; Vocabulary worksheet Unit 13
TEST GENERATOR: Unit test 13

WARMER

Organise the students into small groups and give them an A3 sheet of paper. Ask them to draw a human body. Challenge the groups to label as many body parts as they can in five minutes. Award a point for every part of the body correctly labelled and spelled.

ABOUT YOU

09 You can begin the class and introduce the topic of the unit by showing the video and asking students to complete the video worksheet. Then, read the questions in the *About you* box and have students answer the questions in pairs.

VOCABULARY AND LISTENING

Illness

1 Books closed. Encourage the students to say what can go wrong with some of the parts of the body, e.g. you can have a headache or a toothache. Books open, ask the students to describe the photos and name the parts of the body before they match the sentences to them. If appropriate, point out that we always say *I've got **a** headache* but with other body parts (*toothache*, *stomach ache*, *earache* and *backache*), the article *a(n)* is optional. Also point out that *I'm cold* (= not hot) is different from *I've got a cold* (= I'm ill) and we can't say *I've got cold*.

95

Answers

The answers are recorded for students to check and then repeat.
A I've got a temperature. B My eye hurts. C I've got a cold.
D I've got a headache. E I've got a pain in my foot.
F I feel sick. G I hurt my leg. H I've got a broken arm.
I I've got toothache. J I've got a stomach ache.

96 2 Ask the students to look at the pictures first and say what the difference is between each pair. Encourage them to use the vocabulary in Exercise 1. For example:

1 A His arm hurts.	1 B His leg hurts.
2 A She's got a headache.	2 B She's got a stomach ache.
3 A He's got a cold.	3 B He's got a temperature.

Point out that the students may hear information about both pictures but only one is the correct answer. For example:

Coach: *What's wrong, Martin? Is your arm OK?*
Boy: *My arm's fine. It's my leg! It really hurts.*

Play the recording at least twice. After the students have listened to the recording, ask stronger students to say why the other picture is not correct. (*1 A His arm is fine. 2 B She hasn't got a stomach ache. 3 B He hasn't got a temperature.*)

Answers

1 B 2 A 3 A

96 3 Ask the students to try to match the advice to the health problems before they listen again. Point out that this advice does not appear in the same order on the recording. With a weaker class, play the recording for a third time and stop it after each piece of advice.

Answers

don't do any sports 3	don't walk 1
eat fruit and vegetables 3	rest 3
don't watch TV late 2	go to sleep now 2
go to hospital 1	drink a lot 3

» AUDIOSCRIPT TB PAGE 273

4 First, write the table below on the board (without the examples) for the students to copy into their notebooks, and brainstorm a few examples from the class (see suggestions below). Ask the students in pairs to write down two or three more examples in each column. Write the ideas from the pairs onto the board in the correct column. Then, encourage the pairs to take turns to ask and answer the questions using the ideas in the table.

Bad for your health	Good for your health
don't do any sport	*play more sport*
eat a lot of fast food	*eat healthy food*
watch TV late	*go to bed early*

Answers

Students' own answers

GRAMMAR *should / shouldn't*

1 Books closed. Write these incomplete sentences from the recording on the board:

1 I think you ______ go to hospital.

2 You ______ walk on that leg.

Ask the students to complete them (1 *should*, 2 *shouldn't*). If necessary, play the first conversation from the recording again. Ask the students: 'Which words do we use to give advice?' 'Which one do we use to say something is a good idea? And a bad idea?' 'Which word follows *should* and *shouldn't*?' Books open. Ask the students to do the exercise.

Answers

1 advice 2 good 3 bad 4 always

2 Books closed. First, ask the students to guess how we make questions with *should*. Books open. They match the questions to the answers.

97

Answers

The answers are recorded for students to check and then repeat.

1 Should I stop doing sport? c Yes, you should.
2 Should I take some medicine? a No, you shouldn't.
3 When should I drink it? b Every evening before bed.

» GRAMMAR REFERENCE AND PRACTICE ANSWER KEY TB PAGE 249

3 Point out that the students should match the problem to the advice (a–h) before they complete the advice. With a stronger class, ask the students to cover the advice and then read the problem and try to guess the advice.

MIXED ABILITY

Write the problems (1–8) and complete advice with *should* or *shouldn't* (a–h) onto large strips of paper (16 strips in total). Put them on the board and as a class ask the students to separate them into two columns: problems and advice. Next, as a class, ask them to match each problem to some advice by moving the strips of card. Then, ask stronger students to do the exercise in their books without looking at the board. Allow weaker students to check their ideas with the strips on the board while they do the exercise.

Answers

1 c You shouldn't play tennis.
2 e You should wear more comfortable shoes.
3 b You should take some medicine and go to bed.
4 g You shouldn't eat anything.
5 h You should stop watching TV.
6 f You should go to hospital.
7 a You should go to bed earlier.
8 d You shouldn't go to school.

4 Point out that there is one mistake with how the advice is given in each sentence. Remind students that the verb after *should(n't)* is always the infinitive without *to*.

Answers

1 I think you **should bring** a scarf.
2 You **should** go to the doctor.
3 I **should go** to bed earlier.
4 You aren't well. You **should** stay at home today.
5 You **shouldn't** come to my house today – I am ill.
6 You **shouldn't** watch TV all day.

» GRAMMAR WORKSHEET UNIT 13

ə PRONUNCIATION Silent consonants

5 If necessary, check that students understand the difference between a vowel and a consonant by asking 'Which letters in *should* are consonants and which are vowels?' Point out that a silent consonant is a consonant that we don't pronounce. Ask the students to cross out the silent consonant in each word, reminding them that they are looking at consonants and not vowels.

98

Answers

The answers are recorded for students to check and then repeat.

(The silent consonants are in **bold**)

cas**t**le, clim**b**, ha**l**f, **k**nife, lis**t**en, shou**l**d, ta**l**k, wa**l**k, wou**l**d, **w**rong, **w**rote

6 Read through the example conversation as a class. Model a good answer with a stronger student first. Point out that the students can use one of the problems in Exercise 3 if they want.

FAST FINISHERS

Fast finishers produce a much longer conversation using the health problems on this page or their own ideas, perhaps at a doctor's surgery. They practise their conversation in pairs and then perform it to the class.

Answers

Students' own answers

COOLER

Mime a health problem and ask: 'What's the matter with me?' Encourage the students to ask questions. Then, ask for some advice. They then do the same activity in small groups. For example:

Teacher: *[holding head] What's the matter with me?*
Student A: *Have you got a headache?*
Teacher: *Yes, I have.*
Student B: *Have you got a temperature?*
Teacher: *I think so.*
Student C: *You've got a bad cold.*
Teacher: *What should I do?*
Student D: *You should go to bed and rest.*

GRAMMAR *should / shouldn't*

1 **Look at these examples from the conversations. Then choose the correct words to complete the rules.**

You **shouldn't walk** on that leg.
You **should go** to bed.

1 We use *should* and *shouldn't* to give *advice* / *information*.
2 We use *should* to say something is a *good* / *bad* idea.
3 We use *shouldn't* to say something is a *good* / *bad* idea.
4 The verb after *should* is *always* / *never* the infinitive without 'to'.

2 **Look at these examples from the conversations you heard on page 80. Match the questions to the answers. Notice how we make questions with *should*.**

I should … → Should I … ?

1 **Should** I **stop** doing sport?
2 **Should** I **take** some medicine?
3 When **should** I **drink** it?

a No, you **shouldn't**.
b Every evening before bed.
c Yes, you **should**.

97 **Listen and check. Then repeat.**

» GRAMMAR REFERENCE AND PRACTICE PAGE 150

3 **Read the problems 1–8 and choose the correct advice for each one a–h. Then complete the advice with *should/shouldn't*. There may be more than one possible answer.**

1 My hand hurts a bit today.
2 I've got a pain in my foot.
3 I've got a headache and a temperature.
4 I feel a bit sick.
5 My eyes hurt.
6 I can't move my leg at all. I think it's broken.
7 I feel very tired.
8 I've got a bad cold.

a You ________ go to bed earlier.
b You ________ take some medicine and go to bed.
c You ________ play tennis.
d You ________ go to school.
e You ________ wear more comfortable shoes.
f You ________ go to hospital.
g You ________ eat anything.
h You ________ stop watching TV.

4 **Correct the mistakes in the sentences.**

1 I think you should to bring a scarf.
2 You shoud go to the doctor.
3 I should to go to bed earlier.
4 You aren't well. You stay at home today.
5 You don't come to my house today – I am ill.
6 You no should watch TV all day.

ə PRONUNCIATION Silent consonants

5 **Some words in English have silent consonants. Find one silent consonant in each word.**

castle	climb	half	knife
listen	should	talk	walk
would	wrong	wrote	

98 **Listen and check. Then repeat.**

6 **Read the example conversation. Have similar conversations with your partner. Choose a different question from the box each time. Use health problems and advice from this lesson, or use your own ideas.**

What's wrong?
What's the matter?
Are you OK?

What's the matter?

I've got a temperature. What should I do?

You should rest. You should also drink lots of water. You shouldn't go to school.

READING

1 Read the magazine article. Match the photos A–D to the paragraphs 1–3.

2 Choose the correct headings a–d for the paragraphs 1–3. There is one heading you don't need.

a Different kinds of running races
b Some problems with running
c All the ways running is good for you
d Reasons why running is popular

A
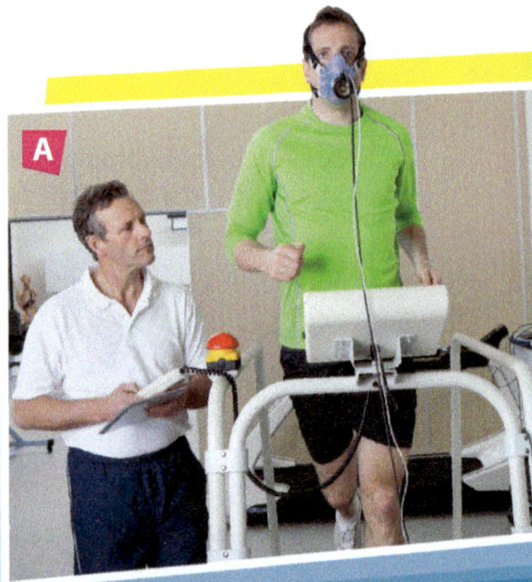

What is so great about running?

B

1 In the past, people didn't need sports like running to stay healthy because they were very active. But these days, many of us spend most of the day sitting down. This means we need to get some exercise in our free time, and running is a cheap and easy way to do it. It's more fun than doing boring exercises in a gym, and all you need is a good pair of trainers and some comfortable clothes. Also, it's a sport that people can do at any age – for example Fauja Singh finished a marathon at the age of 101!

C

2 To make running interesting, you can enter a race. Fun runs are very popular. These are often 5 km long and are great for beginners. You can run with your friends and maybe dress up. For fitter people, there are half-marathons, marathons, or even ultra-marathons. These can be 70–400 km long. One of the most famous is the Marathon des Sables which takes six days and goes through the Sahara desert.

D

3 Running is fun and scientists say it is one of the best ways to keep fit. However, make sure you don't do it every day – it's important to have a rest between runs. Running improves the health of almost every part of your body, including your brain. It can make you feel happier and healthier, and live longer. It also helps you sleep well, and that gives you the energy to enjoy your life more. Perhaps it's the perfect sport!

99

TALKING POINTS

Do you go running? If not, would you like to?
Do you think running is the 'perfect sport'? If not, what is?

READING

WARMER

Ask the students to tell you what you were talking about in the last lesson, i.e. giving advice with *should* and *shouldn't*. Ask: 'How often do you give advice?' 'What on? Who to?' 'Who do you go to for advice: a member of your family or friends?' Tell the class you are going to run a marathon and ask them for some advice.

BACKGROUND INFORMATION

A fun run is a friendly race (running, cycling or even motorcycling or going by snowmobile) where people take part for their own enjoyment rather than for competition. These runs can be short races or even marathons. Participants may wear fancy dress and they will often raise money for charity. *La cursa* is one of the biggest fun runs in the world. Held once a year in Barcelona, Spain over a distance of 10.766 km, this run is now 40 years old. It attracts around 55,000 runners (in recent years, the majority have been women) and unlike many other fun runs, it is free to enter. The *Marathon des Sables* is an annual 251 km ultramarathon (so called because it is longer than the traditional length of a marathon – 42.195 km) held over six days in the Sahara Desert in Morocco. The oldest marathon runner Fauja Singh was born on 1st April 1911 in the Punjab and he's carried the torch at both the Athens and London Olympic Games. There is some disagreement over the youngest runner, but Budhia Singh (born 2002) ran 65 km when he was five and Jennifer Amyx ran a 42 km marathon also when she was five.

1 Ask the students to look at the title of the article and the photos and say what they think the article is about. Point out that each of the photos goes with one of the paragraphs. Encourage the students to describe each photo in pairs and say what they think each paragraph is about. Then, ask the students to read and match the photos to the paragraphs.

Answers

A paragraph 3 B paragraph 2 C paragraph 1 D paragraph 2

99 The Reading text is recorded for students to listen and read.

2 Ask the students in pairs to read each heading and try to decide which paragraph it goes with. Point out that there is an extra heading. Ask them to check their answers by reading each paragraph again.

MIXED ABILITY

With a mixed ability class, for Exercises 1 and 2, divide the class into three groups. Each group reads a different paragraph and matches it to the correct photo(s) and the best heading. Then, reorganise them into groups of three who have read a different paragraph each and ask them to share their answers.

FAST FINISHERS

Fast finishers work in pairs. They cover the article and look at the paragraph headings. They try to say as much as they can about each paragraph.

Answers

Paragraph 1 d Reasons why running is popular
Paragraph 2 a Different kinds of running races
Paragraph 3 c All the ways running is good for you
Not needed b Some problems with running

TALKING POINTS

Read paragraph 3 to the class inviting reactions to the advice. Read the last line 'Perhaps it's the perfect sport!' and add 'Or is it?' Organise the students into groups and ask them to discuss the questions.

14 GETTING AROUND TOWN

VOCABULARY AND READING

Places in town

1 Look at the map and find these things.

EP

bridges bus stops a playground
a roundabout streets traffic lights

2 Look at the map again and find a place where you can:

EP

0 see a film *cinema*
1 send a letter
2 stay the night
3 buy food
4 borrow a book
5 study
6 eat a meal
7 get some money
8 buy petrol
9 find a police officer
10 get better
11 see a play
12 catch a bus
13 learn about history
14 buy things outdoors

3 Talk to your partner. Which of the places in Exercise 2 do you …

- like going to?
- hate going to?
- often go to?
- never go to?

4 Read the description of the town and look at the map in Exercise 1. Find five mistakes in the description.

ABOUT YOU

Do you live in a city, town or village? What is it like?
Do you prefer cities, towns or villages?
What's the best thing about where you live?

ABOUT | GALLERY | CONTACT

This is my town. It's small but very pretty. A river goes **through** the town centre and there are four bridges going **across** it. Between the road and the river, there's a market. **Next to** the market is a really nice café. There are also some shops in the town. **Opposite** the shops, there's a bank, a museum and a restaurant. Behind the museum, there's a children's playground. The restaurant is **near** the train station, and **beside** the train station there's a post office. There's also a sports centre on that street. **In front of** the supermarket, there's a car park. We have a zoo too, but that's **outside** the town.

101

5 20 9

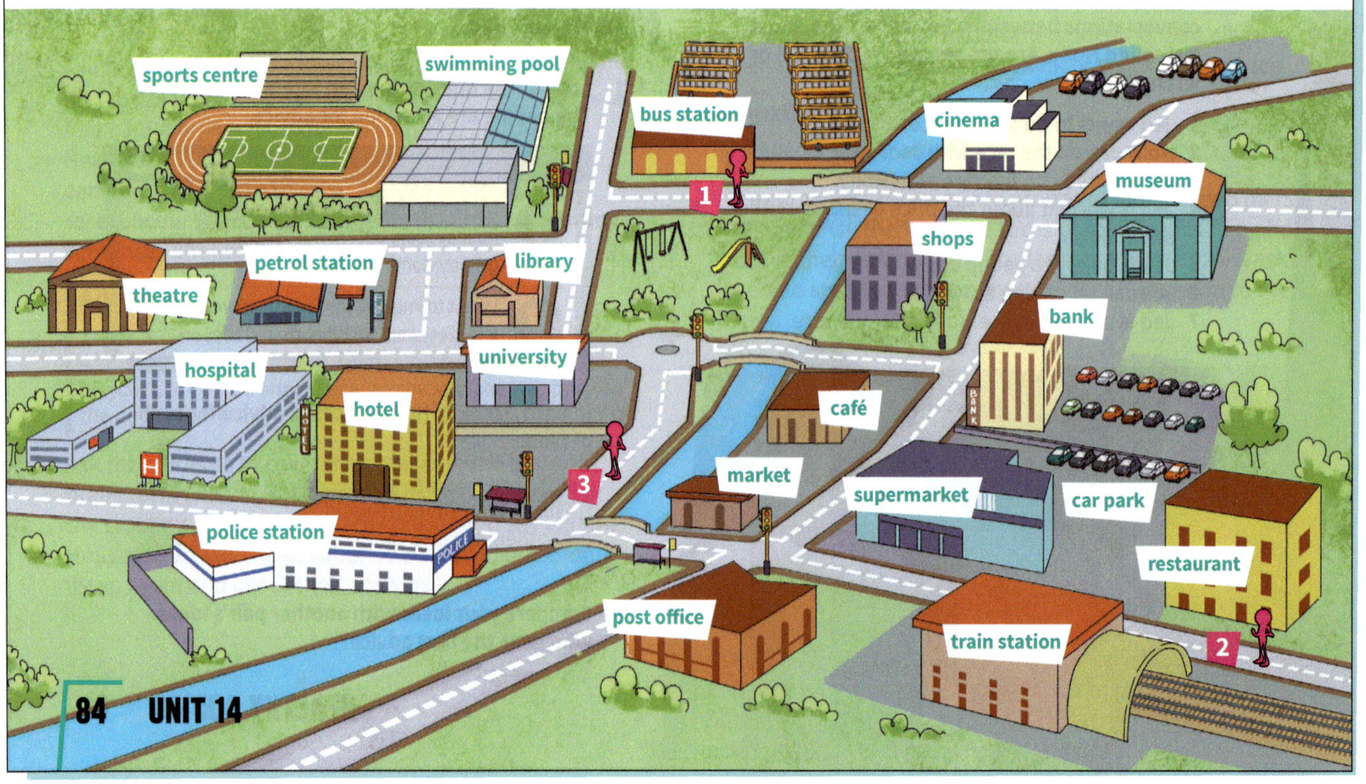

14 GETTING AROUND TOWN

Unit Overview

TOPIC	Places in a town
VOCABULARY	Places in town
AND READING	A description of a town
GRAMMAR	Prepositions
READING	A trip to Edinburgh
VOCABULARY	Compound nouns
PRONUNCIATION	Compound nouns
LISTENING	A conversation about a visit to Edinburgh
WRITING	An article about a city
EXAM TASKS	Listening Part 5

Resources

GRAMMAR REFERENCE AND PRACTICE: SB page 151; TB page 249
WORKBOOK: pages 60–63
PHOTOCOPIABLE WORKSHEETS: Grammar worksheet Unit 14; Vocabulary worksheet Unit 14
TEST GENERATOR: Unit test 14; Term test 2

WARMER

Write *Where I live* on the board and then divide the board into two columns with the headings *things I like* and *things I don't like*. As a class, brainstorm one or two ideas, e.g.:

things I like	things I don't like
lots of parks	*nowhere to go when it rains*

Encourage the students to copy the table into their notebooks and in small groups, write down some more ideas.

ABOUT YOU

If necessary, pre-teach the difference between a village (a rural settlement), a town (an urban area usually with a market and a population of between 1,000 and 20,000) and a city (an urban area usually with more people and a cathedral and/or a university). If you did the Warmer activity, encourage the students to use these ideas when they ask and answer the questions.

VOCABULARY AND READING

Places in town

1 Ask the students to look at the map first and in pairs, describe what they can see. Next, ask them to find the things on the map. Check that they can say the things correctly by asking them to listen and repeat, in particular *bridge* /brɪdʒ/ and *roundabout* /ˈraʊnd.ə.baʊt/.

Answers
Students' own answers

2 In pairs, ask the students to read the descriptions of places and try to name them before they find the places on the map.

FAST FINISHERS

Fast finishers ask and answer questions in pairs about the places on the map, e.g. *Where's the post office? It's here. / It's beside the train station.* If they don't know the preposition, they can point.

Answers
1 post office 2 hotel 3 supermarket 4 library 5 university 6 restaurant 7 bank 8 petrol station 9 police station 10 hospital 11 theatre 12 bus station 13 museum 14 market

3 Encourage the students to look at the map and to take turns to ask full questions and answer in full sentences giving a reason. They can use the words in Exercise 2 to do this. If necessary, demonstrate with a stronger student first; e.g.:

Teacher: *Which of the places do you like going to?*
Student: *I like going to the cinema.*
Teacher: *Why do you like going to the cinema?*
Student: *Because I love seeing films. What about you?*

Answers
Students' own answers

4 Point out that there are five mistakes in the description and that the students will need to check each sentence against the map to do this. If necessary, begin as a class by reading the first three sentences and asking 'Where's the river?' (*students point at the river*) 'Does it go through the town centre?' (*yes*) 'How many bridges are there?' (*three*) 'Is this the first mistake?' (*yes*)

Answers
there are four bridges (there are three bridges)
Opposite the shops, there's a bank, a museum and a restaurant (there isn't a restaurant opposite)
Behind the museum, there's a children's playground. (there's grass behind the museum)
There's also a sports centre on that street. (there's a supermarket)
In front of the supermarket, there's a car park (it's behind the supermarket)

101 The Reading text is recorded for students to listen and read.

READING

1 Look at the map and read the article about Edinburgh. Match places A–E to the names in the box.

Edinburgh Castle
Palace of Holyroodhouse
Scottish Parliament
St Giles' Cathedral
Tourist Information Office

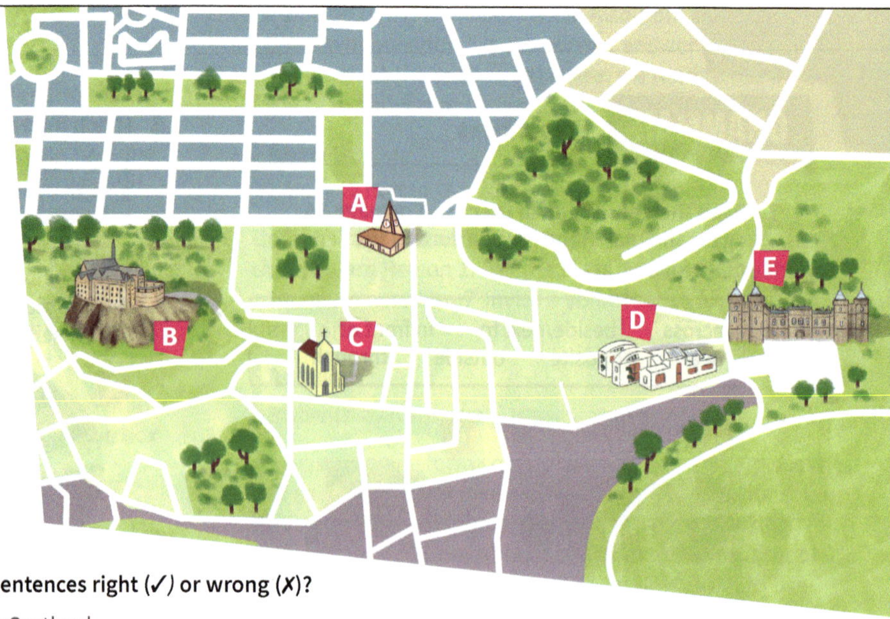

104 Listen and check. Then repeat.

2 Read the article again. Are the sentences right (✓) or wrong (✗)?

1. Edinburgh is the largest city in Scotland.
2. Lots of people visit the castle in the summer.
3. You can walk from Edinburgh Castle to Holyroodhouse.
4. The Camera Obscura museum is about the history of Edinburgh.
5. The Queen sometimes stays at Holyroodhouse.
6. The Scottish Parliament building is closed to visitors.
7. Princes Street is a good place to go shopping.
8. All of Edinburgh's guided tours are on foot.

Hey guys! I'm going to Edinburgh, the capital of Scotland, soon. Have you got any advice for me?

Lucky you! Edinburgh's great. It isn't the biggest city in Scotland, but it's very beautiful and has an amazing history. The best place to start is Edinburgh Castle. This sits up on top of Castle Rock and from here you can see the whole city below you. It gets very busy in the summer.

Next, walk down the Royal Mile, through Edinburgh's 12th-century Old Town. Don't miss St Giles' Cathedral and the Camera Obscura. This amazing museum is all about how we see things, and has floating fish, funny mirrors and a 3D tunnel of stars. They sell great postcards there.

At the bottom of the Royal Mile is the Queen's Edinburgh home, the Palace of Holyroodhouse. When the Queen isn't there, you can visit the rooms and gardens. Next to the Palace is the Scottish Parliament. Spanish architect Enric Miralles designed it. Parts of it look like fishing boats on the beach. There are also roof gardens and fountains. And you can visit it for free!

You should also go to Edinburgh's New Town. This area isn't very new actually – it's over 200 years old! The most famous street in Edinburgh, called Princes Street, is in New Town. Here you find Edinburgh's best shops and department stores.

If you haven't got much time, you can see Edinburgh with a tour guide. Choose from walking tours, cycle tours and even ghost tours. These take you through the narrow streets of the Old Town late at night, and include scary stories from the 18th century.

Don't forget to take a good guidebook – and your raincoat. It often rains in Edinburgh. Have a great time!

105

TALKING POINTS

Would you like to go to Edinburgh? Why / Why not?
What would you like to do there?
Do you enjoy visiting cities?
What kind of museums do you like best?

READING

WARMER

Tell the class that in this lesson, they are going to visit a large city in Europe, but they have to guess which one. They can ask you *Yes/No* questions, e.g. *Is it a capital city? Is it in England?* The answer is Edinburgh.

BACKGROUND INFORMATION

Glasgow is the largest city in Scotland, but Edinburgh is the capital city. The Royal Mile is a series of streets which go from Edinburgh Castle to the Palace of Holyroodhouse. This route measures about one Scottish mile, which is actually slightly longer than an English mile (1 Scottish mile = 1.12 English miles).

A *camera obscura* means 'dark room or chamber'. It's a room with a small hole that projects an image of the outside onto one of the walls. Visitors to the 150-year-old Camera Obscura Museum can see images of Edinburgh.

Building began on the Scottish Parliament building in 1999 and the first debate was held on 7th September 2004.

A traditional musical instrument of Scotland is the bagpipes and you can find bagpipe players on the Royal Mile wearing the Scottish kilt.

1 Books closed. Challenge the class to tell you five true things about Edinburgh, e.g. *it's in the north of Europe; it's in Scotland; it's the capital city; the people there speak English; the money is the pound*. Books open. Pre-teach *castle*, *palace*, *cathedral*, *parliament* and *tourist information* office by asking 'Who lives or works in these buildings?' 'What do they do?'

Then, ask the students to read the article quickly to find and, if appropriate, underline the five place names and then find the places on the map.

104

Answers

The answers are recorded for students to check and then repeat.
A Tourist Information Office B Edinburgh Castle
C St Giles' Cathedral D Scottish Parliament
E Palace of Holyroodhouse

2 Ask the students to read through the sentences in pairs and decide if they are right or wrong before they read the article again. Encourage stronger students to correct the wrong sentences.

Answers

1 × (It isn't the biggest city in Scotland.) 2 ✓ 3 ✓
4 × (It's about how we see things.) 5 ✓
6 × (You can visit it for free.) 7 ✓
8 × (Choose from walking tours, cycle tours, etc.)

105 The Reading text is recorded for students to listen and read.

FAST FINISHERS

Encourage fast finishers to use the sentences in this exercise to write some right and some wrong sentences about where they live, e.g. *Valencia is the largest city in Spain.* (wrong) When the others have finished, the fast finishers read out their sentences for their classmates to say if they are right or wrong. If appropriate, award points for correct answers.

TALKING POINTS

First, ask the students to write down at least three reasons they'd like to go to Edinburgh and at least three reasons why they'd like to go somewhere else. Then, ask them to take turns to ask and answer the questions in pairs using their notes to help them. Remind them to give full answers.

VOCABULARY Compound nouns

Books closed. Ask the class 'Where does a bus stop?' and elicit *bus stop*. Write it on the board. Point out that these words are called compound nouns; some are written as one word (e.g. *bedroom*) and others as two words (e.g. *bus stop*).

1 Books open. Ask the students to look at the map, article and exercises on page 84 to find the 12 compound nouns. If necessary, give the students the first letters of each word in the compound noun to help them, e.g. t______ c______, t______ s______.

Answers
town centre, train station, post office, supermarket, car park, traffic lights, petrol station, sports centre, bus station, police station, swimming pool, police officer

2 If students have access to a dictionary (paper or online), encourage them to check whether the compound noun is one or two words for themselves before telling them the answer.

106

Answers
The answers are recorded for students to check and then repeat.
postcard, cycle tour, walking tour, guidebook, tour guide, raincoat

3 Ask the students to read through the sentences and try to think of a suitable compound noun before they look at their new words in Exercise 2. Make sure they have written each word correctly, i.e. as one or two words.

Answers
1 postcard 2 raincoat 3 tour guide 4 walking tour
5 guidebook 6 cycle tour

» VOCABULARY WORKSHEET UNIT 14

PRONUNCIATION Compound nouns

4 Write *cycle tour* on the board, say the word and elicit which word we stress (*the first*). Then, ask them to listen and underline the stressed word in all the compound nouns in Exercise 2.

Then, ask 'Which word do we usually stress in compounds nouns?' Finally, ask them to listen again and repeat.

107

Answers
The answers are recorded for students to listen and underline, then repeat.
cycle tour, police station, walking tour, town centre, bus station, post office, petrol station, train station, sports centre
The stress usually falls on the first word.

LISTENING

108 1 A2 Key for Schools Listening Part 5.

In this part of the exam, students listen to two people talking and they have to match two lists of items, for example people to their hobbies, or in this task times to places. They may hear two or more words from the list of answers for each question, but only one will be correct. There will be three options from the list A–H that are not answers to any of the questions.

Ask the students to look at the places first and find them on the map in Exercise 1 page 86 before they listen. Play the recording once.

Answers
Students are given answers after Exercise 2.

108 2 Encourage the students to compare their answers, saying why they think their answer is correct before they listen again.

MIXED ABILITY
With a mixed ability class, pair up a stronger student with a weaker student for this stage and encourage the stronger student to explain to their partner why they think their answer is correct. Play the recording again.

Answers
1 Saturday morning F 2 Saturday afternoon A 3 Saturday evening C 4 Sunday morning E 5 Sunday afternoon D

» AUDIOSCRIPT TB PAGE 274

WRITING

PREPARE TO WRITE
An article

GET READY Ask the students to find all the examples of *this* and *these* in the article. Next, ask them to read the paragraph about London, find the nouns which they have to replace, i.e. *buildings*, *St James's Park*, *shows* and *Harrods* and say if it is singular or plural before completing the sentences.

Answers
1 these 2 This 3 these 4 This

PLAN Brainstorm a list of places as a class first, then students choose three and think about where they are, what you can do there, and why they are interesting.

WRITE Encourage the students to use the paragraph about London as a model for their own writing. Stronger students should also look at the longer article about Edinburgh again for useful expressions and ideas for their own writing. Remind them to use *this* / *these*.

IMPROVE Ask the students to read their partner's work. Remind them to check that *this* is used for singular nouns and *these* for plural nouns.

COOLER
Play *Where am I?* Say to the class: 'I'm eating hamburger and chips with my family. I can see the waiter. He's carrying a plate of food. Where am I?' Encourage them to guess (*in a restaurant*).

In teams, the students write four descriptions for different places in the town. Each team reads out their description and the others have to guess where they are. Award one point for a correct guess and two points for a good description.

VOCABULARY Compound nouns

In English, it's possible to make new words by putting two words together: *bus* + *stop* = *bus stop*. These are called compound nouns. Sometimes they are written as one word and sometimes as two. Do you do this in your language too?

1 **Look at the map, text and Exercises on page 84, and find 12 compound nouns.**

2 **Match the words on the left of the box to the words on the right to make compound nouns. Remember some are one word and some are two.**

post	guide
cycle	tour
walking	coat
guide	card
tour	book
rain	tour

106 **Listen and check. Then repeat.**

3 **Complete the sentences with compound nouns from Exercise 2.**

1. I found a ________ with a really nice picture on it to send to my friend.
2. I'm glad I wore a ________ yesterday because the weather was terrible.
3. Our ________ was so funny. I loved her stories about the city.
4. That ________ was fun, but my feet hurt now!
5. I read in the ________ that this castle is 1,000 years old.
6. The ________ was brilliant. We rode all around the city.

PRONUNCIATION Compound nouns

107 **4** **Listen to the compound nouns and underline the stressed words.**

cycle tour

In compound nouns, which word do we usually stress? Listen again and repeat the words.

LISTENING

108 **1** **Listen to Rob talking to a friend about a visit to Edinburgh. Which place did Rob visit at each time?**

0 Friday evening *B*

Times		Places
1 Saturday morning	☐	**A** Scottish Parliament
2 Saturday afternoon	☐	**B** Old Town
3 Saturday evening	☐	**C** Theatre
4 Sunday morning	☐	**D** New Town
5 Sunday afternoon	☐	**E** Museum
		F Edinburgh Castle
		G Cathedral
		H Holyroodhouse

108 **2** **In pairs, compare your answers. Listen again and check.**

WRITING

PREPARE TO WRITE

An article

GET READY Look at the article about Edinburgh again and find all the examples of *this* and *these*. Then complete the paragraph about London with *this* or *these*.

London is the capital city of England, and has lots of interesting buildings you can visit. One of [1] ________ is Buckingham Palace, the Queen's London home. From here you can walk to St James's Park. [2] ________ is a lovely place to stop for a rest and a picnic. Many people like to see shows when they are in London. You can get tickets for [3] ________ online or in Leicester Square. And don't forget about Harrods! [4] ________ shop is famous around the world.

PLAN Make a list of interesting and famous places in a city you know well. Choose three, and make notes about them. You could include information such as:

- where they are
- what you can do there
- why they are interesting.

WRITE Write 50–60 words about your city. Use *this*/*these* in your paragraph.

IMPROVE In pairs, read your own text and your partner's. Did you write about the same places? Check for mistakes with *this*/*these*. Give your partner two ideas to make their text better.

CULTURE

SCOTLAND

FACTFILE Scotland

Scotland is part of the United Kingdom.
Population: Around 5.4 million people
Languages: English, Gaelic and Scots
Capital city: Edinburgh

1 **Read the sentences and look at the map. Match the sentences to the places.**

1. This city is in the west of Scotland. It is the largest city in Scotland.
2. This city is in the north of Scotland. It is the capital of the Scottish Highlands.
3. This city is near the coast in the east of Scotland. It is the capital of the country.

2 **Read and match the photos (A–E) to the texts (1–5).**

109

SCOTTISH HIGHLIGHTS

Are you are looking for a great place to spend your next holiday? Then come to Scotland! Find out more about this interesting country and things you can do, see … and eat!

1 ______ The **Great Highland Bagpipe** is a Scottish musical instrument. It is a woodwind instrument. To play the instrument, the bagpiper fills the bag with air and pushes it out with his elbow.

2 ______ The **Highland Games** happen around Scotland from June to September. People celebrate Highland Games in other parts of the world too. There are different sporting competitions at the games. These test throwing, pulling and strength. The games are competitive but people can also enjoy music and dancing.

3 ______ For special events, like parties, Scottish men often wear a **kilt**. Kilts are skirts. They are usually made of coloured or black wool with a 'tartan' pattern. Members of the same family ('clan') have their own, specific tartan. Men often wear shoes called **Brogues** with their traditional clothes.

4 ______ In Scotland, there is a famous biscuit called **shortbread**. One of the most important things in shortbread is butter. Butter is also an ingredient in a popular Scottish sweet called **fudge**.

5 ______ **The School of Art** and the **Queen's Cross Church** in Glasgow are both buildings by the famous Scottish architect Charles Rennie Mackintosh. There are also a lot of beautiful, historical **castles** in Scotland to visit.

CULTURE

Learning Objectives

- The students learn about Scotland.
- In the project stage, they design a brochure to attract visitors to their area and present it to other students.

Vocabulary

woodwind competitive event pattern architect

Resources

CULTURE VIDEO AND CULTURE VIDEO WORKSHEET: A view of Scotland

BACKGROUND INFORMATION

The UK stands for the United Kingdom of Great Britain and Northern Ireland and consists of four countries: England, Wales and Scotland (which make up Great Britain) and Northern Ireland. The capital cities of each country are London, Cardiff, Edinburgh and Belfast. Scotland is the second largest country in the UK (after England) and has over 790 islands. The official language in Scotland is English, although 1.4% of the population also speak Scottish Gaelic. The currency is the pound (£). Scotland is governed by parliament in London but also has its own parliament which has some control over local issues such as education and housing. For example, the education system is different. In 2014, there was a referendum in Scotland on independence and 55.3% voted against it.

WARMER

Draw or project a map of the UK (see Background information above) onto the board and challenge the students to label the four countries and their capital cities. Then, ask some general knowledge questions about Scotland (see example questions below). If appropriate, do this as a team game and award points.

1 What's the capital of Scotland? (Edinburgh)
2 What's the currency? (the pound £)
3 Does Scotland have a king or a queen? (yes, a queen – Queen Elizabeth II)
4 What is the Scottish flag like? (a white cross on a blue background)
5 What are some of the most popular sports in Scotland? (football, rugby, tennis, golf and hockey)
6 What's the highest mountain in Scotland? (Ben Nevis – 1,344 m)
7 How many people live Scotland? (5.4 million – accept an approximation)
8 What famous wizard went to school in Scotland? (Harry Potter – Hogwarts is in Scotland)

1 Books closed. Challenge the students to tell you everything they can remember about Edinburgh from Unit 14. If appropriate, organise the students into teams and award points. Books open. Next, ask the students to look at the information in the factfile in pairs and find the cities.

Answers

1 Glasgow 2 Inverness 3 Edinburgh

2 Ask the students to look at the title *Scottish Highlights* and the photos and ask 'What do you think *highlights* means?' (*the best or most important things*) Next, ask them to describe the photos in pairs and try to guess what each thing is before they match the photo to its text. If necessary, point out that they should not write the letter (A–E) of the photo in the space as this space is for a heading.

Answers

1 D 2 A 3 C 4 B 5 E

3 Ask the students in pairs to think of a suitable heading for each text (1–5) before they look at the words in the box.

109

Answers

The Reading text is recorded for students to listen and check their answers.
1 Music 2 Sports 3 Clothes 4 Food 5 Buildings

4 Encourage the students in pairs to try to answer the questions before they read the texts again.

Answers

1 air 2 from June to September 3 special events; celebrations 4 butter 5 Glasgow 6 The School of Art and the Queen's Cross Church

5 Ask the students in pairs to find the words in the texts and try to work out the meaning from context before they match it to its meaning.

FAST FINISHERS

Ask fast finishers in pairs to find some more new words in the texts, try to guess their meaning from context, and then check their ideas in a dictionary or with you. If time allows, they can write some multiple choice questions for the others.

Answers

1 pattern 2 architect 3 event 4 woodwind 5 competitive

TALKING POINTS

Ask the students to read the texts again and write down three things they would like to see or do in Scotland and three things they wouldn't like to see or do. Then, organise them into small groups and ask them to share their ideas saying whether they would or wouldn't like to visit Scotland and why.

110
6 Ask the students to read the instructions first and ask 'What do you need to do?' (*choose a or b*)

MIXED ABILITY

For Exercises 6–8, pair up a stronger student with a weaker student. For each exercise, ask the stronger student to make sure their partner knows what they have to listen for and also to share their ideas and answers during each exercise.

Answers

b

110
7 Ask the students to read through the sentences first in pairs and try to decide if they are right or wrong. Ask stronger students to correct the wrong sentences.

Answers

1 × (They are only going to Scotland.) 2 × (She has to choose between two.) 3 ✓ 4 × (You can see four castles.) 5 ✓ 6 ✓ 7 × (Her friend wants shortbread.)

110
8 Encourage the students to copy the table into their books and try to make notes before they listen again.

Answers

Castle Tour: four castles (historical buildings); Loch Lomond
Highland Games: men in traditional clothes; sporting competitions; bagpipes; dance festival

» AUDIOSCRIPT TB PAGE 275

9 Ask the students to look at their table in Exercise 8 again and answer the question in pairs. Encourage them to give reasons for their answers.

Answers

Students' own answers

PROJECT ***A brochure***

If necessary, pre-teach *brochure*: show the class examples or ask 'If you want to go on holiday, what sort of thin book can you get from a travel agency?' (*a holiday brochure*) Ask the students to read the project instructions in bold and ask 'What are you going to design?' (*a brochure about your area*)

Copy the following headings onto the board and brainstorm some ideas as a class: *local events, typical food, important buildings, music.*

Ask the students in pairs to choose at least two things from each column and make some notes on each one. Encourage them to check their information online or in a local guidebook. Encourage the pairs to use the Scotland text as a model for their own brochure. In small groups, pairs show their brochure and also give feedback on each other's work.

PROJECT EXTENSION

Invite a brief classroom discussion on what students liked about each other's brochures and what makes a good one. Then, ask each pair to choose a place in another part of the world, preferably somewhere they would like to visit. Encourage them to look for information about their place, find some photos and produce an electronic or paper brochure to attract visitors. Then, ask the class to look at each other's work and vote for the best three.

CULTURE VIDEO 04: A view of Scotland

When students have completed the lesson, they can watch the video and complete the worksheet.

COOLER

Ask each student to write two questions about their country on a piece of paper (they must also write the answer). Collect in the questions, organise the students into teams and hold a general knowledge quiz.

3 **Match the headings to the texts.**

Buildings   Clothes   Food   Music   Sports

4 **Read the texts again and answer the questions.**

1 What does a bagpipe player fill the bag with?
2 When are the Highland Games in Scotland?
3 When do men wear kilts in Scotland?
4 What ingredient is in shortbread and fudge?
5 Where is Queen's Cross Church?
6 Which buildings are by Charles Rennie Mackintosh?

5 **Match the highlighted words in the article to the meanings.**

1 repeated lines or colours
2 this person draws buildings
3 a social activity with lots of people
4 a type of instrument, like the bagpipes, flute or clarinet
5 trying to win something or get points for something

TALKING POINTS

Would you like to visit Scotland? Why? / Why not?

110 **6** **Listen to Emma talking to her friend about the summer holidays. What does she decide to do with her family?**

a visit a castle **b** watch the Highland Games

110 **7** **Listen to the conversation again. Are the sentences are right (✓) or wrong (✗)?**

1 Emma and her family have plans to go to Scotland and Ireland.
2 Emma needs to choose two activities.
3 Emma really likes geography.
4 You can see 14 castles on the tour.
5 The castle tour leaves the hotel before eight in the morning.
6 They can watch and listen to music and dance in the afternoon at the Highland Games.
7 Emma needs to bring her friend fudge.

110 **8** **Listen again and complete the table.**

	Things to do or see
Castle Tour	
Highland Games	

9 **Which of the two tours would you like to do? Why?**

PROJECT *A brochure*

Imagine you work for a tour company. In pairs, design a brochure to attract visitors to your area.

- Make notes about:
  - local events visitors can go to
  - typical food visitors can try
  - important buildings to visit
  - music they can listen to
- Find or take some **photographs** of your local area, make a brochure.
- Present your brochure to another pair.

10 NOW WATCH THE CULTURE VIDEO

15 MYSTERIES IN NATURE

ABOUT YOU

What are your favourite places or things in nature?
What activities do you like doing outside?
Where do you like doing them?

VOCABULARY AND READING

Geographical features

1 Match photos A–H to the words in the box. Use each word once only.

EP

cliff field island lake mountain
river snow water

111 Listen and check. Then repeat.

2 Look at the photos and complete the sentences with *wide*, *high*, *long* and *deep*.

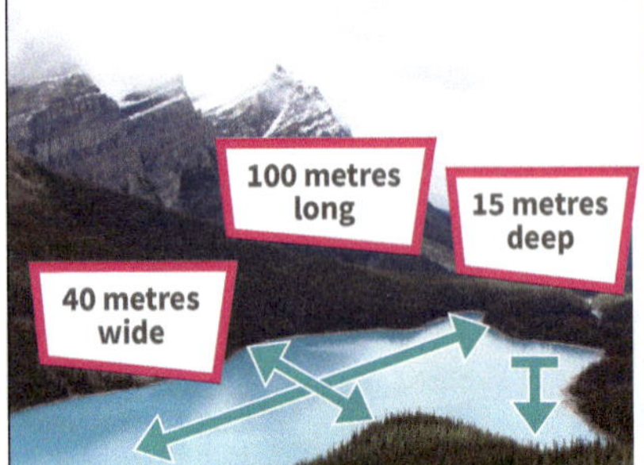

1 Mount Everest is 8,848 metres ________.
2 The Amazon River is 11 kilometres ________ and 6,400 kilometres ________.
3 Lake Titicaca is 107 metres ________.

3 Match the words in Exercise 1 to the adjectives in the box.

EP

deep high long wide

4 Think about your country. Give the names of …

- two high mountains
- an area of deep water
- a long river
- a wide lake.

5 What can you see in the photos on page 91? What do you think this strange story is about?

6 Read the article quickly. Check your answers to Exercise 5.

7 Read the article again. Complete the text with *wide, high, long* and *deep.*

8 In pairs, discuss these questions.

1 Do you think the Yeti is real, or is it just a story?
2 What do you think the footprint in the snow belongs to?

15 MYSTERIES IN NATURE

Unit Overview

TOPIC	Strange things which happen in nature
VOCABULARY	Geographical features
AND READING	Is the story real?
GRAMMAR	Past continuous
PRONUNCIATION	Rising and falling intonation
READING	Loch Ness
VOCABULARY	The weather
LISTENING	A story about looking for the Loch Ness monster
SPEAKING	A story about a strange animal

Resources

GRAMMAR REFERENCE AND PRACTICE: SB page 152; TB page 249
WORKBOOK: pages 64–67
PHOTOCOPIABLE WORKSHEETS: Grammar worksheet Unit 15; Vocabulary worksheet Unit 15
TEST GENERATOR: Unit test 15

WARMER

Put students into small groups and ask each group to draw an island on an A3 sheet of paper. Ask the students to draw and label as many things on their island as they can, e.g. a beach, a river, a forest.

ABOUT YOU

If you did the Warmer activity above, ask whether the students would prefer to live on their island or in a town or a city. Then, ask the students in pairs to take turns to ask and answer the questions using some of the words they drew on their islands.

VOCABULARY AND READING

Geographical features

1 Ask the students to describe the photos first before they match them to the words. Check their pronunciation by asking them to listen and repeat. Point out that the *s* in *island* is silent /ˈaɪlənd/ and that we don't stress the second syllable in *mountain.*

111

Answers

The answers are recorded for students to check and then repeat.
A lake B river C mountain D field E snow F water G cliff H island

2 Books closed. Draw a three-dimensional picture of a swimming pool on the board with a diving board. Invite volunteers to come to the board and label the picture with *long*, *wide*, *deep* and *high* (for the diving board). Books open. The students do the exercise.

Answers

1 high 2 wide, long 3 deep

3 Demonstrate the first word in Exercise 1 as a class:

Teacher: *What are cliffs like?*
Student: *They're usually high.*

Point out that *snow* and *water* are uncountable so the question is *What is snow/water like?* Students continue in pairs.

Answers

cliff: high, wide	mountain: high
field: long, wide	river: long, wide, deep
island: long, wide	snow: deep
lake: long, wide, deep	water: deep

4 In pairs, allow the students about two minutes to think of examples of each one. If appropriate, allow them to check their ideas online. Then, check answers as a class.

Answers

Students' own answers

BACKGROUND INFORMATION

The Yeti, also known as the Abominable Snowman, is a mythical creature which lives in the Himalayas (Nepal, Tibet, Russia and China) and leaves its tracks in the snow. Modern explorers have claimed to have seen their tracks in the snow and some have even brought back samples from Yetis, e.g. skin, hair and teeth. Recent DNA tests have shown that these samples belong to real animals such as dogs and bears.

5 Ask students to describe the two photos on page 91 (the mountain and footprint) and say what they think the story is about.

Answers

Students' own answers

6 Ask students to read the text to check their ideas. Encourage them to say which four words are missing from the text (*wide, high, long and deep*).

Answers

Students' own answers

7 Point out that they will need to use each word once.

112

Answers

The Reading text is recorded for students to listen, read and check their answers.
1 high 2 long 3 wide 4 deep

8 Point out that the students should use their imagination and give their opinions to answer these questions. There are no correct answers.

Answers

Students' own answers

GRAMMAR Past continuous

1 Books closed. Introduce the past continuous by drawing a timeline on the board:

Today

Ask the students 'What did the explorers see in the Himalayas?' (*footprints in the snow*) and write it on the timeline:

footprints in the snow Today

Then, ask the students to describe the explorers' activity at this time and write it on the timeline:

footprints in the snow Today

← They were walking through deep snow →

Finally, ask the students some concept check questions: 'When did they start walking?' 'When did they see the footprints?' 'Did they continue walking afterwards?' Elicit when we use the past continuous.

Books open. As a class, ask the students to look at the table and say what kind of words are missing in 1–4 (*the verb*) before they complete the table.

Answers

1 climbing 2 walking 3 exploring 4 climbing

» GRAMMAR REFERENCE AND PRACTICE ANSWER KEY TB PAGE 249

2 Point out that the students should use the past continuous in all these sentences. Remind them to check their spelling, in particular sentence 1 *running* (double *n*). In 4, they will need to add the subject pronoun for the short answer.

MIXED ABILITY

Allow the stronger students to do the exercise on their own. Invite the weaker students to the board, write the gapped sentences on the board, and complete them together step by step. Encourage the weaker students to look at the table in Exercise 1 as they do this.

FAST FINISHERS

Fast finishers use the table in Exercise 1 to write questions about Eric Shipton and the explorers. When the others are ready, organise the class into small groups with at least one fast finisher in each group. The fast finisher reads their questions and the others answer. If appropriate, the fast finisher can award points for correct answers.

Answers

1 were playing, weren't running 2 Were, climbing, wasn't 3 was watching, wasn't tidying 4 Were the students working, they were

3 Point out that students often make mistakes with tenses, in particular they often use the present when they are talking about the past. Point out that there is one mistake with the tense in each of these sentences. With a weaker class, also point out that the verbs in the present continuous should be in the past continuous.

Answers

1 We **were** playing football in the park yesterday morning.
2 I lost it at the party when we **were** dancing.
3 We **weren't** reading stories about strange animals in class yesterday.
4 She **wasn't** thinking and she dropped her bag.

» GRAMMAR WORKSHEET UNIT 15

ə PRONUNCIATION

Rising and falling intonation

4 The students listen and repeat. Point out that when *was* and *were* aren't stressed (the weak form), we use a schwa /ə/. When they are negative, we generally use the strong form.

113 **Audioscript**

The sentences are recorded for the students to listen and repeat.

My brother was riding his bike.

My dad wasn't working in the garden.

Were they climbing in the mountains?

Were you looking for footprints?

5 Read the example dialogue as a class, pointing out that Student B's answer is a long answer with information about the place, the people and the activity. Encourage the students to give as much information as possible in their answers.

Answers

Students' own answers

COOLER

Hand out a slip of paper to each student. Ask them to write an activity on it that you can do at a party, e.g. *drink lemonade*, *dance*, *listen to music*.

Collect in the slips of paper, mix them up and hand them out again to different students. Tell them they are at a party and when the music starts, they should stand up and do the activity on their paper (and also watch what other students are doing).

Play some 'party music' and allow the students one or two minutes to do their action. Then, turn off the music. Ask the students to sit down. In groups, ask the students to write as many correct sentences as they can using the past continuous, e.g. *Maria was dancing*.

Is the story real?

112

In 1951, a British explorer, Eric Shipton, was climbing in the Himalayas, south of Mount Everest. He wasn't exploring alone. There were several climbers and Sherpas with him. They weren't climbing that day, but they were walking through thick snow on a mountain 6,000 metres [1] ________ when they saw a line of footprints. They followed the footprints for 500 metres. The footprints were 33 cm [2] ________, 20 cm [3] ________ and a few centimetres [4] ________. It wasn't a bear. The footprints were much too big. The Sherpas said the animal usually lived in the forests and didn't often come up into the snow. Their name for the animal was the Yeti, or the Wild Man of the Snows. People still come back from the Himalayas today with stories of seeing the Yeti.

GRAMMAR Past continuous

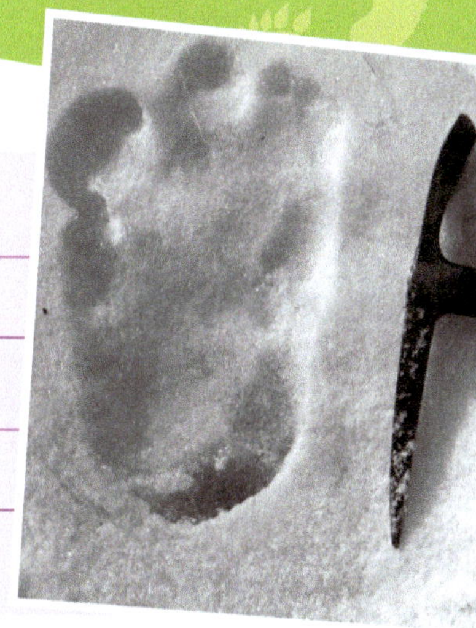

1 **Read the table. Complete sentences 1–4 using the verbs in the article.**

Positive	Eric Shipton The climbers	was were	[1] ________ in the mountains. [2] ________ through thick snow.
Negative	Eric Shipton The climbers	wasn't weren't	[3] ________ alone. [4] ________ that day.
Questions	Was	I/he/she/it	looking for footprints?
	Were	you/we/they	
Short answers	Yes, No,	I/he/she/it	was. wasn't.
	Yes, No,	you/we/they	were. weren't.

» GRAMMAR REFERENCE AND PRACTICE PAGE 152

2 **What was happening yesterday afternoon? Complete the sentences with the past continuous form of the verbs.**

0 '*Was* Suzie *helping* (help) her teacher?' 'Yes, *she was*.'
1 The boys ________ (play) football in the park. They ________ (not run) very fast because the grass was too long.
2 ________ you ________ (climb) that tree?' 'No, I ________.'
3 My friend ________ (watch) TV. She ________ (not tidy) her room.
4 '________ the students ________ (working) on the computer?' 'Yes, ________.'

3 **Correct the mistakes in the sentences.**

1 We are playing football in the park yesterday morning.
2 I lost it at the party when we are dancing.
3 We aren't reading stories about strange animals in class yesterday.
4 She isn't thinking and she dropped her bag.

ə PRONUNCIATION
Rising and falling intonation

113 **4** **Listen and repeat.**

My brother was riding his bike.
My dad wasn't working in the garden.
Were they climbing in the mountains?
Were you looking for footprints?

5 **In pairs, ask and answer the questions.**

What were you doing …
… last Sunday morning at eleven o'clock?
… yesterday at seven o'clock in the morning?
… last Saturday at one o'clock?
… last Monday evening at six o'clock?

What were you doing last Sunday morning at eleven o'clock?

I was at the sports centre. I was swimming with my mum.

READING

1 Look at the photos. What do you know about Loch Ness and the Loch Ness Monster?

2 Read the article quickly and match the pictures A–C to the paragraphs 1–3.

3 Read the article again and answer the questions.

1. When do people think they see things on the loch?
2. What does 'loch' mean?
3. How big is Loch Ness?
4. Which has more water: the lakes of Wales and England or Loch Ness?
5. When did people first see a monster?

A

LOCH NESS

1

Loch is the Scottish Gaelic word for 'lake'. Loch Ness is in the north of Scotland not far from Inverness. The loch is 230 m deep – it's the second deepest loch in Scotland – 36 km long and nearly 3 km wide. There's more water in Loch Ness than all the water in all the lakes in England and Wales. That's a lot of water for something to hide in!

B

2

The weather around the loch changes quickly. One minute it's sunny, the next it's cloudy, the next there's a bit of rain, and then it's sunny again. It can be a windy place, too. Clouds move quickly through the sky and on sunny days the clouds make shadows on the water. It's easy to think you see something in the water. When it's foggy, the fog sits on the loch and it's possible to think you see things then too.

3

The story of the Loch Ness Monster, or 'Nessie', started about 1,500 years ago. Then people called it a giant water animal. In the 1930s, a new road beside the loch brought more people to the area and more people started to see more strange things. In fact, over 1,000 people think they saw a strange animal in the loch.

There are several photos of some of the strange animals. Could any of them be Nessie?

114

TALKING POINTS

Do you think there is a monster living in Loch Ness?
If not, why do so many people think they see something?

READING

WARMER

Introduce the topic of strange stories by saying to the class: 'Something very strange happened at the weekend.' Wait for the students to respond, e.g. *What happened? Tell us more!* before you continue with your strange story. If appropriate, use this one:

I was watching a film, when I heard a strange noise outside. I opened the door and saw a large, white dog. It looked hungry, so I gave it some meat. It ate the meat quickly and disappeared. On Sunday, I told my neighbour about the dog. He said, 'That's strange! A large, white dog lived in your house many years ago but it died just before the owner moved house.'

Invite a class discussion on this story by asking questions: 'Who is the dog?' 'Is it the same dog that lived in the house before?' 'Where is the dog now?' Then, tell the students that they are going to read and listen to some strange stories and at the end of the lesson, they are going to tell their own story about an animal. Encourage them to start thinking of ideas for it.

1 Ask the students to describe the photos and as a class, say what they know about Loch Ness and its monster. Encourage the students to say more by asking 'What is a loch?' 'Where is Loch Ness?' 'What do you think the weather is like there?' 'How deep do you think the loch is?' 'What lives there?' 'When did people first see it?'

Answers

Students' own answers

2 Encourage the students to read the article quickly and check their ideas in Exercise 1. Then, ask them to match the paragraphs (1–3) to the photos (A–C).

MIXED ABILITY

With a mixed ability class, divide the class into three groups for Exercises 2 and 3. Put the stronger students in Group B and the weaker ones in Group A or C. Group A reads part 1, matches it to its photo and answers question 1 in Exercise 3. Group B reads part 2, matches it to its photo and answers questions 2, 3 and 4. Group C reads part 3, matches it to its photo and answers question 5. Then, three students from each group work together and share their answers.

Answers

A 3 B 1 C 2

3 Ask the students to try to answer the questions in pairs before they read the article again.

Answers

1 When there are clouds making shadows on the water or when it's foggy.
2 It is Scottish for 'lake'.
3 It is 36 km long, nearly 3 km wide and 230 m deep.
4 Loch Ness.
5 About 1,500 years ago.

114 The Reading text is recorded for students to listen and read.

TALKING POINTS

Remind the students there is no right or wrong answer to these questions. Ask the students in small groups to take turns to give their opinions. Encourage them to think of as many possibilities as they can for the second question.

16 AMAZING ANIMALS

ABOUT YOU

11 Watch the video then ask and answer the questions in pairs.
What animals do people in your family have?
Do you like visiting zoos? Why? / Why not?
Is there any animal in particular that you like?

A

B

C

D

E

F

G

H

I

J

VOCABULARY AND READING

Animals

1 Match the photos A–J to the words in the box.

EP

bear chicken duck elephant
insect lion monkey mouse
rabbit rat

116 Listen, check and repeat.

2 Complete the table with the words in Exercise 1. Which of the animals can you keep as pets?

Wild animals	Farm animals	Both

Now add other animals that you know.

3 In pairs, discuss the questions.

1 Which of the animals in Exercise 2 can help people?
2 How do they help?
3 What can they do?

4 Look at the photos on page 95. Are these wild animals, pets or farm animals?

Now read the story quickly. Which animal helped Jack?

5 Choose the best title for the story.

1 A quiet walk in the forest
2 Bear to the rescue
3 Alone with a mountain lion

6 Read the story again and answer the questions.

1 What time of year was it?
2 Was Jack walking in this area for the first time?
3 How many bears did he see?
4 Was the bear afraid of Jack?
5 What jumped onto Jack's back?
6 Which was the larger animal, the mother bear or the mountain lion?
7 What did the bear do next?
8 What did the mountain lion do next?

16 AMAZING ANIMALS

Unit Overview

TOPIC	Wild animals and pets
VOCABULARY	Animals
AND READING	Bear to the rescue
GRAMMAR	Past simple and past continuous
READING	Our animal friends
VOCABULARY	Phrasal verbs
PRONUNCIATION	/uː/ and /ʊ/
LISTENING	An interview about looking after pets
WRITING	A story
EXAM TASKS	Reading Part 4; Writing Part 7

Resources

GRAMMAR REFERENCE AND PRACTICE: SB page 153; TB page 249
WORKBOOK: pages 68–71
VIDEO AND VIDEO WORKSHEET: Animals
PHOTOCOPIABLE WORKSHEETS: Grammar worksheet Unit 16; Vocabulary worksheet Unit 16
TEST GENERATOR: Unit test 16

WARMER

Books closed. Write the unit title *Amazing animals* on the board. First, challenge the students to think of an animal or a bird beginning with each letter in the title, e.g. *Ant, Monkey, Alligator, Zebra, Iguana, Newt, Giraffe, Antelope, Nightingale, Insect, Mouse, Armadillo, Lion, Snake*. Then, discuss ways animals are amazing.

ABOUT YOU

11 You can begin the class and introduce the topic of the unit by showing the video and asking students to complete the video worksheet. Then, read the questions in the *About you* box and students answer the questions in pairs.

VOCABULARY AND READING

Animals

1 Ask the students to identify the animals in the photos first before they match them to the words in the box.

116 **Answers**

The answers are recorded for the students to check and then repeat.
A monkey B insect C chicken D bear E elephant F duck G lion H mouse I rabbit J rat

2 Pre-teach *wild* and *farm* by asking 'Where do we find chickens?' (*on farms*) and 'What about bears?' (*in the wild*) Copy the table onto the board and ask a volunteer to write *bear* and *chicken* in the correct column. Ask the students to continue in pairs and then underline any animals which you can also keep as pets. Finally, ask them to add more animals to their table.

Answers

Wild animals: bear, chicken, duck, elephant, insect, lion, monkey, mouse, rabbit, rat
Farm animals: chicken, duck, insect, rabbit
Pets: insect, mouse, rabbit, rat (also accept other animals if students can justify their answer)
Students' own answers

3 Ask the class 'Can an elephant help people?' (*yes*) 'How?' (*by moving heavy objects*) and invite a brief class discussion. Then, encourage the students in pairs to ask these questions about the other animals in Exercise 2.

Answers

Students' own answers

4 First, ask the students to look at the photos at the top of page 95 and identify the two animals they can see (*two black bears and a mountain lion*) and the kind of animals they are. Then, ask them to guess which animal helped Jack before they read the story.

Answers

wild animals
the mother bear

5 Ask the students to think of a good title for the story before they look at the three options (1–3).

Answers

2

6 Encourage the students to try to answer the questions before they read the story again.

FAST FINISHERS

Put the fast finishers into pairs. Student A is Jack and Student B is a friend. Jack should tell his friend what happened and his friend should show interest (e.g. *Really? No?*) and ask more questions (e.g. *What did you do next? Were you scared?*).

Answers

1 It was May / spring.
2 No, it was a place he knew well.
3 He saw three.
4 No, it wasn't.
5 A mountain lion jumped onto his back.
6 The mother bear was larger.
7 The bear pulled the lion off his back.
8 The lion ran away.

117 The Reading text is recorded for students to listen and read.

GRAMMAR Past simple and past continuous

1 Books closed. Ask 'When did the story happen?' (*in the past*) Draw the following on the board:

Today

Jack **saw** a black bear (B)

Ask 'What was Jack doing when he saw the black bear?' (*He was walking along a path.*) Add the first part of the sentence:

Jack **was walking** along a path (A) when … Today

He **saw** a black bear (B)

Elicit the tense of the verbs (*A past continuous, B past simple*) and which happened first (*A*).

Books open. The students answer the questions.

Answers

1 *saw* is past simple, *was walking* is past continuous
2 Action A started first
3 Action B interrupted Action A

» **GRAMMAR REFERENCE AND PRACTICE ANSWER KEY TB PAGE 249**

2 Ask the students to say whether we usually follow *while* with the past simple or past continuous (*past continuous*).

Answers

While Jack was watching the bears, something large and heavy hit him from behind.
2 *was watching* started first.
3 *hit* interrupted *was watching*
Then, while he was fighting it, the mother bear ran towards him.
2 *was fighting* started first
3 *ran* interrupted *fighting*
While the mountain lion was attacking Jack, the bear stood on its two back legs.
2 *was attacking* started first
3 *stood* interrupted *was attacking*

3 Ask the students to highlight the past simple and past continuous in two different colours.

Answers

Past simple: liked, knew, stopped, walked, knew, wasn't, didn't try, tried, didn't attack, attacked, pulled, ran off, went, looked at, walked, recognised, wanted, was (x 5)
Past continuous: was walking

4 Before going over the answers, ask the students to check a) the spelling of their past simple verbs; b) that they have used *was* and *were* correctly; and c) that they have spelled the *-ing* form correctly.

MIXED ABILITY

Pens down. Read the complete sentences (i.e. with the verbs in the correct past simple or continuous form) to the students first and ask them to identify which verb is in the past simple and which is in the past continuous before they do the exercise.

Answers

1 were sleeping, started 2 was reading, rang
3 arrived, were playing 4 was eating, heard
5 fell off, was skating

5 Point out that there is one mistake in each sentence either with the verb in the past simple or the verb in the past continuous.

Answers

1 When we **were** looking for the lions at the zoo yesterday, we found the elephants.
2 Yesterday while I **was coming** back home, I dropped my purse in the road.
3 When I **was** waiting for the bus, I saw a monkey in the trees.
4 When we **were walking** beside the lake, we heard a noise behind us.
5 It **was** snowing when I went there and very cold.

6 Read the two example sentences. Ask the students to look at the animals in the table in Exercise 2 on page 94 and elicit a couple more examples as a class. Then, challenge the students to make at least five more sentences in pairs.

Answers

Students' own answers

» **GRAMMAR WORKSHEET UNIT 16**

COOLER

Write this on the board.

past simple	**past continuous**
1 see a bear	1 play a computer game
2 phone the police	2 ride my bike
3 wake up	3 sleep on the sofa
4 hear a strange noise	4 rain
5 arrive home	5 watch TV
6 fall down	6 have lunch

Demonstrate the activity. Shake the dice; this number gives you the verb in the past simple. Shake it again; this gives the verb in the past continuous. Make a complete sentence with the two verbs and *when/while*, e.g. *My mum phoned the police while we were having lunch.* Point out the order of the two verbs is not important. Students play in groups of six for a few minutes.

One day in May, Jack Smith was walking in Northern Oregon. It was a place he liked walking in and he knew it well. He was walking along a path when he saw a black bear, a female with her two babies. One was about a year old, the other was only a few months. Jack stopped to watch the bears. Because Jack walked along the path regularly, the bear knew who he was. It wasn't afraid and it didn't try to attack him. While Jack was watching the bears, something large and heavy hit him from behind. It was a mountain lion! Jack tried to get away from the mountain lion. Then, while he was fighting it, the mother bear ran towards him. But the bear didn't attack Jack, it attacked the mountain lion. The bear was much bigger than the mountain lion. While the mountain lion was attacking Jack, the bear stood on its two back legs and pulled the mountain lion off Jack's back. The mountain lion ran off into the trees. Then the bear went back onto its four feet and looked at Jack for a moment, before it walked back to look after its babies.

Jack wasn't badly hurt. He was sure the bear recognised him and wanted to save his life.

GRAMMAR Past simple and past continuous

1 **Look at this sentence from the story and answer the questions.**

A — B

*He **was walking** along a path when he **saw** a black bear.*

1 Which verb is past simple, and which verb is past continuous?
2 Which action, **A** or **B**, started first?
3 Which action, **A** or **B**, interrupted the other?

» GRAMMAR REFERENCE AND PRACTICE PAGE 153

2 **Find three sentences with *while* in the story. Answer questions 2 and 3 in Exercise 1 about them.**

3 **Find all the other examples of the past simple and the past continuous in the story.**

4 **Complete the sentences with one verb in the past simple and one in the past continuous.**

0 The boy *was eating* (eat) an ice cream when the monkey *stole* (steal) it.
1 The cats ________ (sleep) outside when the rain ________ (start).
2 While the girl ________ (read) a book, her phone ________ (ring).
3 The teacher ________ (arrive) while Katie and Adam ________ (play) a computer game.
4 Lucy ________ (eat) her lunch when she ________ (hear) the news.
5 The boy ________ (fall off) his board while he ________ (skate) in the park.

5 **Correct the mistakes with the past simple and past continuous.**

1 When we looking for the lions at the zoo yesterday, we found the elephants.
2 Yesterday while I came back home, I dropped my purse in the road.
3 When I waiting for the bus, I saw a monkey in the trees.
4 When we walk beside the lake, we heard a noise behind us.
5 It is snowing when I went there and very cold.

6 **In pairs, take turns to say sentences with *when* or *while* and the past simple or past continuous. Use the verbs in the box and animals from the table on page 94.**

climb	drive	eat	find	open
run	sit	talk	walk	write

While the man was driving along the road, a monkey jumped out of a tree.

I saw a family of rabbits when I was walking by the river.

READING

1 Look at the photos. How are these animals helping people? Do you think it is bad to use animals in this way? Discuss your ideas with your partner.

2 Read Part 1 of the article. Match two of the photos A–C to this part of the article.

3 Read Part 1 of the article again.

1 Find three things that guide horses can do.
2 Find two things that monkey helpers can do.

4 Look at the photos again. What do you think Part 2 of the article is about? Read it quickly to check your ideas.

5 Read Part 2 of the article again. For each question, choose the correct answer (A, B or C) for each gap.

1	**A** busy	**B** free	**C** favourite
2	**A** help	**B** look	**C** make
3	**A** tells	**B** speaks	**C** says
4	**A** arrives	**B** brings	**C** collects
5	**A** shall	**B** need	**C** should
6	**A** project	**B** activities	**C** jobs

6 In pairs, look at all the choices for Exercise 5 again and answer the question.

How did you choose the correct answers?

Our Animal Friends

118

1 Animals can help people in many different ways. They can help people in their homes and in their daily lives. They can also save people when they are in danger, for example in the mountains or in the sea. When people think of animal helpers, most people think of guide dogs for the blind (people who can't see). But do you know about guide horses? These small horses help blind people move around a city or town. For example, they travel with them in taxis, cross roads and even help them get on and get off buses. Horses live much longer than dogs, so they can be with the person for a long time. Other animals can be helpers too. Monkeys are very clever and can look after people in many different ways. They can pick up your phone when you drop it. They can turn on the television for your favourite programme and turn off the television when it finishes. However, many people think that monkeys shouldn't be animal helpers because they are wild animals.

A

2 Most dogs are good at swimming but the dogs in the photo are very, very good at it. They work on [1] ______ beaches in Italy during the summer, keeping people safe in the sea. They can jump from helicopters and fast boats, and [2] ______ people in danger in the water.

'Dogs don't get tired as quickly as we do,' [3] ______ Emilio, their trainer. 'A dog is strong and it can swim fast. It gets to a swimmer faster than we can and then it [4] ______ the person back to the beach.'

It takes three years to teach these dogs everything they [5] ______ to know. Then they are ready to do their [6] ______.

People often think of animals as their friends, but these amazing animals are much more than that.

B

C

TALKING POINTS

Were you surprised by any of the animal helpers in the article? Which ones? Why?
Discuss your ideas with your partner.

READING

WARMER

Write anagrams of some of the animals in this unit on the board, e.g. *ilno* (lion), *art* (rat) and *aber* (bear). Include *dog*, *horse* and *monkey*. Challenge the students to find all the animals within a time limit, e.g. two minutes. Then invite a brief class discussion on how dogs, horses and monkeys can help people.

BACKGROUND INFORMATION

Blind people and dogs have had a special relationship as far back as the first century as shown on a mural in the Roman ruins of Herculaneum. However, people didn't start training dogs to act as guides until after the First World War. It takes about 18 months to train a dog from birth. During this training, the dog is taken to all the places its owner will go to and needs to learn what is safe. Guide dogs are working dogs, so if you see a guide dog, you should not touch, feed or talk to it without asking its owner first.

1 Ask the class to identify the animals in the photos first. Use the photos to pre-teach *guide dog*, *guide horse* and *blind* (ask 'Who does the guide dog or guide horse help?') and then ask them to discuss their ideas in pairs.

Answers

Students' own answers

2 Ask the students to read Part 1 quickly and say which of the two photos on this page go with this part.

Answers

B and C

3 Encourage the students to talk about these things before they read Part 1 again and check their ideas.

Answers

1 travel with them in taxis, cross roads, get on and off buses
2 pick up the phone, turn on and off the TV

4 Now ask the students to look at the remaining photo and try to guess what this part is about. Point out that they should not try to complete the text for now. When they have read the text, ask them some questions to check they have understood it, e.g. 'Where do these dogs work?' (*on beaches in Italy*) 'What do they jump from?' (*helicopters and fast boats*) 'Why are dogs good lifeguards?' (*they don't get tired as quickly as us, they are strong and they can swim fast*) 'How long is their training?' (*three years*)

Answers

swimming dogs which save people

5 **A2 Key for Schools, Reading Part 4.**

In this part of the exam, students fill in six spaces in a text with a word. The main focus is on vocabulary, although there may be a maximum of two grammatical items. Each space has three multiple-choice options. Ask the students to read the complete text again and think about the missing words without reading the options. Then, ask them to look at the options and choose the best word (A, B or C) for each space.

MIXED ABILITY

With a mixed ability class, encourage the stronger students to complete the exercise on their own. With the weaker students, go through the text question by question and help them to find the correct answer by removing one of the incorrect answers for them.

118

Answers

The Reading text is recorded for students to listen, read and check their answers.

1 A 2 A 3 C 4 B 5 B 6 C

6 Encourage the students to say in pairs why the answer they chose is correct and why the other answers are wrong.

Answers

Students' own answers

TALKING POINTS

First, encourage the students to write down at least two new things they learned from the complete article (Parts 1 and 2) before they discuss their answers to the questions with their partner.

VOCABULARY Phrasal verbs

1 Ask the students to find the phrasal verbs in Part 1 of the article and to try to guess the meaning of each one from the context before they look at the meanings (a–f).

Answers

1 d 2 e 3 f 4 c 5 b 6 a

2 Ask the students to read each sentence in pairs first and think about the meaning of the missing phrasal verb. Point out that some verbs will need to be in the past.

Answers

1 pick up 2 get on 3 turn off 4 looked after 5 turned on

» VOCABULARY WORKSHEET UNIT 16

PRONUNCIATION /uː/ and /ʊ/

3 Ask the students to look at *good*, *food* and *foot* and ask 'Do we pronounce the *oo* in the same way in all three words?' (*no:* /gʊd/, /fuːd/ *and* /fʊt/) Play the recording and ask the class to listen. After checking the answers, ask the students to listen to the words again and repeat.

119 **Audioscript**

The words are recorded for students to listen to the sounds.

do, food, foot, good, group, look, move, put, suit, took, true, two

120 **Answers**

The answers are recorded for students to listen and check, then listen and repeat.
/uː/ move: do, food, group, suit, true, two
/ʊ/ look: foot, good, put, took

LISTENING

121 1 Ask the students to identify Jim Townes (the boy) and Sue Green (the girl) in the photo. Read the instructions and ask the students to predict what Sue might say. Write a list on the board. After listening, ask 'How many different things did Sue say?' and 'Did she say any of the things on the list on the board?'

Answers

three – feeding pets, keeping pets clean, treating them as living things, not toys

121 2 Point out that Sue talked about the three things at the top of each column, i.e. *food*, *keeping them clean* and *animals, not toys*. Ask the students in small groups to make notes on what Sue means by each one before they listen again.

Answers

Food: They feed the pet. They can do it every day and learn that animals get hungry and thirsty just like them.
Keeping them clean: Brushing the animal. Animals don't like to be dirty. Cleaning the cage once a week.
Animals are not toys: They are living things. Learning to be kind, playing with them nicely and not hurting them.

» AUDIOSCRIPT TB PAGE 275

3 Have students work in small groups to think of at least three other things we can learn from looking after a pet (*e.g. they can get ill or hurt, they can die, how to be responsible for a living being, respect for others*).

Answers

Students' own answers

WRITING

PREPARE TO WRITE
A story

GET READY In pairs, ask the students to describe what they can see in each picture and then ask them to try to tell the short story. Point out that they should use the past tense. Encourage the students to ask each other (and if necessary you) for useful vocabulary (e.g. *drop her purse*, *pick up her purse*, *a handbag*) using *How do you say X in English?*

PLAN Point out that the students need to write something about all three pictures and encourage them to make notes.

WRITE A2 Key for Schools Writing Part 7.

In this part of the exam, students will need to look at three pictures and write the story shown in the pictures in 35 words or more. Encourage the students to use the past tense for their story and remind them that they should use words like *and*, *but*, *because* and *so* to connect their ideas.

Model answer

One day, while Martha was walking down the street, her purse fell out of her handbag. A little dog was following her. It picked up the purse. Later, Martha was looking for her purse in her handbag when the little dog gave it back to her.

IMPROVE Students should try to give their partner at least two ideas to make their story better. They should check that their partner has used the past tense correctly and also check their partner's spelling.

FAST FINISHERS

Ask fast finishers to write a much longer story (about 70 words) using *when* and *while*, the past simple and past continuous. They could also write about the weather in the story and how the woman was feeling.

COOLER

Have a hot air balloon debate. Organise the class into groups of six. Each member of the group chooses a different animal. Tell the groups that they are animals and they are in a hot air balloon. It is too heavy, so one of the animals has to jump out. Each animal needs to say why they should remain and then, finally, they vote on who has to jump.

VOCABULARY Phrasal verbs

1 **Match the phrasal verbs from Part 1 of the article to the meanings.**

EP

1 get on	**a** start something working
2 get off	**b** stop something working
3 look after	**c** take something off the floor
4 pick up	**d** enter a bus, train, plane or boat
5 turn off	**e** leave a bus, train, plane or boat
6 turn on	**f** help someone when they are ill or cannot do something themselves

2 **Complete each sentence with one of the phrasal verbs in Exercise 1 in the correct tense.**

0 It was starting to rain when I _got off_ the bus, so I opened my umbrella.
1 Please ________ your bags from the floor and put them on the shelf.
2 Finally, the boat arrived to take us across the lake. But it was full and we couldn't ________.
3 I can only do my homework when it's quiet. Please can you ________ the radio?
4 I ________ my mum when she was ill. I made her meals and drinks.
5 I woke up suddenly in the night and it was very dark, so I ________ the light.

PRONUNCIATION /uː/ and /ʊ/

119 **3** **Listen to the sounds /uː/ and /ʊ/.**

Then put the words in the box in the correct columns.

do food foot good
group look move put
suit took true two

/uː/ move	/ʊ/ look

120 **Listen and check. Then repeat.**

LISTENING

121 **1** **Listen to the radio interview between Jim Townes and Sue Green. Sue talks about things children learn from looking after pets. How many things does she talk about?**

121 **2** **Now listen again and make notes in the chart about what Sue says children learn from pets.**

Food	Keeping them clean	Animals, not toys

3 **Do you think Sue is right? What other things can children learn when they look after a pet?**

WRITING

PREPARE TO WRITE
A story

GET READY Look at the three pictures. What does each one show? Compare your ideas with a partner.

PLAN In your story you have to write about all of the pictures. Read the questions and make notes.

1 What happened in the first picture?
2 What happened in the second picture?
3 What happened in the third picture?
4 What was the end of the story?

WRITE Write the story shown in the pictures. Write 35 words or more.

IMPROVE In pairs, read your own story and your partner's. Check for mistakes.
Give your partner two ideas to make their story better. Use your partner's advice and rewrite your story.

LIFE SKILLS SOCIAL RESPONSIBILITY

PROTECTING ANIMALS

LIFE SKILLS

Protecting animals

We can protect pets and animals in the wild by:

- making sure they have food and water
- making sure they have a safe place to live
- being kind to them

1 **Read the sentences in the speech bubbles and answer the questions.**

Animals are not toys.

We should be kind to animals like we are kind to people.

1 Do you agree with the sentences? Why? / Why not?
2 Which sentence do you prefer? Why?
3 Do you have a pet? Have you ever visited an animal reserve or seen a wild animal?

2 **Think of the animals in your country and answer the questions.**

1 Which are in danger? What problems do they have?
2 Can people help them? How?

In pairs, compare your ideas.

3 **Look at the title of the article and the photos. How do bees help us? Why is it important to protect bees? What is the bee collecting in the photo?**

4 **Read the article quickly and check your answers.**

Save the bees!

1 Are bees important?

Bees are a very important part of our ecosystem. Bees pollinate plants. In fact, about 30% of the food we eat depends on bees. Bees help people in other ways too. For example, they make the honey we eat and wax for candles and cleaning wood.

In many areas of the world, bees are in danger. People build houses, offices and factories on their homes. Farmers use strong chemicals on plants to stop insects eating them. But these chemicals also kill bees.

2 How does Mikaila Ulmer help bees?

Mikaila Ulmer, from Texas, is a girl who has her own lemonade company. She gives part of the money she makes selling lemonade and other products to charities to save bees. She teaches people about the importance of bees and how they help us. Mikaila has her own blog called Beelieve Blog. On her blog she shares information about her company and her projects.

3 How can we help bees and other insects?

There are a lot of different ways we can help protect bees and other insects. For example, we can:

- use fewer chemicals on plants
- learn more about organisations and people working to protect insects and their homes
- learn more about insects and how they help us
- start a blog on an animal or insect you think needs our help.

122

LIFE SKILLS

Learning Objectives

- The students learn how they can help and protect animals.
- In the project stage, they make a poster about protecting animals and display them in the classroom.

Vocabulary

wax pollinate charities ecosystem protect

BACKGROUND INFORMATION

There are over 3,000 endangered species of animals in the world, which means unless we do something to protect them, they will disappear from the planet. Animals which are already extinct include the Dodo, the Javan and Bali Tiger and the Elephant Bird. Other species such as the Northern White Rhinoceros only exist in conservation areas; they're extinct in their natural habitat. Species may become endangered due to global warming and climate change, destruction of their natural habitat, hunting or lack of food. The IUCN (International Union for Conservation of Nature) classifies endangered species into five categories: critically endangered, endangered, vulnerable, near threatened and least concern.

WARMER

Read out a list of endangered animals (e.g. Giant Panda, Bengal Tiger, Snow Leopard, African Penguin, Javan Rhino, etc.) and ask the class 'What do these animals have in common?' (*they're all endangered*) Next, invite a class discussion on how animals become endangered and what we can do to protect and save them.

LIFE SKILLS

Protecting animals

Ask the students to read the information in the *Life skills* box and check their ideas from the Warmer. Then, ask the class 'How can we be kind to animals?' (*respect them, support a rescue centre or animal charity, discourage others from being unkind,* etc.)

1 Encourage the students to ask and answer the questions in small groups. If appropriate, encourage the students to talk about the ways we are kind to people and how we should use these ways to be kind to animals (e.g. *we help people who are less privileged, so we should also help animals who are less privileged too*).

Answers

Students' own answers

2 First, brainstorm a list of animals from the students' country as a class. Then, give students time to think about their answers to the two questions before discussing their ideas in pairs.

Answers

Students' own answers

3 Ask the class to read the text title and find the photo of a bee. Next, ask them to look at the photo next to the bee and say what bees give us (*honey and wax to make candles*). Then, ask them to answer the questions in pairs. Don't tell the class the answers for now as they will read the complete text in Exercise 4.

Answers

Students' own answers (they will get the answers in Exercise 4)

4 When the students have read the article, ask them to compare their answers with a partner.

Answers

Bees help us because they pollinate plants (giving us fruit and vegetables). We get honey and wax from bees – we eat honey and we use wax to make candles and clean wood. It's important to protect bees or we might not have fresh produce/flowers. They are an important part of our ecosystem/world. The bee in the photo is collecting pollen.

5 Ask the students in pairs to try to say if the sentences are right or wrong before they read the text again.

Answers

1 × (They are very important.) 2 ✓ 3 ✓ 4 × (The company sells lemonade and other products.) 5 ✓ 6 × (There are different ways we can help.)

122 The Reading text is recorded for students to listen and read.

6 Ask the students to read the meanings first and try to think of a suitable word before they look at the highlighted words in the text.

MIXED ABILITY

Pair up a stronger student with a weaker student for this exercise. Ask the stronger student to help their partner with this exercise. Then, encourage the weaker students to choose four or five more words in the text that they do not understand and to ask their stronger partner for help with its meaning.

Answers

1 wax 2 pollinate 3 charities 4 ecosystem 5 protect

TALKING POINTS

Encourage the students to take turns to ask and answer these questions in small groups. Ask them to think of some more endangered animals which weren't mentioned in the Warmer section.

123 7 Ask the students to read through the sentences before they listen. Point out that they will need to choose one of the three.

Answers

c

123 8 In pairs, encourage the students to try to complete the sentences with the correct name before they listen again.

Answers

1 Alice 2 Jayden 3 Alice 4 Alice 5 Jayden 6 Alice

» AUDIOSCRIPT TB PAGES 275–276

9 Books closed. As a class, brainstorm some ways we can help animals and write them on the board. Books open. Ask the students to compare the list on the board with the list in the book. Then, ask the pairs to reach an agreement on the top three.

Answers

Students' own answers

10 Ask 'What sort of word is missing in each sentence?' (*a verb*) Then, encourage the students to read through the sentences in pairs and try to complete them with a suitable verb before they look at the words in the box.

FAST FINISHERS

Encourage fast finishers in pairs to read through the sentences again and talk together about whether they agree or disagree with each one. If they disagree, encourage them to rewrite the sentence so that they agree with it.

Answers

1 volunteer 2 protect 3 donate 4 make sure

PROJECT *A poster about protecting animals*

Ask the class to read the instructions in bold and ask 'What do you need to make for this project?' Next, ask them to look at the article about bees again and ask 'Is the design attractive?' (*yes*) 'Why?' (*there's a title and photos; it's divided into three short paragraphs; each paragraph has a clear question; there are bullet points in the third paragraph which makes it easier to read*)

Organise the students into small groups and ask them to choose an animal, preferably an animal which is endangered and that they don't know very much about. Encourage the groups to use the article as their model for their poster but with less text. Ask them to read what they need to include on the poster and think about questions for their headings, e.g. *What does [animal] need? How we can help [animal]? How can we protect [animal]?* Next, ask them to find some pictures and also the answers to the three questions.

Encourage them to check their written work for mistakes and then show a draft version of their poster to another group for feedback and ideas for improvement.

Ask the groups to produce their final version. If appropriate, invite another class to come and see the posters and to vote on the best three.

PROJECT EXTENSION

If you created a class blog in Life Skills ICT Literacy page 76–7, encourage the students to write a blog post on how we can protect their chosen animal. If they don't have a blog, ask them to write their blog post by hand. Students could find their ideas online by searching for 'animal rescue centres'. If available and/or appropriate, arrange for someone from an animal rescue centre to visit the school and talk about their work.

COOLER

Encourage the groups to write some quiz questions about their posters (see *Project* box), e.g. *Where does it live? What does it eat? Why is it endangered? How can we protect it?* Ask each group to take turns to read out their questions and also answer the other groups' questions. If the class enjoy competition, award points for correct answers.

5 **Read the text again. Are the sentences right (✓) or wrong (✗)?**

1 Bees are not important animals.
2 Bees help us to make candles.
3 Bees are in danger in some places.
4 Michaela's company only sells honey.
5 Michaela has a blog.
6 We cannot help protect bees and other insects.

6 **Match the highlighted words in the text to the meanings.**

1 we use this to make candles
2 moving pollen from one plant to another
3 organisations helping something or someone and raising money
4 all the plants and animals in one place and how they live together
5 to keep safe

TALKING POINTS

Do you like bees or are you afraid of them?
What other animals are in danger?

123 **7** **Listen to Jayden and Alice talking. What are they talking about?**

a They are talking about making honey.
b They are talking about birds and turtles in the wild.
c They are talking about rescue centres and volunteer jobs.

123 **8** **Listen again and write Alice or Jayden.**

1 ________ is looking at a website.
2 ________ is afraid of bees.
3 ________ says we get honey and wax from bees.
4 ________ finds a centre with rabbits, cats, dogs and rats.
5 ________ has music lessons on Saturday mornings.
6 ________ is going to call to find out more.

9 **Look at the list (a–f). Number the top three ways you think we can help animals. Compare your answers with your partner.**

a We can **donate money.**
b We can **protect** animals.
c We can **volunteer** our time.
d We can **make sure that animals have food and water.**
e We can **protect their homes.**
f We can **find out ways to help** animals.

10 **Complete the sentences with the words in the box.**

donate make sure protect volunteer

1 I want to ________ at an animal rescue centre at weekends.
2 There are a lot of different ways to ________ animals. You can find out more online.
3 I want to ________ part of my pocket money to an animal rescue centre.
4 We need to ________ animals have safe homes, food and water.

PROJECT

A poster about protecting animals

In small groups, make a poster about protecting animals.

- Choose an animal. Is it a pet or a wild animal? How big is it?
- Design a small poster to help people know more about your animal. Include:
  - pictures of your animal or its home
  - what your animal needs
  - how people can help your animal
  - how we can protect it.
- Take turns presenting your posters to another group.
- Display posters in the classroom.

REVIEW 4 UNITS 13–16

VOCABULARY

1 Find the odd word out in each set.

0 lake (cloudy) mountain field
1 duck monkey playground rabbit
2 library insect bridge post office
3 race headache temperature pain
4 helicopter bicycle bus roundabout
5 deep rest wide high

2 Read the definitions and complete the words.

0 When the weather is like this, it's difficult to see where you're going.
f _o_ _g_ _g_ _y_
1 You put this on to keep you dry when it is wet.
r ___ ___ n ___ ___ a ___
2 You stop your car and wait when this is red. You go when it is green.
t ___ ___ ___ f ___ c ___ i ___ h ___
3 We get eggs and meat from this farm animal.
c ___ ___ c ___ ___ ___
4 This is an animal and also something we use with our computers.
m ___ ___ s ___
5 Doing lots of this keeps you healthy.
e x ___ ___ ___ i ___ e

3 Complete the sentences with the correct form of the phrasal verbs in the box.

get on	get off	look after	pick up
turn off	turn on		

1 I was late for school this morning because I ________ the wrong bus!
2 The football match starts in a few minutes. Please can you ________ the TV?
3 While I ________ the train, I fell down and hurt my leg.
4 My sister was ill yesterday, so my dad stayed at home to ________ her.
5 It's important to ________ your mobile phone when you're at the cinema.
6 At the weekends, I ________ rubbish at our local park.

GRAMMAR

1 Choose the correct words to complete the sentences.

1 I ate with my family *out* / *outside* the tent.
2 It's very easy to get to the sports centre because it's *in front of* / *opposite* my house.
3 I took a trip *through* / *down* the River Nile.
4 You *shall* / *should* bring some of your computer games.

Correct the mistakes in the sentences.

5 I enjoyed my holiday. Every day I was going swimming.
6 I liked the tennis match because Nadal and Grigor Dimitrov are playing.
7 In Thailand, I visited many places and the most interesting thing is eating the food there.
8 It is raining in Taipei when we got there yesterday.

2 Complete the sentences with the verbs in brackets. Use the past simple or past continuous.

0 It _wasn't raining_ (not rain) when I _left_ (leave) the house this morning.
1 When I ________ (arrive) at the party, my friend ________ (sing) in the living room.
2 I ________ (walk) around the shops when I ________ (meet) my friend.
3 My dad ________ (call) me while I ________ (do) my homework.
4 I ________ (not run) when I ________ (hurt) my foot. I ________ (dance).
5 I ________ (not see) any animals when I ________ (walk) in the snow.

3 Give these people advice using *should* or *shouldn't*.

0 I've got a temperature and a headache.
You should take some medicine and go to bed. You shouldn't go to school.
1 My running shoes are too small.
2 I really want a pet!
3 The weather's really hot and I want to go to the beach.
4 I've got nothing to wear to my friend's party.
5 I don't know the way to the museum.

REVIEW 4 UNITS 13–16

Overview

VOCABULARY	Illness; Health; Places in town; Compound nouns; Geographical features; The weather; Animals; Phrasal verbs
GRAMMAR	*should / shouldn't*; Prepositions; Past continuous; Past simple and past continuous
WRITING	Write a story
LISTENING	Tessa talking about her friends
SPEAKING	Asking questions; talking about where you live
EXAM TASKS	Writing Part 7; Listening Part 5; Speaking Part 1

Resources

PHOTOCOPIABLE WORKSHEETS: Grammar worksheets Units 13–16; Vocabulary worksheets Units 13–16; Review Game Units 13–16; Literature worksheet; Speaking worksheet; Writing worksheet

WARMER

Organise the students into small groups and give each group a piece of paper or a mini whiteboard* and a board marker. Read out a description of some of the words in Review 4 Vocabulary Exercise 1 and ask the groups to write down the correct word in large letters. As soon as they have finished, they should hold up their word for you to look at and check. If appropriate, award points for correct answers. Repeat this for several different words.

*This can be a laminated piece of paper or a plain sheet of paper inside a plastic wallet.

VOCABULARY

1 Demonstrate this activity first by telling the students to look at the example (0) and asking 'Which word is different?' (*cloudy*) Encourage stronger students to also say why the word in each is different.

Answers

1 playground 2 insect 3 race 4 roundabout 5 rest

2 Point out that some of the letters are given and that there is one space for each other letter in the word.

Answers

1 raincoat 2 traffic light 3 chicken 4 mouse 5 exercise

FAST FINISHERS

Ask fast finishers in pairs to find five more new words in Units 13–16 and write a description for each one. Then, invite them to come to the board, write their descriptions and include the first letter of each answer with a space for all the other letters in the answer. When the others are ready, ask them to read the fast finisher's descriptions and find the words.

3 Ask the students to read the sentences first and think about the missing verb before they read the phrasal verbs in the box. Ask them to read question 1 again and ask 'What form of the verb do I need to use here?' (*the past*) Then, point out that they will need to use the past form in some of the other sentences.

Answers

1 got on 2 turn on 3 was getting off 4 look after
5 turn off 6 pick up

GRAMMAR

1 For questions 1–4, encourage the students to read the complete sentence first before they choose the correct answer. For questions 5–8, point out that there is one mistake with the tense in each sentence.

Answers

1 outside
2 opposite
3 down
4 should
5 I enjoyed my holiday. Every day I **went** swimming.
6 I liked the tennis match because Nadal and Grigor Dimitrov **were** playing.
7 In Thailand, I visited many places and the most interesting thing **was** eating the food there.
8 It **was** raining in Taipei when we got there yesterday.

2 Ask the students to read the whole sentence first and think about which action was happening (past continuous) when the other happened (past simple). With weaker students point out that they will need to use the past simple in one part of the sentence and the past continuous in the other. In question 4, two of the verbs are in the past continuous and the other verb is in the past simple.

Answers

1 arrived, was singing 2 was walking, met
3 called, was doing 4 wasn't running, hurt, was dancing
5 didn't see, was walking

3 Ask the students to read the example first and ask 'Do you think this is good advice?' Next, ask them in pairs to write two pieces of advice for each sentence (*You should … and you shouldn't …*). If time allows, encourage each pair to compare their answers with another pair and decide who has given the best advice for each situation.

Possible answers

1 You should buy a bigger pair. / You shouldn't wear them.
2 You should get a goldfish. / You shouldn't get a big pet.
3 You should put sun cream on. / You shouldn't sit in the sun.
4 You should borrow something from your sister. / You shouldn't worry about it.
5 You should look at the map. / You should ask someone.

WRITING

1 A2 Key for Schools Writing Part 7.

In this part of the exam, there are three pictures which make a story. Students need to write the story in at least 35 words. In pairs, ask the students to look at the three pictures, describe what they can see in each one, and try to make a simple story. Next, ask them to think of some words to connect their ideas, e.g. *and, but, so, because*, etc. Then, encourage them to write their own story using the past continuous and past simple. If time allows, in pairs encourage them to read each other's stories, check for mistakes (spelling, punctuation, past tense, etc.) and give two ideas for ways their partner can make their story better. Ask the students to write their final version.

Model answer

Last weekend, I was spending time with my friends by a lake and we were having great fun. Suddenly, it started to rain, so we all ran into a café. In the café, we played a board game, but it wasn't as good as the lake.

LISTENING

124 **1 A2 Key for Schools Listening Part 5.**

In this part of the exam, the students listen to a longer informal conversation between two people and have to match five items and eight options (there is also an example which uses one of the options, so two options are not used). They will hear the complete conversation twice.

First, ask the students to read the instructions and ask 'Who is Tessa talking to?' (*her father*) 'What about?' (*her friends and their problems*) Next, ask them to look at the example and ask 'What is Eva's problem?' (*She's got a temperature.*) If appropriate, tell them to cross out Problem G. Point out that for each person they may hear two of the options (A–H), but only one answers the question *What problem does each person have?* Play the complete recording and encourage the students to compare their answers and say why they think their answer is correct. Play the recording again and encourage the students to check their ideas.

Answers

1 H 2 C 3 D 4 E 5 A

» AUDIOSCRIPT TB PAGE 276

SPEAKING

1 Remind the students to give full answers when they ask and answer the questions in pairs.

MIXED ABILITY

Help the weaker students by giving them the first word or words of each question.

Answers

1 How do you feel when the school holidays start?
2 What's your favourite animal?
3 What kind of weather do you like best?
4 What do you like doing when it's snowy?

2 A2 Key for Schools Speaking Part 1.

In Speaking Part 1 of the exam, both candidates are first asked the following questions *What's your name?, How old are you?* and *Where do you live?* Then, in Phase 2, candidates are asked questions on two different topics e.g. their home, school, hobbies, etc.

First, encourage the students to answer the question *Where do you live?* with a full sentence, e.g. *I live in Madrid, which is the capital city of Spain.* Next, allow the students time to make notes on where they live before they talk to their partner. Encourage them to consider their house, their street and what is opposite, in front of, near, etc. their house.

Answers

Students' own answers

COOLER

Remind the class that in A2 Key for Schools Speaking Part 1, the examiner will ask them questions on different topics (see Speaking Exercise 2 above). Ask the students to look back through their books and brainstorm a list of things they might be asked to talk about onto the board, e.g. *Tell me about your favourite sport / what you do on a school day / the music you like or play / your last weekend / your favourite room, building or place / your last holiday or your favourite type of holiday / your favourite clothes / your favourite shops / the things you like to eat / your pet or favourite animal*, etc. Next, in pairs, ask them to take turns to be the examiner who chooses a topic and says 'Tell me about …' and the student who answers. Encourage the examiner to listen carefully to their student and to give them some ideas to improve their answer.

WRITING

1 Look at the three pictures. Write the story shown in the pictures. Use 35 words or more.

LISTENING

124 **1** For each question, choose the correct answer. Listen to Tessa talking to her father about her friends. What problem does each person have?

Example:
0 *Eva* [G]

People		Problems
1 Leon	☐	**A** foot hurts
2 Nat	☐	**B** broken arm
3 Maddie	☐	**C** feels sick
4 Ilsa	☐	**D** has a cold
5 Greg	☐	**E** headache
		F leg hurts
		G temperature
		H toothache

SPEAKING

1 Put the words in order to make questions.

1 feel / how / you / start / when / do / school / holidays / the ?
2 your / animal / favourite / what's / ?
3 weather / you / best / of / what / like / kind / do?
4 do / like / you / when / it's / doing / what / snowy / ?

In pairs, ask and answer the questions. Take turns to speak.

2 In pairs, talk about where you live. Take turns to speak.

Tell me about where you live.

I live in a small town. There's a park near the …

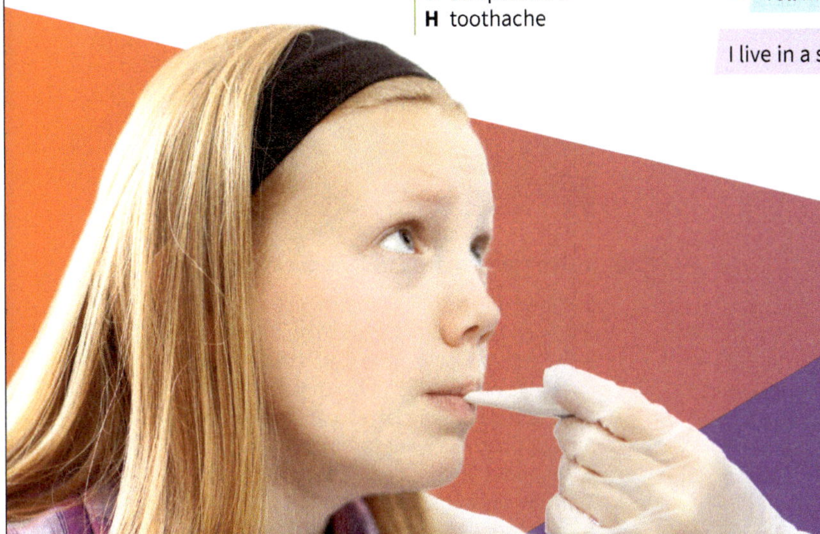

17 WHAT ARE YOU WATCHING?

ABOUT YOU

How often do you watch TV?
Do you watch more TV on your laptop, on your smartphone or on the television?

VOCABULARY AND LISTENING

Television

1 **Complete the sentences with the words in the box.**

EP

cartoons	channels	fan	live
on demand	on TV	programme	
records	remote control	stream	
talent show	the news		

1 It's so easy to watch TV these days. You can ________ anything at any time.
2 I like to know what's happening in the world, so I watch ________ every day.
3 TV with real people is OK, but it's more fun watching ________, like *Tom and Jerry*.
4 Which ________ do you want to watch? There's one about nature or one about music.
5 Please give me the ________. I want to turn on the television and I don't want to get up!
6 Watch our new ________ tonight. There are six young singers and dancers. Choose the best.
7 My brother's a big ________ of Manchester United. He watches all their matches.
8 I think our television can get more than 100 ________. I never know what to watch.
9 I like choosing what to watch and when I want to watch it, so I watch most of my television ________.
10 Ed Sheeran is playing a concert tonight in London and they are showing it ________ on television, so I can watch it while he's playing.
11 When my dad goes on holiday, he ________ his favourite shows and watches them when he gets back.
12 Have you got a newspaper so we can see what's ________ this evening?

125 **Listen and check, then repeat.**

2 **How do you watch television? In pairs, discuss the questions.**

1 Do you often watch shows live, or do you watch them on demand?
2 Which programmes do you usually stream?
3 Do you like talent shows? Which is your favourite?
4 How many channels do you have at home?
5 Which cartoons do you like watching?
6 When do you watch live television?

126 **3** **Listen to the conversation. Ella and Charlie meet in the street. What does Charlie invite Ella to do?**

126 **4** **Listen again and answer the questions.**

1 When is the football match on?
2 Which channel does Ella think the game is on?
3 Why does Ella want to watch the game on a television and not on her laptop?
4 Where does Ella plan to watch the game?
5 Why does Ella want to watch it live?
6 What did Charlie's parents do last week?
7 What does Charlie ask Ella to do?
8 Where does Ella decide to watch the match in the end?

17 WHAT ARE YOU WATCHING?

Unit Overview

TOPIC	Television and entertainment
VOCABULARY AND LISTENING	Television A conversation about watching a football match
GRAMMAR	Future with *going to*
PRONUNCIATION	*going to*
READING	Talent shows
VOCABULARY	Entertainment
LISTENING	A conversation about a talent show
SPEAKING	Talking about TV programmes

Resources

GRAMMAR REFERENCE AND PRACTICE: SB page 154; TB page 249
WORKBOOK: pages 72–75
PHOTOCOPIABLE WORKSHEETS: Grammar worksheet Unit 17; Vocabulary worksheet Unit 17
TEST GENERATOR: Unit test 17

WARMER

Ask the class to look at the unit title and photos at the top of the page and say what this unit is about (*television and entertainment*). Next, ask 'What types of programmes can you see on the four screens?' (*a sports programme, a music programme, a film, a cartoon*) and brainstorm a list of different types of TV programmes onto the board, e.g. *a sports programme, a music programme, a film, a cartoon, the news, a quiz show, a series, the weather.* Next, ask 'What's on TV tonight?' and 'Are you going to watch it?' Wait for several students to give their answers. Then, ask the students to repeat your two questions and write them on the board. Now ask the students to take turns to ask and answer the questions on the board, in pairs. Encourage them to use variations on *yes/no*, e.g. *I'm not sure. / I (don't) think so. / Perhaps. / Of course!* (Students will talk about their favourite TV programmes in the Speaking section at the end of this unit.)

ABOUT YOU

Before the students answer the questions in pairs, as a class, ask them to look at the photos at the top of the page again and identify the different ways they can watch TV.

VOCABULARY AND LISTENING

Television

1 Ask the students to read the sentences and in pairs, try to think of a suitable answer before they look at the words in the box. If they can't think of an answer, ask them to say if the missing word is a noun, a verb or an adjective. Next, encourage them to complete the easier sentences first, e.g. 2 and 3, and cross the answers out so that they can do the more difficult sentences through elimination. If necessary, help the students by saying whether the words are nouns, verbs or adjectives. Check that the students understand the meaning of the more difficult words by asking questions, e.g. 'If Ed Sheeran is playing live, is he playing now or did he play in the past?' (*now*) 'What word means to watch a programme over the internet?' (*stream*) 'Why do people record TV programmes?' (*so they can watch them at another time*)

FAST FINISHERS

Either ask the fast finishers to go around the class helping the others to complete the exercise or in pairs ask them to go onto Exercise 2. When they have finished Exercise 2, ask them to take turns to ask and answer some more questions using some of the other words in Exercise 1.

125

Answers

The answers are recorded for the students to check and then repeat.
1 stream 2 the news 3 cartoons 4 programme
5 remote control 6 talent show 7 fan 8 channels
9 on demand 10 live 11 records 12 on TV

2 Encourage the students to give extended answers to the questions. If necessary, demonstrate by inviting a student to ask you the questions.

Answers

Students' own answers

126
3 Ask the students to look at the photo and describe the two young people. With a weaker class, point out that Ella talks a lot and the students won't hear Charlie's invitation until the end of the recording.

Answers

to watch the European League game at his house

126
4 Ask the students to read the questions and try to answer them before they listen again. With a weaker class, it may be necessary to play the recording for a third time, pausing after each answer.

Answers

1 It's on Saturday evening.
2 She thinks it's on Channel 6.
3 Because their television has a much bigger screen.
4 She plans to watch it at home / her house.
5 Because she hates it when her friends text her to tell her what's happening and she's not watching.
6 They bought a home cinema.
7 Charlie asks her to watch the programme at his house. / Charlie asks her to stop talking.
8 She decides to watch it at Charlie's house.

» AUDIOSCRIPT TB PAGE 276

READING

1 **Do you watch TV talent shows? How many can you name?**

2 **Read the questions and talk about your ideas with your partner.**

a Do talent shows tell people what to say or can they choose?
b What different kinds of talent show are there?
c What do winners of talent shows usually get?
d Who chooses the winners?
e Are talent shows live?

TALENT SHOWS

128

What do you really know about talent shows?

Everyone knows *The Voice*! It's a talent show for people who want to become famous singers. All of the singers on the show are good and some of them are excellent! There are lots of other talent shows around the world as well. In many countries, talent shows are the most popular shows on TV.

1 ____________

There are shows like *Got Talent* for musicians, people doing magic, singers … and lots more. There's a show for dancers, too. It's called *Strictly Come Dancing*. Every year there are new ideas for talent shows. There are even some national talent shows for robots and singing dogs!

2 ____________

Yes, most of the talent shows on TV are live. It's also possible to go to the **studio** and be a member of the **audience**. Then you can watch a talent show live on **stage**.

3 ____________

I'm sure you know the answer to this one. Usually, the people watching the show on TV and in the theatre **vote for** who (or what!) they like best. Sometimes famous people are the **judges** as well. On *Masterchef*, only the professional chefs choose the winner.

4 ____________

In a **competition** there is always a **winner**. The winner of **the final** usually gets a **prize** and sometimes becomes a **star**. On some shows the **runner-up** gets a prize too and a few of them become stars. On a few shows, the winner gets nothing – but they often become famous!

5 ____________

Most of the time, the people on the shows can say, sing or do what they want to. Sometimes, the show tells them the words to say, so they are a bit like actors or **performers**. But this doesn't happen on all the shows.

3 **Read the article quickly and check your ideas. Complete the article with questions from Exercise 2.**

4 **Answer the questions about the article.**

1 What talent show is there for dancers?
2 Where can people go to watch a talent show live?
3 Who are the judges of talent shows?
4 What happens to the runners-up on talent shows?
5 Why are some of the people on talent shows a bit like actors?

TALKING POINTS

Which talent shows are popular in your country? Why?
Which one do you like best? Why?
Discuss with your partner.

READING

WARMER

Write these anagrams on the board and ask the students to put the letters in order to make a type of TV programme (with a weaker class, use a capital letter for the first letter of each word): *eNsw* (news), *aCnoort* (cartoon), *iFml* (film), *oprSst / aegmmPorr* (sports programme), *iQzu / hoSw* (quiz show), *eeirSs* (series), *aeehtrW* (weather), *aelnTt / hoSw* (talent show).

BACKGROUND INFORMATION

The Voice, *Got Talent*, *Strictly Come Dancing* and *Masterchef* are all extremely popular TV shows, where the aim is to find new talent.

The Voice first began in the Netherlands as The Voice of Holland. The aim is to find singers who are not signed to a record label. The winners are decided by viewers.

In the UK, anyone with any sort of talent (singing, dancing, gymnastics, magic, etc.) can audition for a place on *Got Talent*. The winners are chosen both by the show's judges and by the viewers. The final winner performs in a special show in front of the Queen.

Strictly Come Dancing (or *Strictly* for short) is a British TV show where celebrities pair up with professional dancers and take part in a dance competition (ballroom and Latin dancing) in front of panel of judges. It has been on TV since 2004 and is extremely popular.

Masterchef is a cooking competition which began in the UK before being exported to more than 40 other countries around the world (including China, Indonesia and South Korea). *Masterchef Australia* is one of the most watched TV series in Australia. There are also versions for professional chefs, for celebrities and also for children.

1 Ask the students to look at the photos on both pages and identify the type of TV programme first. (They are all types of talent shows – see Background information.) Invite a brief discussion by asking 'Are there these shows on TV in your country?' 'Do you watch them?' 'Why? Why not?' (The students will talk more about talent shows in their country in the Talking points section after doing the reading activities.) Then, ask the students to discuss the questions in pairs. Brainstorm different talent shows the students know and write them on the board. Leave the list on the board for later.

Answers

Students' own answers

2 Point out that the students should share their own ideas with their partner in this exercise.

Answers

Students' own answers

3 Ask the students to read the text quickly and find the answers to the questions in Exercise 2 first. Then, ask them to put each question in the right space but point out that the questions are not in the same order as the paragraphs.

MIXED ABILITY

With a mixed ability class, divide the class into five groups. Each group reads the introduction and one of the paragraphs and then finds the corresponding question.

Then reorganise the groups so that in each group of five, each student has read a different paragraph. Ask them to read their question and then share the answer with the other group members. Either omit Exercise 4 or ask them to continue working in their group of five and help each other answer the questions.

128

Answers

The Reading text is recorded for the students to listen and check their answers.

1 b 2 e 3 d 4 c 5 a

4 Encourage the students to answer the questions in pairs. Point out that they can then check their answers by reading the article again.

Answers

1 There is a show called *Strictly Come Dancing*.
2 They can go to a studio.
3 They are the audience and sometimes they are famous people as well.
4 Sometimes they get nothing, sometimes they get a prize and a few of them become stars.
5 Because the show tells them the words to say.

TALKING POINTS

Refer the students to the list of talent shows on the board that they discussed in Exercise 1 to help them with their discussion.

18 MAGAZINES AND BOOKS

TEEN Magazines

ABOUT YOU

12 Watch the video then ask and answer the questions in pairs.

What books do you like to read?
What's your favourite book?
Why do you like reading it?
Does your school have a school newspaper or magazine?
What do you like reading in your school newspaper/magazine?

Film Fan >

LOL! >

Mountain Bike Monthly >

Footie Time >

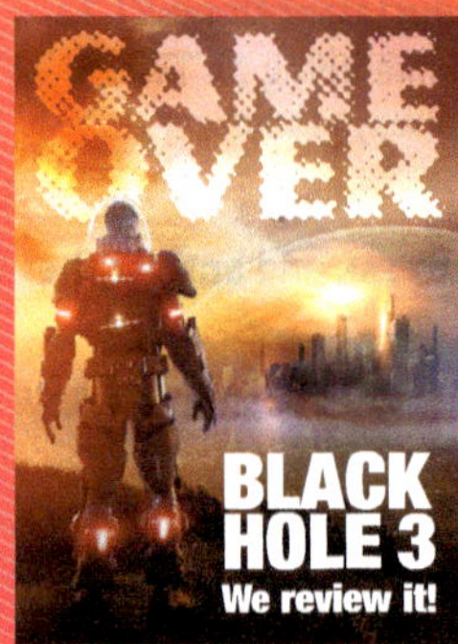

GAME OVER >

I ❤ Animals >

VOCABULARY AND LISTENING

Magazines

1 Look at the magazines on the website. What do you think each one is about? Discuss with your partner.

2 Match the magazine descriptions to the titles in the photos.

1 Out and about on rough roads
2 The latest football news
3 Music, fashion, TV, bloggers and vloggers
4 Information on hundreds of animals
5 The newest and best films
6 All the new video games

3 Which of these magazines would you like to read? Why? Tell your partner.

4 Look at the words in the box for things you find in magazines. Match the words to the definitions.

EP

advertisement	article	cartoon
headline	information	interview
photograph	review	

1 a written opinion about a book, film or TV programme
2 information about a product to make you buy it
3 a picture made using a camera
4 facts about a situation, person or event
5 a funny drawing
6 the title of a magazine story in large letters
7 a written conversation usually between people
8 a piece of writing in a magazine

130 Listen and check. Then repeat.

18 MAGAZINES AND BOOKS

Unit Overview

TOPIC	Magazines, books, plays and films
VOCABULARY	Magazines
AND LISTENING	A conversation about a school magazine
GRAMMAR	Making suggestions
PRONUNCIATION	Intonation
READING	Read and Review
VOCABULARY	*as*, *because*, *so* and *when*
LISTENING	A review of a film
WRITING	A review of a film, play or book

Resources

GRAMMAR REFERENCE AND PRACTICE: SB page 155; TB page 250
WORKBOOK: pages 76–79
VIDEO AND VIDEO WORKSHEET: Books we like
PHOTOCOPIABLE WORKSHEETS: Grammar worksheet Unit 18; Vocabulary worksheet Unit 18
TEST GENERATOR: Unit test 18

WARMER

Write *M _ g _ z _ n _ s / _ nd / b _ _ ks* on the board. Ask the students to complete the unit title with the missing vowels. Brainstorm a list of things that we read onto the board. Challenge the class to think of at least ten, e.g. *book*, *newspaper*, *magazine*, *comic*, *web page*, *dictionary*, *letter*, *cartoon*, *advertisement*, *worksheet*, *postcard*, *message*, *email*. Have a brief discussion on the things the students read by asking 'Do you ever read a newspaper, magazine or comic?' 'How often do you read them?' The students will continue this discussion in pairs in the *About you* box below.

ABOUT YOU

12 You can begin the class and introduce the topic of the unit by showing the video and asking students to complete the video worksheet. When the class has completed the activities, ask them to take turns to ask and answer the questions in pairs.

VOCABULARY AND LISTENING

Magazines

1 Book closed. As a class, brainstorm a list of the different types of magazines you can read, e.g. sports, music, fashion. Books open. Ask the students to compare their ideas with the front covers on the page and ask them to say what they think each magazine is about, e.g. *I think this one is about … because on the front cover there is … .*

Answers
Students' own answers

2 Pre-teach *rough roads* by drawing a picture of a rough and a smooth road on the board and asking 'Where do you usually find rough roads?' (*in the countryside*) 'What sorts of transport travel on rough roads?' (*motorbikes, mountain bikes, 4x4 vehicles*). Next, as a class, match description 1 to the correct cover (Mountain Bike Monthly) and then ask the students to continue in pairs.

Answers
1 Mountain Bike Monthly 2 Footie Time 3 LOL! 4 I ♥ Animals 5 Film Fan 6 Game Over

3 Encourage the students to choose two magazines they would like to read and to think of a reason for each one before they speak to their partner. If necessary, demonstrate a good answer with a stronger student, e.g.:

Teacher: *I'd like to read Film Fan because I like going to the cinema and I'd like to know about the latest films. What do you think?*
Student: *I don't agree. I'd like to read …*

Answers
Students' own answers

4 Before the students look at the exercise, brainstorm a list of things they can find in magazines. Give them two or three examples first, e.g. *the front cover*, *articles*, *photographs*. Then, ask them to read the definitions first and try to think of the word before they match them to the words. After the students have repeated the words, encourage them to note the stressed syllable in each word, especially *advertisement*, *cartoon*, *interview* and *photograph*.

130 **Answers**
The answers are recorded for the students to check and then repeat.
1 review 2 advertisement 3 photograph 4 information 5 cartoon 6 headline 7 interview 8 article

READING

Read and Review

1 Look at two book covers. Do you know these stories? What are they about?

Discuss your ideas with a partner.

2 Read the reviews and check your ideas.

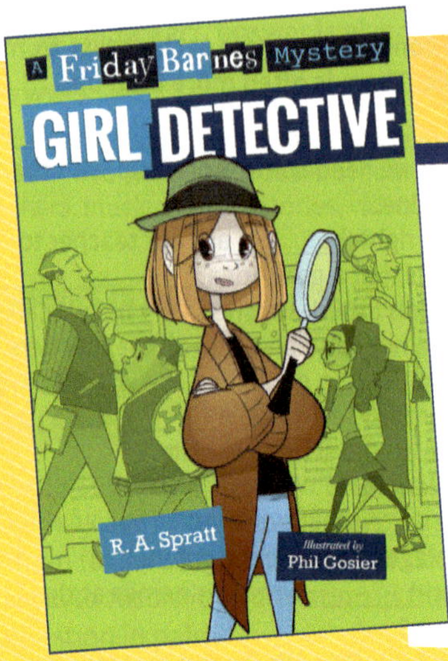

Friday Barnes, Girl Detective

Friday Barnes, Girl Detective is about 11-year-old Friday Barnes. Her parents are always busy, **so** she spends her time reading. She reads lots of detective stories. Then some thieves steal some jewellery and, guess what, Friday is able to help her detective uncle catch them. **When** she gets a reward of $50,000, she spends the money on going to a really good boarding school. The head teacher doesn't like Friday **because** she is different from the other students. Friday is clever, too, and she solves mysteries at the school with her friend Melanie.

I loved the book. I wanted to read it to the end **as** it's very exciting. This is the first Friday Barnes book, and I'm definitely going to read more.

Annika

Charlie and the Chocolate Factory

Charlie Bucket lives in a small house with his family. They're very poor. One day, Charlie finds some money on the street and he decides to buy a Wonka chocolate bar with it. **When** he opens the chocolate bar, Charlie finds a golden ticket inside. It's his lucky day! It's a ticket to visit Willy Wonka's famous Chocolate Factory. Charlie is very excited. Grandpa Joe is excited, too, **because** he can go on the visit with Charlie. **As** there are five golden tickets, four other children visit the factory as well. They all meet Willy Wonka and go around the factory. Lots of strange things happen! Only Charlie is left at the end, **so** he's the winner! What's the prize? Why not read the book and find out?

This book is very funny. I really liked it. It's so popular and there are two films of the book and a musical!

Josh

3 Read the reviews again and answer the questions.

1 How old is Friday?
2 Why does she read a lot?
3 What does she like reading?
4 What does she do with the $50,000?
5 What do Friday and her friend Melanie do at the school?
6 What does Annika think of the book?
7 Where does Charlie get the money for the chocolate bar?
8 Who is Willy Wonka?
9 Who goes with Charlie to the factory?
10 How many golden tickets are there?
11 Who wins the prize at the end?
12 What does Josh think of the book?

TALKING POINTS

Which of the two books would you like to read? Why?

READING

WARMER

Choose eight new words from the previous lesson. Give the students a definition for each word and ask them to write down the word with the correct spelling. The students then swap their lists and correct each other's words. With a weaker class, write the first letter of each word on the board and then add a dash for each of the other letters, e.g. c _ _ _ _ _ _ (*cartoon*).

BACKGROUND INFORMATION

Friday Barnes, Girl Detective is a series of eight mystery novels (as of 2018) about an 11-year-old detective. Set in a boarding school, this series is written by R.A. Spratt, a female author from Australia.

Charlie and the Chocolate Factory is a 1964 children's book by Roald Dahl, made into a film starring Johnny Depp. Dahl may have got his inspiration from the Cadbury's Chocolate factory near his boarding school, which used to ask pupils to test the chocolate.

Romeo and Juliet (Vocabulary section) is a play by William Shakespeare, first published in 1597. Shakespeare wrote 37 plays, classified into three types: tragedy, comedy and history. *Romeo and Juliet* is a tragedy.

The School of Rock (Listening section) is an American musical comedy film starring Jack Black, which is still very popular with young British teenagers. It is now a stage play in London and New York.

1 Ask the students to look at the book covers first and ask 'What are the names of the books?' 'Who wrote them?' 'Are there films or TV series about these books?' before they discuss what they think each one is about in pairs. If necessary, pre-teach *Girl Detective* and *Chocolate Factory* by asking the students to look at the silhouettes next to each book title and to say what each one is. Please note: the vocabulary in *Friday Barnes* is more difficult than *Charlie* and students may need help with the following words: *thief/thieves*, *steal*, *jewellery*, *a reward*, *boarding school* and *solve (a mystery)*.

Answers

Students' own answers

2 Ask 'What are you going to read?' (*two reviews*) Then, ask the students to read the reviews and talk to their partner about what each book is about and also whether the reviewer liked it.

MIXED ABILITY

With a mixed ability class, for Exercises 2 and 3 divide the students into two groups and ask each group to read one review. Ask the stronger students to read about Friday Barnes (more challenging vocabulary) and the weaker students to read about Charlie. Then, pair up one student from each group and ask them to tell each other what their review is about. In Exercise 3, ask them to find the answers from their text and then share their answers with their partner. Questions 1–6 are about *Friday Barnes* and 7–12 are about *Charlie and the Chocolate Factory*.

Answers

Students' own answers

3 Ask the students to read the questions first and try to answer them before they read the reviews again.

Answers

1 She is 11 years old.
2 Because her parents are very busy.
3 She likes reading detective stories.
4 She pays to go to a boarding school.
5 They solve big and small mysteries.
6 She loved it and thought it was very exciting.
7 He finds it on the street.
8 The owner of a famous chocolate factory.
9 His Grandpa, Joe.
10 There are five.
11 Charlie.
12 He thinks it's very funny and he really likes it.

133 The Reading text is recorded for students to listen and read.

TALKING POINTS

Ask the students to think about their answer first and then organise them into small groups to compare. Encourage them to give reasons for their answer.

FAST FINISHERS

Encourage fast finishers to work through Exercise 3 at their own pace. Check their answers and in small groups, encourage them to extend their discussion in Talking points by also asking and answering these questions: *How do you choose a book to read? Do you ever read book reviews? Or do you prefer to ask your friends? Do you prefer to read the book or watch the film? If both, which do you do first?*

VOCABULARY *as, because, so and when*

1 Ask the students to look at the reviews on page 108 again (without looking at this exercise) and ask 'What do the words in blue do?' (*connect sentences*) Once the students have matched the sentence halves, ask 'Which two words give a reason?' (*as*, *because*) 'Which word talks about the consequence?' (*so*) 'Which word do we use to talk about the time something happened?' (*when*)

Answers

1 c 2 a 3 d 4 b

2 Point out there are four more sentences in the reviews with *as*, *because*, *so* and *when* and if appropriate, ask the students to underline them.

Answers

Her parents are always busy, so she spends her time reading.
When she gets a reward of $50,000, she spends the money on going to a really good boarding school.
Grandpa Joe is excited, too, because he can go on the visit with Charlie.
As there are five golden tickets, four other children visit the factory as well.

3 Ask the students to read the title first and say what they know about this story and Shakespeare (see Background information on the previous page). Then, ask them to read the complete review first, without completing it, and say whether the writer of the review liked the play (yes) before they complete the review.

Answers

1 because / as 2 so 3 as / because 4 When

» **VOCABULARY WORKSHEET UNIT 18**

LISTENING

134 1 Read the instructions together, then look at the photos of the people and elicit their names and what they are doing (*Mike – presenter, Phoebe – talking about a film*). Please note: the title of the film has been replaced by a 'beep' noise during most of the conversation so that students have to listen to the end to hear the title.

Answers

The School of Rock

134 2 Ask the students to read the sentences and try to decide in pairs if they are right or wrong before they listen again. Encourage stronger students to correct the wrong sentences.

Answers

1 ✓ 2 ✓ 3 ✗ (The musicians in the band are students.)
4 ✗ (Dewey's old band gets first prize.)
5 ✗ (It was on TV last week.) 6 ✓

» **AUDIOSCRIPT TB PAGE 277**

WRITING

PREPARE TO WRITE
A review

Before the students start this section, brainstorm a list of well-known films, books and plays onto the board – they don't have to be English ones! Write the questions *What's it about? Did you like it? Why (not)?* on the board. Ask pairs of students to ask and answer the questions about at least two of these films.

GET READY If you haven't done so already, ask the students to read the three reviews again and to say which book or play they'd like to read or see first. Next, ask 'What information comes first in a review?' (*the story*) 'What information comes second?' (*the opinion*) and 'Do the reviews tell you what happens in the end?' (*no*)

Then, ask the students to look at the tenses in the review and if appropriate, ask them to underline expressions in all three that they could use in their own review.

Answers

The first paragraph of each review tells the story of the book and the second paragraph gives the writer's opinion.
The present tense.

PLAN Write these questions on the board:

Is it a film, book or play? What's the title?

What's it about?

What's your opinion? Should I read/see it?

Encourage the students to choose a film, play or book and write notes in answer to these questions.

WRITE Point out that they only need to write a short description of the story and remind them that they shouldn't say what happens in the end. Remind them to use *as*, *because*, *so* and *when* if possible.

IMPROVE The students check each other's work for punctuation and spelling.

Answers

Students' own answers

COOLER

Choose some words from this unit and play *Definition, mime or picture*. Organise the students into teams. The teams take turns to choose how they want you to help them with the word. If the team says *definition*, give them a definition of the word, if they say *mime*, mime the word, and if they say *picture*, draw a picture on the board. If appropriate, award a point to the first team to guess the word. Continue with all the words.

VOCABULARY *as, because, so and when*

1 Look at the reviews again. We use the words to connect ideas in sentences.

EP Match the beginnings and endings of the sentences.

1 The Head Teacher doesn't like Friday
2 I wanted to read it to the end
3 When he opened the chocolate bar,
4 Charlie was left at the end,

a as it's very exciting.
b so he was the winner.
c because she is different from the other students.
d Charlie found a golden ticket inside.

2 Find four more sentences with *as*, *so*, *because* and *when* in the reviews on page 108.

3 Complete the review of the play with the words from Exercise 1.

Romeo AND Juliet by William Shakespeare

Romeo and Juliet is a really sad story about two young people. Their families don't want them to marry [1]________ the families hate each other. However, Romeo and Juliet are in love and they get married. They know their families will be very angry, [2]________ they don't tell them. Juliet's family don't know she's married and they find a husband for her. But she can't marry this man [3]________ she's already married to Romeo. Juliet is very unhappy. She drinks something to make her sleep, so her family will think she's dead. Then she goes to sleep. Romeo finds Juliet first and thinks she's dead, so he kills himself. But Juliet isn't dead! [4]________ she wakes up, she sees Romeo is dead and kills herself. And that's the end!

I saw the play at the City Theatre. The actors were all great and I cried at the end. I loved it. Go and see it.

LISTENING

1 (134) Listen to part of the radio programme: *Good Morning Mike*. Phoebe phones in to review a film.

What's the name of the film Phoebe is talking about?

2 (134) Listen to the review again. Are the sentences right (✓) or wrong (x).

1 Phoebe lives in London.
2 The guitar player gets a job in a school.
3 Everyone in the The School of Rock band is a teacher.
4 The School of Rock get first prize in Battle of the Bands.
5 Phoebe watched the DVD of the film last week.
6 Phoebe thinks the film is very good.

WRITING

PREPARE TO WRITE

A review

GET READY Read the three reviews on pages 108 and 109 again.
Which parts of the reviews *tell the story* of the book and which parts are the writers' *opinions*?
What tense do we use for writing a review?

PLAN Think about a film, play or book that you like.
Make notes about:
- the story of the film, play or book.
- your opinion.

Organise your ideas into two paragraphs.
- Paragraph 1: the story of the film
- Paragraph 2: your opinion.

WRITE Write your review of a film, a play or a book in about 50 words. Use the correct tenses and connect your ideas with *as*, *because*, *so* and *when*.

IMPROVE In pairs, read your review and your partner's. Check for mistakes.

Rewrite your review and give it to your teacher for a class magazine.

CULTURE

BRITISH TV AROUND THE WORLD

1 **In pairs, discuss the questions with your partner.**

1 Can you name any British TV programmes?
2 Do you prefer watching cooking shows, nature programmes or dramas?
3 How often do you watch TV in English?

2 **Read and match the photos (A–C) to the texts. Who do you think is the most similar to you?**

3 **Match the headings to the texts.**

Talent shows   Nature shows   Cooking shows

4 **Read the texts again and answer the questions.**

1 What does Brad like doing?
2 What is Ryan's favourite show? Why?
3 When do Eve and her family watch nature programmes?
4 Why does Eve's brother like *The Blue Planet*?
5 What programme do Karen's parents always watch?
6 What music programme does Karen like? Why?

5 **Complete the sentences with the highlighted words in the text.**

1 I love sea animals. I love swimming too and I'm taking a ________ course, so I can go diving on holiday with my family this summer.
2 When I go on nature walks with my family, we like taking photos of birds and animals in their ________.
3 I'm always at home to watch my favourite TV programme on Monday evening at seven o'clock. I never ________ it!
4 We all need to help our ________ and keep it clean.
5 On talent shows people can sing, dance and do magic or ________.

TALKING POINTS

Do you know the programmes Ryan, Eve and Karen are talking about?
Do you watch them?
Which ones don't you like? Why?

FACTFILE British TV

British TV programmes are popular around the world.

According to the BBC, there is in an increase in people watching British TV in different countries. People watch programmes from their own countries too, but thanks to internet and cable TV, it's easier than ever to watch international programmes.

British **talent shows**, **cooking shows**, **nature programmes** and **dramas** are all popular with international viewers.

THAT'S ENTERTAINMENT!

Watching television is a popular free-time activity for many people around the world. Find out more about what young people are watching – and why.

RYAN New Zealand

1 ________

My parents' friend Brad has a small restaurant in Auckland and he loves cooking. I sometimes go to visit him with my parents at weekends. When we go to his house, we walk around town during the day. Then, we love watching shows and competitions about cooking in the evening.

Brad's favourite show is *MasterChef* because it gives him ideas for his restaurant. I prefer *The Great British Bake Off* because I love cooking and eating cakes and sweets!

CULTURE

Learning Objectives

- The students learn about British TV programmes.
- In the project stage, they plan a TV programme timetable and present it to the class.

Vocabulary

scuba diving natural habitat miss planet acrobatics

Resources

CULTURE VIDEO AND CULTURE VIDEO WORKSHEET: The world of British TV

BACKGROUND INFORMATION

The BBC (British Broadcasting Corporation) is Britain's public media service and also the world's oldest (and largest in numbers of employees). It is mainly funded by a licence fee: most people need to pay for a licence to watch British TV, although over 75s can get one for free.

The Great British Bake Off is a baking competition where contestants compete against each other to become the 'star baker'.

The Blue Planet is a nature documentary programme about the oceans narrated by David Attenborough, a famous nature presenter.

Elephant Diaries is a wildlife series which follows the lives of a group of orphaned elephants in a sanctuary in Kenya.

Horrible Histories is based on a series of books with the same name. These programmes narrate historical events in entertaining ways for young people.

For more information on *MasterChef*, *Got Talent* and *The Voice*, see TB Unit 17 page 205 Background information.

WARMER

Write these TV programmes from Unit 17 on the board and ask the class to complete them with the missing vowels:

n_ws	c_rt_ _n	f_lm	sp_rts pr_gr_mm_
q_ _z sh_w	s_r_ _s	w_ _th_r	t_l_nt sh_w

(*news, cartoon, film, sports programme, quiz show, series, weather and talent show*).

Then, ask the students to work in pairs. One of them has just arrived on Earth from another planet, has never watched TV before and needs to ask their partner to explain what one of the programmes is about, when it is on, why people like it, etc.

1 Ask the students to read the factfile and ask 'Which British TV programmes are popular with international viewers?' (*talent shows, cooking shows, nature programmes and dramas*) Then in pairs, ask the students to discuss the questions.

Answers

Students' own answers

2 Ask the students to look at the photos, the title and the introduction in blue and ask 'What are Ryan, Karen and Eve writing about?' (*what they watch on TV*) Next, ask them to match the photos to the texts. Then, ask 'Do any of the three people watch similar programmes to you?' and encourage them to share their answers with their partner.

FAST FINISHERS

Encourage fast finishers to work through Exercises 2–5 at their own pace and check their answers. Then, ask them to use the three texts as a model to write their own short profile about the TV programmes they are watching and why. Collect in their profiles. When the others are ready, read out the profiles and ask the rest of the class to guess who wrote each one.

Answers

1 A 2 B 3 C

3 If appropriate, ask the students to write one of the types of programmes in the box in each of the gaps (1–3).

Answers

1 Cooking shows 2 Nature shows 3 Talent shows

4 Encourage the students in pairs to try to answer the questions before they read the texts again. If necessary, point out that in question 1, Brad is a friend of Ryan's parents.

Answers

1 cooking 2 *The Great British Bake Off*; he loves cooking and eating sweets and cakes 3 on evenings, when it is cold/rainy 4 because he likes scuba diving 5 *Britain's Got Talent* 6 *The Voice*; she likes music, singing and dancing

135 The Reading text is recorded for students to listen and read.

Continued on page 218.

5 First, ask the students in pairs to read the sentences and try to think of a suitable word for each gap. Next, ask them to find the words in the texts and try to work out the meaning from context. Finally, ask them to complete the sentences.

MIXED ABILITY

With weaker students, help them by asking them to choose from two possible answers for each space, e.g. *1 I love sea animals. I love swimming too and I'm taking a* ***scuba diving / acrobatics*** *course, so I can go diving on holiday with my family this summer.*

Answers

1 scuba diving 2 natural habitat 3 miss 4 planet 5 acrobatics

TALKING POINTS

Ask the students to find six TV programmes in the texts and write these on the board (*MasterChef*, *The Great British Bake Off*, *The Blue Planet*, *Elephant Diaries*, *Britain's Got Talent* and *The Voice*). Then, ask the students in small groups to take turns to ask and answer the questions about these programmes (see Background information above for more information about these programmes).

136 6 Ask the students to look at the names of the three programmes and say what they know about any of them before they listen.

Answers

a

136 7 Ask the students to try to choose the correct words (a or b) before they listen again.

Answers

1 b 2 a 3 b 4 a 5 a 6 b

136 8 Before the students listen again, write the table below on the board (examples are given in italics). Encourage the class to say what John likes about each of the programmes and write their ideas in the correct column.

	MasterChef Junior	Horrible Histories
John likes …	*watching the young chefs*	*reading about history*

Answers

MasterChef Junior: He likes watching the young chefs and he loves learning new meals.
Horrible Histories: He loves reading about history in French and in English. He loves telling funny stories.

» **AUDIOSCRIPT TB PAGES 277–278**

PROJECT ***A TV programme timetable***

Ask the students to read the project instructions in bold and ask 'Where do you work?' (*at a TV station*) 'What are you making plans for?' (*a new channel*) 'What do you need to plan?' (*a programme timetable*) 'When for?' (*Saturday mornings from 10 am to 2 pm*). If available, show the class a copy of the TV timetable for Saturday mornings in their own country and brainstorm a list of possible TV programmes onto the board.

Next, organise the students into small groups. Ask the students to choose some programmes from those written on the board (or they can use their own ideas) and think about why they are interesting. Ask each group to copy the table into their notebook and complete it. It may be necessary to do one or two examples together as a class.

Rearrange the groups so that the students are now working with members from different groups and ask them to compare their timetables. Encourage the students to make suggestions for improvement. Then, ask the students to go back to their original group and create a neat copy of their timetable (either on paper for display on the wall or an electronic version). Encourage the class to look at final versions of the different timetables and vote for the best one.

PROJECT EXTENSION

Ask the students to look at their TV programme timetables and decide which of the programmes they would like to watch. Next, tell the groups that they are going to create one of these TV programmes. Ask the students to choose one of the programmes and talk together about how they would produce their show. Then, they should present their ideas to the class for feedback. If time allows, ask the students to work on a script for their show, rehearse their show and then present it to the class.

CULTURE VIDEO 05: The world of British TV

When students have completed the lesson, they can watch the video and complete the worksheet.

COOLER

Ask the class 'Can you guess what I watched on TV last night?' and then give them a description of the programme without saying which one it was, e.g.

Teacher: *I watched a great show on TV last night. Can you guess what programme I watched? There were four young people and they all had to make something for dinner. One of them cooked some fish and another made something with meat. The winner made a Mexican dish which was vegetarian.*

Student: *Was it MasterChef?*

Then, ask the students to continue the activity in small groups.

135

EVE Canada

2 ________
I love going on nature walks with my family and watching wildlife. In the evenings when it's too cold or too rainy to do things outside, my family and I like watching programmes about science or animals at home.
My older brother loves scuba diving so his favourite programme is *The Blue Planet*. Mum and I love watching *Elephant Diaries*. This TV show helps baby elephants return to their natural habitat.

KAREN Northern Ireland

3 ________
I have to do my homework first before I watch TV, but one programme my parents never miss is *Britain's Got Talent*. They love it when there are people on the show doing gymnastics or acrobatics.
I love music, singing and dancing. I get bored watching *Britain's Got Talent* because a lot of people on the programme do other things. I'm a good singer, so I prefer watching *The Voice* in my free time.

136 **6 Listen to John talking to his friend Amber about his homework. Which show is he going to write about?**

a Horrible Histories
b Britain's Got Talent
c MasterChef Junior

136 **7 Listen to the conversation again and choose the correct words, a or b.**

1 John is doing homework
a for his German lesson **b** for his French lesson
2 John likes watching ________ on TV.
a different programmes **b** French programmes
3 Amber ________ watching cooking programmes.
a loves **b** dislikes
4 John likes learning ________.
a new meals **b** new songs
5 Amber ________ what *Horrible Histories* is.
a doesn't know **b** knows
6 John loves ________
a reading about nature **b** reading about history

136 **8 Listen to the conversation again and write the things John likes about the programmes.**

PROJECT

A TV programme timetable

You are working at a TV station and making plans for a new channel. In small groups, plan a programme timetable for Saturday day times from 10 am to 2 pm.

- Make a list of possible programmes you think people like.
- Decide on the times of the programmes.
- Think of why the programmes are interesting and what people can learn from them.
- Fill in the table in your notebook.

Time	Programme *(title/name of programme or type of programme (comedy, nature show, drama …)*	Audience *(children, teenagers, adults)*	Why is the programme interesting?
10 am– ___ am		It is for ________	People can learn ________

- Present your ideas to another group.
- Tell the class about your programme timetable. Decide on which programme timetable you like best.

13 NOW WATCH THE CULTURE VIDEO

19 SCHOOL CAN BE FUN!

A

B

C

D

E

F

G

H

I

J

ABOUT YOU

What kind of school trips do you go on with your school? Do you enjoy them?

What was the last school trip you went on? What did you do?

VOCABULARY AND LISTENING

Trip activities

1 **Look at the photos of people on school trips. What activities are they doing? Match the photos A–J to the words and phrases in the box.** EP

canoeing · cooking on a fire · dancing at a disco · going on a nature walk · going round a museum · going to an amusement park · sailing · visiting a farm · visiting an aquarium · watching a show

137 **Listen and check. Then repeat.**

2 **In small groups, ask and answer the questions.**

1 Which of these activities do you do on school trips with your school?
2 Which ones do you enjoy?
3 Which ones would you like to try?
4 Which ones would you not like to do? Why not?

138 **3** **Listen to a teacher talking to a class about a school trip and answer the questions.**

1 Where is Tall Trees activity centre?
2 Which activities in Exercise 1 do you hear?

138 **4** **For each question, write the correct answer in each gap. Write one word or a number or a date or a time. Then listen again and check.**

End-of-term school trip for Year 8

Name of Activity Centre:	Tall Trees
Date we leave:	1 ________ July
Time to get to school:	2 ________ am
What to bring for the journey:	3 ________

What to pack

✔ for water activities:	4 ________ things
✔ for nature walks:	trainers and 5 ________

19 SCHOOL CAN BE FUN!

Unit Overview

TOPIC	At school
VOCABULARY AND LISTENING	Trip activities A talk about a school trip
GRAMMAR	*have to / don't have to*
PRONUNCIATION	*have to / has to*
READING	The flipped classroom – what's it all about?
VOCABULARY	School collocations
LISTENING	A description of a boarding school
SPEAKING	Giving a presentation about your perfect school
EXAM TASKS	Listening Part 2

Resources

GRAMMAR REFERENCE AND PRACTICE: SB page 156; TB page 250
WORKBOOK: pages 80–83
VIDEO AND VIDEO WORKSHEET: School life
PHOTOCOPIABLE WORKSHEETS: Grammar worksheet Unit 19; Vocabulary worksheet Unit 19
TEST GENERATOR: Unit test 19

WARMER

Challenge the students to guess the unit title *School can be fun!* Write _ _ _ _ _ _/_ _ _/_ _/_ _ _! on the board. Encourage students to take turns to guess the missing letters. Tell them that they can only guess five wrong letters. Next, check that the students understand the difference between *fun* and *funny* by asking 'Which word describes something you like doing or you enjoy?' (*fun*) 'Which word describes something that makes you laugh?' (*funny*) Then, in groups, ask them to write a list of four things that are fun about school and four things that are not fun, e.g.:

fun	**not fun**
meet friends	do homework
go on school trips	do exams
play matches	sit down for a long time
try new activities	get up early

ABOUT YOU

First, brainstorm a list of different types of school trips (e.g. *a visit to a museum, sports activities*) onto the board, then ask the students to take turns to ask and answer the questions in pairs.

VOCABULARY AND LISTENING

Trip activities

1 Ask the students to look at the photos and describe what the young people are doing in each one before they match them to the words and phrases. After the students have repeated the words and phrases, encourage them to note the stressed syllables, in particular *ca<u>noe</u>ing*, *<u>dis</u>co*, *mu<u>se</u>um*, *a<u>muse</u>ment park*, *a<u>qua</u>rium* and *<u>na</u>ture walk*.

137

Answers

The answers are recorded for the students to check and then repeat.
A going on a nature walk B visiting a farm
C going to an amusement park D cooking on a fire
E canoeing F dancing at a disco G going round a museum
H visiting an aquarium I watching a show J sailing

2 Organise the students into small groups and ask them to take turns to ask and answer these questions about the activities in Exercise 1.

Answers

Students' own answers

138 **3** Ask the students to read the questions in Exercise 3 and ask 'What is Tall Trees activity centre, do you think?' (*somewhere where students can do lots of different activities*) As they listen, if appropriate, encourage them to put a tick next to the activities they can do at the centre.

Answers

1 in a forest 2 sailing, swimming, cooking, visiting a museum, visiting an aquarium, canoeing, nature walk, disco

138 **4 A2 Key for Schools Listening Part 2.**

In this part of the exam, students listen to a monologue and need to complete a set of notes with <u>one</u> word or a number, a date or a time. Ask the students to read the notes first and think about what sort of information is missing. Remind them that they may hear two or even three possible words for each space, but only one is the correct answer, for example on the recording, they hear three dates: *We're going on 25th July, next Friday, until Monday 28th July. Please remember you have to give me £200 by Monday 21st July.* The correct answer is 25th July. Have them try to complete the answers first, then play the audio a second time for them to check.

Answers

1 25th / 25 2 8 3 drink 4 swimming 5 trousers

» AUDIOSCRIPT TB PAGE 278

GRAMMAR *have to / don't have to*

1 With a stronger class, ask the students to cover a–e first and try to complete the sentences with their own words. Then, they uncover them and do the matching and compare with their own ideas. Write the answers on the board, with *have to / has to* in a different colour.

FAST FINISHERS

Encourage the fast finishers to work through Exercises 1–3 at their own pace. Then, they write new endings (a–e) for the sentence beginnings (1–5) in Exercise 1 and write these new endings on the board in a different order. When the others are finished, they match the sentence beginnings (1–5) in the exercise to the fast finishers' new endings.

Answers

1e 2d 3b 4a 5c

2 Ask the students to look at the examples on the board (see Exercise 1) and ask 'When do we use *have to* and *don't have to*?' (*to talk about obligation or no obligation*)

Answers

1b 2a

3 Ask the students to look at the examples on the board and use these to complete the table in the book. Ask 'What form of the verb comes after *have to*?' (*the infinitive*)

Answers

Obligation	No obligation	Question form
I/you/we/they have to go He/she/it has to go	I/you/we/they don't have to go He/she/it doesn't have to go	Do I/you/we/they have to go? Does he/she/it have to go?

» GRAMMAR REFERENCE AND PRACTICE ANSWER KEY TB PAGE 250

139 4 Ask the students to read the list and guess what Leo has to or doesn't have to do on the trip. The students then listen and check.

Answers

Ticked: get up early every day, go swimming, leave his phone at home, share a bedroom, help with the cleaning

» AUDIOSCRIPT TB PAGE 278

5 Read the examples as a class. Remind students that we use *don't have to* to say that something isn't necessary; they should use *can't* to say if he isn't allowed to do something. Put the students into pairs and ask them to write at least two more pairs of sentences.

MIXED ABILITY

Ask weaker students to write three more sentences with *He has to* or *He doesn't have to* only.

Possible answers

He has to go swimming, but he doesn't have to go to the disco. He can stay in his room if he likes.
He can't bring his mobile phone. He has to leave it at home.
He has to share a bedroom. He can't sleep in his own room.
He doesn't have to do any school work, but he can if he wants to.

6 Point out there is one mistake with *have to* in each of the sentences, and that although there are different ways of correcting some of the sentences, they should correct them all with *have to / don't have to.* You may also wish to point out that in number 4 they'll need to change *nothing*.

Answers

1 You don't **have to** bring anything – it's not necessary.
2 Please, you **have to** come! It's going to be a great concert.
3 We **don't have** to pay for the skate park.
4 You **don't have to** pay **anything** for the disco. It's free!
5 We **have to** get up early to go sailing.
6 You **have** to pack warm clothes for the school trip.

» GRAMMAR WORKSHEET UNIT 19

PRONUNCIATION *have to / has to*

7 Ask the students to listen to the six sentences first, without repeating them, and say how the *to* is pronounced in each sentence (/tə/).

140 **Audioscript**

The sentences and questions are recorded for the students to listen and repeat.

1 I have to go shopping.
2 He has to do his homework.
3 Do you have to go now?
4 Does he have to pay today?
5 We have to write a story.
6 She has to win this match.

8 First, ask the class to repeat the example *Do you have to visit anyone this weekend?* Ask the question for the second thing on the list, i.e. *Do you have to do any homework?* Point out that the answer is *Yes, I do. I have to … or No I don't. I can … if I want to*. Then, have students ask and answer questions in pairs about the rest of the things on the list.

Answers

Students' own answers

COOLER

In groups, the students write some questions about the things they have to and don't have to do at home, e.g. *Do you have to do your homework before dinner? Do you have to share a bedroom?* Then, reorganise the groups so students from different groups are working together. The students take turns to ask and answer their questions.

GRAMMAR *have to / don't have to*

1 **Match the two halves of the sentences.**

1 Everyone has to be at school
2 Mr Peters has to check
3 You have to wear
4 You don't have to bring anything
5 Do we have to wear

a to eat.
b smart clothes to the disco.
c our uniform on the journey?
d your names.
e at eight o'clock

2 **Now read the examples and then complete the rules with a and b.**

Everyone *has to* be at school at eight o'clock.
You don't *have to* bring anything to eat.

1 *have to* means ______
2 *don't have to* means ______

a no obligation: you have a choice and you can do this if you want.
b obligation: You have no choice. You can't say 'no'!

3 **Complete the table with the correct form of** *have to*.

Obligation	No obligation	Question form
I/you/we/they ______ go He/she/it ______ go	I/you/we/they ______ go He/she/it ______ go	______ I/you/we/they ______ go? ______ he/she/it ______ go?

» GRAMMAR REFERENCE AND PRACTICE PAGE 156

139 **4** **Listen to Leo asking about the school trip. Tick (✓) the things he has to do.**

- get up early every day ☐
- go sailing ☐
- go swimming ☐
- go to the disco ☐
- leave his phone at home ☐
- share a bedroom ☐
- help with the cleaning ☐
- do any school work ☐

5 **Make pairs of sentences about Leo using** ***have to/ doesn't have to*** **and** ***can/can't*****.**

He has to get up early. He can't stay in bed late.

6 **Correct the mistakes in the sentences.**

1 You don't bring anything – it's not necessary.
2 Please, you need come! It's going to be a great concert.
3 We haven't to pay for the skate park.
4 You pay nothing for the disco. It's free!
5 We have get up early to go sailing.
6 You has to pack warm clothes for the school trip.

ə PRONUNCIATION *have to / has to*

140 **7** **Listen and repeat.**

1 I have to go shopping.
2 He has to do his homework.
3 Do you have to go now?
4 Does he have to pay today?
5 We have to write a story.
6 She has to win this match.

8 **In pairs, ask and answer about what you have to do/don't have to/can/can't do this weekend. Use these ideas or your own.**

visit anyone?
do any homework?
get up early/ late?
go shopping?
do any cleaning?
go to bed early / late?

Do you have to visit anyone this weekend?

No, I can stay at home if I want to.

READING

1 Read the first paragraph of the article. Do you think the flipped classroom sounds like a good idea? Why / why not?

141

THE FLIPPED CLASSROOM

What's it all about?

In a normal classroom, the teacher stands at the front of the room and gives a lesson and the students listen and take notes. Then they go home and do their homework. In a flipped classroom, everything is the other way around. Students study at home from a textbook or online videos, and then discuss the topic and do 'homework' exercises or projects in class. Lots of schools are trying it, but is it a good idea? We spoke to a teacher and two students to find out more.

Penny – *teacher*

The flipped classroom is hard work for the teacher, especially at the beginning. You have to make videos of every topic in the textbook for the students to watch on their computers at home. That takes a really long time! But it means I can spend time in class helping students one-to-one. I love that – I wasn't able to do it before.

Caitlin – *student*

I love coming into the classroom ready to talk about the topic and feeling I understand it. In a normal class, I often feel nervous, because if I don't understand, I have to ask the teacher to stop the lesson and explain. But with a video, I can watch it as many times as I like until I understand it. It's great!

Dylan – *student*

We tried the flipped classroom for one term in maths, but there were a few problems. Some students didn't watch the videos before the lesson, so they couldn't do the exercises in class. Also, when the teacher was going round helping people, we found it really easy to stop working and just chat. We did a test at the end of the term and we all got terrible marks. I usually pass every test, but I failed that one.

2 Read the article and answer the questions. Write *P* (Penny), *C* (Caitlin) or *D* (Dylan).

Who said this about the flipped classroom?

1 I If I need to, I can repeat parts of the lesson.
2 I like being able to explain things during the lesson.
3 Lots of us spent too much time talking to each other.
4 There were people who did not prepare for the classes.
5 I don't have to be scared about what's going to happen in the lesson.
6 Getting everything ready wasn't easy.

3 In pairs, discuss the questions.

1 What do you think are the best/worst things about flipped classrooms?
2 Would you like to try it? For which subjects?

TALKING POINTS

14 Watch the video about a school called Redroofs. Then ask and answer the questions with a partner.

What do you like about your school?

Is your school bigger or smaller than Redroofs?

How many children are in your year?

What subjects do you study?

What are your teachers like?

READING

WARMER

Write *The perfect school* on the board as a title. Underneath that, write *They don't have to study*. As a class, brainstorm a list of more characteristics of a perfect school, e.g. *They don't have to do tests; they don't have to wear a uniform; they don't have to do homework; they can choose their own subjects.* In the Speaking section at the end of this unit, the students will have to make a presentation on their perfect school.

BACKGROUND INFORMATION

In a traditional classroom, the teacher often stands at the board and lectures while the students take notes. In a flipped classroom however, students learn about the lesson content at home through videos, slide presentations, podcasts, etc. and class time is freed up to spend on practice. People often say that Alison King's journal article 'From Sage on the Stage to Guide on the Side' in 1993 inspired the move towards the Flipped Classroom. In her work, King suggested that teachers should move away from being transmitters of information: moving from the Sage (or wise person) on the Stage towards the role of Facilitator or the Guide on the Side. Another important contributor is Salman Khan, founder of the Khan Academy, which is a free education platform where students can watch more than 6,500 different video tutorials at their own pace. In ELT (English Language Teaching), the students could watch a video tutorial about *have to/don't have to* at home so that in class, they can spend more time using the language to talk about their perfect school.

1 Ask the students to look at the photo of the classroom and ask 'What's different about this photo?' (*it's upside down*) Next, ask them to read the title and ask 'What's a flipped classroom?' Invite suggestions. Next, ask them to read the first paragraph to check their ideas. Then, ask them in pairs to talk together about whether a flipped classroom is a good idea.

Answers

Students' own answers

2 This exercise is loosely based on A2 Key For Schools Reading Part 2 where students need to read three short texts about three different people and answer questions beginning *Which person …?* Ask the class the look at the names at the top of the three short texts and ask 'Are Penny, Caitlin and Dylan students?' Ask the students to read the three short texts to get a general idea. Ask 'What did Penny, Caitlin and Dylan think of the flipped classroom?' (*Penny and Caitlin liked it but Dylan didn't.*) Next, ask them to try to answer the questions. Then, ask them to read the texts again and if appropriate underline the answers. Remind them that they will not find the same words in the text as in the questions.

Answers

1 C 2 P 3 D 4 D 5 C 6 P

141 The Reading text is recorded for students to listen and read.

3 If necessary, brainstorm a list of school subjects onto the board and encourage the students to ask and answer question 2 about these subjects.

Answers

Students' own answers

TALKING POINTS

14 After the students have completed the video activities, encourage them to ask and answer the questions in pairs. If necessary, point out that the final question *What are your teachers like?* is asking about the students' opinion of their teachers. (It doesn't ask about their teachers' preferences; this would be *What do your teachers like?*)

VOCABULARY School collocations

1 Ask the students to find the verbs on the left in the article on page 114 and try to guess the meaning from context before they do the exercise. Next, ask them to cover the verbs on the left, look at the nouns on the right, and try to remember which verb goes with each one. Finally, ask them to check their answers with the words in the articles.

Answers

do: an exercise, a project, homework, a test
fail: a test
get: marks, homework
give: a lesson, homework, (good/bad) marks, a test
pass: a test
study from: notes, a textbook
take: notes, a lesson, a test

2 Encourage the students to read the whole sentence first, to think both about meaning and also the nouns which go with each verb, before they choose the correct answer.

FAST FINISHERS

Ask fast finishers to write a new sentence with the incorrect word, e.g. *We're doing a project on schools around the world.*

Answers

1 notes 2 pass 3 textbooks 4 exercises 5 mark 6 project

3 First, ask the students to look at the phrases in Exercise 1 and brainstorm a list of things about a school which uses the flipped classroom onto the board, e.g. *do homework exercises or projects in class*, *do tests*, *get marks*, etc. Then, ask the students in pairs to compare these things with their own school.

Answers

Students' own answers

» VOCABULARY WORKSHEET UNIT 19

LISTENING

142 1 Pre-teach *boarding school* by asking the students to read the instructions for the exercise and asking 'What's a boarding school?' Then, ask them in pairs to describe what they can see in each photo before they listen to Maya. With a weaker class, play the recording for a second time and pause it after each answer.

Answers

1 B 2 E 3 C 4 D 5 A

142 2 Ask the students to read the article first, say what type of word is missing in each space, and then try to complete the gaps before they listen again. Point out that they should use one or two words only in each gap. If time allows, invite a brief class discussion on whether the students would like to go to a boarding school.

MIXED ABILITY

With a mixed ability class, pair up a stronger student with a weaker one. Ask the stronger student to help the weaker student to complete the article before they listen again. Then, after listening, they compare their answers and the stronger student helps their partner again.

Answers

1 600 2 three 3 photos 4 6 pm / 6 o'clock 5 Saturday 6 games 7 dining room 8 cleaning 9 tennis

» AUDIOSCRIPT TB PAGE 278

SPEAKING

1 In pairs, ask the students to write notes for each point about their own perfect school. If they are slow to start, brainstorm some possible answers onto the board.

Answers

Students' own answers

2 Organise the students into groups of four. Each pair should give a short presentation of their school using the notes they made in Exercise 1. Encourage the pair who are listening to think of at least two questions they would like to ask about the school at the end of their presentation. If necessary, demonstrate this activity by inviting a stronger pair to come to the front and present their perfect school. When they have finished, ask them two appropriate questions about their presentation, e.g. *Do the students have to do exams? Why do they have to do PE?*

Answers

Students' own answers

COOLER

In small groups, the students design a perfect school timetable. They should include times of the classes, the names of the subjects and the break times.

VOCABULARY School collocations

1 EP **Match the verbs to the nouns to make phrases. Use the article on page 114 to help you. Some verbs go with than one noun.**

do	an exercise
fail	a project
get	homework
give	a lesson
pass	marks
study from	notes
take	a textbook
	a test

2 **Choose the correct words to complete the sentences.**

1 I took lots of *notes* / *projects* in my last lesson.
2 I really hope I *pass* / *fail* this test!
3 Some people like studying from *textbooks* / *projects* and other people prefer videos.
4 The maths teacher gave us six *exercises* / *homework* to do at home.
5 What *mark* / *test* did you get in your science exam?
6 I'm doing a history *project* / *homework* at the moment, about the Romans.

3 **In pairs, compare your school with the one in the article. Use the phrases in Exercise 1.**

They study from the textbook at home, but we use ours in class.

LISTENING

142 **1** **Maya goes to a boarding school. She sleeps there and only goes home for holidays. Listen to her describing her school. Number the photos in the order you hear about them.**

142 **2** **Listen again. Complete the article Maya wrote about her school with the missing words.**

I go to a boarding school called Hartland School. It has about [1] ________ students.

I have to share a bedroom with [2] ________ other girls. We can put [3] ________ of our family on the walls.

There's a library where we do our homework. We start studying at [4] ________ every evening.

We work really hard at my school. We even have lessons on [5] ________ mornings!

After homework, we can go to the [6] ________ room to have some fun.

We have meals in a big [7] ________ and we have to help with the [8] ________ afterwards.

We have to do sports at my school. Next term, we're going to do [9] ________.

SPEAKING

1 **Make a presentation about your perfect school. Work with a partner. Plan what you want to say. Think about:**

- a name for your school
- the size of your school
- places in your school
- what students can/can't do
- what students have to / don't have to do
- what the teachers are like
- what subjects you study

2 **Present your ideas to another pair. Which school sounds most fun to go to?**

20 FAMILIES

VOCABULARY AND LISTENING

Family

1 Complete the table with the words in the box and the family words from About you. EP

aunt cousin grandchild
granddaughter grandfather
grandmother grandparent grandson
nephew niece uncle

Male	Female	Male or female

143 Listen and check. Then repeat.

144 **2** Listen to Kate describing her family. Complete her family tree with the names in the box.

Iris Jana Kasia Liz Rory
Sue Wiktor

ABOUT YOU

In pairs, tell your partner three things about your family. Use some of these words:

brother/sister child/children daughter/son
father/mother husband/wife

144 **3** Listen again and match the people in the photos to their names in the family tree.

4 Make eight sentences about Kate's family tree. In pairs, compare your sentences with your partner's. Are any of your sentences the same?

Tony is Jessie's grandfather.

Marek is Jana and Karolina's dad.

5 Look at the photos. Describe the people using some of the words in the box. EP

beautiful blonde dark fair
good-looking old pretty short
slim tall young

6 Draw your own family tree. In small groups, describe the people in your family.

116 UNIT 20

20 FAMILIES

Unit Overview

TOPIC	Different families
VOCABULARY AND LISTENING	Family A talk about a family tree
GRAMMAR	Adverbs of manner
PRONUNCIATION	The letter *i*
READING	What's it like to grow up in a big family?
VOCABULARY	Adverbs of degree
LISTENING	Descriptions of families
WRITING	A description of your family
EXAM TASKS	Reading Part 5

Resources

GRAMMAR REFERENCE AND PRACTICE: SB page 157; TB page 250
WORKBOOK: pages 84–87
PHOTOCOPIABLE WORKSHEETS: Grammar worksheet Unit 20; Vocabulary worksheet Unit 20
TEST GENERATOR: Unit test 20; Term test 3; End of Year test

WARMER

Write the unit title *Families* on the board. Brainstorm common family words onto the board, e.g. *brother*, *sister*. In pairs, the students ask and answer questions about the things members of their family have to (and don't have to) do, e.g.:

A: *Does your mother have to visit anyone on Saturdays?*

B: *No, she doesn't. Does your brother have to do homework after school?*

ABOUT YOU

Check that the students understand the meaning of the words, in particular *husband/wife* by asking 'Are your father and mother married?' 'Who's your father's wife?' 'Who's your mother's husband?' Point out that *children* is the plural form and we never say *childrens*. If necessary, give an example for you first, e.g. *I've got two brothers and a sister. I'm married. My husband's name is Peter …*

VOCABULARY AND LISTENING

Family

1 Do the first three words as a class to check that the students know what to do. Point out that some words, e.g. *child/children* and *cousin* can refer to male or female. Then, ask the students to complete the table with the words in the box.

143

Answers

The answers are recorded for the students to check and then repeat.
Male: brother, father, grandfather, grandson, husband, nephew, son, uncle
Female: aunt, daughter, granddaughter, grandmother, mother, niece, sister, wife
Male or female: child/children, cousin, grandchild, grandparent

144 2 Ask the students to look at the photos and elicit that it shows a family tree. Ask them to find Kate's name. Then, ask the students to listen and complete the tree. Note that the numbered spaces on the family tree are not in the same order in which they appear in the recording.

MIXED ABILITY

With a mixed ability class, it may be necessary to play the recording several times, pausing after the answers are given so that the students can complete Exercises 2 and 3.

Answers

1 Iris 2 Sue 3 Liz 4 Wiktor 5 Kasia 6 Rory 7 Jana

144 3 Encourage the students to try to identify the people in the photos before they listen again.

Answers

A Sue and Tony B Jana and Karolina C Liz, Wiktor and Kate D Rory, Phil and Helen E Iris

» AUDIOSCRIPT TB PAGES 278–279

4 Ask the students to choose eight people in Kate's family and write a sentence about each one.

Possible answers

Karolina is Jana's sister.
Sue is Iris's daughter.
Helen is Kate's aunt.
Ursula is Karolina's grandmother.
Tony is Sue's husband.
Helen is Liz's sister.
Kate is Jessie's cousin.
Helen is Phil's wife.

5 Check that the students can pronounce the words correctly first by asking them to listen and repeat, in particular *blonde* /blɒnd/, *slim* /slɪm/ and *young* /jʌŋ/.

Possible answers

Iris is beautiful with short hair.
Kate is pretty, with blonde hair.
Rory is young.
Jana and Karolina are slim.
Helen has long, dark hair.
Wiktor has fair hair.
Sue is good-looking.

6 Draw your family tree on the board and encourage the students to ask you questions, e.g. *Who's your mother's brother?* and *What's your brother like?* Then, ask them to draw their own tree and then in groups take turns to ask and answer questions about their families.

Answers

Students' own answers

GRAMMAR Adverbs of manner

1 Either write the example sentences on the board or ask the students to read them. Ask 'Is Kate's cousin Jana a good piano player?' 'How do you know?' 'What are the words in purple?' 'Do they describe **what** something or someone is like or **how** something or someone does something?' 'How do we usually form them?' The students then choose the correct word to complete the sentences.

Answers

1 how 2 many

» GRAMMAR REFERENCE AND PRACTICE ANSWER KEY TB PAGE 250

2 First, ask the class to look at the five adverbs in purple in Exercise 1 and say what the adjective is, i.e. *fast – fast, good – well, easy – easily, hard – hard, careful – carefully*. Then, ask them to say which three adverbs do not finish in *-ly*.

Answers

fast, good, hard

3 Check that the students understand the meaning of the adjectives first. Then, ask them the spelling rules and, in pairs, have them take turns to say what these rules are. Write the answers on the board and ask the students to check their spelling carefully.

Answers

badly, easily, loudly, noisily, quickly, quietly, wonderfully

4 Do the first question as an example by inviting the class to give you possible adverbs. Encourage them to look at Exercises 1 and 3. Then, ask them to complete the rest of the questions. Remind them to be careful of their spelling and point out that more than one adverb may be possible in each question.

FAST FINISHERS

Ask fast finishers to make new questions with the adverbs they haven't used and then take turns to ask and answer their new questions.

Answers

1 carefully / quickly / well 2 fast / quickly 3 well / loudly / quietly 4 quietly / loudly 5 loudly / quietly 6 easily / quickly

5 Ask the students to find the adjective or adverb in each sentence and where necessary, correct it. If necessary, remind students that adjectives describe nouns (*what* something is like) and adverbs describe the verb (*how* we do something).

Answers

1 I liked the competition because both teams played very **well**.
2 I thought that film was really **bad**.
3 You should think about that very **carefully**.
4 My friend ran really **fast** in the race.
5 You can find **my house easily**.

» GRAMMAR WORKSHEET UNIT 20

PRONUNCIATION The letter *i*

6 Ask the students in pairs to read the words in the box to each other first and say how many different sounds they hear for the letter *i*. They should hear two different sounds, /ɪ/ and /aɪ/.

145 **Answers**

The answers are recorded for the students to check and then repeat.
/ɪ/ milk: children, interesting, quickly, sing, sister, slim
/aɪ/ night: child, find, kind, quite, wife

7 Ask the students to read the title first and ask 'What is the information about?' Then, ask them to cover the words in the box, read the six pieces of advice, think about whether the missing word is an adverb or adjective, and try to think of a suitable one for each gap. Next, they compare their ideas with the words in the box. Finally, in pairs encourage them to complete the gaps with the correct adjective or adverb form of the words in the box.

Answers

1 interesting / important 2 difficult 3 happily / interestingly 4 carefully 5 important 6 correctly / carefully

8 Begin this exercise on the board as a class. Ask them to look at their own family tree (Vocabulary and Listening Exercise 6 page 116) and choose some people to write about from there. Encourage the students to write about at least four members of their own family.

Next, organise the class into small groups and ask them to tell each other about the family members in their table. Encourage them to ask some follow-up questions. Point out that if a family member is no longer alive, they will need to use the past.

Answers

Students' own answers

COOLER

Write the word *quickly* on the board. Give the class some instructions, e.g. *Stand up! Sit down!* and tell them to follow the instructions in the manner of the adverb, i.e *Stand up!* (students stand up quickly)

Now ask a student to come to the front and face away from the board. Write a new adverb on the board (e.g. *loudly*), give the class instructions, and ask them to follow them in the manner of the new adverb. The student at the front watches them and tries to guess the adverb. Continue this activity as a class or in small groups.

GRAMMAR Adverbs of manner

1 **Look at the sentences from the listening and think about the words in purple. These are adverbs of manner.**

I know a bit of Polish but when people speak fast, I can't understand them!
Jana plays the piano really well.
She wins easily every time we play!
Her family worked hard and sent her to England to study music.
I have to hold them carefully because they're very old.

Choose the correct words to complete the rules.

1 Adverbs of manner describe *how* / *when* we do things.
2 We make *many* / *all* adverbs of manner by adding *-ly* to an adjective.

» GRAMMAR REFERENCE AND PRACTICE PAGE 157

2 **Look at the sentences in Exercise 1. Find three adverbs that don't end in *-ly*. Write their adjectives.**

3 **Look at the spelling rules below and then write the adverbs for the adjectives in the box.**

bad easy loud noisy quick quiet wonderful

Adjective	Adverb
slow	slowly (add *-ly*)
happy	happily (change *y* to *i*)
careful	carefully (double the *l*)

4 **Complete the questions with adverbs from Exercises 1 and 3. Then in pairs, ask and answer the questions.**

1 Do you do your homework ________?
2 Can you run ________?
3 Can you sing ________?
4 Do you speak ________ on the bus?
5 Do you play music ________ in your bedroom?
6 Can you make friends ________?

5 **Correct the mistakes in the sentences.**

1 I liked the competition because both teams played very good.
2 I thought that film was really badly!
3 You should think about that very careful.
4 My friend ran really fastly in the race.
5 You can find easily my house.

PRONUNCIATION The letter *i*

6 **Work with a partner. Look at the underlined letters. What sound does *i* make in the words? Put them into the correct column in the table.**

child children find interesting kind quickly quite sing sister slim wife

/ɪ/ milk	/aɪ/ night

145 **Listen and check. Then repeat.**

7 **Complete the advice with the words in the box. Change the adjective into an adverb where necessary.**

careful correct difficult happy important interesting

How to find out about your family history

1 Every family has lots of ________ stories in its past.
2 It's not too ________ to find out about your family history.
3 Ask older family members about their parents and grandparents. They will talk ________ for hours about this.
4 Listen ________ and write down what they tell you.
5 The most ________ thing you need to find out is when and where people were born.
6 Write everything down ________ because you don't want mistakes in your family tree.

8 **Complete the table about your family. Under *Interesting information*, put an adjective (e.g. *clever*) and a verb plus adverb (e.g. *sings badly*). Then in small groups, talk about the people in your table.**

Family member	Interesting information
Mum	*clever sings badly*

READING

1 Look at the photo and describe it. What do you think it's like living in a big family? Write three ideas. Read the article quickly to see if your ideas are included.

What's it like to grow up in a big family?

by Ella Blackstone

I am the oldest of eight children. To me, my family is completely normal, but other people find it amazing. So, for everyone who's interested, here's what it's like to grow up in a big family!

Remembering the names, ages and birthdays of all your family members is really difficult. My parents often call my brothers and sisters by the wrong names. This is probably why our pets never had names.

Some of my friends get money for doing jobs around the house, but we certainly don't. In our house, the dishwasher is on nearly all the time, there are always clothes to wash or put away, and the tidying up never ends. We all have to help, even the little ones.

Every shelf in our house is full of prizes, for basketball, tennis, cricket and rugby. We are all really competitive. The clever ones want to be the cleverest, the pretty ones the prettiest, and the funny ones the funniest.

Being slow is not a good thing in a big family. You have to move quickly to get into the shower or to get the best seat in the minibus (big families don't have cars). And you have to eat fast, especially if there's cake in the house!

Yesterday, I saw my 7-year-old sister in my old dress. She probably got it from my 15-year old sister, who gets most of my things. We have to share bedrooms, toys, and even our parents' time. Sharing is not always easy, but we are quite good at it, luckily.

Life in a big family has its ups and downs, but I love it.

146

2 Read the article again. Are the sentences right (✓) or wrong (x)?

1 Ella has seven younger brothers and sisters.
2 Her family enjoyed choosing names for their pets.
3 Ella and her brothers and sisters earn money from helping around the house.
4 The younger members of Ella's family also have to do jobs.
5 The children in Ella's family do well at sport.
6 Ella says being fast is useful in a big family.
7 She says she gave an old dress to her seven-year-old sister.
8 Her family hate sharing everything with each other.

In pairs, compare your answers.

TALKING POINTS

Do you come from a big family?

YES → How is your family the same/different to the one in the article?

NO → Would you like to be part of a big family? Why/Why not?

READING

WARMER

Write the following family words from Unit 20 on the board. Invite volunteers to come and complete them:

a _ _ t	b r _ _ _ _ r
c h _ _ d	c _ _ _ _ n
d _ _ _ _ _ _ _	f _ _ _ _ r
g r _ _ _ c _ _ _ d	g r _ _ _ d _ _ _ _ _ _ r
g r _ _ _ s _ n	g r _ _ _ f _ _ _ _ r
m _ _ _ _ _	g r _ _ _ m _ _ _ _ r
s _ _ _ _ r	s _ n
u _ _ _ e	

Answers

aunt	brother
child	cousin
daughter	father
grandchild	granddaughter
grandson	grandfather
mother	grandmother
sister	son
uncle	

Now rub out the words from the board and organise the class into teams. Give a definition for each family word and award a point to the team who puts up their hand first, gives the correct answer and can spell it correctly, e.g. 'My mum's sister is my …' (*A-U-N-T*)

BACKGROUND INFORMATION

A nuclear family is one where the parents live with one or more children. An extended family is one where other relatives such as the grandparents, aunts, uncles or cousins also live with the family. A single-parent family is where there is only one parent. In some cultures, like Spain, a large family is where there are three or more children, whereas in China, families could only have one child until 2016. Famous people with large families include Wolfgang Amadeus Mozart, who was the seventh of seven children, Madonna, who has six children and Angelina Jolie and Brad Pitt, who also have six children.

1 Tell the class that they are going to read about Ella and her really big family. Ask them to look at the photo and find Ella's parents. Then, ask 'How many brothers and sisters has Ella got?' and let them count. Now ask the students to read the question in the title, i.e. *What's it like to grow up in a big family?* and ask 'What does *grow up* mean?' (*become older or an adult*) Next, ask if anyone has got a big family (i.e. three or more siblings) and if so, what it's like. If they haven't, ask what they think it's like. Invite some ideas from the class and ask the students to write down three ideas each. Then, ask them to read the article quickly and answer the question *Does Ella enjoy living in a really big family?* (yes)

Answers

Students' own answers

146 The Reading text is recorded for students to listen and read.

2 Ask the students to read the sentences and decide if they are right or wrong before they read the text again. If appropriate, ask them to underline their answers in the text. Encourage stronger students to correct the wrong sentences. When the students compare their answers, ask them to say *why* by showing each other the part of the text they have underlined, e.g. *Why did you put 'right'? Because here she says …*

FAST FINISHERS

Fast finishers write some questions about the article. When the others are ready, the fast finishers read out their questions and the others answer. If your class enjoy competitions, do this as a team game.

Answers

1 ✓ 2 ✗ (Our pets never had names.) 3 ✗ (Some of my friends get money … but we certainly don't.) 4 ✓ 5 ✓ 6 ✓ 7 ✗ (She probably got it from my 15-year-old sister, who gets most of my things.) 8 ✗ (Sharing is not always easy, but we are quite good at it, luckily.)

TALKING POINTS

Ask the students to read the first question *Do you come from a big family?* (= three or more brothers and sisters) and write down their own answer: *Yes, I do* or *No, I don't.* Then, ask them to think of a suitable answer to their follow-up questions. Demonstrate this activity with a stronger student:

Teacher: *Do you come from a big family?*
Student: *No, I don't.*
Teacher: *Would you like to part of a big family?*
Student: *No, I wouldn't.*
Teacher: *Why not?*

Then, organise the students into small groups and ask them to take turns to ask and answer the questions.

VOCABULARY Adverbs of degree

1 Ask the students to find the adverbs in blue in the article and see if they can work out the meaning from the context before they answer the questions.

Answers

1 really 2 nearly 3 quite 4 certainly 5 probably

2 Ask the students to complete the sentences using the adverbs.

Answers

1 really 2 nearly 3 quite 4 certainly 5 probably

3 Demonstrate this activity first as a class by telling the class some true and false things about your family (see examples below in Mixed ability).

MIXED ABILITY

Encourage stronger students to write as many true and false sentences as they can in the time allowed for this exercise. With the weaker students, write five example sentences (see below) on the board about your family. Then, ask them to choose four of the sentences and change them so that they are true for them, e.g.:

My brothers are really tall.

My sister listens to music nearly all the time.

I work really hard at school.

My mother is quite good at music.

My grandmother certainly cooked very well.

Answers

Students' own answers

» VOCABULARY WORKSHEET UNIT 20

LISTENING

147 1 Ask the students to look at the three silhouettes of family groups and describe what family members they can see in each one before they listen.

Answers

A Sally B Sammy C Harry

147 2 Ask the students to read the sentences and try to decide who says each one before they listen again. Point out that they won't hear the answers in the same order as the sentences and they won't hear the same words on the recording but rather words that have a similar meaning. With a stronger class, in preparation for the writing stage below, choose six useful expressions from the recording. Play the recording again and stop it after each expression for them to write down.

Answers

1 Sally 2 Harry 3 Sammy 4 Sally 5 Harry 6 Sammy

» AUDIOSCRIPT TB PAGE 279

WRITING

PREPARE TO WRITE
A description of your family

GET READY A2 Key for Schools Reading Part 5.

In this part of the exam, the students will need to read a text with six gaps and write one word for each gap. These words are generally grammar words. In this exercise, the first gap has been completed as an example and students only complete five gaps.

Books closed. Ask the class to say what they remember about Sally's family from the recording. Books open. Ask them to read her description of her family and think about what kinds of words are missing. They shouldn't complete the gaps for now. Point out that they should use one word only in each gap and this word should be spelled correctly. Then, get the students to complete the gaps.

Answers

grammar words like prepositions, conjunctions, pronouns, auxiliaries, etc.
1 with 2 to 3 them 4 a 5 your

PLAN Ask the students to look at Sally's description again and think about what questions she answers in each sentence. Brainstorm a list of these questions onto the board. For example:

Have you got any brothers or sisters?

Do you live with any other members of your family?

What are they like? How old are they?

Who do you like spending time with in your family?

How often do you see them?

Now ask the students to make notes in answer to these questions. Remind them to look at the notes they wrote in Grammar Exercise 8 page 117 for help.

WRITE Remind the students that they can use Sally's description to help them by using her sentences but changing the information.

IMPROVE Ask the students to check that the description is interesting, there are some adjectives and adverbs, and the spelling is correct.

COOLER

Play *Stand up and change seats if ….* Arrange the chairs so the students are sitting in a circle.

Choose some statements about family from this lesson, e.g. the sentences in Vocabulary Exercise 2 page 119, and/or in Sally's description of her family. Write them clearly on a piece of paper (the students will need to be able to read these).

Say one of the sentences, e.g. 'Stand up if a grandparent lives with you.' Those students stand up. Remove one of the seats. Say 'Now change seats and sit down.' Those students standing change seats but one student will be left without a seat. This student becomes the teacher and reads out the next sentence. Continue as a class or in small groups. If moving the chairs isn't possible, tell the students standing to swap seats and sit down. The last student to sit down becomes the teacher.

VOCABULARY Adverbs of degree

1 **Look at the adverbs in the article and match them to the meanings.**

EP

1. Which one means 'very much'?
2. Which one means 'very close to'?
3. Which one means 'not completely'?
4. Which one means '100% true'?
5. Which one means 'maybe'?

2 **Complete each sentence with a different adverb from Exercise 1.**

1. Sally's my best friend. I ________ like her.
2. In my family, we all eat dinner together ________ every night.
3. I'm not sure about this colour. It's ________ nice, I suppose.
4. I don't know if Grace is coming to the party, but Tim ________ is. I know that for sure.
5. 'What's the time?' 'I'm not sure but it's ________ about 2 o'clock.'

3 **Work in pairs. Write three true and three false sentences about your family using the adverbs in Exercise 1. Take turns to read your sentences and guess which are true and which are false.**

My brother's really tall. My mum's probably driving at the moment.

LISTENING

147 **1** **Listen to three young people talking about who they live with. Match the speakers to the pictures of families A–C.**

A

B

C

147 **2** **Listen again. Who do you think is talking? Write Sammy, Sally or Harry next to the sentences.**

1. I live with one of my grandparents.
2. I have to travel quite a long way to see my dad.
3. My sister is getting married soon.
4. I don't spend a lot of time with my cousins.
5. My brother and I sleep in the same room.
6. There are two families in my home.

WRITING

PREPARE TO WRITE

A description of your family

GET READY Read Sally's description of her family. What kinds of words are missing from the gaps: grammar words or vocabulary words?

Complete the description. Write ONE word for each gap.

Example: 0 *my*

Reply Forward

To: Sally
From: Gabrielle

I live with 0 ________ parents in a three-bedroom house. I'm the only child in the family – I haven't got any brothers or sisters. My grandfather lives 1 ________ us as well – he's in the room next 2 ________ mine. He's 78, and he tells lots of interesting stories. I've also got four cousins, and I love seeing 3 ________ too. They're 4 ________ bit older than me, and they don't look like me. I'm quite tall and I've got dark hair, but they're short and they've got fair hair.

Write soon and tell me all about 5 ________ family.

PLAN Make notes about your family.

WRITE Write a description of your family in 70 words or more.

IMPROVE In pairs, read your description and your partner's. Check for mistakes. Give your partner two ideas to make their description better. Use your partner's advice to rewrite your description.

LIFE SKILLS EMOTIONAL SKILLS

A

BEING A GOOD FRIEND

LIFE SKILLS

Being a good friend

A good friend
- understands your feelings
- says sorry when they are wrong
- understands you and knows when you have a problem

1 **Read the sentences and answer the questions.**

It is better to have a few good friends than a lot of friends.

To know how someone else feels, put yourself in their shoes.

1 What do you think the sentences mean?
2 Do you agree with the sentences? Why? / Why not?
3 Which sentence do you prefer? Why?

2 **Choose two qualities that you think are important in good friends. In pairs, compare your ideas.**

They listen carefully
They make me feel good
They are there for me when I have problem
They help me do my best
They give me their opinion
They trust me

3 **Read the text quickly. Match sections 1–3 to photos A–C. Are you a good friend?**

1 ....

Friends are an important part of our lives. It's sometimes difficult to make friends and it's not always easy to keep them. To have close friends, it's essential to be a good friend. The big question is what can you do to be a good friend and keep your friends?

B

4 **Complete the sentences with highlighted words from the text.**

1 It's .... to be a good friend to have friends.
2 It's not always easy to make and keep .... friends.
3 Maybe your friend is worried about a bad .... in an exam.
4 Good friends give.......... and they tell you the best thing to do in a difficult situation.
5 It is sometimes important to be .... so you can know yourself.
6 Remember that the longest .... you have is with yourself.

LIFE SKILLS

Learning Objectives

- The students consider what a good friend is.
- In the project stage, they make a helpful poster with advice and present it to other students.

Vocabulary

essential close mark advice alone friendship

BACKGROUND INFORMATION

IQ (Intelligence Quotient) has always been linked to academic success. However, in the 1990s, journalist Daniel Goldman in his book *Emotional Intelligence: Why it can matter more than IQ* suggested that emotional intelligence can also contribute to this academic success. Emotional intelligence, also known as EQ (Emotional Quotient) is the ability to identify and manage your own emotions and the emotions of others. For example, it may be acceptable to shout loudly and get angry when your favourite team loses a match, but it is probably unacceptable to shout loudly and get angry with a teacher in class. Teachers can help their learners improve their emotional intelligence by encouraging them to (among other things):

- be active listeners (really listening and understanding others, using body language to show this)
- develop their vocabulary for feelings (e.g. understanding the difference between *angry*, *sad* and *frustrated*)
- develop self-awareness (realising how they appear to others)
- show empathy (being able to put yourself in someone's else's shoes).

WARMER

Organise the students into small groups and give each group two pieces of A3 paper and some board markers. Ask the groups to write *A good friend …* at the top of one and *A bad friend …* at the top of the other. Then, ask them to write down at least three qualities of each in a list with bullet points, e.g.:

A good friend …	A bad friend …
listens to you	talks a lot but doesn't listen
makes you laugh	laughs at you

Then, display the posters on the walls. Invite the students to stand up, read the posters and tell each other whether they agree or disagree with the ideas.

LIFE SKILLS

Being a good friend

If the students did the Warmer, ask them to compare their ideas of what a good friend is with the ideas in the *Life skills* box. If they didn't do the Warmer, ask them to read the ideas in the box and say whether they agree with them.

1 Encourage the students to ask and answer the questions in small groups. Ask the students if they have a similar expression to *put yourself in their shoes* in their own language.

Answers

Students' own answers

2 If necessary, pre-teach *trust* by asking the students to read through the qualities and say which verb means 'you believe that this person will not hurt you'. Next, ask the students to compare the list in the book with their ideas on their posters on the walls (see Warmer) and to identify which are the same and which are different. Then, ask them to choose the two most important qualities from the book and/or the posters and compare their ideas with a partner.

Answers

Students' own answers

3 First, ask the class 'What does each photo say about being a good friend?' and encourage the students to answer this question in pairs before they read the text. Encourage the students to answer the question *Are you a good friend?* in pairs and to say why.

Answers

1 A 2 C 3 B

148 The Reading text is recorded for students to listen and read.

4 Encourage the students in pairs to read the sentences first and think of a suitable word before they look for the words in the text.

MIXED ABILITY

Give the weaker students the answers but in a different order. Ask them to find these words in the text first before they complete the sentences.

FAST FINISHERS

Encourage fast finishers to work through Exercises 3 and 4 at their own pace. When they have finished, encourage them to think of a suitable title for the whole article and also a heading (this could be a question) for sections 1–3.

Answers

1 essential 2 close 3 mark 4 advice 5 alone 6 friendship

149 **5** Ask the students to read the three sentences (a–c) first before they listen. Encourage them to try to guess who Alex is.

Answers

b

149 **6** Ask the students to try to answer the questions before they listen again.

Answers

1 school bell ringing / leaving school 2 He had an argument with Alex. 3 He sent a text message to Alex. 4 They help each other when times get difficult. 5 No, she tells him to wait. / No she doesn't. 6 tomorrow / the next day

TALKING POINTS

Brainstorm a list of situations where students may need help and support onto the board first, e.g. difficult homework, too many exams, want to join a sports club, etc. In small groups, encourage the students talk about the people they talk to for each of the different situations.

149 **7** Ask the students to try to match the sentence halves first before they listen and check their answers. Play the recording again and ask them to listen and repeat.

Answers

1 d 2 a 3 b 4 c

» **AUDIOSCRIPT TB PAGE 279**

PROJECT *A helpful poster*

Ask the class to read the instructions in bold and ask 'What do you need to do first?' (*read the two problems and choose one*) 'And then?' (*talk together and write some advice using the expressions in the Useful language box*). Ask the students on their own to read both problems and choose one.

Organise the students into small groups and ask them to choose the problem together. Remind them to use the useful language in Life Skills Reaching an agreement page 32 and to write down some advice using the useful language in Exercise 7.

Next, encourage the groups to talk about what sort of picture could illustrate the situation and then ask them to nominate someone to draw it. If appropriate, the students could take a photo to illustrate the situation instead.

Ask the groups to produce a poster with both a picture and the advice. Next, display the posters on the walls and ask each to present their poster to another group. Encourage the other group to give some advice on how the posters could be improved (using the useful language).

PROJECT EXTENSION

Brainstorm a list of typical situations where students may need help and support onto the board again (see Talking points above). Encourage the students to include academic ones, e.g. coping with exams, study habits (taking notes, recording new language, revising, etc.) and some more social ones (e.g. making new friends, changing school, city or country). Ask the class to vote on the ones that concern them the most. Give each group one of the chosen situations and ask them to create a poster with sensible advice.

COOLER

Encourage the students to look critically at the posters they created at the beginning of the class (see Warmer). Encourage them to talk together about whether they would like to add or remove anything from their lists in the light of this lesson. Then, if appropriate encourage a class discussion on what emotional skills are by using the information in Background information above.

2 ....

Good friends usually share interests and like doing the same things. They have fun together but they help each other in difficult times, too. For example, when someone gets a bad mark in an exam, does not get on the football team or feels sad or alone, a good friend tries to understand the situation and offers help.

Your friend is sad and you don't know what to do. Maybe you can call them, visit them or make them a card. When a friend is worried about an exam, you can help them study. If your friend doesn't get on the football team, you can practise together after school.

Remember, a good friend listens carefully and gives advice when possible. So, listening to people and putting yourself in their shoes helps make, and keep, friends.

3 148

It's important to have friends to help you, but it's also necessary to know how to be alone and to be sure of yourself. Don't forget, the longest friendship in your life is with yourself!

C

149 **5 Listen to Karl talking to Martha. What does Martha do?**

a She tells Karl her problems.
b She listens to Karl and tries to help him.
c She calls Alex.

149 **6 Listen again and answer the questions.**

1. How do you know where Karl and Martha are?
2. Why is Karl feeling sad?
3. What did Karl do immediately after the argument?
4. According to Martha, what do good friends do?
5. Does Martha think Karl should call Alex that day?
6. When does Martha tell Karl to send a message?

TALKING POINTS

Who do you talk to when you need help and support? A friend? A family member? A teacher?

149 **7 Now listen again and match the two halves of the sentences.**

USEFUL LANGUAGE

1 Why don't you …	**a** wait until tomorrow.
2 I think you should …	**b** worry.
3 You shouldn't …	**c** to wait.
4 It's a good idea …	**d** send him a message?

PROJECT *A helpful poster*

In small groups, choose problem A or B below. Talk together and think of some advice and write ideas in your notebook. Use expressions from Exercise 7.

- Draw a picture of the situation you chose.
- Make a poster with your advice and a picture.
- Present your poster to another group or to the class.

A I have no idea what to do. My best friend always says bad things about our friend Jack when he isn't with us. What should I do?

B My friend Anna is very sad these days. She spends her weekends alone and doesn't want to go out. I'm worried about her. How can I help her?

BEING A GOOD FRIEND 121

REVIEW 5 UNITS 17–20

VOCABULARY

1 **Write a word to link each group of words.**

Complete the words for the groups.

0 aunt cousin nephew niece
f *a m i l* y

1 study pass fail teach
s ___ o ___

2 dance music friends fun
d ___ ___ ___ o

3 headline photographs articles advertisement
m ___ ___ ___ z i ___ e

4 channel remote control the news programme
t ___ ___ e ___ i ___ ___ ___ n

5 winner performer prize talent show
c ___ ___ p ___ ___ ___ ___ ___ ___ ___ n

2 **Put the words in order to make questions. Then complete the answers with adverbs.**

1 can / dance / well / you / ?
No, I dance ________.

2 easily / you / new / do / things / learn / ?
No, I have to work very ________.

3 always / you / school / speak / do / at / quietly / ?
No, sometimes I speak ________.

3 **Complete the sentences with the words in the box.**

album	cartoons	fan
reviews	star	the final

1 The film got good ________ in the newspapers.

2 I love Ed Sheeran's first ________. His music's really good.

3 My little brother watches ________ on TV when he gets home from school.

4 It's ________ of the talent show tonight. Then we'll know the name of the winner!

5 My favourite film ________ is Jennifer Lawrence.

6 I'm a big ________ of rock music. I love it!

GRAMMAR

1 **Read the rules about entering the talent show. Complete Emma's email to Lauren with the words and phrases in the box.**

can	can't	don't have to	have to x3

TALENT SHOW

Rules for entering

AGE: 14 or over

GROUPS: possible but only up to five people

PRICE TO ENTER: £10 per person

Just fill in the form on our website! Pay by 31 July.

To: Lauren
From: Emma
Date: 2 May
Reply Forward

I've got some information about the talent show. You [1] ________ be 14 or over to enter. We [2] ________ enter as a group, but the group [3] ________ have more than five people in it. If we want to enter, we [4] ________ pay £10 each, and we [5] ________ fill in a form on the website. We [6] ________ pay yet; we can wait until the end of July. What do you think? Shall we do it?

2 **Choose the correct words to complete the sentences.**

1 He drives very *good* / *well*.

2 The weather there was very *good* / *well*.

3 *Shall* / *Can* you come to my house at 7 pm?

Correct the mistakes in the sentences.

4 Why not to see a film?

5 You don't bring anything except your clothes and your money.

6 Why not trying phoning her later.

7 Lets choose some more photographs for the magazine.

REVIEW 5 UNITS 17–20

Overview

VOCABULARY	Television; Entertainment; Magazines; *as*, *because*, *so* and *when*; Trip activities; School collocations; Family; Adverbs of degree
GRAMMAR	Future with *going to*; Making suggestions; *have to / don't have to*; Adverbs of manner
LISTENING	Owen talking about his family
READING	A postcard from a school trip
SPEAKING	Asking questions; talking about school trip activities
EXAM TASKS	Reading Part 5; Speaking Part 2

Resources

PHOTOCOPIABLE WORKSHEETS: Grammar worksheets Units 17–20; Vocabulary worksheets Units 17–20; Review Game Units 17–20; Literature worksheet; Speaking worksheet; Writing worksheet

WARMER

Play Backs to the board. Put the students into pairs. Ask them to sit so that Student A has their back to the board and so can't see it. Next, write six words from Units 17–20 (see examples below) on the board. Tell Student B that they need to give a description of each word on the board for Student A to guess the word. When the first pair has finished, they shout *Stop!* and the game stops. Ask Student A to change seats with B, so that Student B can't see the board. Repeat the activity with six new words from Units 17–20 (see examples below).

Student A	Student B
headline	advertisement
pass	fail
prize	performer
aunt	nephew
sailing	canoeing
cartoon	channel

VOCABULARY

1 Books closed. Read the first set of words in the example (*aunt*, *cousin*, *nephew* and *niece*) and ask 'What do they have in common?' (*they are members of the family*) Books open. Ask the class 'What do you have to do in this exercise?' Point out that some of the letters are given and there is a space for each other letter in the word.

Answers

1 school 2 disco 3 magazine 4 television 5 competition

2 Ask the students to write the three questions first. With a weaker class, tell them the first word in each question. For the answers, point out that the answer is *No*, so they will need to think of an adverb with an opposite meaning. If time allows, encourage them to ask and answer the questions in pairs and give true answers.

Answers

1 Can you dance well? No, I dance badly.
2 Do you learn new things easily? No, I have to work very hard.
3 Do you always speak quietly at school? No, sometimes I speak loudly.

3 Ask the students to read the sentences first and think about the missing word before they read the words in the box.

MIXED ABILITY

Give stronger students the first letter of each missing word and ask them to try to complete the sentences without looking at the words in the box. Give very weak students pairs of words to choose from for each space, e.g. 1 *reviews / cartoons*, 2 *review / album*, 3 *albums / cartoons*, 4 *reviews / the final*, 5 *star / fan* and 6 *star / fan*.

Answers

1 reviews 2 album 3 cartoons 4 the final 5 star 6 fan

GRAMMAR

1 Ask the students to read the information about the talent show first and ask 'What are the rules?' Encourage them to explain the rules using *have to/don't have to* or *can/can't*, e.g. *You have to be 14 or over / You can't be 13 or under*. Next, ask them to read the whole email and think about the missing verb (*have to/don't have to* or *can/can't*). Then, ask them to complete the gaps, checking that they use *(don't) have* + *to* + infinitive or *can/can't* + infinitive (without *to*).

FAST FINISHERS

Ask fast finishers in pairs to write a suitable reply to Emma's email answering the two questions at the end.

Answers

1 have to 2 can 3 can't 4 have to 5 have to 6 don't have to

2 For questions 1–3, encourage the students to read the complete sentence first before they choose the correct answer. For questions 4–7, point out that there is one mistake in each of the sentences and if necessary, point out that there are two mistakes with punctuation.

Answers

1 well
2 good
3 Can
4 Why **don't we** see a film?
5 You don't **need to** / **have to** bring anything except your clothes and your money.
6 Why not **try** phoning her later?
7 **Let's** choose some more photographs for the magazine.

LISTENING

150 **1** Ask the students to read the instructions and ask 'What do you have to do?' Point out that one of the people is Owen and encourage them to guess who it is. Play the recording twice.

Answers

A Max B Rob C Lily D Grace E Abby F Nora G Colin H Liam I Owen J Ryan

» **AUDIOSCRIPT TB PAGE 279**

READING

1 **A2 Key for Schools Reading Part 5.**

In this part of the exam, the students read a short email or message and need to complete six gaps with one word. The focus in this part is on grammar.

With a strong exam-focussed group, ask them to do the exercise as an exam. Allow them about ten minutes to do it. Encourage them to compare their answers before you check them as a class.

Answers

1 a 2 the 3 Her 4 from 5 than 6 of

SPEAKING

1 With a weaker class, help the students by giving them the first word or words of each question. Then, remind them to give full answers when they ask and answer the questions in pairs.

Answers

1 What kind of TV programmes do you like?
2 Which magazines do you like reading?
3 What activities do you do after school?
4 Which family members live at home with you / with you at home?

2 **A2 Key for Schools Speaking Part 2.**

In the first part of the exam, students will need to look at some pictures of different things, e.g. different hobbies, sports, outdoor activities, holidays, etc. and answer a general question such as *Do you like these different hobbies/sports/activities? Why? / Why not?* For this part, the two students are expected to talk together and not to the examiner for between one and two minutes.

Point out that in the exam, the examiner will give them one to two minutes to do this activity, but they should try to keep talking to their partner until the examiner asks them to stop.

Answers

Students' own answers

3 In the next part of the exam, the examiner will ask the students in turn 'Do you think … ?' questions, which are related to the pictures. If the students give very short answers, the examiner will ask *Why? / Why not?* or turn to the other student and ask *What do you think?* At the end of the activity, the examiner will ask each student in turn *Which of these sports/hobbies/activities do you like best?* The examiner will allow between one and two minutes for this part.

Encourage the students to take turns to ask the questions, answer in full sentences and also finish their answer by asking *What about you?* where appropriate.

Answers

Students' own answers

4 In the last part of the exam, the examiner will ask one of the students a more open question, e.g. *Is it better to go on trips with your school or with your family? Why?* and then invite the other to give their opinion by asking *And what about you?* Then, the examiner will ask the other student a more open question and also invite their partner to give their opinion by asking *And you?*

Encourage Student A to ask Student B the first question and ask Student B to finish with *And what about you?* Student A should answer. Then, ask Student B to ask Student A the second question and ask Student A to finish with *And you?* Student B should answer. Stop this activity after two minutes.

Answers

Students' own answers

COOLER

Organise students into two teams for an end of coursebook quiz. Ask the five questions below and give teams time to find the answers in the Student's Book. Award points for correct answers.

1 How often do the Paralympic Games take place? (Every four years – Culture 1 page 22)
2 What or who is Tamburello? (a sport from North Italy played with a tambourine – Review 1 page 35)
3 What information can you find on kidzcationz.com? (travel advice from kids for kids – Reading Unit 10 page 64)
4 What or who is Ponchiki? (Russian doughnuts – Speaking Unit 11 page 71)
5 How old is Friday Barnes? (11 – Reading Unit 18 page 108)

LISTENING

150

1 **Listen to a boy called Owen talking about a picture of his family. Listen and write the correct letter beside each name.**

Nora	....	Colin	....
Abby	....	Lily	....
Rob	....	Liam	....
Grace	....	Max	....
Ryan	....		

Which person is Owen?

READING

1 **For each question, write the correct answer in each gap. Write ONE word in each gap.**

Dear Daisy

I'm ⁰ *having* a great time on my school trip here in Spain. I've made ¹ .... new friend. She's staying in ² .... same activity centre as me. ³ .... name is Natalya and she comes ⁴ .... Russia. She's a year older ⁵ .... me.

Yesterday morning, we went to visit a museum. There were lots ⁶ .... very interesting things there.

See you soon.

SPEAKING

1 **Put the words in order to make questions.**

1 kind / programmes / TV / like / you / do / what / of / ?
2 magazines/ like / do / which / reading / you / ?
3 activities / do / after / what / you / do / school / ?
4 which / home / live / members / at / you / family / with / ?

In pairs, ask and answer the questions. Take turns to speak.

2 **Here are some pictures of different school trip activities. Do you like these activities? Say why or why not. Talk about the activities with your partner.**

3 **In pairs, ask and answer these questions. Take turns to speak.**

Do you think …
going to museums is boring?
visiting theme parks is expensive?
going camping is fun?
visiting a castle is interesting?
going on a nature walk is exciting?

Which school trip activities do you like best?

4 **In pairs, talk about school trips. Take turns to speak.**

Which is more fun, learning in a classroom or learning on a school trip?

What school trips would you like to do in the future?

EXTRA ACTIVITIES

UNIT 10 VOCABULARY AND READING, PAGE 62

2

Quiz result?

More *Yes* than *No* answers.
You are careful with your money and want to buy things for a good price. You usually think and look before you buy.

More *No* than *Yes* answers.
You love clothes and shopping, and you like spending money. You don't always think before you buy and you spend a bit too much sometimes.

UNIT 10 PREPARE TO WRITE, PAGE 65

Well, I found a great jacket on the internet. It was black and it had a really cool design on the back. You can't pay in cash of course, so my mum paid for it with her credit card. After that, we waited and waited but it didn't come. After two weeks I emailed the company, but they didn't answer. Then, six days later, it finally arrived. But the jacket was the wrong size. It was too small *and* it was blue. I returned it and asked them to send me the right one, but they emailed me to say they didn't have one in my size in black. And my mum is still waiting for them to return her money.

UNIT 12 GRAMMAR, PAGE 73

7 **Write true sentences with superlatives. Use the ideas below or your own ideas.**

The most famous person in my country is the president.

easy
famous
good
old
popular

school subject
person in my country
computer game I play
show on TV
place in my country

Compare your answers with a partner.

UNIT 18 GRAMMAR, PAGE 107

7 **In small groups, plan a class magazine.**

Think about the questions.

What would you like:
- your class magazine to be called?
- to include in your class magazine?

Do you want it to be a paper magazine or an online one?

Is the magazine going to be weekly, monthly, termly or yearly?

Step 1 Suggest as many ideas as you can in your group for your class magazine.

Let's …
Why don't we … ?
Shall we … ?
Why not … ?

Step 2 Choose the five best ideas to share with the class. Tell the class.

Step 3 As a class, discuss and choose the best three ideas.

UNIT 11 SPEAKING, PAGE 71

3 Student A will ask you for information about dishes A–C. Answer his or her questions.
Then ask Student A questions about items D–F on page 71. Use the following questions to help you.

What are the ingredients in ...? | Does ... contain meat? | What is ...?

How much is a bowl of ...? | Where is ... from?

Then choose the dish you want to buy.

A

American barbecue

Large burger £5.00
Ingredients: Meat, bun

Burger with cheese £5.50
Barbecue sauce 50p
Ingredients: Meat, cheese, bun

B

Aloo tikki 50p each
Ingredients: potatoes, peas, chilli, onions

C

Shish kebab £4.00
Ingredients: Chicken or lamb, onions, spices

UNIT 11 SPEAKING, PAGE 71

3 Student A, ask Student B questions about items A–C on page 71. Then choose the dish you want to buy. Use the following questions to help you.

What are the ingredients in ...? | Does ... contain meat? | What is ...?

How much is a bowl of ...? | Where is ... from?

Student B will ask for information about these dishes. Answer his or her questions.

D

Yakisoba

Fried noodles with vegetables, meat and onions

small bowl £2.00

large bowl £3.00

E

Zapiekanka

Bread with mushrooms and cheese £1.50

or grilled meat served with fried onions £3.20

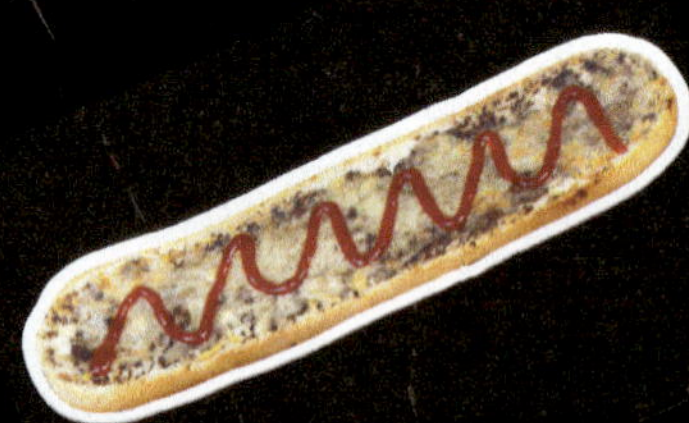

F

Ponchiki – 50p each

Lovely sweet doughnuts!

GRAMMAR REFERENCE AND PRACTICE ANSWER KEY

STARTER UNIT BE / THERE IS / THERE ARE

1 **1** Is there … , Yes, there is.
2 Are there … , No, there aren't (are not).
3 Are there … , Yes, there are.

HAVE GOT

2 **1** have not (haven't) got
2 have ('ve) got
3 has not (hasn't) got; has ('s) got
4 Have … got; have

CAN

3 Students' own answers

UNIT 1 ADVERBS OF FREQUENCY

1 **1** play **2** doesn't (does not) go **3** watches **4** Does … go **5** don't (do not) play **6** studies

2 **1** We never play badminton.
2 My dad doesn't (does not) often go running (or My dad doesn't go running often.)
3 My friends and I sometimes go cycling.
4 We aren't (are not) usually bored in our sports lesson.
5 Are you often tired in the morning?

3 *(Possible answers)*
1 Do you and your friends often go sailing? No, we never go sailing.
2 Are you sometimes bored at home? Yes, I'm (am) often bored on Sunday afternoon.
3 How often do you cook dinner? I often cook dinner.
4 How often does your best friend watch TV? She always watches TV after dinner.
5 Do you sometimes go running alone? Yes, I often go running alone.

UNIT 2 PRESENT CONTINUOUS AND PRESENT SIMPLE

1 **1** We're (are) serving dinner now.
2 I'm (am) not going to school this morning.
3 What are you making?
4 My friends aren't (are not) going cycling at the moment.
5 Is your best friend sitting next to you?

2 **1** never eat **2** go **3** 's sleeping **4** do you usually have **5** watching, I'm not **6** isn't working **7** always go

3 *(Possible answers)*
1 For breakfast, I often have toast and hot chocolate.
2 My friends and I sometimes play football after school.
3 At the moment, my best friend is sitting next to me and she's doing this exercise.
4 I'm wearing a T-shirt, trousers and shoes today.
5 On Friday afternoon, I usually go to my grandparents' house and we have pizza.
6 I'm doing this exercise now.

UNIT 3 LIKE, DON'T LIKE, HATE, LOVE + -ING

1

verb	only add *-ing*	remove -e and add *-ing*	double the consonant and add *-ing*	*-ing* form
get up			✓	getting up
have		✓		having
make		✓		making
open	✓			opening
play	✓			playing
shop			✓	shopping
sit			✓	sitting
swim			✓	swimming
watch	✓			watching

2 **1** playing **2** living **3** driving **4** going **5** wearing **6** getting up

3 *(Possible answers)*
2 I don't like listening to rock music.
3 I hate studying for exams.
4 I really like having pizza for dinner.
5 I quite like swimming in the sea.

UNIT 4 PAST SIMPLE OF BE

1 **1** were **2** was not (wasn't) **3** were not (weren't), was **4** were **5** was not (wasn't), was

2 **1** Was your first teacher tall? Yes, he/she was.
2 Were his shoes broken? Yes, they were.
3 Were you and your friends cold? No, we weren't.
4 Was your mobile phone in your bag? No, it wasn't.
5 Were we near the lake? Yes, we were.

3 *(Possible answers)*
1 Were you late for school on Monday? No, I wasn't.
2 Were your friends tired at 9 am this morning? No, they weren't.
3 When was your best friend born? In 2006.
4 What day was it yesterday? It was Tuesday.
5 Was this exercise difficult? No, it wasn't.

UNIT 5 PAST SIMPLE: REGULAR VERBS

1

climb → climbed	change → changed	carry → carried	play → played	stop → stopped
walked	died practised	tried studied	stayed enjoyed	shopped planned

2 **1** played **2** watched **3** listened **4** climbed **5** tried **6** finished

UNIT 6 PAST SIMPLE: NEGATIVES AND QUESTIONS

1 **1** didn't (did not) cook **2** didn't (did not) work **3** didn't (did not) use **4** didn't (did not) climb **5** didn't (did not) open

2 (*Possible answers*)
1 My mum didn't listen to rock music yesterday.
2 My classmates didn't walk to Paris yesterday.
3 I didn't study for five hours yesterday.
4 My friends and I didn't play rugby yesterday.
5 This class didn't start at 7 pm yesterday,

3 **1** Did … help, Yes, she did.
2 Did … finish, Yes, they did.
3 Did … start, No, it didn't.
4 Did … enjoy, Yes, I/we did.
5 Did … rain, No, it didn't.

4 (*Possible answers*)
1 What time did you start school? I started school at 9 o'clock.
2 Did you use a computer last night? Yes, I did.
3 What did you study yesterday? I studied maths and history.
4 Did you visit another country on holiday? Yes, I did. I visited Italy.
5 When did you finish Unit 5? We finished it last week.

UNIT 7 PAST SIMPLE: IRREGULAR VERBS

1 **1** go **2** rode **3** see **4** swam **5** take **6** arrived **7** carry **8** enjoyed **9** live **10** stopped **11** watch

2 **1** <u>went</u>, go **2** <u>had</u>, have **3** <u>rode</u>, ride **4** <u>ate</u>, eat **5** <u>bought</u>, buy

3 **1** gave **2** rode **3** bought **4** got up **5** saw **6** could

4 **1** enjoyed **2** Did … go **3** stayed **4** did … do **5** swam **6** was **7** visited **8** did … eat **9** had **10** took

UNIT 8 *SOMEONE, ANYONE, ETC.*

1 **1** anything **2** nothing **3** everything **4** someone **5** no one **6** somewhere

2 **1** any **2** any **3** Every **4** any **5** some

3 **1** someone, no one **2** anywhere, somewhere **3** anything, nothing **4** Everyone

UNIT 9 PRONOUNS AND DETERMINERS

1 **1** My **2** His **3** Their **4** her **5** Our **6** your

2 **1** His **2** yours **3** mine **4** hers **5** yours **6** Ours

3 **1** our **2** yours **3** his **4** mine **5** your **6** My **7** yours **8** theirs

UNIT 10 *SOME, ANY, A LOT OF, A FEW, A BIT OF*

1

Countable	Uncountable
earring, egg, jacket, photo, purse, T-shirt, wallet	jewellery, juice, make-up, milk, money

2 **1** any **2** some **3** any **4** some **5** any **6** any

3 **1** a lot of **2** a bit of **3** a few **4** a lot of **5** a few

4 **1** any **2** some **3** a **4** a bit of **5** lot **6** a

UNIT 11 *AS … AS*

1 **1** The Burger Bar is as popular as the Pizza Restaurant.
2 Ireland is as wet as Scotland.
3 Lemonade isn't as sweet as cola.
4 Your shorts aren't as dirty as your T-shirt.
5 My mum's pizza is as good as the pizza at Harry's Café.

COMPARATIVE ADJECTIVES

2 **1** younger **2** more interesting **3** easier **4** farther/further **5** bigger

3 **1** The train is faster than the bus.
2 Istanbul is hotter than London (today).
3 The pizza was better than the burger.

UNIT 12 SUPERLATIVE ADJECTIVES

1 **1** nearer, the nearest **2** larger, the largest **3** thinner, the thinnest **4** friendlier, the friendliest **5** happier, the happiest **6** more beautiful, the most beautiful **7** better, the best **8** worse, the worst **9** farther/further, the farthest/the furthest

2 **1** the longest **2** the most famous **3** the best **4** the friendliest **5** the biggest **6** the funniest

3 **1** My sister is the fastest person in our school.
2 Russia is the largest country in the world.
3 Salad is the healthiest food in this café.
4 I'm the worst singer in my class.
5 My brother is the best player in his team.

4 **1** more **2** faster **3** the healthiest **4** the best **5** more **6** the tallest

UNIT 13 *SHOULD/SHOULDN'T*

1 **1** shouldn't (should not) **2** shouldn't (should not) **3** should **4** should **5** should **6** shouldn't (should not)

2 **1** You shouldn't (should not) drink a lot of cola and lemonade.
2 You shouldn't (should not) eat a lot of sweets and chocolate.
3 You should eat healthy food.
4 You should sleep well.
5 You shouldn't (should not) watch a lot of TV.

3 **1** Should my brother buy a fast car? No, he shouldn't (should not).
2 Should my friends go to bed earlier? Yes, they should.
3 Should we have a party? No, we (you) shouldn't (should not).
4 Should I stay at home? No, you shouldn't.

4 (*Possible answers*)
1 You should buy her some jewellery.
2 No, you shouldn't. You should go to bed early.
3 You should go to Turkey. It's beautiful.
4 He should play baseball. It's fun.
5 Yes, you should. You should join a sports club.

UNIT 14 PREPOSITIONS

1 **1** near **2** across **3** opposite **4** near **5** next to **6** in front of

2 **1** Outside **2** across **3** next to **4** near **5** opposite

3 (*Possible answers*)
1 No, it's in my town.
2 My favourite shop is the sports shop. It's next to the library.
3 Yes, it does.
4 I walk across a bridge when I go to school.
5 Yes, there's a museum opposite the cinema.

UNIT 15 PAST CONTINUOUS

1 **1** was doing **2** was cooking **3** weren't playing **4** weren't wearing **5** weren't having **6** were climbing

2 **1** was crying **2** wasn't (was not) sleeping **3** was reading **4** were surfing **5** was sitting **6** wasn't (was not) watching **7** was listening **8** was raining

3 **1** Were your friends riding their bikes? Yes, they were.
2 Were you shopping with your friends? Yes, I was. (Yes, we were.)
3 Was your mum working? No, she wasn't.
4 Was I having a shower? No, you weren't.
5 Were you and your friends swimming at the lake? Yes, we were.

4 (*Possible answers*)
1 What were you doing at 8 am this morning? I was having breakfast.
2 Were you wearing blue socks yesterday? No, I wasn't. I was wearing white socks.
3 Were you and your friends watching a film after school yesterday? No, we weren't. We were doing our homework.
4 Was it raining yesterday evening? No, it wasn't.
5 What were your friends doing on Saturday morning? They were playing tennis.

UNIT 16 PAST SIMPLE AND PAST CONTINUOUS

1 **1** came, were playing **2** didn't call, heard **3** was getting off, started **4** arrived, was making **5** was climbing, fell **6** didn't meet, were shopping

2 **1** when **2** while **3** when **4** When **5** when **6** While

3 **1** was travelling, felt **2** started, wasn't (was not) talking **3** was carrying, fell **4** were running, saw **5** was doing, rang **6** didn't visit, were staying

4 (*Possible answers*)
2 When I got to school, my friends were playing football.
3 The teacher came into the classroom while we were doing our homework.
4 When I arrived home, I rang my friend.
5 While I was doing my homework, my brother came into my room.

UNIT 17 FUTURE WITH *GOING TO*

1 **1** We aren't ('re not or are not) going to ride our bikes to school tomorrow.
2 My friends are going to watch the talent show on TV.
3 My mum isn't ('s not or is not) going to play tennis later.
4 My dad's (is) going to make pizza.
5 My cousins aren't (are not) going to visit us next weekend.

2 **1** 're (are) going to stay **2** 'm (am) going to buy **3** 're (are) going to watch **4** 'm (am) not going to go **5** 'm (am) going to travel **6** 'm (am) going to work **7** 'm not (am not) going to serve

3 **1** are … going to watch **2** are … going to wear **3** Is … going to work **4** are … going to see **5** Are … going to travel **6** Are … going to study

4 (*Possible answers*)
1 We're going (are going) to watch a soap opera.
2 I'm going (am going) to wear my school uniform.
3 No, she isn't. She's going (is going) to stay at home.
4 We're going (are going) to see my grandparents.
5 Yes they are. My best friend's going (is going) to go to Italy.
6 Yes, I am. I'm going (am going) to study in Barcelona.

UNIT 18 MAKING SUGGESTIONS

1 **1** use **2** Shall we **3** Let's **4** Shall **5** Why not **6** Why don't we

2 **1** Let's watch

2 Shall … have (Why don't … have)

3 Why not (Why don't we or Shall we) ride

4 Let's read

5 Shall … take (Why don't … take)

3 (*Possible answers*)

1 Let's have a party.

2 Let's go to the cinema.

3 Shall we write down some ideas and plans?

4 Why don't we use the computer?

5 Why not make some pancakes?

6 Shall we write a music review?

UNIT 19 *HAVE TO / DON'T HAVE TO*

1 **1** have to get fit **2** don't have to go **3** have to leave **4** have to wear **5** doesn't have to wear **6** don't have to make

2 **1** don't have to buy **2** don't have to help **3** have to do **4** has to stay **5** don't have to bring

3 **1** Does your mum have to work five days a week at the museum? No, she doesn't.

2 Do you have to turn off your smartphone at school? Yes, I/we do.

3 Does your dad have to travel for his work? No, he doesn't.

4 Do we have to do Exercise 5? No, you/we don't.

5 Do your friends have to make their beds? Yes, they do.

4 (*Possible answers*)

1 What time do you have to get up on a school day? I have to get up at 7 o'clock.

2 Do you have to speak English in your English class? Yes, I do.

3 How much homework do you and your classmates have to do every day? We have to do a lot of homework.

4 What do you have to do if you miss a class? My mum has to phone the school or write a note.

5 Do you have to buy a ticket before you get on a bus in your town? No, I/you don't.

UNIT 20 ADVERBS OF MANNER

1 **1** carefully **2** well **3** happily **4** quietly **5** wonderfully **6** heavily **7** hard **8** badly **9** angrily **10** fast **11** noisily

2 **1** hard **2** quickly **3** badly **4** carefully **5** well

3 (*Possible answers*)

1 How many languages can you speak well? I can speak Spanish and English well.

2 How often do you do your homework slowly and carefully? I always do my homework slowly and carefully.

3 Do you eat quickly? No, I don't. I eat very slowly.

4 How far is your school from your house? Can you walk there easily? It's five kilometres. No, I can't walk there easily. I have to go by car or by bus.

5 Do you play in a sports team? Does it play badly or well? Yes I do. It plays quite well.

WORKBOOK ANSWER KEY AND AUDIOSCRIPTS

GET STARTED!

VOCABULARY

1 **1** door **2** computer **3** board **4** exercise book **5** chair **6** bag **7** coat **8** pens **9** teacher **10** ruler **11** rubber **12** map **13** textbook **14** window **15** poster

2 Students' own answers

3 Possible answers: **1** door **2** board **3** pens **4** poster **5** chairs **6** exercise books **7** bag **8** teacher **9** ruler **10** rubber **11** map **12** textbook

4 **1** teacher **2** computer **3** coat **4** window **5** bag

GRAMMAR

1 Students' own answers

2 **1** Are there **2** Is there **3** Is there **4** Are there **5** Is there **6** Is there

3 Students' own answers

4 **1** have got **2** haven't got **3** hasn't got **4** have got **5** haven't got **6** haven't got **7** has got **8** hasn't got

5 **1** Have your friends got pens? **2** Has your dad got a computer? **3** Have you got a best friend? **4** Has your teacher got a blue coat? **5** Have you got a pet?

6 Students' own answers

7 Students' own answers

VOCABULARY

1 **1** fourteen **2** 18 **3** twenty **4** 23 **5** thirty-one **6** 40 **7** fifty-six **8** 62 **9** seventy-one **10** 85 **11** ninety **12** 100

2 **1** September **2** July **3** March **4** August **5** May **6** December **7** June **8** January **9** October **10** February **11** November

3 **1** February **2** March **3** April **4** May **5** June **6** July **7** August **8** September **9** October **10** November **11** December

4 **1** 16th September **2** 30th June **3** 7th October **4** 23rd February **5** 13th December **6** 21st August

5 Students' own answers

GRAMMAR

1 **1** b **2** e **3** a **4** h **5** d **6** f **7** g

2 **1** Can you make a cake? **2** Can you play tennis? **3** Can you ride a bike? **4** Can you run 5 km? **5** Can you speak three languages? **6** Can you stand on your head? **7** Can you swim underwater?

3 Students' own answers

4 Students' own answers

5 **1** like **2** love **3** hasn't got **4** has got **5** likes **6** plays **7** doesn't play **8** likes

6 **1** What books do you like? **2** Do you like drawing pictures? **3** What sports do you play at school? **4** Do you like watching TV? **5** What is your favourite animal?

7 Students' own answers

8 Students' own answers

WRITING

1 **1** d **2** b **3** f **4** a **5** c **6** e

2 Students' own answers

UNIT 1 Sports and games

VOCABULARY

1 **1** volleyball **2** skating **3** badminton **4** hockey **5** snowboarding **6** cycling **7** gymnastics **8** baseball **9** table tennis **10** athletics **11** sailing **12** surfing

2

play	go	do
badminton baseball hockey rugby table tennis volleyball	cycling sailing skating snowboarding surfing	athletics gymnastics

3 **1** go **2** do **3** plays **4** play **5** go

GRAMMAR

1 **1** never **2** sometimes **3** often **4** usually

2 **1** My sister usually goes cycling with my dad. **2** I never play rugby with my friends. **3** Snowboarding is sometimes dangerous. **4** My friends often do gymnastics after school. **5** My grandparents always play table tennis on Sundays.

3 **1** Do you usually go cycling in the city? **2** Do your parents often play badminton? **3** How often do you go snowboarding? **4** Do your friends sometimes play rugby at school? **5** Do you always go sailing in the summer?

4 Students' own answers

5 **1** I **always go** swimming on a Sunday. **2** I **am often** tired in the evening. **3** People **sometimes go** cycling with their friends. **4** At the weekend, **I usually** do sports. **5** In the holidays, we **sometimes go** sailing.

VOCABULARY

1

a	b	e	s	g	b	h	k	b	d	i
f	o	o	t	b	a	l	l	n	p	i
e	a	c	i	d	t	r	u	g	b	y
i	r	a	c	k	e	t	m	y	a	g
g	d	a	k	f	b	e	g	s	l	c
m	r	h	p	r	t	n	h	d	l	i
h	o	c	k	e	y	n	a	o	c	e
c	b	s	u	r	f	i	n	g	n	f
i	d	k	e	f	a	s	u	n	f	b

2 **1** stick **2** ball **3** balls **4** bat **5** racket **6** board

READING

1 every week, on Saturday

2 **1** B **2** C **3** B **4** A

3 **1** 2 **2** 13 **3** a ball, a swimming pool **4** head, hands, feet

LISTENING

1 plays tennis, cycles, studies, reads, goes to the cinema

2 **1** ✓ **2** × **3** × **4** ✓ **5** ✓ **6** ×

3 **1** play tennis **2** 6.00 am **3** play tennis **4** do homework **5** play tennis

01 **Barry:** Hello and welcome to the Sports Day Podcast with me, Barry Stephenson. I've got a very special guest here today. Her name's Andrea Murray. She's Britain's number one teen tennis player. Hello, Andrea. Welcome to the show.

Andrea: Hi, Barry. It's good to be here. I always listen to your show.

Barry: That's great. So, Andrea, our listeners want to know about your family.

Andrea: Well, Barry, my family is sporty. My mother, Sandra, plays badminton and goes sailing. My father, Tony, plays rugby for a team in our town.

Barry: Do you have any brothers and sisters, Andrea?

Andrea: Yes, I do. I have a brother and a sister.

Barry: Do they do sports?

Andrea: Yes, they do. My brother, Dan, goes snowboarding and skating. And my sister, Amy, plays volleyball.

Barry: What a fit family! Can you tell us about a typical day for you?

Andrea: I'm often very busy and I never get up late. I always play tennis for two hours before school.

Barry: What time do you get up?

Andrea: I usually get up at five o'clock.

Barry: Five o'clock? That's early!

Andrea: Yes. I get up at five o'clock from Monday to Friday and I get up at six o'clock at the weekend.

Barry: Do you play tennis at the weekend?

Andrea: Yes, I do. On Saturdays, I usually cycle to the tennis courts after breakfast and then I play tennis all day. On Sundays, I do my homework in the morning and then I usually play tennis after lunch. Practice is very important.

Barry: Do you get very tired, Andrea?

Andrea: Yes, I'm usually tired, but I love playing tennis. I want to be the best tennis player in the world.

Barry: What do you do in your free time?

Andrea: Sleep! But I love reading and going to the cinema with my friends too.

Barry: Well, thanks for talking to us, Andrea. Good luck!

WRITING

1 all the questions

2 **1** faborite - favourite **2** Does you - Do you **3** to - two **4** bal - ball **5** two - to **6** sometime - sometimes **7** I also in a team - I'm/I am also in a team **8** We playing - We play **9** becase - because **10** its - it's

3 Students' own answers

4 Students' own answers

UNIT 2 This is my day

VOCABULARY

1 **1** tidy **2** leave **3** wake **4** have **5** check **6** get **7** prepare **8** put **9** brush

2 **1** wake up **2** get dressed **3** have breakfast **4** check your messages **5** tidy your room **6** prepare your school bag **7** brush your hair **8** clean your teeth **9** put on your shoes **10** leave the house

3 **1** check my messages **2** have breakfast **3** get dressed **4** clean my teeth **5** prepare my school bag **6** leave the house

GRAMMAR

1 **1** present simple **2** adverbs of frequency **3** present continuous **4** *today*, *now* and *at the moment*

2 **1** always **2** always **3** now **4** today **5** at the moment **6** usually

3 **1** tidy **2** watch **3** is cooking **4** doesn't work **5** isn't working **6** are you reading

4 **1** I **am studying** now because I've got an exam tomorrow. **2 Do you know** Katy? She's my sister. **3** My brother **is** watching TV with his friends. **4** My mum is a doctor. She **usually works** at weekends. **5** Every day we **drink** tea for breakfast.

VOCABULARY

1 **1** cereal, bread, honey **2** cheese, tomatoes **3** fish, rice, vegetables **4** fruit

2 **1** c **2** g **3** e **4** b **5** f **6** a **7** d

3 Students' own answers

READING

1 **1** Y **2** L **3** A **4** Y **5** Y **6** L **7** A

2 **1** She has cereal and milk. **2** She walks. **3** It starts at 7.30 am. **4** She usually has sandwiches and fruit. **5** She watches videos on the internet. **6** She does her homework in the evening.

LISTENING

1 They're in a shop / supermarket.

2 **1** J **2** J **3** G **4** G **5** G **6** J

3 **1** working **2** on holiday **3** make eggs **4** 1.30 **5** chocolate **6** likes

02 **Jasmine:** Hi, George!

George: Oh, hello, Jasmine! What are you doing here?

Jasmine: I'm shopping for my parents. They usually go to the supermarket at weekends, but this week my mum is away for work and my dad is too busy.

George: That's a pity. Where's your mum?

Jasmine: She's in Canada. She says it's really cold there. So, why are you here? Don't you always play football on Saturday afternoon?

George: There isn't any football today. Everyone in the team is on holiday.

Jasmine: Oh, right. So, why are you here? You hate the supermarket!

George: Yeah, I do. I'm getting some eggs. My sister is home from university and she wants to cook. She wants to make eggs and chips. She loves them! Well, actually, I love chips too.

Jasmine: And I like eggs! What time does she want to have lunch?

George: At half past one.

Jasmine: You haven't got much time then!

George: I know. So, what are you buying?

Jasmine: Oh, lots of things. I'm getting bread, apples, eggs – and some chocolate.

George: I like chocolate, but I don't eat it often. I prefer biscuits.

Jasmine: I never eat chocolate, but my dad eats it every day. Well, I've got to go now. I've got lots of things to buy.

George: See you at school on Monday.

Jasmine: Bye.

WRITING

1 **1** d **2** e **3** f **4** g **5** b **6** a **7** c

2 I get up at 7 o'clock **and** get dressed. My breakfast is cereal **or** toast. Then I prepare my school bag **and** go to school at 8 o'clock. I usually walk to school **but** sometimes I go on the bus. School starts at half past eight **and** finishes at 3 o'clock. Lunch is at 1 o'clock. I usually have sandwiches **or** a salad. After school I go home. Dinner is at half past seven. After dinner, I do my homework **and** go on the internet. I go to bed at half past nine.

1 and **2** but **3** or

3 **1** and **2** or **3** but **4** or **5** but **6** and

4 Students' own answers

5 Students' own answers

UNIT 3 Great sounds

VOCABULARY

1 **1** rap **2** opera **3** rock **4** hip-hop **5** jazz **6** classical music **7** soul

2 **1** piano **2** electric guitar **3** saxophone **4** keyboard **5** violin **6** drums

3 **1** c **2** a **3** d **4** e **5** b

GRAMMAR

1 **a** 4 **b** 2 **c** 3 **d** 1

2 **1** writing **2** running **3** catching **4** making **5** practising **6** swimming

3 **1** My brother doesn't like doing homework. **2** I hate playing the piano. **3** My sister loves rapping **4** My best friend likes reading books. **5** My dad likes playing the violin.

4 **1** I like **going** shopping at weekends. **2** He doesn't **like watching** opera on TV. **3** I don't like **playing** football at school. **4** She **loves** reading books. **5** We love **listening** to music.

VOCABULARY

1 **1** famous **2** a concert **3** in a band **4** a singer **5** on tour **6** music **7** an album **8** a music video

2 **1** plays **2** become **3** teaches **4** become **5** record **6** giving **7** make **8** goes

3 **1** actor **2** record **3** keyboard **4** instruments **5** rock **6** festival **7** musician

READING

1 Young people between 10 and 16 who want to be actors, dancers and singers, and adults.

2 **1** ✗ **2** ✗ **3** ✓ **4** ✓ **5** ✗

3 **1** in London **2** Leona Lewis and Dua Lipa **3** on Mondays, Tuesdays and Wednesdays **4** dancing, singing or acting classes

LISTENING

1 the violin

2 **1** Tuesdays **2** 25 **3** park **4** Driscoll **5** 643599

03

Mrs Driscoll: Hello?

Sam: Oh, hello. Is that the Park Music School?

Mrs Driscoll: Yes. How can I help you?

Sam: I'm phoning to ask about violin lessons. Are you the violin teacher?

Mrs Driscoll: Yes, I am. My name's Mrs Driscoll. What do you want to know?

Sam: Can I have lessons after school? We finish at half past three.

Mrs Driscoll: Yes, you can come here at four o'clock.

Sam: And how long are the lessons?

Mrs Driscoll: An hour. How many lessons do you want?

Sam: Er, maybe two a week. Can I come on Wednesdays and Fridays?

Mrs Driscoll: Er, let's see. Erm, I teach another student on Wednesdays, but you can come on Tuesdays and Fridays.

Sam: Yes, that's great. How much is each lesson?

Mrs Driscoll: Well, it's usually £30. But because you're having two lessons a week, it's £25 an hour.

Sam: That sounds good. Where are the lessons?

Mrs Driscoll: At the music school. It's 18 East Road. Catch the number eight bus from the theatre and get off at the park. The music school is near there.

Sam: OK, thanks. Er, can you say your name again, please?

Mrs Driscoll: Of course! It's Mrs Driscoll. That's D–R–I–S–C–O–double L. Let me give you my mobile phone number. Have you got a pen?

Sam: Er, yes.

Mrs Driscoll: OK. It's 643 5 double 9.

Sam: Uh huh. Thanks. See you next week then.

Mrs Driscoll: Oh, wait, what's your name?

Sam: Oh, it's Sam.

Mrs Driscoll: See you next week, Sam.

Sam: Yes, thanks. Bye.

Mrs Driscoll: Bye.

WRITING

1 **1** pop and hip-hop **2** Beyoncé and Taylor Swift **3** the electric guitar

2 **Music and me**

My name's Kate and I'm 13 years old. My friends and I all like listening to music. I think pop and hip-hop are exciting but jazz is boring. My favourite singer is Beyoncé. She's a really good singer. I also like Taylor Swift. Her music is great.

I listen to music at home and it's fun, but I love playing music, too. I'm in a band called The Pink Elephants! I play the electric guitar. It's great!

3 **1** also **2** also **3** and **4** and **5** also **6** also

4 Students' own answers

5 Students' own answers

UNIT 4 It was awesome!

VOCABULARY

1 **1** amazing **2** wonderful **3** fine **4** terrible **5** really good **6** OK **7** fantastic **8** great **9** horrible **10** brilliant **11** lovely **12** perfect

2

very, very good	all right	very bad
amazing, wonderful, really good, fantastic, great, brilliant, lovely, perfect	fine, OK	terrible, horrible

3 **1** brilliant **2** awesome **3** terrible **4** OK **5** horrible **6** really good

GRAMMAR

1 **1** We weren't at school. **2** It was very cold. **3** I was at a party. **4** She wasn't at the park. **5** Was he at home? **6** You were very happy.

2 **1** was **2** weren't **3** Were, was **4** wasn't **5** was **6** weren't

3 **1** weren't **2** was **3** Was **4** was **5** was **6** Were **7** were **8** wasn't **9** were **10** was

4 **1** Where **were** you yesterday? **2** Yesterday, it **was** sunny. **3** I **was** very happy because the test was easy. **4** We **were** at the beach last weekend. **5** The film **started** at 4 o'clock. **6** My parents **were** at a party on Saturday night.

VOCABULARY

1 **1** worried **2** upset **3** interested **4** sorry **5** happy **6** nervous **7** glad **8** afraid **9** surprised **10** angry

2 **1** sorry **2** afraid **3** happy **4** nervous **5** upset **6** surprised

READING

1 **1** B a trip in a hot-air balloon **2** A bungee jumping **3** C a day at a theme park

2 **1** good **2** was **3** worried **4** bad **5** liked **6** wants

3 **1** view **2** quiet **3** horrible **4** adults

LISTENING

1 **1** C **2** B **3** A **4** A **5** A

04 **1** Where was Olivia on Saturday?

Tom: You weren't at the football game on Saturday.

Olivia: No, I wasn't. I was at home. It was my brother's birthday party.

Tom: Oh, how old was he?

Olivia: He was seven. He was so happy with all his new toys.

Tom: Great!

2 What was the weather like at the theme park?

Girl: How was your trip to the theme park?

Boy: Brilliant! It was a really great day.

Girl: Was the weather good? It was rainy here and the wind was terrible!

Boy: Really? It was lovely at the theme park! The sun was out all day.

Girl: I want to go with you next time!

3 Where were Joni's parents last weekend?

Luke: How was your weekend, Joni?

Joni: It was fantastic. I was with my friend Carla because my mum and dad were away. We were in the shopping centre all day on Saturday with her parents, and had lunch at a great restaurant.

Luke: And where were your parents?

Joni: Visiting my sister at university. They were there all weekend.

4 When was Amy's birthday?

Jenny: Hi Amy. How was your weekend?

Amy: It was great. All my family were at my house on Saturday for my birthday.

Jenny: Was it your birthday on Saturday?

Amy: No, my birthday was on Friday and it was my mum's birthday on Sunday. The party was for me and my mum.

5 Who was at the swimming pool?

Lizzy: Hi Jamie. Were you at the swimming pool last Sunday?

Jamie: Yes, it was brilliant!

Lizzy: Oh, really? Were your parents there?

Jamie: No, it was me and my friends. There was a group of us.

Lizzy: That sounds fun. Was your friend from England there too?

Jamie: No, he wasn't. He was with his brother at the beach.

WRITING

1 Question 4

2 **1** special **2** expensive **3** tired **4** fantastic

3 Students' own answers

4 Students' own answers

UNIT 5 Moments in history

VOCABULARY

1

p	u	b	l	i	s	h	e	d
l	c	l	i	m	b	e	d	i
a	b	d	f	i	l	p	r	e
y	r	e	c	o	r	d	e	d
e	i	k	h	m	r	u	c	o
d	g	c	r	o	s	s	e	d
p	a	i	n	t	e	d	i	h
d	j	m	f	j	b	t	v	k
t	r	a	v	e	l	l	e	d
g	l	o	p	e	n	e	d	o

2 **1** died **2** painted **3** received **4** travelled **5** played

3 **1** travelled **2** climbed **3** crossed **4** painted **5** opened **6** published

GRAMMAR

1

in	on
2017	10th March
August	Sunday
October 2012	12th June 1999
the 20th century	

2 **1** on **2** in **3** on **4** in **5** in

3 **1** completed **2** cooked **3** copied **4** enjoyed **5** finished **6** invited **7** joined **8** phoned **9** played **10** studied

4 **1** I practised the guitar. **2** I cleaned the bathroom. **3** I played badminton with my friends. **4** I phoned my brother. **5** I studied maths, English and history.

5 **1** Yesterday I **went** to school at 8 o'clock. **2** I **received** an email from my teacher. **3** Last weekend, I **played** football in the park. **4** My brother **watched** TV yesterday. **5** In the afternoon, it **started** to rain and we went home.

VOCABULARY

1 **1** palace **2** castle **3** cathedral **4** church **5** square

2 **1** roof **2** floor **3** stairs **4** ceiling **5** statue

3 **1** floor **2** statue **3** castle **4** roof **5** square **6** ceiling

READING

1 an earthquake and a fire

2 **1** × **2** ✓ **3** × **4** ✓ **5** × **6** × **7** ✓

LISTENING

1 **1** b **2** d **3** c **4** a

2 You hear facts 2, 4, 5 and 7. The other facts are all true.

05 **Host:** Good evening and welcome to *Our History*. Today, we've got a special guest, Harry Harper. Harry teaches at a university and he knows everything about history!

Harry: Hello.

Host: So, who has a question for Harry? Yes? What's your name?

Robert: Um, I'm Robert.

Harry: Hello, Robert. What do you want to know about?

Robert: Can you tell me a fact about Henry VIII of England?

Harry: Yes, of course, Robert. He had six wives! OK, another question? Yes?

Lisa: Hi, Harry. I'm Lisa. Can you tell me an interesting fact about the footballer Pelé?

Harry: Well, Lisa. I can tell you Pelé played international football for Brazil 92 times! Who's next? Yes, you.

Rachel: I'm Rachel. What do you know about the scientist Marie Curie? What is interesting about her?

Harry: A lot of things, Rachel! Marie Curie won the Nobel Prize in 1903. But maybe you don't know that her daughter was also a scientist and she also won a Nobel Prize in 1935! All right. Who wants to go next?

Leon: Me! I'm Leon and I want to know about women and the history of space travel.

Harry: OK. Everybody knows that Yuri Gagarin was the first man to travel to space, but who was the first woman? Well, she was an astronaut and her name was Valentina Tereshkova. She travelled to space in 1963. OK, another question. Yes, you? What's your name?

WRITING

1 **1** 1829 **2** 1888 **3** 1975 **4** Now, today

2 **1** invented **2** connected **3** ordered **4** started **5** enjoyed **6** saved

3 Students' own answers

UNIT 6 What a great job!

VOCABULARY

1 **1** farmer **2** cook **3** dentist **4** an artist **5** an actor **6** factory worker **7** model **8** pilot

2 **1** artist **2** farmer **3** actor **4** factory worker

3 **1** cook **2** mechanic **3** sports coach **4** model **5** shop assistant **6** engineer

GRAMMAR

1 **1** didn't do **2** didn't study **3** didn't like **4** didn't go **5** didn't meet **6** didn't walk

2 **1** What time did the shop open? **2** Did you go to work yesterday? **3** Did your parents work in a factory? **4** Did she come to the office? **5** What did you do yesterday? **6** Did he enjoy his job?

3 **a** 4 **b** 5 **c** 1 **d** 6 **e** 3 **f** 2

4 **1** I **didn't** go to school yesterday. **2** Did you **watch** the film on TV yesterday? **3** It was rainy and we **didn't** play football. **4** Did you **get** a nice present for your birthday? **5** She didn't **have** English homework yesterday.

VOCABULARY

1 **1** boss **2** earn **3** office **4** busy **5** customers **6** staff

2 **1** office **2** busy **3** staff **4** customers **5** boss **6** earn

READING

1 Students' own answers

2 **1** C **2** C **3** A **4** B **5** A

LISTENING

1 **1** Ben **2** Ben **3** Lauren **4** Lauren **5** Ben

2 **1** She wanted to work in an office or a shop. **2** Because the factory was near her house. **3** Because he did lots of different things. **4** Ben started work at 9.00 am. **5** He wore a jacket and trousers with a clean white shirt. **6** She worked with Anna, a girl from school and some older boys from another school.

06 **Ben:** What did you do for your work experience, Lauren?

Lauren: Well, I wanted to work in an office or a shop. But I worked in a factory.

Ben: Did you enjoy it?

Lauren: Yes, it was fun. Thanks, Ben.

Ben: Did you get the bus every day?

Lauren: No, I didn't. The factory was near my house, so I just used my bike.

Ben: Really? For my work experience, I had to get up early to go by train.

Lauren: Oh, where did you work?

Ben: I worked in an office in a computer company.

Lauren: Was it good?

Ben: Yeah, great.

Lauren: Did you work on a computer all day?

Ben: No, I didn't. I did lots of different things. It was interesting.

Lauren: So, what time did you start?

Ben: At nine o'clock every day, but I got up at half past six to get the train at quarter to eight.

Lauren: I started at 8 am.

Ben: That's early. When did you get home?

Lauren: At four o'clock. It was a long day. But it was great because the people were very nice.

Ben: That's good.

Lauren: So, what did you wear to work, Ben? Did you wear a jacket?

Ben: Yes, I did, with trousers and a shirt. I wanted to wear a T-shirt, but they said no. I wore a clean white shirt each day. How about you? What did you wear?

Lauren: I wore jeans and a T-shirt.

Ben: Were there any other people there from our school?

Lauren: Only Anna. There were two boys from another school in our group.

Ben: Were they the same age as you?

Lauren: No, they were older. They really helped us.

WRITING

1 **1** He worked in an office in a school.
2 Yes, he did.

2 My dad worked in an office in a school. **He** started work at 8 o'clock and he finished at 3 o'clock. He **didn't** earn a lot of money, but the people were very friendly and he liked the students. **My** dad used a computer at work for the first time in 1981. **My** **dad's** job was fun because it was busy.

3 **1** b **2** e **3** d **4** c **5** a

4 Students' own answers

UNIT 7 An exciting trip

VOCABULARY

1 **1** f **2** b **3** g **4** h **5** d **6** a **7** e

2 **1** do water sports **2** buy presents **3** go camping **4** take photos **5** go sightseeing **6** lie on the beach **7** stay at a hotel **8** ride a bike

3 **1** stay at a hotel **2** take photos **3** do water sports **4** buy presents **5** lie on the beach **6** go sightseeing **7** ride a bike **8** go camping

GRAMMAR

1 **1** ride **2** have **3** give **4** take **5** go **6** see **7** buy **8** get up **9** come **10** swim **11** do **12** eat

2 **1** rode **2** had **3** gave **4** took **5** went **6** saw **7** bought **8** got up **9** came **10** swam **11** did **12** ate

3 **1** went **2** came **3** had **4** ate **5** took **6** saw **7** rode **8** gave **9** bought

4 **1** Where did you go on holiday last year? d **2** Who did you go with? a **3** Did your sister go sightseeing with you? e **4** What food did you eat? b **5** Did you and your family enjoy the holiday? c

5 **1** I **went** to France last summer. **2** I **went** sightseeing when I was in New York. **3** I **bought** some postcards and a T-shirt. **4** My parents **gave** me some money for my birthday last year. **5** Did you **eat** some nice food in Italy?

VOCABULARY

1 **1** coach **2** ferry **3** flight **4** guidebook **5** map **6** passport **7** station **8** suitcase **9** ticket **10** tourist **11** tour guide

2 **1** arrived at **2** pack **3** got on **4** took **5** travel by **6** got off **7** catch

READING

1 **1** Ibn Battuta **2** 1304 **3** 44 countries and cities, including India, China, Granada, Beijing and Cairo **4** Portugal **5** 1480 **6** Africa and India, the Atlantic and Pacific Oceans and the Philippines

2 **1** He studied and never travelled far from his home in Morocco. **2** He travelled for almost 30 years. **3** He went to 44 countries. **4** He wrote about his travels when he was an old man. **5** He became a sailor in 1505. **6** The journey from Spain to the Philippines took about 18 months. **7** He used maps and the stars to find his way.

LISTENING

1 Manchego / Spanish cheese

2 **1** R **2** R **3** P **4** R **5** P **6** R

3 **1** b **2** f **3** d **4** a **5** e **6** c

07 **Rebecca:** Hi, Paul. How was your holiday?

Paul: Oh. Hi, Rebecca. Yeah, it was great! How was yours?

Rebecca: Good, thanks. Where did you go?

Paul: Spain.

Rebecca: Really?

Paul: Yes, why?

Rebecca: I went to Spain, too!

Paul: That's amazing! We were there at the same time!

Rebecca: How long did you go for?

Paul: Two weeks. And you?

Rebecca: Only a week. Who did you go with?

Paul: I went with my parents. What about you?

Rebecca: I went with my mum and my brother. My dad didn't come.

Paul: We stayed in a great hotel near the beach in Valencia. There was a brilliant swimming pool there, too. Where did you stay?

Rebecca: Oh, we went camping near Barcelona. I loved it. The campsite was great and the weather was really good. Did you try Spanish food?

Paul: Yes, I did. I love Spanish food. We had it every day. Actually, I bought you a present. Here you are.

Rebecca: Oh, that's nice of you. Err, what is it?

Paul: It's *Manchego*. It's a Spanish cheese.

Rebecca: It's lovely. Thank you!

WRITING

1 **1** ✓ **2** ✓ **3** ✓ **4** ✓ **5** ✓ **6** ✓ **7** ×

2 Students' own answers

3 Students' own answers

UNIT 8 Favourite places

VOCABULARY

1 **1** carpet **2** curtains **3** armchair **4** bookshelf **5** lamp **6** cupboard **7** mirror **8** blanket **9** photographs **10** cushion **11** chest of drawers

2 **1** mirror **2** bookshelf, chest of drawers, cupboard **3** carpet **4** lamp **5** blanket

3 **1** curtains **2** armchair **3** carpet **4** cushions **5** bookshelf/cupboard **6** photograph

GRAMMAR

1 **1** everything **2** everyone **3** somewhere **4** something **5** anywhere **6** anyone **7** nowhere

2 **1** No one **2** anything **3** nothing **4** somewhere **5** anyone **6** everywhere

3 **1** c **2** e **3** f **4** h **5** a **6** b **7** d **8** g

4 **1** **Someone** gave me a T-shirt. **2** He didn't bring **anything** to the party. **3** We stayed at home all day and we didn't go **anywhere**. **4** You didn't tell me **anything** about it! **5** Please bring **something** to eat to the party.

VOCABULARY

1 **1** draw **2** play **3** write **4** listen to **5** read **6** paint

2 **1** computer **2** songs **3** drums **4** wind **5** pictures **6** stories

READING

1 blankets, chest of drawers, armchair, cushions

2 **1** B **2** B **3** A **4** B **5** B **6** C

LISTENING

1 It's very big.

2 **1** B **2** B **3** A **4** B

3 **1** ✓ **2** ✓ **3** × **4** × **5** ✓ **6** ×

08 **Jeremy:** Hello. You're watching *The Home Show*. I'm Jeremy Snow. Tonight, we meet the famous blogger KJ Neal. KJ's blog is famous all over the world. KJ is from Wales and she's only fourteen years old!

KJ: Thirteen, Jeremy. I'm fourteen in January. And I'm not from Wales. I'm from Scotland.

Jeremy: Oh. OK, right. Sorry about that! Anyway, welcome to the show. Now, KJ, what's your favourite place in your home? Is it your living room or maybe your bedroom?

KJ: Well, I love my bedroom, but it isn't my favourite place.

Jeremy: OK. So which place is it?

KJ: It's my writing room.

Jeremy: You've got a writing room? Wow!

KJ: Well, it's not really *my* room. I share it with my mum and dad.

Jeremy: What's it like?

KJ: It's got long, red curtains, some bookshelves and an old lamp. I'm very happy there.

Jeremy: And what's your favourite thing in your writing room? Is it your old lamp?

KJ: No, it's not. It's an armchair. It's very old, and it's green. I sit in the armchair and write my blog.

Jeremy: Do you sometimes write in your bedroom?

KJ: No, I don't. I never write there. It's quite small and there isn't much light.

Jeremy: What about the writing room? Is it a big room or a small one?

KJ: It's very big! That's why it's my favourite place!

Jeremy: Well, KJ, thank you for telling us about it. OK, now the next thing I wanted to ask you about was …

WRITING

1 **a** 3 **b** 2 **c** 5 **d** 4 **e** 1

2 I like it because they look very happy. My dad gave it to me when I was little so it's special. **1** because **2** so

3 **1** because **2** so **3** so **4** because

4 Students' own answers

5 Students' own answers

UNIT 9 Clothes and fashion

VOCABULARY

1 **1** tie **2** sunglasses **3** swimming costume **4** trainers **5** socks **6** boots **7** jumper **8** swimming shorts **9** gloves **10** suit **11** scarf **12** cap

2 Possible answers:

at the beach	on your feet	on your head	when it's cold	at work in an office
sunglasses swimming costume swimming shorts	boots socks trainers	cap scarf	boots gloves jumper scarf socks	suit tie

3 **1** bright **2** black **3** pale **4** blue

GRAMMAR

1 **1** d **2** a **3** e **4** f **5** b **6** c

2 **1** hers **2** mine **3** yours **4** ours **5** theirs

3 **1** She watches TV in **her** free time. **2** Can I borrow **your** new sunglasses? **3** It's **my** birthday on Sunday. I'm having a party. **4** My mum bought **me** some new trainers for school. **5** This jacket isn't **yours**. It's mine.

4 **1** his **2** my **3** your **4** mine **5** their **6** her

VOCABULARY

1 **1** wool **2** cotton **3** leather **4** plastic **5** metal **6** cork

2 **1** cotton **2** metal **3** wool **4** plastic **5** leather

READING

1 C

2 **1** ✓ **2** ✓ **3** × **4** × **5** ✓

3 **1** environment **2** swap (v) **3** charity shop **4** recycling centre **5** damaged

LISTENING

1 She doesn't know what to make for the School Family Day.

2 **1** Saturday **2** children **3** pasta / macaroni **4** yellow, T-shirts **5** mum

09 **Julie:** Dad, I really need some help.

Dad: What's the matter, Julie?

Julie: Well, we've got to make things to sell at the School Family Day.

Dad: What's the School Family Day?

Julie: Well, it's next Saturday. We all go to school with our families and there are games. This year all the students have to make or bring something to sell as well.

Dad: Why are you selling things?

Julie: We want to send money to help children in poor countries.

Dad: That's good! So, what's the problem?

Julie: I don't know what to make. Can you help me?

Dad: Of course! Hmm, I know! You can make necklaces.

Julie: How?

Dad: With macaroni pasta. You can paint the pasta different colours and put them on a string to make a necklace.

Julie: That's a good idea! I can make necklaces. But I want to take more things.

Dad: OK, well … I've got another idea. You can take some of the clothes that you don't wear anymore.

Julie: Oh yes, my yellow dress is too small and I have some T-shirts from when I was nine years old. They're very nice but I can't wear them now.

Dad: You can ask your mum – she'll help you find some clothes and it's good to recycle.

Julie: Yes, maybe she's got some clothes she doesn't want as well.

Dad: I can give you some of mine too! And I want to go with you on Saturday.

Julie: Great! Thanks, Dad.

WRITING

1 **1** parents **2** wear **3** cotton **4** made **5** trainers **6** leather **7** park **8** green

2 **1** blue **2** summer **3** school **4** jacket **5** weekend **6** white **7** shorts **8** beach

3 Students' own answers

4 Students' own answers

UNIT 10 Buying things

VOCABULARY

1

o	b	p	r	i	c	e	c
d	n	t	e	r	d	p	w
i	c	d	c	h	e	t	a
s	a	l	e	s	m	g	l
c	s	f	i	b	i	l	l
o	h	w	p	u	r	s	e
u	p	g	t	i	w	s	t
n	c	s	o	b	n	r	u
t	l	l	k	i	c	f	e

2 **1** cash **2** price **3** discount **4** sale **5** receipt

3 **1** sale **2** wallet/purse **3** purse/wallet **4** receipt **5** bill **6** price

GRAMMAR

1 **1** positive **2** negative **3** countable and uncountable **4** countable **5** uncountable

2 **1** There were a lot of people in the café. **2** I would like some books for my birthday. **3** Do you have any money? **4** My brother hasn't got any football boots. **5** My sister wants to buy a few biscuits. **6** Would you like a bit of cake?

3 **1** a lot of **2** a few **3** any **4** a bit of **5** some **6** a lot of

4 **1** I've got **some** bread and an apple. **2** There aren't **any** cookies in the kitchen. **3** There are **a lot of/many** new students in my class. **4** I've got **a** lot of books in my bag. **5** These trainers cost **a lot of** money.

VOCABULARY

1 **1** c **2** e **3** d **4** a **5** f **6** b

2 **1** pay for **2** buy, for **3** sell, for **4** have, for **5** is, for

READING

1 Students' own answers

2 **1** in Canada **2** yes **3** an amusement park **4** yes **5** in 2008 **6** 200 **7** fish underneath you **8** dentist, police officer, work in a restaurant or a supermarket

LISTENING

1 **1** B **2** C **3** A **4** B **5** A

10 **1** You will hear Katie talking about a present for her mother. What did she buy?

Katie: I went out on Saturday to buy Mum's birthday present. I wanted to get her some sunglasses, but they were very expensive. There were some chocolates in the sweet shop but I got her chocolates last year, so I went to the bookshop to get that new book by her favourite author.

2 You will hear two friends talking during their lunch break. What do they decide to do together after school?

Girl: Do you want to come to my house after school? We can finish the history project.

Boy: I can't today. I have to go to my swimming class at six. But we can go to the library and take out that book about the Romans.

Girl: That's a good idea. Then you can go to the pool afterwards.

3 You will hear a man talking to his daughter. What does his daughter want to buy?

Girl: Dad, you know we have the school party next week?

Dad: Yes, what do you want?

Girl: Well, I've got a new red dress and black jacket but I've only got trainers or my old blue shoes and they're ancient. I really want some black ones. Can you come shopping with me?

Dad: OK.

4 You will hear a teenager talking to his mother. What does he want to do?

Boy: Mum, you know my old bike?

Mum: Yes, the one in the garage.

Boy: Well, I think I can repair it and find someone to buy it.

Mum: That's a good idea. You don't ride it anymore. Then you can use the money for your holiday.

5 You will hear a boy talking to a shop assistant. Why does he buy the yellow T-shirt?

Boy: Excuse me. I'd like a T-shirt, please.

Assistant: Do you like this blue one?

Boy: Well, I like it but it's very big. It's for my brother. He's only eight.

Assistant: Ah, this one is smaller. It's £10.

Boy: I've only got £7.

Assistant: There's a bright yellow one here. It's £5.

Boy: That's great!

WRITING

1 a jacket and a pizza

2 Students' own answers

3 Students' own answers

UNIT 11 Eating out

VOCABULARY

1 **1** ice cream **2** cola **3** burger **4** chicken legs **5** pasta

2 **1** glass **2** pizza **3** piece **4** lemonade **5** bowl **6** plate

3 **1** Cream **2** tomato **3** chicken legs **4** salad **5** lemonade **6** strawberries

GRAMMAR

1 **1** as old as **2** n't/not as tall as **3** n't/not as big as **4** as interesting as **5** n't/not as expensive as **6** as popular as

2 **1** longer **2** healthier **3** shorter **4** more exciting **5** hotter **6** more popular

3 **1** more popular **2** hotter **3** longer **4** shorter **5** more exciting **6** healthier

4 **1** as big **2** dirtier **3** nicer **4** colder **5** interesting as

5 **1** older **2** easy **3** bigger **4** younger **5** better

VOCABULARY

1 **1** noodles, pancakes **2** chilli, curry **3** omelettes, chips, onions **4** sweets **5** seafood, grilled meat

READING

1 A

2 **1** burger and chips **2** chocolate cake **3** omelette and salad **4** fruit salad and cream **5** chicken legs **6** nothing

3 **1** Because it was his birthday. **2** Next to the cinema. **3** Yes, it was busy. **4** The manager. **5** Nothing, it was free.

LISTENING

1 **1** curry

2 **1** Wednesdays **2** 5.30 pm **3** £15 **4** 13 **5** pizza **6** 01632 960875 **7** a restaurant

11 **Lily:** Hi, Josh!

Josh: Hi, Lily. I'm phoning to ask about those cooking classes you go to. Are they fun?

Lily: Yes. They're really good! Do you want to learn to cook?

Josh: Yes, I can make pasta, but I want to learn more. When are the classes?

Lily: Well, I go on Wednesdays, but there are classes on Thursdays as well.

Josh: I'd like to go to the same class as you. What time do they start?

Lily: At five thirty, so we have time to go home after school finishes at four. The class is two hours long.

Josh: How much does the class cost?

Lily: You've got a student card, haven't you?

Josh: Yes, is it cheaper for students?

Lily: That's right. It's usually £20 a month but for us it's £15.

Josh: Are there many people in the class?

Lily: Not many. There are thirteen people in my group.

Josh: And what do you learn to make?

Lily: Well, last week we made pizzas with cheese and mushrooms. Next week the teacher says it's India week, and we're making curry.

Josh: Great! I love curry. Can you give me the teacher's phone number?

Lily: Umm, wait a minute … yes, it's 01632 960875.

Josh: Let me repeat that: 01632 960875, right?

Lily: Yes. Oh and it's on London Road, in the little restaurant on the corner.

Josh: That's Bob's restaurant. I know it. OK, thanks, Lily. See you there next week.

Lily: Bye, Josh.

WRITING

1

Type of food	Main courses	Desserts	Drinks	Opinions
Italian Mexican Spanish	burger and chips cheese pizza omelette and salad pasta with meat	chocolate cake fruit salad strawberry cheesecake vanilla ice cream	cola lemonade mineral water orange juice	brilliant lovely wonderful

2 **1** summer **2** dancing **3** meat **4** cola **5** hot

3 Students' own answers

4 Students' own answers

UNIT 12 The latest technology

VOCABULARY

1 Down: **1** headphones **4** screen **5** keyboard **6** mouse **8** e-reader **9** speaker

Across: **2** laptop **3** printer **7** console **10** smartphone **11** tablet **12** tracker

2 **1** (fitness) tracker **2** headphones **3** laptop **4** mouse **5** e-reader **6** printer **7** console **8** smartphone **9** tablet **10** screen **11** keyboard **12** speaker

3 **1** headphones **2** e-reader **3** console **4** screen **5** printer **6** laptop

GRAMMAR

1 **1** best **2** worst **3** fastest **4** most exciting **5** heaviest **6** most famous **7** cleverest **8** thinnest

2 **1** heaviest **2** best **3** cleverest **4** most famous **5** worst

3 **1** friendliest **2** oldest **3** most **4** higher **5** best **6** more

4 **1** is the most exciting footballer in the league.
2 was the fastest runner in the world in 2017.
3 is the most popular computer game in our class.
4 has the best hot chocolate in my town.

5 **1** It was the **greatest** holiday ever. **2** You should go to the MetroCentre because it's the **biggest** shopping centre in the UK. **3** You can wear your **oldest** clothes for this job. **4** The **easiest** subject at school is PE. **5** The most expensive cost £900 and the **cheapest** cost £400.

VOCABULARY

1 Possible answers:

buy	chat to	download	visit	watch
clothes, films, music, pictures, shoes, videos	family, friends	films, music, pictures, videos	websites	films, videos

2 **1** memory **2** save **3** digital **4** virus **5** machines **6** software

READING

1 A and C

2 **1** C **2** A **3** B

LISTENING

1 **1** B **2** A **3** C **4** B **5** A

12 You will hear Matt talking to his friend Sara about a technology festival.

Matt: Hi, Sara. Would you like to go to the Technology Festival with Amelia and me on Sunday?

Sara: Yes! I love computers. Is it in the shopping centre near the station?

Matt: Not this year. It's in the library. You know they've got three big rooms.

Sara: That's good. It's not far from my house. What's in the festival? Have they got any robots?

Matt: Yes, my dad says there are robots that walk and talk.

Sara: Wow! I saw an amazing robot online. It can clean the house and make food.

Matt: But robots can't do your homework for you!

Sara: I know. I'd like a robot to do my English homework! Let's go to the festival. How much will it cost? It was £8 last year.

Matt: Last year it was only £6, Sara. This year it's £10.

Sara: Can we buy things at the festival?

Matt: I think so. I'd like a new camera, but I haven't got much money. I got a really good mouse last year.

Sara: I need a new mouse. What about computer games? Do you want a new computer game?

Matt: Not now. My mum bought me one for my birthday.

Sara: OK. So, when shall we meet?

Matt: Well, the festival starts at 11 o'clock, so let's meet outside your house at a quarter to eleven and walk there together. Amelia is coming later, at about 12 o'clock, because she has tennis lessons in the morning.

WRITING

1 **1** e **2** c **3** f **4** a **5** b **6** d

2 **1** Are you busy on Saturday? **2** What are you doing on Sunday? **3** Would you like to go swimming on Friday? **4** Do you want to go to the park this afternoon?

3 **a** 6 **b** 1 **c** 5 **d** 4 **e** 3 **f** 2

4 Students' own answers

UNIT 13 Healthy bodies

VOCABULARY

1 **1** broken **2** headache **3** toothache **4** stomach ache **5** cold **6** hurt **7** sick **8** temperature **9** pain

2 **1** toothache **2** temperature **3** sick, stomach ache **4** pain **5** hurt, broken

3 **1** B **2** A **3** C **4** B

GRAMMAR

1 **1** should **2** should **3** shouldn't **4** should **5** shouldn't **6** should

2 **1** play tennis this afternoon **2** go to bed **3** sit down **4** eat so much chocolate **5** study hard tonight **6** drink lots of water

3 **1** × **2** ✓ **3** ✓ **4** × **5** ×

4 **1** I think you **should** take a coat. **2 Should I** bring a DVD? **3** correct **4** You **shouldn't** eat sweets in class. It's a school rule. **5** You **should** bring some water. It's very hot today. **6** correct

VOCABULARY

1 **1** get fit **2** have a rest **3** eat well **4** stay healthy **5** sleep well **6** do some exercises **7** enter a race

2 **1** d **2** c **3** a **4** b **5** e

3 **1** get **2** have **3** get **4** feel **5** enter **6** do

READING

1 2, 4, 5, 9

2 **1** She cycles to school. **2** At lunchtime she swims in the school swimming pool. **3** On Saturdays she enters races. **4** She won six triathlons last year. **5** She wants to be in the Olympics. **6** She has a rest on Sundays.

LISTENING

1 **A** 3 **B** 4 **C** 1 **D** 2

2 **1** × **2** ✓ **3** × **4** ✓ **5** ×

3 **1** should **2** matter **3** wrong **4** about

13 **1**

William: Good morning, Mum.

Mother: How's your stomach ache, William? Why are you out of bed?

William: Oh, it's much better, Mum. But I've got a headache now.

Mother: Really? You should take some medicine and go back to bed. It's good there's no school today.

William: OK, Mum. You're right. I'm happy it's Saturday. I'll go to bed now.

2

Teacher: What's the matter, Susie? You aren't saying much in class today.

Susie: I don't feel very well.

Teacher: What's wrong? Have you got toothache again?

Susie: No, I've got a pain in my arm. My teeth are fine.

Teacher: Well, you don't look very well. Go to the school office and call your parents.

3

Doctor: OK, Carla. Tell me what's wrong?

Carla: I don't feel very well and I think I've got a temperature. I feel hot and cold.

Doctor: OK. Can you sit on the bed here? I'll check. You came last week when you hurt your eye. How is it now? Does it still hurt?

Carla: No, it's much better, thanks.

4

Tom: Catch the ball, Marek!

Marek: OK. I'm trying … Ow!

Daisy: What's the matter, Marek?

Marek: My foot really hurts. Ow, I think it's broken.

Daisy: Oh no! What about your hand? Does it hurt, too?

Marek: My hand is OK. Ah, can you help me walk?

WRITING

1 Some advice about how to get into the school football team and how to get fit

2 **1** exercise **2** running **3** gym **4** football **5** park **6** healthy

3 **1** every day **2** to the gym **3** her friends **4** healthy food, like fish and vegetables

4 Students' own answers

UNIT 14 Getting around town

VOCABULARY

1 **1** library **2** traffic lights **3** bridges **4** bus stops **5** streets **6** roundabout

2 **1** d **2** f **3** a **4** c **5** e **6** b

3 **1** petrol **2** post **3** centre **4** street **5** station **6** pool

GRAMMAR

1 **1** opposite **2** next to **3** in front of **4** beside **5** opposite

2 **1** outside / near **2** next to / beside **3** opposite **4** next to / beside **5** through **6** across **7** opposite

3 **1** way **2** on **3** near **4** Turn **5** where **6** Go **7** next **8** after

4 **1** next to **2** supermarket **3** outside **4** along **5** across

VOCABULARY

1 **1** d **2** a **3** b/e **4** f **5** c **6** b/e

2 **1** guidebook **2** postcard **3** walking tour **4** tour guide **5** raincoat **6** cycle tour

3 **1** walking tour **2** tour guide **3** guidebook **4** raincoat **5** postcard

READING

1 1, 2, 3, 5, 7

2 **1** × **2** × **3** ✓ **4** ✓ **5** ✓ **6** ×

LISTENING

1 **1** C **2** F **3** H **4** G **5** D

14 You will hear Lucas talking to a friend about his trip to Cardiff with his family. Which place did each person visit on Saturday?

Girl: Hi, Lucas. How was your weekend?

Lucas: It was great, thanks. I went to Cardiff on Saturday morning with my family.

Girl: What did you do there?

Lucas: We all went to different places! I spent the morning in the museum.

Girl: And what did your sister do?

Lucas: She wanted some new jeans and a dress, so she went off to get those.

Girl: Did your mum go with her?

Lucas: Not this time. She met a friend and they went out for a meal together. They usually go to the cinema but there was nothing on they wanted to see.

Girl: Did your brother come with you?

Lucas: Yes, he had tickets for the big international rugby match, so he went to watch that.

Girl: Wow, lucky thing!

Lucas: I know! My dad wanted to go but he already had plans to see that new musical. We weren't interested so he went with a friend from work.

Girl: Did they enjoy it?

Lucas: Yes, a lot! My grandfather's decided to go next month. He spent Saturday in the park. He said it was too hot to go to the castle.

WRITING

1 **1** these **2** these **3** this **4** this **5** these **6** this

2 **1** This **2** this **3** These **4** These **5** This

3 **1** Galicia, in Spain **2** beautiful **3** lovely beaches **4** young people and families **5** a lot of shops **6** sell clothes and food **7** the museum **8** it has an old photograph of my street

4 Students' own answers

UNIT 15 Mysteries in nature

VOCABULARY

1 **1** long **2** wide **3** deep **4** high

2 **1** long **2** high **3** deep **4** wide

3 **1** mountain **2** island **3** lake **4** cliff **5** field **6** river

4 **1** in the field **2** cliff **3** lake **4** island **5** river **6** snow

GRAMMAR

1 **1** She wasn't doing her homework. She was playing with her games console. **2** He wasn't playing the piano. He was reading. **3** He wasn't reading a magazine. He was listening to music. **4** They weren't playing football. They were playing tennis. **5** She wasn't standing up. She was sitting down.

2 **1** Was he helping his parents? **2** Were Tia and Karl swimming in the sea? **3** Were they doing their homework? **4** Was your friend playing volleyball? **5** Were you reading a book?

3 **1** they weren't **2** I was / we were **3** she wasn't **4** they were **5** he wasn't

4 **1** I **enjoyed** my birthday party last week. **2** correct **3** correct **4** I liked it because **my favourite team was playing**. **5** When we were on holiday we **swam** every day.

VOCABULARY

1 **1** fog **2** ice **3** rain **4** snow **5** sun **6** wind

2 **1** snow **2** rainy **3** icy **4** fog **5** sunny

READING

1 They met after one girl found a balloon with a message from the other girl.

2 **a** 7 **c** 4 **d** 2 **e** 8 **f** 5 **g** 3 **h** 6

LISTENING

1 2, 3, 5, 6

2 **1** b **2** d **3** e **4** f **5** c **6** a

15

Sam: How was your holiday, Jack?

Jack: Oh, it was OK. Cornwall's a beautiful place. But the weather was really bad.

Sam: Oh, no! Was it bad every day?

Jack: Well, we got to Cornwall on Saturday morning. It was OK for the first hour, but then it started raining. It rained all day. We sat on the beach holding umbrellas. We didn't have much fun!

Sam: What about on Sunday? Was the weather any better then?

Jack: No, it was worse. It was really cold and windy on Sunday. We stayed in the hotel all day. We played some games but it wasn't very interesting.

Sam: Really? What about the next day? Did you leave the hotel on Monday?

Jack: Yes! We went out on Monday morning. It was sunny that day. But it wasn't very warm, so we didn't swim in the sea.

Sam: Was Monday the only sunny day?

Jack: Yes, it was! On Tuesday, it was foggy. We went to the town to go shopping but we couldn't see the sea. On Wednesday, it was very cloudy but we had a meal in a nice restaurant. We enjoyed that day because it wasn't raining.

Sam: Your last day was Thursday, wasn't it?

Jack: Yes, that's right. Guess what happened that day.

Sam: What?

Jack: It snowed!

Sam: In May?

Jack: Yes, in May! We're never going to Cornwall again!

WRITING

1 **1** e **2** c **3** d **4** a **5** b **6** f

2 **1** The people in the town were scared. **2** The Bondar was living in the forest. **3** One night he went to a house. **4** A little boy gave him some food. **5** The Bondar became friends with the boy.

3 **1** lives **2** hair **3** big **4** mountains **5** saw **6** forest

4 Students' own answers

UNIT 16 Amazing animals

VOCABULARY

1 Down: **1** elephant **2** monkey **4** rabbit **7** chicken
Across: **3** lion **4** rat **5** bear **6** insect **8** duck **9** mouse

2 Possible answers: **1** insect **2** chicken, duck **3** duck, insect **4** elephant, rabbit **5** rat, mouse, rabbit **6** lion

3 **1** insects **2** duck **3** bear **4** chickens **5** a mouse **6** Rats

GRAMMAR

1 **1** c **2** f **3** e **4** b **5** a **6** d

2 **1** were playing, started **2** was walking, found **3** was watching, called **4** were you doing **5** bought, was shopping **6** were waiting, drove

3 **1** when **2** While **3** while **4** When

4 **1** B **2** A **3** B **4** B **5** B

VOCABULARY

1 **1** turned off **2** got on **3** looked after **4** got off **5** turned on **6** picked up

2 **1** off **2** off **3** on **4** up **5** after **6** off

READING

1 **1** She was four years old. **2** He was taking a photo (of a bird). **3** She was in the forest (four kilometres away). **4** Because Lua was making a noise. **5** Because she was sleeping with Lua.

2 **1** A **2** C **3** B **4** C **5** A **6** A

LISTENING

1 **1** (her) rat **2** (an) elephant(s)

2 **1** c **2** d **3** e **4** b **5** a

3 **1** × **2** ✓ **3** ✓ **4** × **5** ✓ **6** ✓

16 **Donny**: Good morning and welcome to *Animal World*. I'm Donny Forrest. Today on *Animal World*, we're talking to Kirsty Smith. Welcome to the programme, Kirsty.

Kirsty: Hello, Donny. Thank you for inviting me.

Donny: Now, Kirsty, you're twelve years old. Is that right?

Kirsty: I'm thirteen.

Donny: Ah, right. Now tell us how many animals you've got, Kirsty.

Kirsty: I've got 34.

Donny: 34! That's amazing. How many dogs and cats have you got?

Kirsty: Well, I've got five dogs and twelve cats.

Donny: What other animals have you got?

Kirsty: I've also got nine rabbits and three birds.

Donny: Is that it?

Kirsty: No! I've got a rat, a fish and a sheep. Oh, and two horses.

Donny: Why have you got so many animals?

Kirsty: I love animals! I really enjoy looking after them.

Donny: Do you have a favourite?

Kirsty: Of course not. I love all my animals. Well, perhaps I love Jolly a bit more than the others.

Donny: Who's Jolly?

Kirsty: He's my rat. Some people think rats are horrible, but I think they are beautiful and intelligent animals.

Donny: Do you have a very big garden, Kirsty?

Kirsty: No, we don't. Our garden is quite small. But we live next to some fields. The animals run around and play there.

Donny: Is it true that you had seven monkeys a few years ago?

Kirsty: Yes, it is true! But we only had them for a few months. Then they went to live in a zoo. Do you know what animal I would like to have?

Donny: Oh, let me guess … a lion?

Kirsty: No, not a lion. I'd like to have elephants. But we'd need a much bigger garden!

Donny: How many elephants would you like to have?

Kirsty: I'd be very happy with two.

Donny: Well, thanks for coming on the show today, Kirsty. Next time you must bring one of the animals, but not an elephant!

WRITING

1 **1** was drawing **2** saw **3** went **4** opened **5** came **6** sat **7** saw **8** was

2 **A** One day **B** while **C** Then **D** Finally

3 Possible answers: **1** It was windy. **2** They were playing football in the garden. **3** She saw a kite. **4** It went into the tree. **5** Can you help me?/Can I/you get my kite? **6** They got the kite.

4 Students' own answers

UNIT 17 What are you watching?

VOCABULARY

1 **1** f **2** c **3** a **4** b **5** e **6** d

2 **1** fan **2** live **3** channel **4** remote **5** stream **6** demand **7** news

3 **1** talent show, stream **2** fan, live **3** demand, programmes

GRAMMAR

1 Possible answers: **1** He's going to swim. / He's going to jump in the pool. **2** She's going to open / close her laptop. **3** They're going to watch a match. **4** He's going to make a cake. **5** She's going to do her homework.

2 **1** He isn't going to finish his lunch. **2** I'm going to visit my mum in hospital. **3** She isn't going to phone her friend. **4** We're going to invite our friends to the party. **5** They aren't going to stream the film. **6** We aren't going to go to the concert.

3 **1** correct **2** I**'m** / I **am going** to play tennis and football. **3** I'm happy because you**'re** / you **are** going to come to my house. **4** correct **5** We**'re** / We **are** going to get to the sports centre by car. **6** I hope you**'re** / you **are going to** have a lovely time in my town.

4 **2** Is he going to make a cake? Yes, he is. It's for his mother's birthday. **3** Are they going to play volleyball this Saturday? No, they aren't. There are no games this weekend. **4** Are you going to walk home after school today? Yes, we are. Do you want to come with us?

VOCABULARY

1 **1** studio **2** competition **3** performer **4** judge **5** audience **6** vote for **7** winner **8** the final **9** prize **10** runner-up **11** stage **12** star

2 **1** winner **2** runner-up **3** stage **4** judge **5** star **6** studio **7** audience

READING

1 In the UK / England

2 **1** the United States/America **2** a cartoon **3** the parents **4** three **5** on TV or on his tablet **6** at home **7** a little girl's voice **8** yes

LISTENING

1 She's going to open a restaurant. She's going to enjoy her life and have a holiday.

2 **1** because she won *MasterChef* **2** (in a restaurant) in Manchester **3** He's in the music business. **4** £50,000 **5** have a holiday **6** have fun with cooking

17 **Interviewer**: Good evening. I'd like to welcome Josie Sutton, the winner of one of the most popular programmes on TV at the moment, *MasterChef*. She is here to tell us about her plans for the future.

Josie: Good evening. I'm very happy to be here.

Interviewer: So, Josie. What are you going to do now you are famous?

Josie: Well, I was working in a restaurant in Manchester but now I'm going to open a new restaurant in London.

Interviewer: What kind of restaurant are you going to have?

Josie: I'm not sure, but I'd like to have good food and music. My boyfriend is in the music business, so we wanted to do something together.

Interviewer: That sounds great! Are you going to have live music?

Josie: Yes, we are. We can have a stage where the performers can sing and tables where people can eat.

Interviewer: When are you going to do this?

Josie: Not till next year. I won fifty thousand pounds so I'm going to enjoy my life for a few weeks. I'm going to have a holiday and after that I'm going to start making plans for the restaurant.

Interviewer: Can you give our audience some advice about cooking? What is the best way to become a good cook?

Josie: I think there are three important things. First, you should always use fresh vegetables, meat or fish. Second, you should practise making different dishes, and finally, the most important thing is to have fun with cooking. Invite your family and friends to try your new dishes and enjoy eating with them.

Interviewer: That's good advice! Thank you for coming on our programme today.

Josie: Thank you.

WRITING

1 **1** *The Voice Kids* **2** three **3** Jess **4** The Vamps **5** Yes, Jenna's friends

2 Students' own answers

3 Students' own answers

UNIT 18 Magazines and books

VOCABULARY

1 **1** headline **2** interview **3** advertisement **4** photograph **5** cartoon

2 **1** c **2** d **3** e **4** b **5** a

3 **1** advertisement **2** review **3** information **4** article **5** cartoon **6** interview **7** headline **8** photograph

GRAMMAR

1 **1** b **2** d **3** a **4** c

2 **1** Shall **2** Why **3** don't **4** let's **5** not

3 Possible answers: **1** Why don't we have lunch at my house? **2** Shall we play football in the park on Sunday? **3** Why not go to the mountains? **4** Let's have a party on Saturday. **5** Why don't we play computer games at your house?

4 How are you? Thanks for your email. Yes, I'm free on Saturday. Lets go to the cinema! Why not seeing the new *Hidden Figures* film? Shall we to go to the cinema café before the film? They have great cakes! Why doesn't we meet in front of the cinema at 5 o'clock? Is that OK for you? Why not to call me tonight and we can talk about it?

5 **1** **Let's** go to the cinema! **2** Why not **see** the new *Hidden Figures* film? **3** Shall **we go** to the cinema café before the film? **4** Why **don't** we meet in front of the cinema at 5 o'clock? **5** Why **not call** me tonight and we can talk about it?

VOCABULARY

1 **1** c **2** d **3** a **4** b

2 **1** because, as **2** so **3** When **4** because, as **5** so **6** when

READING

1 Alyssa and Lily

2 **1** his parents **2** another world **3** cycling **4** because it's expensive **5** every night before she goes to sleep **6** She thinks it's brilliant.

LISTENING

1 **A** 3 **B** 5 **C** 4 **D** 2 **E** 1

1, 3

2 **1** Film of the Week (Cinema) **2** *My Wonderful Cousin* 3 £5 **4** New Film (Café) **5** chocolate and carrot

18 Hello and thanks for calling the Film of the Week Cinema. The Film of the Week Cinema is the place to come for all the great new films. We are open in the evening with special sessions on Saturday and Sunday mornings. This week's new film is called *My Wonderful Cousin*. Choose one to hear information about this week's new film. Choose two to hear about next week's new film. Choose three to hear information about the New Film Café. Choose four to talk to one of our assistants. Choose five to buy tickets.

Thank you. *My Wonderful Cousin* is about a bored teenager. Her name is Zoe and she's thirteen. During the long summer holidays, she goes to stay with her cousin Lucas in London and learns to play the guitar. She makes new friends and meets the musicians in a rock band. It changes her life. The film is on from Tuesday to Friday at 7 pm, and at 11 am at the weekend. Tickets are £5.

Thank you. The New Film Café is the perfect place to go before or after a film. The café is at the entrance to the cinema, so it's a great place to meet your friends. We offer coffee, tea, lemonade, orange juice and mineral water. Why don't you try one of our delicious cakes? We have chocolate cake and carrot cake. We also have our fantastic lemon ice cream. It's made in the café with real lemons!

WRITING

1 Yes, the writer likes it.

good – great, really interesting, brilliant, fun

bad – boring

2 Good opinion: amazing, brilliant, exciting, fantastic, great, interesting

Bad opinion: awful, boring, horrible, terrible

3 **1** loved **2** boring **3** sure **4** should **5** Go

4 Students' own answers

5 Students' own answers

UNIT 19 School can be fun!

VOCABULARY

1 **1** e **2** c **3** f **4** a **5** b **6** d

2 **1** on **2** at **3** park **4** on **5** round **6** show

3 **1** disco **2** museum **3** aquarium **4** sailing **5** river **6** fire **7** walk **8** farm **9** show **10** amusement

GRAMMAR

1 **1** We have to be quiet in class. **2** We have to wear a uniform. **3** We have to start school at 7.30. **4** We have to go to school on Saturdays. **5** We have to learn Spanish.

2 **1** doesn't have to **2** has to **3** don't have to **4** doesn't have to **5** have to **6** don't have to

3 **1** have **2** have **3** I have **4** have **5** don't have **6** We have

4 **1** can, don't have to **2** can, can **3** doesn't have to, can't, have to

VOCABULARY

1 **1** d **2** a **3** g **4** b **5** h **6** e **7** f **8** c

2 **1** lessons **2** tests **3** marks **4** textbooks **5** projects **6** notes **7** homework **8** exercises

READING

1 1, 3, 4

2 **1** × **2** ✓ **3** × **4** × **5** ✓ **6** × **7** × **8** ✓

LISTENING

1 **1** 10.30 **2** drinks **3** hat **4** aquarium **5** Thursday

19 You will hear a teacher telling his class about a school trip.

Teacher: Right class, I'm going to talk to you about the school trip next week, so please listen carefully. As you know, we're going to Ireland. Ireland is a beautiful country and I'm sure you're all going to have a brilliant time there. You need to get to the airport at eight o'clock in the morning, because our flight leaves at half past ten.

Lots of people have asked me, 'Do we need to bring anything for the journey?' and the answer is, yes, you do. The journey is quite long, so you should bring something to eat, like crisps or fruit. Oh, and don't forget to bring drinks, too. Water or juice is better than cola.

Now, what clothes do you need to pack? You should bring comfortable clothes and trainers, as you're going to do a lot of outdoor activities. It can be quite sunny at this time of year in Ireland, so please remember to bring a hat, too. You don't need to bring your uniform, so please leave that at home.

Last week, we gave you a timetable of activities for the trip, but this has changed. Unfortunately, we can't visit the museum on Saturday afternoon because it's closed. We're going to visit the aquarium instead. Remember, we return from Ireland on Tuesday. You don't have to come to school on Wednesday because you'll be tired, so I'll see you all back here on Thursday.

WRITING

1 1, 2, 3, 5, 9

2 Students' own answers

3 Students' own answers

UNIT 20 Families

VOCABULARY

1 Across: **1** grandson **2** aunt **3** granddaughter **4** husband **6** wife **7** grandmother **10** uncle

Down: **1** grandfather **5** niece **8** nephew **9** cousin **10** grandparents

2 grandchild

3 **1** old **2** young **3** beautiful **4** dark **5** slim **6** good-looking **7** fair **8** tall **9** pretty **10** blonde **11** short

4 **1** dark **2** slim **3** young **4** tall **5** short

GRAMMAR

1 **1** badly **2** noisily **3** hard **4** carefully **5** quickly **6** happily **7** easily **8** well **9** fast **10** quietly

2 **1** hard **2** badly **3** fast **4** loudly **5** well **6** slowly

3 **1** We study together very **happily**. **2** Be **careful** with the dog. **3** The team was playing very **badly**. **4** You can find my house very **easily**. **5** It was my favourite match because both teams played very **well**. **6** I liked it a lot because the players played **wonderfully**.

4 **1** quickly **2** well **3** carefully **4** happily **5** badly **6** loudly

VOCABULARY

1 **1** probably **2** quite **3** really **4** really **5** certainly **6** nearly

2 **1** really / certainly **2** certainly **3** nearly **4** quite **5** probably

READING

1 **1** than **2** the **3** our **4** to **5** when / after **6** because / as

2 **1** A hotel near the beach or in the mountains. **2** He's teaching them to climb. **3** She helps her with her homework. **4** She's an engineer. **5** She makes pasta for all the family when they're busy.

LISTENING

1 Sunday

2 **1** f **2** e **3** c **4** b **5** a **6** d

3 **1** ✓ **2** × **3** × **4** ✓ **5** ✓ **6** ×

20 **Teacher:** OK, so who's next to tell the class about their family? Um, Mason. It's your turn.

Mason: Thanks, Miss Harris. Good morning, everyone. I'm going to talk about my family. I live with my parents, my grandmother and my two sisters. My mother's called Sam. She's forty-two years old. She's a doctor. She works very hard during the week and sometimes on Saturdays, so I only see her in the evenings or on Sundays. My father's called Matthew. He's forty-one years old. He's a writer. He writes books for children and he works at home. I often help him make the dinner and I love his stories. My older sister's called Katie and my younger sister's called Natalie. Natalie's nine and Katie's sixteen. Natalie loves dancing and sometimes we go to watch her in class on Friday evenings. Katie is very intelligent and studies very hard. She is always in her bedroom with her books. My grandmother's called Anita. She's sixty-three. She's a wonderful person. She always teaches me lots of things. She's interested in everything. We talk about music and physics, cooking and sport, and history. In the evenings, she often goes out with her friends, but she always makes a wonderful lunch for all the family on Sundays. Oh, and there's one more member of our family: George, my uncle. He's an actor and he's forty years old. He often comes to stay with us for the weekend because he lives in the city but he likes coming to our village to relax.

WRITING

1 **1** than **2** in **3** because **4** me **5** don't

2 **1** My aunt lives quite near my house. **2** She has got really long hair. **3** She is almost as old as my mother. **4** I certainly enjoy seeing her.

3 Students' own answers

4 Students' own answers

STUDENT'S BOOK AUDIOSCRIPTS

02 Starter Unit, Student's Book page 10

1 Man: Are there any rulers on the tables?
2 Man: Is there a teacher in the room?
3 Man: Are there any bags on the floor?
4 Man: Is there a yellow bag under the teacher's table?
5 Man: Are there any pencils on the floor?

07 Starter Unit, Student's Book page 12

1 Woman: It's the first of March.
2 Woman: It's the twelfth of October.
3 Woman: It's the eighth of May.
4 Woman: It's the twenty-fifth of February.
5 Woman: It's the twenty-second of July.
6 Woman: It's the thirty-first of December.
7 Woman: It's the third of April.
8 Woman: It's the eleventh of August.

14 Unit 1, Student's Book page 17

Interviewer: Hi, Marco. Can you describe your sport for me, please? Is it a team sport?

Marco: OK. Yes, it's a team sport and there are four players in each team. The players are on horses. It's a bit like polo – in polo the players also ride horses.

Interviewer: So, do the players use sticks or bats to hit a ball, like polo too?

Marco: No, they don't use sticks, they use their hands to pass the ball from one person to another. In fact, players can only use their right hand to pass the ball.

Interviewer: That sounds difficult! What does the ball look like? Is it small?

Marco: No, it's not very small. It's unusual – it's got six handles.

Interviewer: Ah, that makes it a bit easier to pass. So the players hold the ball by one of the handles?

Marco: Yes, that's right.

Interviewer: And one player takes the ball off another player by the handle?

Marco: Yes.

Interviewer: How do the players score goals?

Marco: There's a net at each end of the field. It's bigger than a basketball net and players throw the ball into it to score a goal.

Interviewer: Wow, and I'm sure the horses are moving fast.

Marco: Yes, they are! The players need to be good at passing the ball and excellent horse riders too. But it *is* fun to play.

Interviewer: So, what's the name of the sport?

Marco: Oh, yes sorry. It's called Pato.

16 Unit 2, Student's Book page 18

Maddie: Hello everyone, it's me, Maddie! Welcome to another video. Don't forget to click the 'like' button if you enjoy watching it!

Today I'm talking about my morning routine on a school day. OK, so … my alarm goes off really early – at half past six. I wake up and turn on my phone. I always check my messages in the morning. I get up at about a quarter to seven and go downstairs for breakfast. I sometimes have toast and butter, but I'm having cereal and fruit today! It's healthy and tastes great.

At about seven o'clock, I go upstairs to wash my face and clean my teeth. I don't usually have a shower in the morning. I prefer to do that in the evening.

Then at about a quarter past seven, I choose my clothes and get dressed. I usually wear my uniform, but I'm not wearing my uniform today. We've got a trip this afternoon, so at the moment I'm wearing my favourite T-shirt and a pair of black jeans.

After I get dressed, I brush my hair. Then I tidy my room and check the time. It's usually about 7.30. Time to prepare my school bag! Today I'm not taking many books with me!

At twenty to eight, I put on my shoes, and I'm ready to go to school. OK, I'm leaving the house now. Bye. See you later!

21 Unit 2, Student's Book page 21

Alice: Hello, I'm Alice Brown and you're listening to Radio Gold. Today we're talking about getting up in the morning. For some people, it's really difficult! So, are there ways to make it easier? Well, I'm at Wilton School to find out. With me are some students from class 3B. Now, can I start with you? Tell me about your routine. What's your tip for a perfect morning?

Girl 1: Well, my alarm clock goes off at seven and I leave the house at half past. My tip is that when your alarm goes off, get up immediately. Don't lie in bed checking your messages! Open the curtains and make the room really bright. That will wake you up and make you feel good.

Alice: Thanks! And what's your tip?

Boy 1: Well, before I have my shower or have my breakfast, I do some exercise. I do some star jumps, or maybe a bit of yoga. I never feel tired after that.

Alice: OK, sounds good. And do you have another tip for us?

Girl 2: Yes! My favourite tip is to put your alarm clock on the other side of the room. I always do that! If it's next to me, I switch it off and go back to sleep.

Alice: Great. And what about you?

Boy 2: I get up at about seven and have a shower. Then I tidy my room and go downstairs for breakfast. I always have some orange juice and that really helps me to wake up!

Alice: OK, well that's easy. And how about you?

Girl 3: Well, my tip is to have a cold shower in the morning. The first time you do it, it's quite difficult, but it makes you feel amazing. Then have a good breakfast after your shower and it's the perfect start to the day.

Alice: Ooh, I'm not sure about that one! But thank you. OK, we've got time for one more. Tell me about your tip.

Boy 3: Well, when I'm having my breakfast, I always do a puzzle. Sometimes it's a Sudoku and sometimes a crossword. It makes me think hard and after that, I don't feel tired any more.

Alice: That's a really unusual idea! Well thanks everyone for your excellent tips. And we'd love to hear more from our listeners. Just send a text or email to … [fade]

23 Culture: The Paralympic Games, Student's Book page 23

Interviewer: Welcome back to our show Young Athletes. Today we are talking to eleven-year-old Martha Dirksen. How are you Martha?

Martha: I'm fine, thanks. It's nice to be here.

Interviewer: So Martha, you love playing tennis, right?

Martha: I do! I practise almost every day. There's a court near my school.

Interviewer: Martha is a special tennis player. Martha plays wheelchair tennis, and she dreams of being in the Paralympic Games one day. Isn't that right, Martha?

Martha: Yes, that's right.

Interviewer: Is it difficult to play wheelchair tennis?

Martha: Well, I'm used to it but, yes, it is difficult sometimes.

Interviewer: To play wheelchair tennis, players need to move their wheelchairs quickly on the court and hit the ball too!

Martha: You do make it sound difficult.

Interviewer: Do you have any sports heroes, Martha?

Martha: Yes! I think David Wagner is amazing! He has lots of medals.

Interviewer: True. David Wagner is from the United States and he is one of the best wheelchair tennis players in the world.

Martha: He is! He's a really strong player. He gets up early every day to play tennis.

Interviewer: How about you? Do you get up early every day to play tennis?

Martha: Well, I get up at half past six to get ready for school. I have breakfast at eight o'clock and then I take the bus to school. After school, I have tennis practice on Mondays, Wednesdays, Thursdays and Fridays. I usually get home at about five o'clock.

Interviewer: Wow! I get tired just listening to your day! What do you do at weekends?

Martha: Uhhh … Not much. I have competitions at the weekend.

Interviewer: Well, let's hope we see you in the Paralympic Games one day.

Martha: I hope so!

Interviewer: That's all the time we have today. Many thanks for joining us Martha and good luck to you.

Martha: Thank you.

26 Unit 3, Student's Book page 25

Mia: That was fantastic. I really loved it. It's her new album, right?

Jason: Yes, it is. And I think it's her best album. What other types of music do you like?

Mia: Well, I love listening to rap and jazz. We often listen to jazz at home. My parents and my older brother like it.

Jason: Really? Jazz is ok, but it's not my favourite type of music. I like rock and hip-hop best. I don't like listening to opera. But my parents love it! They listen to it all the time.

Mia: Well, I think a lot of older people like classical music, but it's not so popular with young people.

Jason: Some like it. My sister plays the violin in an orchestra and in a band. So she likes playing classical music *and* rock.

Mia: Oh, I'd love to see her play. Tell me when she's got her next concert.

Jason: Ok. We can go together.

Mia: Great! Can *you* play the violin?

Jason: No, I hate playing the violin. I tried but it's so difficult!

Mia: So what's your favourite instrument then?

Jason: Well, I really love playing the electric guitar. It's a great instrument. I like playing the keyboard as well. What about you?

Mia: My favourite instrument is the saxophone … I love playing the saxophone. I quite like playing the piano, too.

Jason: What about the drums?

Mia: No way. I hate listening to the drums – they're too loud – and I certainly don't want to learn to play them!

Jason: I agree! So it's your turn to choose an album. Which one do you want to play?

Mia: How about this?

30 Unit 3, Student's Book page 27

Emma: Hi Shona. Great to hear from you.

Shona: Hi Emma, so tell me about your first week at the music school. Do you like it?

Emma: Yes, it's fantastic. It's so different from our old school. We have lessons in the mornings, but they're all about music. And then in the afternoon we have school lessons like maths.

Shona: What do you do in the morning lessons? Do you learn to play different instruments?

Emma: Yes. You can choose two instruments, and then you learn them for the first year. I'm not sure what to choose. I love playing the electric guitar, so maybe the guitar and … the keyboard.

Shona: Yes, and then you can play your songs – and sing them too.

Emma: And record an album!

Shona: Do you only do music in the mornings?

Emma: No, we learn about the history of music too, but that starts next week. I can tell you about that next Friday.

Shona: Lucky you! I want to be at music school, but my mum and dad can't pay for me.

Emma: This music school is free!

Shona: Really? What's the name of the school?

Emma: It's called The Clarke School. That's C-L-A-R-K-E.

Shona: Right … C-L-A-R-K-E.

Emma: You play in a band, Shona. You can come here too! Ask your parents to phone the school.

Shona: Wow! Ok. What's the phone number?

Emma: 0-1-5-7-2 3-double 9-6-8-7.

Shona: 0-1-5-7-2 3-double 9-6-8-7. Ok. Got that. And what's the name of the head of the school?

Emma: The head's name is Ms Phillips. That's P-H-I-double L-I-P-S.

Shona. P-H-I-double L-I-P-S. Ok great. My parents can phone tomorrow.

Emma: Oh, and here's the email. They can email as well. It's info-at-clarke 4, as the number, music-dot-com

Shona: info-at-clarke4music-dot-com. Ok. Thanks, Emma.

Emma: Good luck!

31 Unit 4, Student's Book page 28

Conversation 1

Boy 1: Were you and your brother at the football match on Saturday?

Girl 1: No, we weren't. We were at a theme park. It was his birthday.

Boy 1: Wow, awesome! I love theme parks.

Girl 1: Yes, it was amazing. I can't wait to go again.

Conversation 2

Girl 2: Were you at home yesterday?

Boy 2: No, I wasn't. I was out with my family. We were at a barbecue near the beach.

Girl 2: Was it fun?

Boy 2: It was OK. The weather wasn't great. It was a bit cold. And there weren't many people there.

Girl 2: How was the food?

Boy 2: It was fine. Nothing amazing.

Conversation 3

Boy 3: How was your weekend? Were you at the festival?

Girl 3: Yes, I was. I was there with a few of my friends. It was brilliant! The weather was perfect and all the bands were fantastic.

Conversation 4

Girl 1: Where were you on Saturday?

Boy 1: I was at my sister's wedding.

Girl 1: Oh, wonderful!

Boy 1: Yes, it was a really lovely day. There was music and dancing, and the food was really good.

Conversation 5

Boy 2: Where were you yesterday afternoon? You weren't in class.

Girl 2: I was in a football match.

Boy 2: Really? Was it good?

Girl 2: No, it was terrible. Usually I love playing with my team, but yesterday it was horrible! I hate losing!

Conversation 6

Boy 3: Where were you last night? You weren't at the party.

Girl 3: No, I was at home – I wasn't very well. Was it fun?

Boy 3: Yes, it was. It was great. Hope you can come next time!

35 Unit 4, Student's Book page 31

1 What was Bella happy with at the party?

Boy 1: How was the party Bella?

Bella: It was OK. The food was excellent, but the music wasn't great.

Boy 1: Oh, what a shame!

Bella: Yes. And there weren't many people there.

2 Where is Kyle's ticket?

Girl 1: You look worried Kyle. Are you OK?

Kyle: I can't find my ticket for our trip to the theme park tomorrow. It was in my bag this morning, but it's not there now. And it's not on the classroom floor.

Girl 1: What about your jacket pocket? Maybe it's there.

Kyle: Of course – that's it! Thanks!

3 What was the weather like?

Boy 1: Was the weather good for your camping trip?

Girl 2: I'm afraid not! There was no rain, but there was a lot of wind.

Boy 1: Oh, that's a pity!

Girl 2: I know. But at least it wasn't cold.

4 How much was the boy's T-shirt?

Girl 2: I really like your new T-shirt. Was it expensive? They usually cost a lot when you buy them at concerts.

Boy 2: Not really. It was £10.

Girl 2: That's amazing! T-shirts like that are usually £15 or more.

Boy 2: I know. My brother's got one that was £25!

5 Where was the girl on Saturday?

Boy 2: Where were you on Saturday? You weren't at home at 2 pm.

Girl 2: No, sorry. I was shopping in town with my parents.

Boy 2: Oh, I hate shopping. I like having fun with friends or playing sport at weekends.

Girl 2: Me too. Let's play tennis together next Saturday.

37 Life skills: Reaching agreement, Student's Book page 32

Lola: Hi, Daisy! Hi Oscar! What's up? What are you doing?

Oscar: Hello Lola! Well, it's Michael's birthday next weekend. We're deciding what to do.

Daisy: We want to get him a present and organise a surprise party.

Lola: Great idea! Can I help?

Oscar: Sure! Brilliant!

Daisy: OK, let's see. The first thing we need to decide is the day. What do you think?

Oscar: I think it's a good idea to have the party on Sunday night.

Lola: Sunday night? Hmmm … I disagree. We have an important maths exam on Monday morning. Maybe another day is better.

Daisy: I agree. Sunday is not a good day. I think Saturday afternoon is a better idea.

Lola: Me too!

Oscar: OK, fine. Saturday it is.

Daisy: Right. The next thing we need to decide is a present.

Lola: How about a basketball shirt?

Daisy: That's an awesome idea Lola!

Oscar: Sorry, but I don't agree. Michael has a lot of sports clothes. I think it's a good idea to get him a CD, or a book.

Lola: OK. I think a CD is a better idea than a book.

Oscar: I think that a CD is perfect. Michael loves listening to music.

Daisy: Can we get both? A CD *and* a book?

Oscar: That's a great idea!

Daisy: Let's see. Now we just need to think about the friends to invite and the cake!

Lola: We can buy a cake in the shop opposite the school.

Oscar: Hey! I have a better idea!

Daisy: What?

Oscar: I can *make* a cake – I love cooking!

Lola: You do? Well, that solves that problem! Sorry, Daisy, sorry, Oscar, I have to go. I need to help my mum.

Daisy: Ok! Thanks for your help. Let's call Michael's parents to tell them the plan.

Oscar: Great idea, Daisy. See you in class tomorrow! Bye!

38 Review 1: Units 1-4, Student's Book page 35

1 What time do they agree to meet?

Girl 1: Does the tennis match start at two thirty tomorrow?

Boy 1: Yes, but we need to be at the tennis club at two o' clock.

Girl 1: OK. So … I leave home at one o'clock … see you at the bus stop at half past one?

Boy 1: Perfect, see you then!

2 Which instrument does Mona need to practise tonight?

Boy 2: Can you come to my house tonight Mona? I want to show you my new drums!

Mona: Oh wow – new drums! I'd love to see them. But I can't come tonight, sorry. I need to practise for the school concert.

Boy 2: Are you learning a new song on the guitar?

Mona: It's for the piano, actually. I'm not very good yet!

3 What is Finley's brother doing?

Girl 1: Hi Finley. Is your brother at home? I need to ask him something about the volleyball match.

Finley: I'm afraid he's sleeping.

Girl 1: What? But it's ten o'clock.

Finley: I know. He never gets up early at the weekend. He usually has his breakfast at about midday.

4 Where were they in the morning?

Boy 1: What a great morning! Thanks for coming with me.

Girl 2: No problem. It's a brilliant pool. I love swimming there.

Boy 1: Me too. But I'm hungry now. Shall we get some lunch at the café?

Girl 2: OK. And then let's go home. I'm really tired!

5 What does the girl want to have for dinner?

Girl 1: What's for dinner Mum? I hope it's not fish again.

Mum: It's rice with vegetables. Don't worry – it's really nice.

Girl 1: Ohh! Can't we have pasta with tomato sauce?

Mum: Maybe tomorrow. Now come and help me with the vegetables.

Girl 1: OK.

40 Unit 5, Student's Book page 36

Women in History.

1 Man: Cleopatra, Queen of Egypt and the last pharaoh, died in 30 BCE.

2 Man: Marie Curie received the Nobel Prize in chemistry in December 1911.

3 Man: Valentina Tereshkova travelled into space on the 16th of June 1963.

4 Man: Amelia Earhart crossed the Atlantic Ocean, alone, by plane in 1932.

5 Man: Coco Chanel opened her first shop in Deauville, France in the 20th century.

6 Man: Frida Kahlo painted her self-portrait with parrots in 1941.

7 Man: Serena Williams played her first match at Wimbledon in 1998.

8 Man: Junko Tabei climbed Mount Everest on the 16th of May 1975.

9 Man: J. K. Rowling published her first Harry Potter book in June 1997.

10 Man: Ella Fitzgerald recorded her first song in 1936.

44 Unit 5, Student's Book page 39

Dave: And welcome to Living History: I was there! My name is Dave Brown and today's caller is Janet from Manchester, in the north-west of England. Hi Janet.

Janet: Hello Dave.

Dave: So Janet, tell us about the moment in history you remember.

Janet: Well Dave, I remember something that happened in the 1960s. I lived with my mum and dad and older brother in a flat in the city. There were no computers, or mobile phones in those days, you know. There were televisions, but only black and white ones.

Dave: What do you mean Janet, black and white ones?

Janet: I mean the televisions only showed black and white films and programmes; there was nothing in colour!

Dave: That's not like today, Janet!

Janet: I know. You didn't know what colour people's clothes were, or anything like that! Anyway, the day I want to tell you about was in 1967. It was the day colour televisions arrived in the shops. My dad wanted to get one of the first ones. So he and I waited outside the shop early in the morning. Then when it opened, we hurried in to buy one. My dad and uncle carried it back to our flat in its box. It was big and heavy, and it was hard work for them to carry it up the stairs to the flat. We were all so excited. When everything was ready, Mum turned on the TV, we waited and then – there was the picture … in colour!

Dave: A great moment!

Janet: Yes, and the first programme we watched was tennis – green grass, white balls – it was fantastic.

Dave: And now everything we see on TV is in colour, and we don't think about it.

Janet: Yes, I know. Things change so fast.

Dave: Well, thank you Janet for sharing your memory with us.

Janet: Thank you Dave. Bye.

Dave: Goodbye Janet.

49 Unit 6, Student's Book page 43

Girl: Hi Joe. How was your job last week?

Joe: It was great. I loved it.

Girl: Where did you work?

Joe: I worked in the museum.

Girl: Oh no! That sounds boring.

Joe: It wasn't boring, it was fun!

Girl: Really? What did you do all day?

Joe: I worked in the museum shop. I talked to the customers. I helped them find things to buy, and I answered their questions.

Girl: What time did you start?

Joe: I started at eight o'clock in the morning. The shop didn't open until nine, but we needed to get things ready.

Girl: How did you travel to work every day? Did you go by bus?

No, I didn't. I walked. The museum is quite close to my house.

Girl: Oh, I didn't know that. And how did you get the job? Did the school find it for you?

Joe: No. I called the museum and asked for a job. At first, they said no, but I tried again, and they said yes!

Girl: Wow! Well done Joe – that's brilliant!

52 Culture: Saturday jobs, Student's Book page 45

Olivia: Hey Dad. Can I ask you something?

Dad: Sure. Go ahead.

Olivia: I'm thinking of getting a Saturday job.

Dad: Really? Why's that?

Olivia: Well, it's good experience, and I can earn some extra pocket money.

Dad: Sounds good to me. What ideas have you got?

Olivia: Mrs Wilson needs someone to help in the garden.

Dad: You have experience helping us in the garden and you're good with plants. She has a big garden behind her house, right?

Olivia: Yes, she does. The only problem is she needs someone on Saturday mornings, and I have piano lessons then.

Dad: Hmmm. Any other options?

Olivia: Well, there's a job offer in the newspaper for someone to do a paper round.

Dad: Where?

Olivia: In the town centre.

Dad: Do you have any experience for a job like that?

Olivia: No, not really. I don't have any experience, and I haven't got a bike.

Dad: How about dog-walking? My friend Daniel's son walks dogs in the park.

Olivia: Really?

Dad: Yes, I see him on Saturday afternoons. He's always there with three or four small dogs.

Olivia: That sounds like a lot of dogs!

Dad: Well, you've experience walking *our* dog and it's bigger than the dogs Robert walks. Speaking of walking dogs, it's time for you to take Pongo for his walk.

Olivia: OK Dad. Can you call your friend for me?

Dad: Of course!

54 Unit 7, Student's Book page 46

Callum: How was your summer holiday, Lottie?

Lottie: It was brilliant, Callum! We went camping and stayed at a really nice campsite in France. We could walk to the beach in five minutes! My friend Annabel came with us and we swam in the sea every day and rode our bikes. I didn't want to leave!

Callum: Did you get up early every day?

Lottie: Of course not! We got up late and we went to bed late. We had a really good time. We lay on the beach and did lots of water sports too.

Callum: Did you take any photos?

Lottie: Yes, I did. I took hundreds of them! Look, here's one.

Callum: Wow, that's good!

Lottie: Thanks! My parents gave me a new phone before the holiday. It's got a great camera. What about you Callum? How was your holiday? Where did you go?

Callum: It was awesome! I went to Istanbul, in Turkey. We stayed at a little hotel in the city.

Lottie: Really? What did you do?

Callum: We went sightseeing every day. I saw some really interesting places.

Lottie: Oh no, I hate sightseeing!

Callum: What? It's the best thing about holidays!

Lottie: Well – I don't think so! Anyway – what was the weather like?

Callum: It was fine. There was just one day when it rained, and we changed our plans for the day.

Lottie: And what about shopping? Did you buy me a present?

Callum: Of course I bought you a present.

Lottie: Really? What is it?

Callum: It's Turkish Delight. It's a kind of sweet.

Lottie: Oh great, I love sweets. Thanks, Callum. Er, Callum – the box is open!

Callum: Oh … yes … sorry, Lottie! But I only ate one, I promise!

59 Unit 7, Student's Book page 49

Marion: This happened six months ago. I went to Scotland for a holiday with my family. We went to a small island and it took a very long time to get there! We left home in the evening and took a taxi to the train station. First, we bought a ticket. Then we got on the train. It was a special train with beds and we slept really well. Anyway, we arrived in Scotland in the morning. We had some breakfast and then we got on a coach. I sat next to my brother. He ate sweets and listened to loud music all the way! When we got off the coach, we got onto a boat. I enjoyed it, but my brother didn't feel very well. Mum said it was because of all the sweets. Then, when we arrived at the island, we caught a bus to our hotel. It's funny – We now know there's an airport on the island and you can fly there! Next time we'll do that.

65 Unit 8, Student's Book page 53

George: Hi, my name's George. You asked me about my favourite place. That's a difficult one. Let me explain. I don't really have anywhere of my own because our flat's too small, and we don't have a garden. I share a bedroom with my brother, so I don't get much time to myself. But when he goes out or goes to play with his friends, I can be alone in our bedroom, and at those times the bedroom is my favourite place. I put all the cushions on my bed, lie there and read. What do I like reading? Well, mostly stories and sports magazines.

Abby: Hello, I'm Abby. My favourite place – hmmm let me think …

OK, don't laugh – my favourite place isn't anywhere inside the house. It's outside, in the park down the road. I can walk there in five minutes. There's this amazing tree right on the top of the hill, and there's usually no one around. I like sitting under the tree and writing my diary every day. The sound of the wind in the trees is brilliant. It helps me remember everything about my day. No one else reads my diary. Only me.

Jo: Hi, I'm Jo. Yes, I've got a favourite place. It isn't in the house though and it isn't outside. It's in the garage! We don't have a car, so my mum and dad let me use the garage for my music. I started playing the guitar when I was six and that's what I do in the garage. And sometimes I sing. I write all my own songs, but I don't like anyone listening to them. It's quite comfortable. There's an armchair in the corner and I've got pictures on the walls. It really is my favourite place.

67 Life skills: Safety at home, Student's Book page 55

Teacher: OK everyone, come in and sit down, please. We have a special visitor today. This is Marina Armstrong. She's a firefighter and she's here to talk to us about being safe at home. Let's give her a warm welcome.

Firefighter: Thanks very much. It's great to be here at your school. OK, your teacher wants me to talk to you about the dangers of fires at home and burns. Let's start. What are these? Yes?

Boy 1: Matches and a lighter.

Firefighter: Yes, that's right. Please remember that it is not a good idea to use matches or lighters when there isn't an adult at home. Using things wrongly can start home fires, and fires are dangerous, so please be careful. Who knows what this is? Yes?

Girl 1: A fire extinguisher.

Firefighter: We can use fire extinguishers to stop fires. In a moment, I'm going to teach all of you how to use it.

Girl 2: Awesome!

Firefighter: Remember, it's a good idea to have a fire extinguisher at home. If you don't have a fire extinguisher, it's important not to panic, but to stay calm and try to put out the fire with a wet towel. Another accident we see a lot – burns.

Teacher: What can burn us at home? Yes?

Boy 2: Hot tea … or soup!

Firefighter: That's right. Yes?

Girl 1: What about irons? They get hot.

Teacher: You're right! You need to be careful with hot irons. Anything else?

Boy 1: Uhhh … heaters?

Firefighter: Yes, good one. Some heaters can burn you, and putting wet clothes on heaters can start fires. You need to be careful when the cooker is on too! It can get very hot. If your parents are not at home and something happens, you can ring someone for help. It's good to have emergency numbers next to the phone or on your mobile phone.

Teacher: Very interesting information indeed. Does anyone have any questions?

Girl 2: Can I use the fire extinguisher now?

74 Unit 9, Student's Book page 61

Henry: Hi, my name's Henry, and I've got this excellent idea. What have most people got lots of in their homes? Newspapers and magazines! Well, we have anyway. My dad wanted to throw them away, but I stopped him. I cut them up and made a jacket. It looks really great. I even have something to read when I'm bored.

Molly: Hello, my name's Molly and I *know* my idea's brilliant. It just is! There's something I love eating, and one day, I thought, hey yes, I can make jewellery from it, so I did. I made a really pretty little necklace and everyone liked it. But I didn't think about the weather. It was a really hot day, and it started to get soft … so I ate the necklace. Oh, I didn't say. The necklace was made of … chocolate, of course!

Lauren: Hi, I'm Lauren. My idea is just so clever. It's clothes made of money. Yes, money! Notes are best because they're light and quite big. I made some shorts from notes, and they looked really cool. But I was out with my friends, and we didn't have enough money for the cinema, so I used some from my shorts. It was really funny.

79 Unit 10, Student's Book page 65

1 Two friends are talking at the shopping centre. Why is the boy at the shopping centre?

Girl 1: Hi, Chris. What are you doing here at the shopping centre? You usually do all your shopping online.

Chris: Well, not today. I need to go to one of the shops here.

Girl 1: Why? Do you need to look at something in the computer shop?

Chris: No. My computer's fine, but I read there's a great new clothes shop here.

2 A boy, Adam, is talking about shopping. What did he buy?

Adam: Guess what? I was in the market yesterday doing some shopping for my mum. She wanted me to buy some fruit and some bread. I got the bread first and then on the way into the fruit shop, a dog jumped up, took the bread in its mouth and ran away!

3 A woman is talking to her daughter about a present for her son, Matt. What is the present?

Mum: Emily, when you go to the shops today, please can you collect Matt's birthday present for me? It's not very big, so you can put it in your school bag. He has lots of jumpers, but this one is different. I hope he likes it.

Emily: OK Mum. Where do I need to go?

4 Two friends are talking at one of the friend's houses. What is the boy doing?

Boy: Did you find that information for our history project?

Girl: No, I don't know where the list of websites is. Have you got it?

Boy: Yes, in my homework diary. Anyway, look at this site. These are the shoes I like. And they've got my size.

Girl: Well, buy them quickly. Then we can find the website for school.

5 A teacher is talking to the class about a school trip. What is he telling them to do?

Teacher: So, class, please don't forget about tomorrow's trip. Make sure you arrive at school at the usual time. It's warm at this time of year and you usually wear T-shirts and shorts, but it isn't warm by the lake so don't forget to bring a jacket.

81 Culture: Shopping, Student's Book page 67

Gemma: Hi. My name's Gemma. We're doing a shopping survey in class. Can I ask you some questions?

Leo: Sure.

Gemma: OK, first of all, what's your name and how old are you?

Leo: My name's Leo and I'm thirteen years old.

Gemma: Great. Thanks. Now, let's see. Where do you normally shop?

Leo: I like going to small shops, but I normally go to the shopping centre at weekends.

Gemma: Why do you go to the shopping centre?

Leo: I like meeting my friends there and I like window shopping.

Gemma: Perfect. OK. Last question. What do you usually buy at the shopping centre?

Leo: Hmmm. I haven't got a lot of pocket money and I don't usually spend a lot of money. I sometimes buy a music magazine or some sweets.

Gemma: Thanks for your time, Leo.

Leo: No worries. Bye.

Gemma: Bye.

Gemma: Hi Mum! Can I ask you a couple of questions for a survey?

Mum: Ok. Go ahead.

Gemma: I know your name and how old you are.

Mum: Yes, you do.

Gemma: Next question. Where do you normally shop?

Mum: As you know, I love going to the Farmers' Market. I go on Mondays, Wednesdays and Fridays.

Gemma: Why do you go to the Farmers' Market?

Mum: Well, I like helping local farmers and the prices are good.

Gemma: OK. Last question. What do you usually buy at the Farmers' Market?

Mum: I always buy fresh fruit and vegetables. I sometimes buy cheese. Your dad *loves* the cheese from the market.

Gemma: Me too!

Mum: That's true!

Gemma: Thanks Mum.

Mum: That's OK. Now, can you help me do the washing up, please?

85 Unit 11, Student's Book page 71

Boy: Hi, Nadia. Listen, I'm going to a street food festival with my family. Do you want to come with us?

Nadia: Of course! You know I love food! But when is it? We're away on holiday from the 3rd to the 16th of July.

Boy: That's OK – it's next weekend, Saturday and Sunday. It's the 28th and 29th of June. We want to go on Sunday.

Nadia: OK. I can ask my mum. Do we need tickets?

Boy: Yes, you can get them from the festival website. It's www.foodzone.com. That's F-double O-D-Z-O-N-E.

Nadia: Got that, thanks. Do you know how much the tickets are?

Boy: Well, for adults it's £10, but it's cheaper for us because we're under 16. We pay just £8.50. And we get three plates of food for that! Each plate of food after that is £2.50.

Nadia: Fantastic! And what time is it on?

Boy: Let's see ... It opens at nine thirty in the morning.

Nadia: Oh no, that's too early!

Boy: I agree! And it closes at midnight. My parents want to go at about two o'clock. Is that OK for you?

Nadia: Yes, I think so. I need to check with Mum first. Where is it?

Boy: It's in the market square on Green Avenue. Two buses go that way – the 74, and the 89. The 74 is easier for me because it stops outside my house.

Nadia: That's good for me too. I'll speak to my mum and call you back.

Boy: Sure, no problem. Speak to you later Nadia.

86 Unit 11, Student's Book page 71

Girl: Excuse me, what are you selling?

Seller: It's called paella. It's from Spain. It's made with seafood, rice, vegetables and chicken.

Girl: Oh. What's it like?

Seller: It's wonderful! Would you like some?

Girl: Yes please. How much is it?

Seller: It's £4.50 for a small plate or £6.00 for a large plate.

Girl: I'll have a small plate, please.

Seller: That's £4.50, please.

Girl: Here you are.

Seller: Thanks. I hope you enjoy it!

91 Unit 12, Student's Book page 75

You will hear Ella asking her friend Andy about his new computer.

Ella: Nice new laptop, Andy! When did you get it?

Andy: Yesterday. My old one broke a month ago and last week, Dad agreed to buy me this.

Ella: Where did he get it? I need a new computer too.

Andy: He asked a friend for advice and then bought it online. It was cheaper than buying it in a shop.

Ella: Really? How much was it?

Andy: £250. There were cheaper ones, starting at £150. The most expensive ones were over £2,000!

Ella: Wow, that's a lot! And has it got everything you need?

Andy: Almost. I can print on the printer downstairs, and I don't need a mouse. But I'd like to get a better camera for it.

Ella: Good idea. So what do you use the computer for?

Andy: Most things. I can't play my computer games on it, though. It hasn't got enough memory. But I do my homework on it, and chat to my friends on the internet.

Ella: So you're happy with it?

Andy: Very! It's got a nice big screen and the keyboard is really comfortable to use. But the speakers are the best thing about it. My music sounds great on them!

Ella: Brilliant!

93 Life skills: Writing a blog, Student's Book page 76

David: Hello Mrs Wilson. Uhm, is Katie home?

Katie's mum: Oh, hello David, nice to see you. Please come in. She's in the living room working on her blog. She's waiting for you.

David: Thanks, Mrs Wilson. Hiya Katie. Katie? Katie?

Katie: Ah, oh, hi David. Sorry! I'm working on my blog.

David: Great! How's it going?

Katie: It's going well.

David: Is it easy to do?

Katie: Yes, for someone like you! You're good at using computers, David. To start a blog, all you have to do is choose a platform, a title, a design and a topic, and you're ready.

David: Wow! That sounds OK! You're not posting your address on your blog, are you?

Katie: No, it isn't safe to post personal information.

David: Phew! Is your blog about music? I know you like music.

Katie: No, it's not. I like music but my blog is about cats. Look, I'm going to post some photos of my cousin's cat.

David: It looks good. I like the design and the colours. Um. Yeah. Cute cat. I don't like cats. Is it difficult to organise your ideas?

Katie: A little! That's why I have a notebook here next to the computer. Look at my list of posts. I'm going to write a post about my neighbour's cat soon. I have a video of my piano teacher's cat too.

David: Hmmm, more cats? You can do a blog post on my *dog* or my *hamster* when you want!

Katie: No, sorry David, only cats!

David: OK, OK, I get it. Do you want a lot of people to follow your blog?

Katie: No, my blog is just for my friends and family. Look, some friends and family are following me and reading my posts. Here's the list. They can leave comments or share links.

David: Let's see. Hey! There are some nice comments about your photos, Katie.

Katie: Yes, there are.

David: That's great!

Katie: It is! Thanks. So, what will *your* blog be about?

94 Review 3: Units 9-12, Student's Book page 79

1 Listen to two friends talking together in a shop. Why does Ruby want to buy the sunglasses?

Emily: Aren't those sunglasses too expensive Ruby?

Ruby: Mm, £20 *is* a lot of money – it's more than I wanted to spend. But they fit me really well. The others are all too small.

Emily: OK. But are you sure you want black again? These are quite similar to your old ones.

Ruby: Well, all the nice bright ones are really uncomfortable to wear.

2 Listen to a man and a girl talking about what they want to eat. Where are they?

Father: What do you want eat Anna? There are burgers, fish dishes, curry …

Anna: I'd like to try lots of different things. The price of the ticket includes three small plates of food, doesn't it?

Father: Yes. Shall we start with a small plate of curry?

Anna: Then we can walk around and find something else to have.

3 Listen to a boy talking to a girl about his laptop. What does the girl offer to do?

Emily: What's the matter Lucas? You look really annoyed!

Lucas: Oh hi, Emily. Yeah – my laptop's not working. I've tried all the usual things and I can't get it to start.

Emily: Oh no! Well, we've got a couple of spare ones at home. You can borrow one of those while yours is in the repair shop.

Lucas: Thanks Emily!

4 Listen to a message in a shopping centre. What change do customers need to know about?

Shop announcer: Thank you for visiting Green Wood Shopping Centre. Please note that from today our business hours are different. All shops stay open until 10 pm. That gives you two extra hours of shopping! Also, don't forget that today is the last day of the big sale at Parker's Department Store. So go there today and get a great discount!

5 Listen to a girl talking about a party. What did she like about it?

Anna: Hi Jessica. I'm ringing to tell you about the party last night. We all missed you! We went to that new pizza restaurant in town. The party room was a bit small and dark and the music was so loud! But the pizzas were delicious – the nicest I've ever had. I can't wait to go back and have another one!

96 Unit 13, Student's Book page 80

1

Martin: Here, here! Ahhh!

Coach: What's wrong Martin? Is your arm OK?

Martin: My arm's fine. It's my leg! It really hurts.

Coach: Right. I think you should go to hospital.

Martin: Ahhh!

Coach: No, no, don't stand up. You shouldn't walk on that leg. We'll carry you to the car.

2

Girl: Mum, I'm really worried!

Mother: Why?

Girl: I've got an important football match tomorrow, but I don't feel well.

Mother: Oh dear. What's the matter?

Girl: I've got a headache.

Mother: Have you got a stomach ache as well?

Girl: No.

Mother: Mmm – I think you should go to bed now. You'll feel better in the morning. You know, you shouldn't watch TV or use the computer late at night. That's why you get headaches!

3

Patient: Hello Doctor.

Doctor: Hello. How can I help you?

Patient: Well. I get lots of colds. I had one last month and I've got another one now.

Doctor: I see. Well, you haven't got a temperature, but you look tired. You should rest when you have a cold.

Patient: I see. Should I stop doing sport?

Doctor: Yes, you should. You should also eat well. Have lots of fresh fruit and vegetables.

Patient: OK. And should I take some medicine?

Doctor: No, you shouldn't. You should drink a lot. Try water or lemon juice and honey.

Patient: OK. When should I drink that?

Doctor: You should have it every evening before bed.

100 Unit 13, Student's Book page 83

Jed: Holly, look at this. There's a five kilometre race we can enter. Let's do it!

Holly: Oh – umm … I'm busy that weekend. But you should do it Jed.

Jed: That's a shame! I'd really like to do it with you Holly.

Holly: Never mind – I can help you prepare. I know all about keeping fit. I can give you lots of advice.

Jed: Oh … OK then! There. My name's on the list!

Holly: Right, well, the first thing to do is to buy some special running clothes.

Jed: Really?

Holly: Yes, and you should get some new trainers.

Jed: Oh dear! That sounds expensive.

Holly: But it's important. Now, how much time have you got before the race?

Jed: Six weeks. Maybe I should download one of those apps. You know – 'couch to 5k in 6 weeks'. My mum uses one and says it's really good.

Holly: No, you don't need that! Listen to me. You should start tomorrow. Get up early and go running before school.

Jed: But I hate getting up early.

Holly: Well, you should go running every day. You need to go to bed early every night now Jed. No more TV or computer games.

Jed: Uhh?

Holly: You want to finish the race, don't you?

Jed: Well, yeah.

Holly: Remember – you should eat well and drink lots of water. And you shouldn't have any chocolate or cake. Oh, and as well as running, you should go swimming or cycling.

Jed: But I haven't got a bicycle.

Holly: And you should do exercises to make your legs stronger. You should do lots and lots of those Jed.

Presenter: Six weeks later.

Holly: Well done Jed. You did it!

Jed: Uhh? What are you doing here? You said you were busy!

Holly: Oh, did I? Err … Sorry Jed!

Jed: Wait till I catch you!

Holly: Help!

102 Unit 14, Student's Book page 85

Conversation 1

Man 1: Excuse me. Is there a (beep) near here?

Woman 1: Yes, there is. There's a really nice one on the other side of the river.

Man 1: How do I get there?

Woman 1: Walk along this road and go across the bridge.

Man 1: OK.

Woman 1: Then turn right.

Man 1: Right.

Woman 1: Walk down the road and when you get to the supermarket, turn left. The (beep) is opposite the train station.

Conversation 2

Boy 1: Excuse me. Which way is the (beep) ?

Woman 2: Ah, let me think. OK, walk along this road. Go past the train station.

Boy 1: OK.

Woman 2: When you get to the traffic lights, turn right. Then keep walking straight on. It's on the right, next to the bank. It's opposite the cinema and some shops.

Boy 1: Thanks.

Conversation 3

Woman 1: Excuse me. Do you know how to get to the (beep) ?

Man 2: Yes, I do. It's not far from here. Drive along this road until you get to the roundabout. Then turn left.

Woman 1: Turn left at the roundabout. OK.

Man 2: Then go straight on and the (beep) is on your right. It's past the petrol station and in front of the sports centre.

Woman 1: OK, so turn left at the roundabout … and then go straight on, past the petrol station. Thanks very much.

Man 2: No problem.

108 Unit 14, Student's Book page 87

Listen to Rob talking to a friend about a visit to Edinburgh. Which place did Rob visit at each time?

Girl: Hi Rob. How was your trip to Edinburgh?

Rob: It was amazing!

Girl: When did you get there?

Rob: On Friday evening. We had some dinner and then we did a ghost tour with a guide. We walked through all the little streets of the Old Town and heard lots of scary stories!

Girl: And what did you do on Saturday?

Rob: Well, in the morning we went to Edinburgh Castle. The views were great from there – we could see the New Town and Princes Street really well.

Girl: And what about Saturday afternoon? Did you go to St Giles' Cathedral?

Rob: We walked past it, but we didn't go inside because we wanted to see Holyroodhouse. But the Queen was there and it was closed! So we went to the Scottish Parliament building instead.

Girl: Did you go out on Saturday evening?

Rob: Yes. We went to the Edinburgh Playhouse. I don't usually enjoy the theatre, but this show was really good.

Girl: And what did you do on Sunday morning? Did you go shopping in the New Town?

Rob: My brother wanted to, but we went to a museum instead. It's called Camera Obscura.

Girl: Oh – I went there. It's amazing, isn't it? So, did you come home on Sunday afternoon?

Rob: Yes, our train was at half past four. But before that we looked around the New Town and walked along Princes Street. Just to keep my brother happy!

110 Culture: Scotland, Student's Book page 89

Mum: Come in Dan. Emma's in there.

Dan: Hey Emma, what are you doing?

Emma: Hi Dan. My family and I are going to Scotland this summer. My mum wants me to make plans for the second day of our trip.

Dan: OK. What choices have you got?

Emma: Well, my mum gave me two ideas: a castle tour or a day trip to watch the Highland Games.

Dan: Let's see. The castles look interesting and you love studying history.

Emma: My favourite subject is geography but I like history too. Look, the tour goes to four different castles. Two of them are north of Glasgow. Another castle is on Loch Lomond, the biggest lake in Scotland.

Dan: Ah, that sounds nice.

Emma: Yes, the castles look beautiful, but the tour leaves the hotel at seven in the morning. I love studying history, but I hate getting up early. I don't want to get up at six for a tour!

Dan: How about the Highland Games?

Emma: There are some games on in a place near our hotel.

Dan: Look at that picture. What are those men wearing?

Emma: Ah, those are kilts. A lot of men wear traditional clothes to the games.

Dan: Look there. What are they doing?

Emma: Those are pictures of the sporting competitions in the morning. There's a bagpipe and dance festival in the afternoon.

Dan: That looks like fun! So, which one do you prefer?

Emma: Hmmm. Well, I think we should go to the Highland Games.

Dan: Good idea! It's going to be awesome! Can you bring me back some shortbread biscuits?

Emma: Sure! Thanks for your help.

115 Unit 15, Student's Book page 93

Peter: My friend Ollie and I were on holiday in Scotland and we were camping in a field near Loch Ness. I was hoping to get a photo of Nessie, the Loch Ness monster. I know everyone wants to take one, but you never know!

So, that morning – it was a Wednesday, I remember – I woke up first. It was early. It wasn't raining, but there was fog over the water. I was sitting and watching the loch. The fog was getting thinner and thinner, and then, I could see across the loch to the trees on the other side. Suddenly, I saw something in the water. Nessie at last! The Loch Ness monster! I shouted to Ollie to bring the camera. 'Right. Just a minute' he said. 'Quickly' I called. By the time he arrived with the camera, it was foggy on the loch again and we couldn't see anything. Slowly the fog got thinner and I was ready to take the photo. 'Look, Ollie. Can you see Nessie?' I said to him. He laughed. 'That's not Nessie,' he said. 'That's a duck!' I know Ollie didn't believe me, but I'm sure I really saw something that morning.

121 Unit 16, Student's Book page 97

Interviewer: Hello, Jim Townes here. Welcome to today's *Pet Spot*. We have Sue Green in the studio. Good morning Sue. So what's in the news about pets?

Sue: Good morning, Jim. Thank you for inviting me on the show. This article says that children can learn a lot from looking after a pet. The things they learn can help them in other parts of their lives.

Interviewer: Is this news? Children love dogs, cats and small animals. We know that.

Sue: Ah yes, but what do they learn? I'd like to talk about that.

Interviewer: OK. So what's the first thing they learn?

Sue: Perhaps the most important is food. Children often feed the pet, even young children can do this. Usually they do it because an adult tells them to. But when children do it every day, they learn that the pet feels hungry and thirsty just like they do.

Interviewer: OK, I can understand that. I remember when I was a boy, we had a dog and I brushed its coat.

Sue: Well that's my next point about looking after animals – keeping animals clean. Animals don't like to be dirty. With small animals like rats or mice, we clean their cages once a week. Older children can do that and younger children can help their older brothers and sisters or their parents.

Interviewer: Yes, true. So, is there anything else children learn from looking after pets?

Sue: Just one more thing ... animals are not toys. They're living things like you and me. When children have animals around them, they learn to be kind to them, to play with them nicely and not to hurt them.

Interviewer: Well, that's very interesting, Sue. Thanks for coming on today's programme. Bye.

Sue: Thanks Jim. Bye.

123 Life skills: Protecting animals, Student's Book page 99

Jayden: Hello, Alice! What are you doing?

Alice: Hey, Jayden. I'm reading a website about a girl from Texas. She has her own company and she donates money to protecting bees.

Jayden: She protects bees? I'm afraid of bees, they're horrible!

Alice: Bees are not horrible, Jayden. Thanks to bees, we have fruit, vegetables and flowers. We get honey and wax from them too.

Jayden: OK. I believe you, but I'm still afraid of them.

Alice: If you don't like bees, there are other animals you can protect. For example, here's an animal rescue centre that needs volunteers on Saturday mornings.

Jayden: What animals do they care for?

Alice: Let's see. They have dogs, cats, ducks, chickens, rabbits – and two rats at the centre. They live in cages. No bees.

Jayden: What do they need?

Alice: Well, they need people to give food and water to the animals and to clean their cages.

Jayden: That sounds interesting – there's only one problem.

Alice: What?

Jayden: I can't volunteer on Saturdays, I have guitar lessons.

Alice: Well, you can help in different ways on other days. People can donate money or things for the animals, too. There's a list of things they need here. Look, here's another option. This centre protects dogs and cats, and it's in our neighbourhood. They organise events on Sundays, and they sometimes need volunteers.

Jayden: That sounds perfect! I love animals and I want to help protect them.

Alice: Me too! I'm going to call for more information.

Jayden: Great. Thanks Alice!

124 Review 4: Units 13-16, Student's Book page 101

Listen to Tessa talking to her father about her friends. What problem does each person have?

Dad: What time is Eva's party, Tessa?

Tessa: The party's not happening, Dad. Eva's got a temperature, and our other friends aren't well either.

Dad: Oh no! What's wrong with Leon? Is he OK? I know he hurt his leg skiing last month.

Tessa: Yes – but that's all better now. At the moment, he's got toothache. He needs to see the dentist on Monday.

Dad: And what about Nat?

Tessa: He ate something bad yesterday and feels really sick. It's the same problem Maddie had a few days ago.

Dad: So what's wrong with Maddie now?

Tessa: She's got a terrible cold. She stayed in bed all day yesterday and most of today, but she still feels ill.

Dad: Oh dear – I hope you don't get it.

Tessa: Me too. I'm OK at the moment. Not like Ilsa. She phoned me earlier to say her head hurts and she doesn't want to go out.

Dad: Poor Ilsa! And what about Greg? His broken arm's better, isn't it?

Tessa: Yes, but now he's hurt his foot. He plays too much rugby!

Dad: I agree! Well, I hope they all feel better soon!

Tessa: That's nice of you, Dad!

126 Unit 17, Student's Book page 102

Charlie: Hi, Ella.

Ella: Oh, hi, Charlie.

Charlie: Great to see you!

Ella: Yeah, good to see you too.

Charlie: Ella, are you free on Saturday evening? Would you like to …

Ella: Sorry, Charlie, I can't. It's an important European League game and I'm going to watch it live. I'm a big football fan.

Charlie: I know! Me too. Look, how about coming …

Ella: I can't remember which channel it's on – is it Channel 6? Anyway, I'm not going to stream it on my laptop – the screen's much too small for something like that! I'm going to watch it on TV at home because our TV screen's really big.

Charlie: Yes, I agree. The thing is, we've just got …

Ella: I'm going to watch it live because I hate it when my friends text me to say what's happening and I'm not watching it. Most of the time I watch TV on demand, so I can watch when I want – but not sport! I always watch that live.

Charlie: Ella! Stop talking a minute!

Ella: Oh, dear … am I talking a lot? Sorry!

Charlie: The thing is, we've got a home cinema – my mum and dad bought it last week. It's like being at the cinema but at home, and the TV screen is *huge* and the sound's great too. Would you like to come round to mine to watch it? Several other friends are coming.

Ella: Would I like to? I'd love to! That's fantastic! Why didn't you say so before?

Charlie: I tried to!

129 Unit 17, Student's Book page 105

Evie: Hi Ben. I know it's Saturday and it's only nine o'clock. I hope it's not too early. But I wanted to know – did you watch the final of *Singer Search* last night?

Ben: Hi Evie. No, it's OK. I'm going to help my mum with some shopping this morning. Yes, I did watch it. Wasn't it amazing!

Evie: Yeah. I so wanted Jason to win. When he came onto the stage, everyone started clapping and shouting, and then when he started singing – a fantastic voice. Maybe he didn't choose the best song, but he could really sing. I think he's got lots of talent.

Ben: You're right – but I thought the singer before him …

Evie: AJ. She was called AJ.

Ben: I know! AJ. I thought she had a great voice. Her song was much better than his.

Evie: Yes, you're right. She was good too and I loved her song, but she didn't sing as well as Jason and she was a bit nervous.

Ben: Yes, and I think the other two had more experience on stage. Anyway, it was really hard to choose. When it was time for the TV audience to vote, I got ready and then I wasn't sure who to vote for – Jason or AJ. In the end, I voted for AJ.

Evie: You didn't! I chose Jason.

Ben: But then I couldn't believe it when Kris won! Her song wasn't anything special and she wasn't a brilliant singer. But I suppose she looked good on stage– she had fantastic clothes.

Evie: You're right. I was really surprised too. But for me she wasn't the best.

Ben: No, I agree. Well at least AJ was the runner-up.

Evie: And Jason came third. But I don't think the best singer won.

Ben's Mum: Ben … Ben!

Ben: Oh, sorry Evie. Got to go. Mum's calling me.

Evie: OK. Speak later. Bye.

Ben: Bye.

131 Unit 18, Student's Book page 107

Oliver: Hey, Aboudi. You're late!

Aboudi: Sorry, guys. I was reading and I didn't notice the time.

Serena: OK … we've only got a few minutes to think about the school magazine. There's a meeting about it at four o'clock.

Oliver: Why don't we write down some ideas now?

Aboudi: OK. Let's include music. We can write an article about the best new albums.

Serena: Cool! And we can have reviews of films and video games.

Oliver: Sounds good … and books too. How about we interview teachers about the books they like.

Serena: Good idea. OK … films and video games and an interview with a teacher.

Aboudi: Let's have some stories too … and some cartoons.

It's good to have something funny!

Oliver: True. And shall we have an information page?

Serena: Good one!

Oliver: Yeah. That's important in a monthly magazine.

Serena: Shall we include advertisements?

Oliver: What type of advertisements?

Serena: I don't know.

Aboudi: We don't need any.

Serena: I agree.

Oliver: Yeah, no advertisements.

Aboudi: I think the magazine should be online. It's much cheaper and easier to do it like that.

Serena: You're right. Oliver, why not ask your dad about it?

He does websites for people, doesn't he?

Oliver: Excellent idea. I can ask him tonight.

Aboudi: OK, is that everything?

Oliver: Yes I think so. Let's talk later.

Serena: All right.

Aboudi: OK. Bye.

Oliver: Bye

Serena: See you.

134 Unit 18, Student's Book page 109

Mike: This is the part of the programme when we ask you to call in with a review of a film. Today we've got Phoebe, calling from London. Hello, Phoebe.

Phoebe: Hello, Mike.

Mike: So let's hear your review.

Phoebe. Thanks, Mike. Well, it's about a guitar player called Dewey Finn. He leaves his band because the band members don't want him to play with them anymore. But then he doesn't have any money, so he looks for a job. When he gets a job as a teacher in a school, the students really like him. They think he's funny and a little bit mad!

Mike: OK Phoebe, so this guy is a teacher now. But he was a musician in a band. Is that right?

Phoebe: Yes – and then Dewey, the teacher who was a musician, decides to start a rock band as there are lots of good musicians in his class at the school. They call the band 'The School of Rock'. The band enters a competition called 'Battle of the Bands' and well, then it all gets a bit complicated.

Mike: But do they win the competition?

Phoebe: No, actually The School of Rock don't win. Dewey was in a different band at the beginning. His old band wins!

Mike: Oh no! That's not a very good ending.

Phoebe: Oh, but it's OK because everyone in the audience likes The School of Rock and wants them to keep playing.

Mike: OK. Is it a new film Phoebe? Oh, and what's it called?

Phoebe: Sorry, It's called *School of Rock*. No, it's an old film but it was on TV last week, so I watched it. I really loved it. Make sure you see it one day! It's great. And now it's a musical too, on the stage.

Mike: Thanks for the review of *School of Rock*, Phoebe. Now for some more music.

136 Culture: British TV around the world, Student's Book page 111

Amber: Hi John. You look serious. What are you working on?

John: I'm doing my French homework.

Amber: What do you need to do?

John: I need to write a paragraph about my favourite TV programme.

Amber: That sounds easy. What's the problem?

John: Easy? You know I love watching different programmes on TV.

Amber: Yes, I do. So?

John: So, I can't decide!

Amber: Ah, I see. What are your choices?

John: Well, I can write about *Britain's Got Talent*.

Amber: That's a good idea.

John: Yeah, but I don't know enough words in French to describe all the things they do on the programme.

Amber: Hmmm. What other programmes can you write about?

John: I can write about *MasterChef Junior*.

Amber: Do you like *MasterChef Junior*? I hate cooking programmes.

John: Really? I like watching the young chefs, and I love learning new meals.

Amber: Interesting … Any other ideas?

John: Hmmm. I like the idea of writing about *Horrible Histories*.

Amber: What's that?

John: You don't know? It's a programme about history. It tells stories of events in history but in a funny way. I love it!

Amber: Do you know any history vocabulary in French?

John: I do! And I love reading about history – in French and in English!

Amber: You love telling funny stories, too!

John: Good point! I do! Right. That's it … I'm going to write about *Horrible Histories*!

Amber: Good luck!

138 Unit 19, Student's Book page 112

You will hear a teacher telling students about a school trip.

Teacher: OK everyone, please listen carefully. I want to tell you about the end-of-term school trip. This year we're going to an activity centre called Tall Trees. It's in the middle of a forest, and it's really beautiful. Look it up online this evening! You can do all sorts of amazing activities there – sailing, swimming, cooking outside and lots of other things. We're going on the 25th of July, next Friday, until Monday the 28th of July. Please remember you have to give me £200 by Monday the 21st of July.

On Friday, the bus leaves at 8.30. But everyone has to be at school at eight o'clock. Before we leave, Mr Peters has to check your names and put the suitcases into the bus.

Now, every year, students ask me 'Do we have to wear our uniform on the journey?' And the answer is, yes, you do! This is because on the way we are going to stop at a few places: first a museum, and then an aquarium.

You don't have to bring anything to eat on the journey. We're going to bring food for all of you. But don't forget a drink, that's important!

The next question is always – 'What do I have to pack?' Well, of course swimming things for all the activities on water, such as canoeing and sailing. And for the nature walks, trainers and old trousers. But don't bring jeans – they're not comfortable when they get wet. Oh and don't forget the disco on the last night. You have to wear smart clothes!

OK, any more questions?

139 Unit 19, Student's Book page 113

Leo: Do I have to get up early every day?

Teacher: Yes, of course.

Leo: Do I have to go sailing?

Teacher: No, you don't have to. But try it. It's fun.

Leo: Do I have to go swimming?

Teacher: Yes. Everybody has to do that.

Leo: Do I have to go to the disco?

Teacher: No, you don't. You can stay in your room instead if you want to.

Leo: Can I bring my phone with me?

Teacher: No, you can't. You have to leave your phone at home.

Leo: Do I have to share a bedroom?

Teacher: Yes, you do. There are six people in each room.

Leo: And do I have to help with the cleaning?

Teacher: Yes. You have to help clean the kitchen and the dining room.

Leo: And do I have to do any school work?

Teacher: No, of course you don't have to do any school work! But you can if you want to.

142 Unit 19, Student's Book page 115

Maya: Hello, and welcome to my school. It's called Hartland School and it has about 600 students.

Let me show you where I sleep first. I share this room with three other girls. We have to keep it really tidy, but we can put posters and photos of our family on the walls, so it feels a bit like home.

This is the library where we do our homework. We have to do homework here every night between six and eight o'clock. We have to work really hard at this school. We even have lessons on Saturday mornings. There are tests and exams all the time! But we have fun too.

This is our games room. It's the best place in the school! We can't use it during the day, but we can come here at weekends and in the evenings to watch TV or play on the computer.

And here's the dining room. Breakfast is at eight o'clock and lunch is at one o'clock. We have to arrive on time, or we don't get any food! And we have to help with the cleaning after meals. Some of us clean the floors and others take the dishes to the kitchen.

And now, if we go outside, this is the sports field. This term we're doing hockey, and next term we're going to do tennis. Some people hate sport, but everyone has to do it. Well, that's my school – hope you like it.

144 Unit 20, Student's Book page 116

Kate: My name's Kate and this is my family tree. My mother's English and my father's Polish. His name's Wiktor and all his family live in Poland, so I go there quite often. I know a bit of Polish but when people speak fast, I can't understand them! I stay with my grandparents, my Uncle Marek, his wife Kasia and my two cousins, Jana and Karolina. They're both slim and pretty and have fair hair. Jana plays the piano really well, and Karolina is good at tennis. She wins easily every time we play!

My mother's name is Liz. She's tall and she's got blonde hair. Her sister, Helen, is married to Phil and they have two small children – a son called Rory and a daughter called Jessie. They're very sweet but very noisy! My granny is called Sue and she grew up in South Africa. That's where she met my grandpa, Tony. They were both very good-looking when they were young. They've both got grey hair now, but Granny's was fair when she was young and Grandpa's was dark.

Granny often tells me stories about her mother – my great-grandmother. She was called Iris, and she was born in 1910 on a small farm in South Africa. She was very musical and loved singing. Her family worked hard and sent her to England to study music. She got married and her husband was called Frank. She became a singer and sang in some of the most famous theatres in London. She had dark hair and she was very beautiful. Granny has a big box of old photographs of Iris. I love looking at them, but I have to hold them carefully because they're very old. Granny's trying to find out about Iris's parents and grandparents now. I'm sure there are lots more interesting stories in my family history.

147 Unit 20, Student's Book page 119

Sammy: There are seven of us living in my family home. There's me, my mum and dad, my brother Arvinder, his wife and baby, Ashia, and my sister, Deepa. She's going to get married soon. I like living with so many people. There's always something happening and someone to talk to. Ashia, my baby niece, likes it too. She never gets bored or unhappy, because there are so many people to play with her.

Sally: I live with my parents in a three-bedroom house. I'm the only child in my family – I haven't got any brothers or sisters, but my grandfather lives with us. He's 78, and he's got lots of interesting stories to tell. I've got four cousins and I love seeing them too. They're a bit older than me, but I don't see them very often because they live quite far away.

Harry: I live with my mum and my two brothers. We live in a flat and I share a bedroom with my brother. My grandma, aunt and uncle live on our street as well, and we all spend a lot of time together. I'm really close to all my cousins. My dad and his second wife live 50 kilometres away, but my brothers and I also spend time with them.

149 Life skills: Being a good friend, Student's Book page 121

Martha: Time to go home. What's up, Karl? You look upset.

Karl: I feel sad today. Alex and I had a big argument and now we're not talking. I don't know what to do.

Martha: Alex is a very good friend of yours, isn't he? He always helps you study for your exams and you share interests. Why don't you send him a message?

Karl: I sent him a text message immediately after the argument, but there's no reply from him yet. What should I do?

Martha: You should be patient. Good friends help each other when times get difficult, like you and Alex.

Karl: OK, you're right. Do you think I should call him?

Martha: I think it's a good idea to wait. Give him time to think. You shouldn't worry.

Karl: Alex and I have fun together and our friendship makes me happy. When do you think I should contact him again?

Martha: I think you should wait until tomorrow. Relax – this is not the end of the world!

Karl: OK, OK. Thanks for listening, Martha.

Martha: No problem Karl.

Karl: It's Alex!

Martha: That's great news! I have to get home to study, but good luck with Alex.

Karl: Thanks, Martha! See you tomorrow. Bye! Hey Alex! I'm so happy to hear your voice …

150 Review 5: Units 17-20, Student's Book page 123

Owen: Hi. My name's Owen. Here's a picture of my family. We were all together in my house for my grandma's 70th birthday party. You can see her here at the front with some flowers. Her name's Nora. My grandpa's standing next to her. His name's Colin. My grandma and grandpa have three children. The oldest is my mum. She's called Abby. She's the one in the blue dress. Then there's my aunt – her name's Lily. She's talking to my mum. And the youngest is my uncle. He's called Rob. He's got short dark hair, and he's wearing jeans and a T-shirt. The other man in the picture is my Dad. He's a bit older than Rob. His name's Liam. I've got three cousins. Grace is the youngest. She's Aunt Lily's daughter and she's only one. My other two cousins are boys. They're Rob's sons. Max is seven years old – he's really interested in football! And Ryan is five years old. He loves playing with his cars. He's under the table playing with them!

Acknowledgements

The authors and publishers acknowledge the following sources of copyright material and are grateful for the permissions granted. While every effort has been made, it has not always been possible to identify the sources of all the material used, or to trace all copyright holders. If any omissions are brought to our notice, we will be happy to include the appropriate acknowledgements on reprinting & in the next update to the digital edition, as applicable.

Teacher's Book

All the texts, photographs and illustrations are used from the Student's Book.

Front cover photography by Hero Images/iStock/Getty Images Plus/Getty Images.

VIDEOS

Key: C = Culture

Photography

All the photographs are sourced from Getty Images.

C2: Hero Images/DigitalVision; Fran Polito/Moment; Hero Images/ DigitalVision; Caiaimage/Robert Daly/OJO+; H. Armstrong Roberts/ ClassicStock/Archive Photos; bubaone/DigitalVision Vectors; VICTOR/DigitalVision Vectors; Ariel Skelley/DigitalVision; Hero Images; Thomas Barwick/DigitalVision; Hero Images; Yellow Dog Productions; Jena Ardell/Moment; Thomas Barwick/DigitalVision; PeopleImages/iStock/Getty Images Plus; **C4:** davidhills/iStock/ Getty Images Plus; Chanon Kanjanavasoontara/Moment; Peter Zoeller/Perspectives; CarmanPetite/Moment; ImageGap/iStock/ Getty Images Plus; MarioGuti/iStock/Getty Images Plus; Kenny McCartney/Moment; John Lawson, Belhaven/Moment.

Video clips

The following video clips are sourced from Getty Images.

C1: Trevor Williams/Image Bank Film; shironosov/Creatas Video+/ Getty Images Plus; FatCamera/Vetta; miodrag ignjatovic/Creatas Video; Faithfulshot/Getty Images Editorial Footage; Pressmaster/ DigitalVision; Thomas Barwick; Pressmaster/DigitalVision; Simonkr/Image Bank Film: Signature; Trevor Williams/Image Bank Film; Rocketclips/Verve+; shironosov/Creatas Video+/Getty Images Plus; imyskin/Creatas Video+/Getty Images Plus; Photosiber/ Creatas Video+/Getty Images Plus; Mariia Kozub/Creatas Video+/ Getty Images Plus; 5432action/Creatas Video; helivideo/Creatas Video+/Getty Images Plus; Pressmaster/DigitalVision; Simonkr/ Image Bank Film: Signature; Trevor Williams/Image Bank Film; shironosov/Creatas Video+/Getty Images Plus; alexisstock/Creatas Video+/Getty Images Plus; Andersen Ross/Verve+; slavemotion/ Vetta; ITN; Trevor Williams/Image Bank Film; BlackLight Films - Louie Schwartzberg/Image Bank Film; Pressmaster/DigitalVision; shironosov/Creatas Video+/Getty Images Plus; **C2:** shironosov/ Creatas Video+/Getty Images Plus; FatCamera/Creatas Video; miodrag ignjatovic/Creatas Video; Mark Andersen/Image Bank Film: Signature; saskami/Creatas Video; BC Video Inc/Archive Films: Creative; Smith Collection/Archive Films: Creative; Bread and Butter Productions/Archive Films: Creative; sdominick/Creatas Video; Smith Collection/Archive Films: Creative; JaimeByrd/ Creatas Video+/Getty Images Plus; FatCamera/Creatas Video; SolStock/Vetta; Wavebreakmedia/Creatas Video+/Getty Images Plus; **C3:** Stusya/Creatas Video+/Getty Images Plus; Hate Kills Man/ Image Bank Film: Signature; Bill Bachmann/Image Bank Film; pigprox/Creatas Video; Kkolosov/Creatas Video+/Getty Images Plus; Spoonfilm/Moment Video RF; Gal Productions/Image Bank Film; Counter Production/Image Bank Film: Signature; Zhang Peng/Image Bank Film; Roy JAMES Shakespeare/DigitalVision; KreangchaiRungfamai/Creatas Video+/Getty Images Plus; Doug Armand/Photodisc; Henglein And Steets/Image Bank Film; Multi-bits/Image Bank Film; Picture Palace/Image Bank Film; Roy JAMES Shakespeare/Image Bank Film; Rick Steves/Image Bank Film; Toshi Sasaki/Image Bank Film; Mckyartstudio/Creatas Video; vichie81/Creatas Video; Henglein And Steets/Image Bank Film; Footage of the World/DigitalVision; footagefactory/Image Bank Film; Galloabraham/Image Bank Film; C R Laing/Image Bank Film; ImagesBazaar/Photolibrary Video; **C4:** Hal Bergman/Image Bank Film; C R Laing/Photodisc; C R Laing/Photodisc; Nils Ruinet/ Image Bank Film; Skyworks/Image Bank Film; Komplett Media/ Image Bank Film; Mattia Bicchi Photography/Moment Video RR; Hal Bergman/Photodisc; Mattia Bicchi Photography/Moment Video RF; Skyworks Places/Image Bank Film; Richard Elliott/Image Bank Film; © www.jangoris.com/Moment Video RF; footagefactory/ Image Bank Film; Eric Harrison/Creatas Video+/Getty Images Plus; f11photo/Creatas Video; serdarcan/Creatas Video+/Getty Images Plus; Skyworks/Image Bank Film; kali9/Vetta; Hal Bergman/ Image Bank Film; JohnFScott/Creatas Video; David Gould/ Image Bank Film; Gal Productions/Rights-ready; perinjo/Vetta; Gal Productions/Image Bank Film; topnatthapon/Creatas Video; Hal Bergman/Image Bank Film; Pekic/Creatas Video; gigidread/ Creatas Video+/Getty Images Plus; Color Red Media/Image Bank Film; **C5:** vins_m/Creatas Video+/Getty Images Plus; yucelyilmaz/ Creatas Video+/Getty Images Plus; monkeybusinessimages/Creatas Video+/Getty Images Plus; Warner Bros. Studios/Warner Bros. Entertainment; Photolibrary Pty Limited/Oxford Scientific Video; John Downer Productions/Image Bank Film; Multipedia/Creatas Video+/Getty Images Plus; Multipedia/Creatas Video+/Getty Images Plus; simonkr/Vetta; uzhursky/Creatas Video+/Getty Images Plus; Picture Palace/Image Bank Film: Signature; John Ambrose/ DigitalVision; BFI HD Collection/Archive Films: Creative; ReeldealHD Ltd/ReeldealHD Ltd; vins_m/Creatas Video+/Getty Images Plus; yucelyilmaz/Creatas Video+/Getty Images Plus; Stockboutique/ Creatas Video; Moon Production/Creatas Video+/Getty Images Plus; Motortion/Creatas Video+/Getty Images Plus; Motortion/ Creatas Video+/Getty Images Plus; PetroglyphFilms/Image Bank Film; Train_Arrival/Creatas Video+/Getty Images Plus; DGLimages/ Creatas Video+/Getty Images Plus; alekleks/Creatas Video+/Getty Images Plus; Do Diligence Inc./Image Bank Film: Signature; A&E Television Networks/Archive Films: Creative; David Kashakhi/ Creatas Video+/Getty Images Plus; A&E Television Networks/ Archive Films: Creative; RaptTv/Creatas Video+/Getty Images Plus; Alona Khylia/Creatas Video+/Getty Images Plus.

Audio

All music clips are sourced from Getty Images.

Intro: LP_MUSIC/SoundExpress;

C1: Andrea Bellina/SoundExpress; Sergii Pavkin/SoundExpress; **C2:** Yevgen Entertainment/SoundExpress; Jason Garner/SoundExpress; Cagdas Takmaz/SoundExpress; **C3:** Stuart Geerts Entertainment/ SoundExpress; Judson Lee Music/SoundExpress; Frobisher/ SoundExpress; **C4:** Enrique Molano/SoundExpress; craig goult/ SoundExpress; Roman Chyzhevskyy/SoundExpress; **C5:** Stoutheart Entertainment/Damon Stout/SoundExpress; Claudia Obländer/ SoundExpress; Claudio Giovann Colombo/SoundExpress.

The publishers are grateful to the following contributors: cover design and design concept: restless; typesetting: Mouse Life, S.L.; project management: Louise Davoren ; videos in units 3, 6, 7, 11, 12, 13, 16, 18 and 19 produced by Purple Door Media Ltd.